CYNTHIA R. CHAPMAN is the Adelia A.F. Johnston and Harry Thomas Frank Associate Professor of Biblical Studies at Oberlin College. She is the author of *The Gendered Language of Warfare in the Israelite-Assyrian Encounter.*

The House of the Mother

THE ANCHOR YALE BIBLE REFERENCE LIBRARY is a project of international and interfaith scope in which Protestant, Catholic, and Jewish scholars from many countries contribute individual volumes. The project is not sponsored by any ecclesiastical organization and is not intended to reflect any particular theological doctrine.

The series is committed to producing volumes in the tradition established half a century ago by the founders of the Anchor Bible, William Foxwell Albright and David Noel Freedman. It aims to present the best contemporary scholarship in a way that is accessible not only to scholars but also to the educated nonspecialist. It is committed to work of sound philological and historical scholarship, supplemented by insight from modern methods, such as sociological and literary criticism.

John J. Collins
General Editor

THE ANCHOR YALE BIBLE REFERENCE LIBRARY

The House of the Mother

The Social Roles of Maternal Kin in
Biblical Hebrew Narrative and Poetry

CYNTHIA R. CHAPMAN

 Yale UNIVERSITY PRESS   NEW HAVEN AND LONDON

"Anchor Yale Bible" and the Anchor Yale logo are registered trademarks of Yale University.

Copyright © 2016 by Yale University.
All rights reserved.
This book may not be reproduced, in whole or in part, including illustrations, in any form (beyond that copying permitted by Sections 107 and 108 of the U.S. Copyright Law and except by reviewers for the public press), without written permission from the publishers.

Yale University Press books may be purchased in quantity for educational, business, or promotional use. For information, please e-mail sales.press@yale.edu (U.S. office) or sales@yaleup.co.uk (U.K. office).

Set in Adobe Caslon type by Newgen North America.
Printed in the United States of America.

Library of Congress Control Number: 2016934919
ISBN 978-0-300-19794-5 (hardcover : alk. paper)

A catalogue record for this book is available from the British Library.

This paper meets the requirements of ANSI/NISO Z39.48-1992 (Permanence of Paper).

10 9 8 7 6 5 4 3 2 1

For Daniel, Christine, and Jonah

Contents

Acknowledgments, ix

List of Abbreviations, xiii

Introduction: Disrupting the Begats (*tôlēdôt*), 1

1. House (*bayit*), 20
2. The House of the Mother (*bêt 'ēm*), 51
3. Chamber of Her Who Conceived Me (*ḥeder hôrātî*), 75
4. My Brothers, the Sons of My Mother (*'aḥay bĕnê-'immî*), 91
5. No, Son of My Womb (*ma-bar-biṭnî*), 110
6. Like a Brother to Me, One Who Had Nursed at My Mother's Breasts (*kĕ'āḥ lî yônēq šĕdê 'immî*), 125
7. The One Who Opens the Womb (*peṭer reḥem*), 150
8. The House of the Father of His Mother (*bêt-'ăbî 'immô*), 173
9. Like Rachel and Leah Who Together Built Up the House of Israel (*kĕrāḥēl ûkĕlē'â 'ăšer bānû šĕtêhem 'et-bêt yiśrā'ēl*), 200

Notes, 229

Index of Subjects, 303

Index of Ancient Sources, 325

Acknowledgments

This book began unexpectedly when I cross-registered for a seminar in the anthropology department at Harvard University in 1996. Taught by Professor James L. Watson, the course focused on kinship as theorized within Chinese social anthropology. I took the course out of an interest in China and Hong Kong, where I have lived for several years at various times in my life. The material in the course, however, ended up providing me with a new lens for reading kinship as described in the biblical text. Some of the assigned readings by Rubie Watson and Margery Wolf helped me to pay closer attention to the social and political roles of women in biblical texts that clearly valued patrilineality while preserving complex stories of mothers, sisters, and daughters. In the two decades since, I have continued to read anthropological studies of kinship and ethnographic studies of professed patrilineal societies. This dynamic and continually developing academic discourse has helped me recognize and theorize the maternally specific Hebrew kinship terms that delineate relationships within the biblical house of the mother.

Numerous friends and colleagues have supported me over the past two decades as I've researched, presented, and written portions of this book. While still a graduate student, I presented the outline of this book to a group of graduate women colleagues who met to share research: Martien Halvorson-Taylor, Vivian Johnson, Valerie Stein, and Rhetta Wiley. I especially thank Martien Halvorson-Taylor and Vivian Johnson, who have continued to serve as critical readers on several chapters over the course of two decades. I have been fortunate to be able to present various chapters from this book in academic settings that have helped me develop my argument and clarify my ideas. Christine Neal Thomas invited me to present a portion of what is now chapter 7 at a conference she organized at Harvard in 2007 on "Women in the Field: Gender and Research in the Hebrew Bible and the Ancient Near East." While I was a visiting professor at the Chinese University of Hong Kong in the spring of 2010, Lo Lung-kuang, then dean of the Chung-Chi Divinity School, invited me to present a three-lecture series focusing on my research into the biblical house of the mother. Pamela Barmash invited me to present chapter 6 at Washington University in St. Louis in the spring of 2011. Chapter 9, which deals with the Hebrew *'ummâ* (mother-unit), was written in honor of my doctoral advisor and ongoing mentor, Peter Machinist, in acknowledgment of his continued impact on my scholarly development. I have presented several chapters at the annual meetings of the Society of Biblical Literature, and I especially thank David Chalcraft of the Social Sciences and the Interpretation of Hebrew Scriptures program unit where I have been fortunate to present several times. I am indebted to the members of the Colloquium for Biblical Research where I presented a chapter of this book in August 2011 and where I continue to find invaluable support for my ongoing research and writing. I would like to thank Elizabeth Bloch-Smith, Susan Niditch, Mark S. Smith, and Abraham Winitzer for generously sharing their specific areas of expertise and reading particular sections of this book. I am grateful to Marc Brettler and Michael Coogan, who took an interest in this book and helped move it forward in the publication process.

Time is an essential ingredient to any book project, and I want to thank the Oberlin College Religion Department and the Office of the Dean for approving my leave requests and supporting my research goals. In 2009, I received a National Endowment for the Humanities summer research stipend that facilitated full-time work on chapter 9. I also want to thank my students at Oberlin College who have helped propel this project forward by asking incisive questions and pointing to important textual links. Several students deserve special mention. Dexter Brown and Benjamin Morrison, 2011 religion majors, read and provided valuable insights on portions of this manuscript. Rachel Webberman, a 2015 double major in religion and classics, helped to proofread the full manuscript and completed the final formatting for the endnotes. Ondrea Keith, a 2010 biology major with minors in studio art and religion, read the full manuscript and worked with me to "disrupt the patriline" artistically and graphically. She produced concept drawings for the line drawings in the book, and Bill Nelson, a graphic designer and artist, rendered the final line drawings. Sophia Weinstein, a 2016 double major in Jewish Studies and studio art with a minor in religion, provided research assistance and the beautiful artwork for the cover of this book. Finally, I want to express my gratitude to three friends who have listened to me talk about this book for far too long: Stacia Dearmin, Shawnthea Monroe, and Kristin Sweeney.

I want to thank Yale University Press and John Collins, the general editor of the Anchor Yale Bible Reference Library, for bringing this book to publication. I am especially grateful to Susan Ackerman, who read and provided helpful feedback on the full manuscript; this book is stronger as a result of her generous gift of time and expertise. Heather Gold was especially responsive and helpful throughout the publication process, and Margaret Hogan brought clarity and precision to the manuscript through her expert copyediting.

Finally, I thank my husband, Wai Wah Sung, and my three children, Daniel, Christine, and Jonah. They constitute the innermost circle of my *bayit* and bring me joy, pride, and the occasional challenge.

Abbreviations

AB	Anchor Bible
ABD	*Anchor Bible Dictionary.* Edited by D. N. Freedman. 6 vols. New York, 1992.
ASV	American Standard Version
AYB	Anchor Yale Bible
BA	*Biblical Archaeologist*
BASOR	*Bulletin of the American Schools of Oriental Research*
BDB	Brown, F., S. R. Driver, and C. A. Briggs. *A Hebrew and English Lexicon of the Old Testament.* Oxford, 1907.
CAD	*The Assyrian Dictionary of the Oriental Institute of the University of Chicago.* 21 vols. Chicago, 1956–2014.
CAT	Commentaire de l'Ancien Testament
CBQ	*Catholic Biblical Quarterly*
CC	Continental Commentaries
COS	*The Context of Scripture.* Edited by W. W. Hallo. 3 vols. Leiden, 1997– .
DCH	*Dictionary of Classical Hebrew.* Edited by D. J. A. Clines. 5 vols. Sheffield, Eng. 1993– .
DJD	Discoveries in the Judaean Desert
Eng.	English
HALOT	Koehler, L., W. Baumgartner, and J. J. Stamm. *The Hebrew and Aramaic Lexicon of the Old Testament.* Translated and edited under the supervision of M. E. J. Richardson. 4 vols. Leiden, 1994–1999.

HSM	Harvard Semitic Monographs
JANES	*Journal of the Ancient Near Eastern Society*
JBL	*Journal of Biblical Literature*
JCS	*Journal of Cuneiform Studies*
JHS	*Journal of Hebrew Scriptures*
JPS	Jewish Publication Society
JSOT	*Journal for the Study of the Old Testament*
JSOTSup	Journal for the Study of the Old Testament: Supplement Series
KJV	King James Version
KTU	*Die keilalphabetischen Texte aus Ugarit.* Edited by M. Dietrich, O. Loretz, and J. Sanmartín. Alter Orient und Altes Testament 24/1. Neukirchen-Vluyn, West Ger., 1976. 2nd enlarged ed. of *KTU: The Cuneiform Alphabetic Texts from Ugarit, Ras Ibn Hani, and Other Places.* Edited by M. Dietrich, O. Loretz, and J. Sanmartín. Münster, 1995 (= *CTU*).
LXX	Septuagint (the Greek Old Testament)
MT	Masoretic Text
NCBC	New Cambridge Bible Commentary
NEA	*Near Eastern Archaeology*
NIV	New International Version
NKJV	New King James Version
NRSV	New Revised Standard Version
OTL	Old Testament Library
OTS	Old Testament Studies
SAA	State Archives of Assyria
SAACT	State Archives of Assyria Cuneiform Texts
SAAS	State Archives of Assyria Studies
SBL	Society of Biblical Literature
TDOT	*Theological Dictionary of the Old Testament.* Edited by G. J. Botterweck, H. Ringgren, and H.-J. Fabry. Translated by J. T. Willis, G. W. Bromiley, and D. E. Green. 15 vols. Grand Rapids, Mich., 1974–2015.

UF	*Ugarit-Forschungen*
VT	*Vetus Testamentum*
WC	Westminster Commentaries
ZAW	*Zeitschrift für die alttestamentliche Wissenschaft*

The House of the Mother

Introduction: Disrupting the Begats (*tôlēdôt*)

One of the popularly known features of the Bible is its penchant for genealogies, often described in the King James language as the "begats." Genesis 4 provides the first human genealogy, recording seven generations from Adam to Lamech. A section of this genealogy reads, "Irad begat Mehujael; and Mehujael begat Methusael; and Methusael begat Lamech" (Gen 4:18),[1] an unbroken chain of fathers and presumed firstborn sons. At the generation of Lamech, however, the begats give way to narrative, and the narrative introduces new categories of kin into the patriline: wives, a younger brother, and a younger sister. Lamech, we read, "took unto him two wives: the name of the one was Adah, and the name of the other Zillah." Adah had two sons, and Zillah had a son and a daughter. The introduction of these two mothers with their pairs of children interrupts the patrilineal flow. The seven generations of named men represent the biblical authors' organization of the known world into a single family, a neatly schematic patriline. In the culminating seventh generation, however, wives introduce social and economic divisions among men. Adah becomes the mother of pastoralists "who dwell in tents" and musicians "who play the lyre and pipe." Zillah's descendants become metallurgists (Gen 4:19–22).

We also find that at the seventh generation, the lines of kinship relatedness shift from the lineal father-son linkage to the lateral wife-mother-son-sibling linkage. If we imagine a genealogical chart, the line from Cain through Lamech would descend vertically down from father to son to grandson.[2] At the generation of Lamech, when the language of paternal begetting gives way to maternal bearing, the line splits laterally into two maternal groupings.[3] Even here, however, each mother is described only as

1

"bearing" her firstborn son; the second child of each mother is introduced as the sibling of the son of the same mother. And so for Adah, we read, "Adah bore Jabal. He was the father of pastoralists who dwell in tents, *and the name of his brother* was Jubal" (Gen 4:20–21; emphasis added). Jubal, the younger son, is not tied directly to either his mother or father; his primary kinship bond is to "his brother," and through his brother to his mother. The similarity in the sound of the two brothers' names contributes to a sense of connectedness between these sons of the same mother.[4] We find a similar pattern of connectedness between Zillah and her children. Zillah is tied directly to her firstborn son, Tubal-Cain, as the one who "bears" him (Gen 4:22), but Zillah's daughter, Naamah, is introduced through her older brother as "the sister of Tubal-Cain." At the generation of Lamech, therefore, women and maternally aligned children disrupt and divide the paternal line. Stated differently, at the generation of Lamech, the patriline becomes a paternally named household, what elsewhere in the Bible is referred to as "the house of the father." Lamech's house is complex, containing two maternally headed sub-houses, each comprising two maternally identified siblings (fig. 1).

What we see in this single text is actually a biblical pattern: exclusively paternal genealogies give way to narratives that introduce households, and these households contain fathers, mothers, wives, concubines, slave wives, firstborn sons, second-born sons, daughters, foreigners, and slaves. The introduction of women and maternally defined subgroups of kin disrupts the neatness of a patrilineal genealogy, marking divisions within a paternal line. This book focuses on these disruptions, namely, on complex biblical houses that are named for founding male ancestors but include socially marked women and maternally identified kin. When the biblical patriline becomes a noisy, fully peopled house, we find not only a father and his firstborn son but a series of maternally aligned kin groups with specific kinship labels that delineate maternal sub-houses within the larger house of the father.

In a sense, the King James language with the repeated translation "begat" appropriately evokes an archaic ideology of patrilineality that biblical writers and modern biblical scholars alike have been too ready to present as a totality, the full picture of ancient Israelite kinship. Certainly, biblical authors valued and recorded exclusively paternal lines in the form of genealogies, but they also preserved the far more inclusive house of the father. Any study that attempts to account for the full picture of biblical kinship must include both of these mechanisms for describing kinship relatedness.

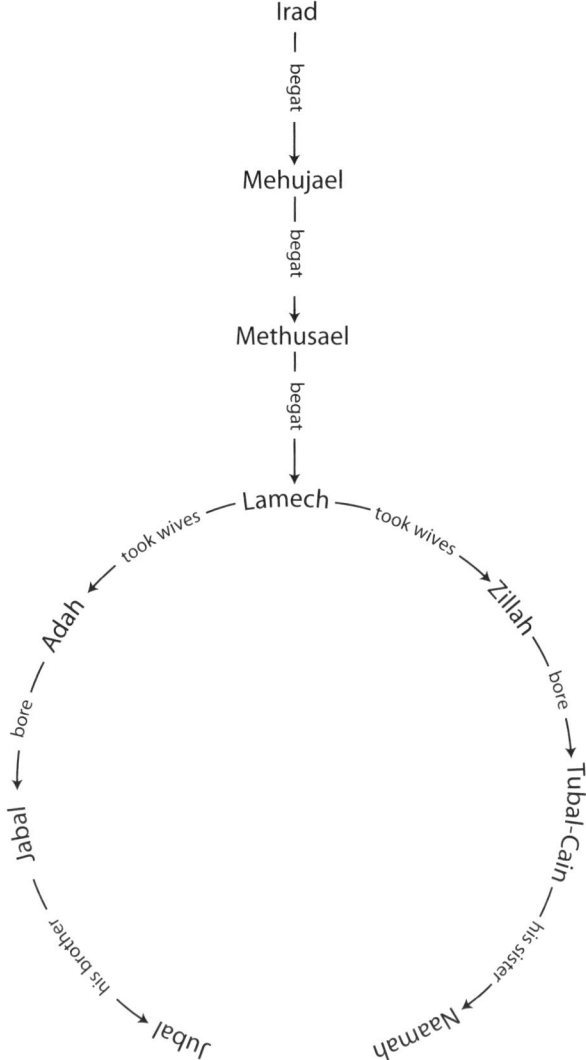

Figure 1. *Disrupting the patriline, Gen 4:18–22. Illustration by Bill Nelson.*

The Patriline in the Bible

In biblical Hebrew the term that most closely approximates the concept of "patrilineage" is *tôlēdôt*, which is usually translated "the generations" and in some cases "the story." The word *tôlēdôt* is associated with the priestly author, who uses the term to provide an "account of men and their descendants," a story of "successive generations," and an accounting of "genealogical divisions."⁵ Ronald S. Hendel considers the *tôlēdôt* an "ethnic genre" specific to Hebrew literature, a biblical category used to denote "genealogical time." He also notes that the word literally means "the begettings" and is appropriately translated "lineage."⁶ While these translations and explanations of the term are appropriate, at its most basic level, *tôlēdôt* means "the paternal begettings"; it denotes male reproductive generation of select males. The priestly *tôlēdôt* feature a series of men who "beget (*hôlîd*)" single sons. Both the noun *tôlēdôt* and the verb *hôlîd* are based in the *hip'il* stem of the verb *y-l-d*, which is explicitly masculine—"to cause to bear"— and therefore always translated "beget."⁷ Claus Westermann captures the exclusively male aspect of the *tôlēdôt* when he notes that at every generation a man is introduced "in such a way that it is the begetting of any individual by his father, not his birth, that is mentioned in the previous part."⁸

Even as we acknowledge that the term *tôlēdôt* approximates the idea of a patriline, we have to note its limited use, occurring only thirty-nine times in the Hebrew Bible.⁹ Given this limited use and its concentration in the priestly source, we can hardly argue that the Bible's primary framework for understanding kinship is the patriline. In Genesis, the *tôlēdôt* serve as a literary "structuring clause," and they likely represent an early genealogical source adapted and used by the priestly writers.¹⁰ As a literary structuring device, however, the *tôlēdôt* frame narratives that feature maternally marked subgroups within a paternal line. Again, we return to the pattern of women and maternally identified kin disrupting the neatness and predictability of the patriline.

An examination of the *tôlēdôt* clauses in the ancestral narratives of Genesis demonstrates that even within these paternal genealogies, wives, additional sons, and daughters are present, named, and important. The Primeval History concludes with the *tôlēdôt* of Shem, Noah's son (Gen 11:10–26). There are ten generations of named men between Shem and Abram; the first nine are listed as a pure patriline, naming only a father and his first-begotten son at each generation. At the generation of Terah, the patriline segments, and we learn that Terah had three named sons: Abram, Nahor, and Haran. As in the case of Lamech, the *tôlēdôt* of Terah introduce a household rather than a patriline, and Terah's household includes a firstborn son, two younger sons, named wives, and a named grandson (Gen 11:27–30). What follows the *tôlēdôt* of Terah is a complex narrative cycle that ultimately presents the household of Abram/Abraham as a paternally named kinship unit that divides into three maternal subunits: Sarah and Isaac; Hagar and Ishmael; and Keturah and her six sons (Gen 25). The *tôlēdôt* of Ishmael include a reference to his mother, Hagar, and her mistress, Sarah, meaning in the *tôlēdôt* sequence that he heads, Ishmael is introduced as part of a maternally named subunit within the house of Abraham (Gen 25:12–18). The *tôlēdôt* of Isaac, the chosen son in the subdivided house of Abraham, also introduce a narrative and household with a wife and twin sons (Gen 25:19–24). The *tôlēdôt* of Esau immediately divide his line into maternal subunits, each containing a grouping of sons and daughters (Gen 36:1–14). Finally, the *tôlēdôt* of Israel's eponymous ancestor Jacob focus immediately on the single son Joseph and introduce the full and maternally subdivided household of Jacob in the story of Joseph (Gen 37:2). This brief overview of the *tôlēdôt* in Genesis demonstrates that even when we focus our attention on those places in the Bible that use the word that most closely approximates a pure patriline, we find that each patriline yields to a more complex and often maternally subdivided household.

The Patrilineal Model in Anthropology: A Historical Overview

The tension between an articulated value of patrilineality and the simultaneous preservation of narratives that demonstrate the importance of mothers and maternally related kin is something that anthropologists have recognized and begun to theorize. If we trace the development of kinship studies within anthropology over the past fifty years, we can document a complete reformulation of anthropological approaches to kinship. One of the key areas of critique and rethinking centers on the concept of patrilineality. Because biblical scholars' understanding of ancient Israelite kinship is so heavily indebted to anthropology, an understanding of the transformation within this field becomes an essential starting point for any new work on kinship in the Bible.

The first thing one notices when beginning research on kinship in the field of anthropology is a series of references to kinship studies as "reconfigured," "revived," "reformulated," "transformed," and "reconstituted."[11] These descriptors bear witness to an upheaval within the area of kinship studies; they have been written in the aftermath of a methodological crisis. Anthropologists have described this situation as the "death" and "reconstitution" of kinship studies.

Turning first to what was initially thought to be the "death" of kinship studies, we begin with the scholarship of David M. Schneider, the anthropologist credited with bringing about this death. Starting with a 1965 article titled "Some Muddles in the Models: or, How the System Really Works" and culminating in his 1984 monograph *A Critique of the Study of Kinship*, Schneider and his students have systematically called into question the very assumptions on which anthropological models of kinship and relatedness have been based.[12] A central tenet of Schneider's critiques is his overarching distrust of anthropologists' use of "models," including the patrilineal model, as too theoretical, esoteric, rigid, and all-encompassing.[13] In 1972, Schneider presented an influential paper entitled "What Is Kinship All About?" at the centennial of the death of Lewis Henry Morgan, the anthropologist identified as "the father of kinship studies."[14] In this paper, Schneider reiterated his critique of the use of models and the evolutionary charting of kinship systems from "primitive Others" to the creation of a "family" "resting on marriage between single pairs" (258). According to Schneider, kinship was something that Morgan "invented" and only existed "as a theoretical notion in the mind of the anthropologist" (269). A central critique within his paper focuses on the concept of "descent"; Schneider discredited the idea that kinship was based solely or even primarily on biological descent (270–71). Instead of studying societies based on preconceived anthropological models, Schneider advocated studying societies based on their own systems and terms for understanding relatedness. Once one turned to native categories, he argued, one could no longer justify treating kinship as a "distinct, discrete, isolable subsystem of every and any culture" (270).

Linda Stone recently summarized the impact of this 1972 paper as the "dropping of a bomb on the field of anthropology": "Schneider's bomb was nearly lethal for kinship studies: it spread shrapnel outward into other areas of anthropological inquiry, and its powerful echoes are still reverberating today. This bomb is summed up in Schneider's now famous pronouncement that kinship 'does not exist in any culture known to man.' He declared that kinship—the very soul of anthropology, the subject that Robin Fox (1967:10) had said was to anthropology what the nude was to art—was thus a 'non-subject.'"[15] The effect of Schneider's critique can be seen, as noted by Stone, in the twenty-year period from the mid-1970s to the mid-1990s, during which no major publications on kinship in anthropology appeared.[16]

As it turned out, however, Schneider's scholarly challenges to the classificatory systems within the study of kinship did not bring about the death of kinship studies within anthropology. Instead, when significant publications within the study of kinship began to reemerge after a twenty-year hiatus, they described kinship studies as "reconfigured," "revived," or "reconstituted." When we look at the shared trends within recent works of reconfigured kinship studies, we see the lasting impact of Schneider's critiques. First, there is a decisive move away from the use of any universalizing model to describe kinship systems as a whole. In place of an overarching model, anthropologists now focus on the specific historical and cultural context of the society or group they are studying. Rather than impose known European kinship terms on non-European societies, researchers retain indigenous terms and systems of classification for relatedness within a group.

Feminist and gender studies approaches have been a driving force in determining the parameters of reconfigured kinship studies. Their emphasis on power differentials in a given group has allowed for the emergence of "multiple ethnographic voices." Anthropologists now pay attention to the social positions of different members of a given group and show how one's position in a group determines one's view of a classificatory system and one's place within it. Differently positioned members within a group employ diverse strategies within a given kinship system in order to secure or improve their positions. These strategies are often keyed to ethnicity, gender, and class.[17]

The decisive move away from universalizing models and the new emphasis on women and gender resulted in a sustained critique and reworking of the concept of patrilineality. Once again, terminology provides our first clue to a methodological shift. Instead of referring to societies like ancient Israel as "patrilineal," many anthropologists have begun to qualify the term, describing societies as favoring, preferring, or valuing male kinship links over female kinship links while nonetheless depending on both. Researching a wide variety of societies, anthropologists have concluded that the "pure" patrilineal model always represents an expressed ideal rather than a lived, practiced reality. Biblically, we have seen that the exclusively paternal record of history found in the *tôlēdôt* is most often juxtaposed with a narrative that details the roles of mothers, younger sons, and daughters. What anthropologists have shown should hardly surprise us: "professed" patrilineal societies depend on women and maternally related kin for their perpetuation and hierarchical ordering. Women and relationships established through women, scholars observed, introduce social and political divisions and hierarchies among men in professed patrilineal societies. Maternally marked hierarchies are not temporary. They do not simply reflect a personal rivalry or jealousy among wives in a domestic household at a given point in time; instead, the hierarchies defined through mothers had an impact on the social and political positions of their children and grandchildren that endured for generations.

In an article focusing on the Nuer, Susan McKinnon creatively captures the skepticism among anthropologists concerning the patrilineal model in her subheading "Patri-? Lineage?"[18] Her skepticism is echoed in the descriptive phrasing of other anthropologists who label patrilineality "an illusion," something that is "at least partly mythical," an "ideology" that is part of a "cultural dogma."[19] Greg Urban argues that anthropologists "fantasized" the importance of descent groups and then "project their own images willy-nilly onto the tabula rasa of indigenous communities."[20]

While some anthropologists have argued for the complete elimination of the term patrilineality,[21] I have found the work of anthropologists who nuance, critique, and reframe it more helpful for biblical material. The authors of the Bible clearly valued patrilineality, and they recorded their history giving pride of place to foundational paternal ancestors. Biblical Hebrew has the indigenous term *tôlēdôt*, and biblical authors and redactors used the *tôlēdôt*, the lists of paternal begettings, as the connective tissue in their story of national origins. Therefore, it is appropriate to consider ancient Israel as a professed patrilineal society, a "male-favoring society," while at the same time recognizing the idealized nature of the claim.

Susan McKinnon is one of the anthropologists who critiques the notion of a "pure patrilineal society" while at the same time recognizing patrilineality as an expressed ideal among the Nuer people. She reexamines E. E. Evans-Pritchard's three-volume work on the ostensibly patrilineal Nuer people, showing how he created "artificial domains" in order to sustain the illusion of pure patrilineality. Evans-Pritchard, she argues, understood his three volumes on the Nuer to represent three discrete domains: *Kinship and Marriage among the Nuer* (1951) focuses on the "domestic" domain; *Nuer Religion* (1956) deals with religious and ritual domains; and *The Nuer: A Description of the Modes of Livelihood and Political Institutions of Nilotic People* (1960) covers the "politico-jural" domain.[22] Evans-Pritchard, McKinnon notes, limited his treatment of bilateral and affinal relationships to the domestic domain.[23] Namely, he argued that relationships established through one's mother or through marriage were only important or worthy of analysis within the domestic domain. This is because Evans-Pritchard, along with Meyer Fortes and Alfred R. Radcliffe-Brown, understood only male, segmentary relations of descent to endure over time, meaning that patrilineal descent alone had an impact on social and political formations over generations. Relationships established through women, they argued, only linked individuals like a husband and a wife or a son and his maternal uncle. Women did not link groups nor did they establish bonds that endured beyond a single generation.[24] McKinnon's reassessment of the Nuer demonstrates that women and relationships established through women were, in fact, essential to understanding what Evans-Pritchard had isolated as the purely patrilineal, politico-jural domain. McKinnon argues that these falsely constructed domains allowed Evans-Pritchard and others to "exclude from the comparative study of political systems all that they have relegated to the substructural 'domestic' domain—including bilateral kinship, affinal relations, and the 'internal' differences in status between persons, individuals, and categories."[25]

According to McKinnon, the practice of domaining also allowed anthropologists to lay claim to several false achievements. She identifies the clear, elegant diagrams of patrilineal descent as one of these false achievements. In her view, the simplicity of these models is only possible through the suppression of domestic and religious dimensions of social life. Ignoring matrilateral kin results in a political model that fails to account for the social hierarchies that such kin introduce into the dominant lineage. The religious and domestic domains are the venues where many of these social hierarchies are formed and practiced.[26] Other researchers have reached similar conclusions. Margery Wolf, whose work focuses on the people of rural Taiwan, argues that the exclusive focus on men in a patrilineal system may cause a researcher to miss "the system's subtleties and also its near fatal weaknesses."[27] For Louise Lamphere, it is the exclusive focus on the "rights and duties" of men in patrilineal models that fails to account for "power and strategies to gain power" where women play active roles.[28]

While anthropologists today emphasize the constructed and fictive nature of the pure patrilineal model, they do not reject the idea that these professed patrilineal societies valued relationships established through men over those established through women. McKinnon, for example, notes that among the Nuer paternal kinship ties were the most valued, but relationships established through female links still had considerable "potency and political force."[29] Edouard Conte recognizes that within Arab societies, marriage between children of paternal brothers is the expressed ideal, but in reality, he argues, the Arab kinship system is cognatic and "characterized by marked asymmetry of gender relations."[30] Lila Abu-Lughod, who studied a Bedouin community in Egypt, recognizes that within this community, "agnation has indisputable ideological priority in kin reckoning" and "descent, inheritance and tribal socio-political organization are conceptualized as patrilineal."[31] Nonetheless, she adds, maternal kin are "strategically useful," even though the bonds formed through maternal kin are conceptualized in terms of "sentiment"—"closeness, identification, common interests, and loyalty."[32] The Bedouin preference for "kin ties established through agnation" found full expression in the way couples presented their marital ties. Even if a couple were more closely related through maternal kin, they would present their relationship in terms of their paternal kin.[33] This is an excellent example of the ways a cognatic reality may be hidden by an agnatic ideology.

Karen Sinclair, who studies the Maori, likewise notes that among the Maori, there is a decided "preference" for "patrilocal residence and transmission of property to patrilineal descendants." But pure patrilineal descent and primogeniture are best understood as "values" held by the Maori; they are part of Maori "dogma."[34] Maori dogma articulates a worldview where older brothers are "pure," "legitimate," and "system sustaining," while younger brothers and women are "polluted," "antisocial," and "system threatening" (168). Maori myth, on the other hand, celebrates women and younger brothers as allied teams who "herald creative transformative feats" (157). Again, what we see is the coexistence of a professed patrilineal ideal with a messier reality that involved women and lower-status men.

A repeated observation within these reexaminations of purportedly patrilineal or male-favoring societies is that maternal kin introduce politically significant and generationally enduring hierarchies and internal group divisions. Maternal kinship bonds are not transient nor are they limited to the domestic household.[35] Abu-Lughod concludes that outside of agnation, "the two most important bonds between individuals were maternal kinship and co-residence."[36] The Maori, who had a clear preference for patrilineal inheritance, still practiced what Sinclair calls "descent group recruitment through women" as a "second best" but useful choice.[37] Finally, Wolf concludes her study of the patrilineal and polygynous villages of rural Taiwan by emphasizing that "the descent lines of men are born and nourished in the uterine families of women, and it is here that a male ideology that excludes women makes its accommodations with reality."[38] This ongoing critique of the patrilineal model suggests that biblical scholars engaged in kinship studies need to theorize women and the relationships established through women. Instead of "domaining" women and matrilateral kin out of the treatments of political and social structures, we need to theorize all relationships within one lens, "as part of one integral system."[39]

To summarize, the anthropological investigation of kinship structures has moved away from universalizing models in favor of culturally and historically specific investigations of individual societies. The historical and cultural integrity of a society is maintained in part through the retention of indigenous kinship terminology. Anthropologists recognize the language of a pure patriline as an articulated ideal rather than a practiced reality, and so they have expanded their investigations of kinship structures to include multiple players in a given household and society. Scholars now theorize the differently positioned members of a household and the multiple strategies each uses to gain a secure position. Most important for this study, women and the relationships formed through maternal ties are central to understanding internal and multi-group hierarchies in professed patrilineal societies.

Biblical Scholarship and the Reevaluation of Kinship in the Bible

The thoroughgoing critique of the patrilineal model within anthropology requires that biblical scholars working today reevaluate earlier treatments of ancient Israelite kinship. Many scholars have already begun this process, and their work serves as a foundation for my own.[40] Here, I briefly mention only a few studies that have made important advances. In the 1960s, George E. Mendenhall and Mary Douglas had already rejected the use of universalizing models and evolutionary schemes in interpreting the historical development of ancient Israel.[41] Robert Wilson, Ronald Hendel, Elizabeth Bloch-Smith, and many others have demonstrated the ideological and socially constructed nature of biblical genealogies.[42] Similarly, Lawrence E. Stager and David J. Schloen have outlined the ideological and symbolic language that the Bible uses to articulate its social and political organization through "the house of the father."[43] Biblical scholars have noted the ambiguity of specific Hebrew kinship terms and identified their ideological function in the biblical text and their participation in social hierarchies within the house of the father.[44] They have shown multiple meanings for specific Hebrew kinship terms like *na'ar* (young man) and *na'ărâ* (young woman), *'āb* (father) and *bat* (daughter), *běkôr* (firstborn or designated heir), *bêt 'āb* (house of the father), and *mišpāḥâ* (clan, family).⁴⁵ Most important for my study are the many scholars who have demonstrated the important social, economic, and political functions of women in the house of the father and in village, religious, and political spheres as well. I engage the work of these scholars in all of the chapters that follow.

The Bible as the Primary Source for Biblical Kinship

In this book I identify and define indigenous Hebrew kinship terms that are maternally specific. Since these terms are found in the narratives and poetry of the Hebrew Bible, the Bible is my primary source text; it is the literary context within which we can define and attempt to understand Hebrew kinship terms. Greg Urban's discourse-analysis approach to social organization is helpful in determining the nature of the Bible as a source document. He notes that a community's "discourse" or "talk" about kinship does not simply describe that community as it already exists; it participates in the community-building process.⁴⁶ Moreover, during times of transition or community upheaval, a community's discourse on kinship shapes its identity and can provide "seeming fixity with respect to a reality in flux."⁴⁷ This becomes important when we consider that biblical narrative was shaped into a nation-defining document during and following sequential exiles, historical periods marked by extreme uncertainty and communal upheaval.⁴⁸ For Judeans during and following the period of the Babylonian exile, the discourse of biblical narrative, poetry, and genealogical lists would have created a fixed or stable image of themselves that confronted their constantly shifting reality.⁴⁹ Several features of the evolving biblical story presented Judeans with an image of stability and purpose. Family narratives that offered migrant Judeans a discourse about being part of the "House of Israel" and descending from Jacob gave meaning to their return to the land. Discourse about the national god Yahweh as the god of their direct ancestors—Abraham, Isaac, and Jacob—helped a fractured community begin to feel connected. "Talk" about standing in a direct line of inheritance for the land of Israel empowered returning Judeans in their resettlement of Judah and what had been Israel. Finally, elevating this narrative to the status of scripture presented this evolving discourse on national identity as an agreed-upon image of the resettled Judah.

The Bible is not an ethnographic report of ancient Israelite society and therefore does not provide a direct window into the lives, values, and beliefs of average ancient Israelites from a particular time period. Multiple ethnographic voices, however, are discernable even though the Bible is not per se an ethnographic report. Biblical family narratives provide differing vantage points on a house, village, society, or kingdom through multiple characters' voices. The male-favoring values found in the begats and in some proverbs give voice to a cultural ideal. Family narratives like those focusing on the household of Abraham or Jacob allow the voices of "underdogs and tricksters," women and younger sons, to be heard.[50] We can even consider the Bible's multiple sources, its redactional layers, as ethnographic voices; one generation comments on the values of a previous generation by adding a family member or changing a kinship label in order to give precedence to a particular view of history. In this book, we see how references to maternal kin can elevate or discredit a particular house's claim to insider status.

Maternally specific kinship terms appear most concentrated in the biblical books that feature well-known foundational family narratives: the houses of Abraham, Isaac, and Jacob in Genesis 12–50; the house of Levi leading up to Moses in Exodus 1–6; the house of Gideon/Jerubbaal in Judges 6–9; the house of David in 1 and 2 Samuel. The core of the stories about these origin houses dates to the pre-exilic period.[51] We then have additional texts, likely dating to the exilic and postexilic periods, that update, expand upon, and revise these family histories. Ruth comments on an existing tradition of the house of David.[52] Song of Songs, with its attribution and punctuated references to King Solomon, assumes an existing lore about Solomon's royal house. Texts in Numbers reorganize the house of Jacob to reflect postexilic priestly ideals.[53] While it is outside of the scope of this book to provide a diachronic analysis of each maternally specific kinship term, there are some historical patterns that can be discerned in the development of the Bible's foundational family narratives. First, birth stories, which tend to provide information about the mothers of foundational ancestors, seem to develop late in the process of building a biography of a hero. Second, where we can trace a diachronic development of a hero's narrative, later additions seem to add genealogical complexity by including mothers or mothers' names, adding additional wives, or changing the label for a wife. In each of these cases, later authors use women in the hero's family ideologically to present a certain line, one to which the author likely belongs, as legitimate, ascendant, and divinely chosen. They also use the addition of wives and mothers to clarify other lines as outsiders to the people of Israel or as marginal within the power structures of a resettled Judah. So while this book is in general synchronic in its approach to identifying and defining maternally specific kinship terms, there are certain places where a diachronic analysis helps to show the ideological function of wives and mothers in the ongoing construction of the Bible's foundational houses.

Extra-Biblical Literary Sources from the Ancient Near East

The anthropological emphasis on examining cultures within their specific historical and linguistic contexts argues against any effort to make sweeping kinship claims about "the ancient Near East." This book focuses on biblical kinship terminology and does not attempt to draw comprehensive analogies with the broader ancient Near East. Nonetheless, there are strong arguments for bringing in some ancient Near Eastern sources that feature the same maternally specific kinship terms that we are attempting to understand. As Semitic languages, Ugaritic and Akkadian can provide a broader cultural, linguistic, and historical framework for understanding specific kinship labels. Many of the biblical kinship terms that I cover in this study are found in Ugaritic and Akkadian texts, even to the extent of replicating word pairs and using them in similar social contexts. Moreover, these kinship terms are found in texts of a similar literary genre, namely the foundational narratives of human and divine kings.[54] For example, the biblical word pair "my brother, the son of my mother," is also found in the Ugaritic Baal Cycle and in the Akkadian language Succession Treaty of Esarhaddon.[55] The examples of this word pair in the Bible are sufficient, in and of themselves, to establish the meaning of the kinship term and its expected social functions. Ugaritic and Akkadian parallels strengthen the argument made based on biblical source material alone. Moreover, the early dating of the Ugaritic and Akkadian texts demonstrates that the kinship structure within which maternal kin carried out important social functions was not a late Hebrew or postexilic innovation. Instead, the social function of maternal kin is as enduring historically as the male-favoring social structure within which it is embedded.

Modern Ethnographies

Throughout this study, I, like so many biblical researchers before me, have turned to anthropological studies of kinship and to ethnographic studies of specific societies as a secondary source base for the study of biblical kinship. Ethnographies documenting societies that are historically, culturally, and linguistically removed from ancient Israel cannot be used to fill in the gaps in our historical record of ancient Israel. They cannot provide definitive answers to a biblical researcher's questions. Instead, modern ethnographic studies help to make biblical researchers such as myself aware of the cultural box within which we read and analyze texts and generate questions for the text. Once we are aware of our own cultural box, we can attempt to inhabit other cultural boxes in order to broaden our vantage point and generate new sets of questions and a wider range of possible answers. Ken Stone is correct here when he notes that "anthropological concepts can help us to construct and continually reassess our reading frames—that is to say, our ideas about the possible context of symbols and beliefs in terms of which the texts seem to make sense—in a way that at least mitigates our tendency to interpret biblical texts in terms of our own assumptions."[56] While modern ethnographies do not fill in the gaps in the biblical record, they can remove cultural blinders allowing biblical scholars to see patterns and make connections that might not otherwise have been possible. Still, only biblical and epigraphic evidence in Hebrew and related Semitic languages can provide the answers to questions raised by a biblical researcher's encounter with another society through a recorded ethnography.

One especially clear example from this book is found in chapter 6. My reading of ethnographic studies made me aware for the first time of multiple societies that considered breast milk to be a substance that transmitted ethnic identity and social status from mother or wet nurse to suckling. This new interpretive possibility led me to reconsider the Bible's understanding of breastfeeding and breast milk and helped me to recognize the indigenous Hebrew phrase, "O that you were like a brother to me, *one who had nursed at my mother's breasts*," as a kinship term. It also suggested that I pay attention to the ethnic and status markers that were present within biblical narratives that featured breastfeeding. A less specific example, but one that has proven essential to my research, is the prominent role of uterine siblings in polygynous societies. Uterine siblings are siblings born to the same mother in a household where the father has more than one wife. Jabal and Jubal, for example, are uterine siblings within the house of Lamech. Even though we cannot make a universalizing statement about the function of uterine siblings in male-favoring, polygynous societies, we can observe that this relationship is an important and strategic one that deserves scholarly attention.

There are a couple of checks and balances we can use when bringing ethnographic material to bear on the biblical text. First, any concept, kinship term, or cultural pattern that is suggested by a comparative ethnography and subsequently "recognized" within the biblical text should be present within the biblical text through indigenous terminology and modes of expression. Second, if an anthropologically generated term or concept is authentically present within the world of the biblical text, it will solve rather than create textual problems. In this book, we see how the concept of "patrilineage" led scholars repeatedly to emend the biblical text in order to maintain the illusion of a pure patriline. Restoring women and maternally identified kin to the house of the father shows that in multiple cases textual emendation is not necessary.

Archaeology

While my primary source base is the biblical text, in chapters 1 and 3 I examine the archaeological scholarship on the pillared house and on gendering the house in order to elucidate the Bible's division of the house of the father into maternal subunits. One of the main differences between the Bible's houses and the excavated houses of ancient Israel is that biblical houses are much larger and more complex than the houses of average ancient Israelites. In some ways, the excavation of elite houses, royal palaces, and temples might provide more valuable data for understanding the multi-chambered, multi-tented, or multi-dwelling houses like those of Abraham, Jacob, Gideon, David, or Solomon. Still, some of the larger, rural household compounds that contained multiple dwellings opening onto a shared courtyard or linked by a contiguous wall help to provide a brick-and-mortar anchor for house-related vocabulary that emerges in biblical narrative.

Methodology: A Discourse Analysis of Indigenous Hebrew Kinship Terms

This study takes as its starting point current anthropological emphases on retaining indigenous kin terms and respecting the historical specificity of a given community. Additionally, my study of maternal kinship in the Bible is attentive to multiple strategies for survival and ascendance that are in evidence within biblical family narratives. The first chapter of this study introduces more fully the indigenous Hebrew terms "house" (*bayit*) and "house of the father" (*bêt 'āb*), both of which are foundational to any study of biblical kinship. Each of the following chapters then identifies maternally specific, indigenous kinship terms that are associated with the house or house of the father, terms that have not been recognized properly as distinct kinship classifications. These terms are sometimes dismissed from comment and other times emended to reflect patrilineal ideals. English translations frequently erase the maternally specific nature of these kinship terms. In my analysis, I retain the Hebrew for the kinship terms and offer literal translations into English. Hebrew grammar, syntax, and literary context help to uncover the social, political, and ritual functions that the biblical text associates with each maternally specific kinship term.

Because indigenous terminology represents the starting point for this study, I sketch my approach to identifying and defining these kinship terms. According to Stanley K. Stowers, the purpose of a definition is to classify a term, compare it to like terms, and provide an interpretation of the term that attempts to explain it.[57] In my case, I am confining my study to the "house" (*bayit*) and to maternally specific kinship terms that appear in relationship to the biblical house. In the chapters that follow, I provide new or emended definitions for Hebrew terms such as "house"; "house of the mother"; "my brother, the son of my mother"; "son of my womb"; "a brother who nursed at my mother's breasts"; "the womb-opener"; and "the house of the father of my mother." Defining these terms ultimately shows their connectedness one with another but also their connection to and indispensability within other known kinship entities such as the "house of the father," the "nation" or "people," and the "kingdom."

As soon as we label a Hebrew term a "kinship term" and translate it into English, we confront a problem. While definitions can be heuristic, they can also mislead, and the danger with translating and defining Hebrew kin terms into English is that we might impose foreign assumptions onto indigenous terms. If definition is a form of redescription, then it necessarily requires that the researcher take a native or local term and redescribe it in ways that serve the researcher's interests.[58] A definition can also suggest a kind of universality and fixity in the understanding of a term, when in reality language is dynamic, shifting, and perspectival. To avoid falsely restricting the meaning of a given term, I first retain the Hebrew when possible and provide literal translations for Hebrew kinship terms. I also show how the understanding of many kinship terms shifts depending on the speaker, the social context, and the words that emerge juxtaposed to it. In short, I allow for what Edouard Conte has called "extreme semantic latitude" in the definition of kin terms.[59] Greg Urban locates the distinction between real and ideal kinship relations in the area of discourse. He argues that researchers have to distinguish between kinship terms and *talk* about kinship terms.[60] He defines "social organization," his preferred term for "kinship," as "the interpretation of the social world through discourse."[61] This study retains indigenous terminology and categories, acknowledges multiple native-speaker understandings of a single term, and recognizes the difference between ideal categories and lived practice of kin and kinship functions.

In order to keep my focus on an indigenous understanding of each of the kinship terms and to identify additional terms, I depend on Hebrew grammar and syntax where the juxtaposition or co-emergence of terms communicates connectedness. A key insight in this regard has come from Hebrew word pairs, whether in apposition or divided in a parallelistic line. Hebrew kinship designations often take the form of parallel lines with split word pairs wherein the second element of the word pair narrows, specifies, and defines the first. Some examples that are covered in this book include "into the house of my mother, into the chamber of her who conceived me" (Song 3:4); "my brothers, the sons of my mother" (Judg 8:19); "like a brother, one who had nursed at my mother's breasts" (Song 8:1); and "No my son, no son of my vows, no son of my womb" (Prov 31:2). I cover biblical scholarship on word pairs and my application of this scholarship to maternally specific kinship terminology in chapter 3.

In order to arrive at an indigenous understanding of Hebrew kinship terms, I subject each narrative example to the following set of questions:

1. How and when does the kinship term emerge, and in what literary contexts?
2. When a term occurs, what kinds of ideals and assumed realities are present?
3. What narrative expectations are set up with the introduction of a maternally specific kinship term?
4. When does a person enter a narrative with a kinship label? Does the person also have a name or only a label? To whom does the kinship label connect the person? Does this particular kinship label obscure other possible kinship relations?
5. When do kinship labels shift or disappear in a narrative and what does this signal?

6. What additional terms co-emerge with this term? How are these additional terms grammatically and/or syntactically related to the term under consideration?[62]

This study ultimately provides a more robust picture of the biblical house of the father, refusing to reduce it to a simple patriline and instead uncovering the presence and significance of maternal kin at all levels of social organization. For the first time, this book identifies, gathers together, and theorizes a collection of indigenous Hebrew kinship terms for maternally related kin. I analyze and define terms like "house of the mother"; "my brother, the son of my mother"; "child who opens the womb"; and "the house of the father of my mother," showing how together these terms outline the unique composition and multilayered social functions of the house of the mother. When we include all of these maternally specific kinship terms in the analysis, it becomes clear that the biblical house of the father divides into maternally defined, unequal subunits. The house of Jacob divides into four subunits, two that trace their ancestry to wives and two that trace their ancestry to secondary, maidservant wives. In the history of ancient Israel and Judah, the sons born to wives found royal and priestly houses while the sons born to maidservant wives are for the most part grouped together anonymously, allocated peripheral land parcels, and remain insignificant in political and sacerdotal realms. For all that we associate the "begats" with kinship in the Bible, they only tell one part of the biblical story. The far more significant part of the story is found within and between biblical "houses" where men and women of varying statuses speak, act, and jockey for control of the historical narrative.

1 House (*bayit*)

The starting point for any study of ancient Israelite kinship structures is the biblical unit known as the "house" or *bayit*, which is often found as part of the construct chain "house of the father" (*bêt 'āb*). Scholars have long recognized the *bêt 'āb* as "the basic building block of the tribal structure"[1] or "the basic unit of Israelite society,"[2] and descriptive translations aim to capture its kinship dimensions: "the joint family,"[3] "family household,"[4] and "ancestral household."[5] There are two pathways for primary research and exploration of the ancient Israelite house. The first is linguistic and literary through the biblical text, and the second is archaeological, focusing on the excavation of Iron I and Iron II "pillared houses."[6] In the Bible, the Hebrew word *bayit* can refer to multiple entities, including an extended-family household, a subunit within a domestic household, a palace, a temple, a nation, and a dynasty. Archaeologists have excavated common village dwellers' houses and common and elite urban houses, and these excavations have contributed enormously to our understanding of the ancient Israelite house described in the Bible. Archaeologists have also excavated palaces and temples in the Levant, and these structures also add to our understanding of the ancient Israelite conception of the house as not only a unit of domestic production but also one of social, political, and religious organization.

Theorizing the Biblical *Bayit*

Unlike the patriline that we examined in the introduction, the Hebrew kinship unit labeled the "house" (*bayit*) is ubiquitous in Hebrew narrative, poetry, and law.[7] Ancient Israel articulated its social organization at all levels from the nuclear family to the nation through the rubric of the Hebrew word for house. This single word describes multiple social, political, physical, and symbolic entities. Israel imagined its own nation as a house, *bêt yiśrā'ēl* (1 Sam 7:2, 3; 2 Sam 1:12; 6:5, 15; 12:8; 16:3), and later as a divided house, *bêt yiśrā'ēl* and *bêt yĕhûdāh* (1 Kings 12:21, 23; 2 Kings 19:30). Israel's king lived in a *bayit* as did its god, and common people lived in *bāttîm* (houses). One frequently cited text features a wonderful interplay on the multiple meanings of the Hebrew *bayit*, where the word describes King David's palace, the temple David hoped to build for Yahweh, and the eternal dynasty that Yahweh promised to David (2 Sam 7). Surrounding nations viewed Israel and Judah as "houses" as well. The Aramaic Tel Dan Stele refers to the "house of David." The Black Obelisk of Shalmaneser III of Assyria mentions the "house of Omri," and in the inscription on the Mesha Stele, King Mesha looks down on "the son of Omri" and on "his house."[8]

At its most basic level, *bayit* describes both a physical dwelling place and the group of people who reside within it.[9] In 1958, Roland de Vaux captured this dual identity well: "The 'family' is a 'house'; to found a family is 'to build a house.'"[10] The biblical house is found most frequently as part of the construct phrase "house of the father" (*bêt 'āb*), and this is where scholars have often blurred the line between a patriline and a paternally named house. Several biblical scholars have used the English term "lineage" as a translation of *bayit* or as a description for what *bayit* signifies.[11] This creates the illusion that a Hebrew equivalent of the word "lineage" is woven throughout the biblical text when in reality biblical scholars are theorizing the "house" through the imposed lens of a patriline.

I support the consensus view among scholars that the *bêt 'āb* was a kinship designation that encompassed both shared residence and dependent, possibly biological relationships to a founding male ancestor.[12] De Vaux, for example, defined the *bêt 'āb* as comprising "those who are united by common blood and common dwelling-place."[13] Two decades later Norman K. Gottwald affirmed this dual usage, suggesting that the *bêt 'āb* was "a compromise formation involving kinship and residence."[14] More recently, Phillip J. King and Lawrence E. Stager have described the *bêt 'āb* as "a group of families with descent from the same *paterfamilias* and dwelling in the same region or village."[15] They also point to the inclusive nature of the *bêt 'āb*, defining its social composition as a father, "his wife or wives, sons and their wives, grandsons and their wives, the unmarried sons and daughters, slaves, servants, *gērîm*, aunts, uncles, widows, orphans, and Levites."[16]

The biblical *bayit* is a fuller representation of ancient Israelite kinship than what is presented in the *tôlēdôt*. A named, foundational house in the Bible, like the house of Jacob or the house of David, did include and privilege a living, senior male head of household and his designated heir (*běkôr*).[17] At the same time, however, it also included men of varying statuses who moved in and out of the household over the course of its existence: sons of the single-portion inheritance; illegitimate, non-inheriting sons;[18] sons-in-law;[19] adopted sons;[20] slaves; levite priests; and dependent workers (*gērîm*).[21] We also find numerous women in named foundational houses, and like the men, they were of varying statuses: the mother of the male head of household,[22] primary and secondary wives of each generation of men,[23] concubines,[24] unmarried sisters and daughters,[25] married daughters,[26] and female slaves.

One of the most important houses described in the Bible is that of Jacob, a domestic household that later morphs into the national house of Israel. At the domestic level, the story of Jacob describes an individual man who ultimately obtains four wives and has twelve sons and a daughter. On the national level, the house of Jacob is the origin house for what becomes the house of Israel. The twelve sons of Jacob become the twelve tribes of Israel, or simply "the sons of Israel" (*běnê yiśrā'ēl*), a phrase that is usually translated as "the Israelites," showing that this kinship term is properly understood to designate a nationality. While scholars have developed social and political theories that show how the twelve sons of Jacob formed a twelve-tribe "amphictyony," or the twelve-tribe "confederation," the four wives of Jacob have not been central to discussions of nation and state formation.[27] From a theoretical perspective, women and relationships formed through maternal ties have remained locked behind the doors of the domestic household (fig. 2).

As a collection of writings written and edited over centuries, the Bible preserves the origin stories for foundational houses that date to multiple periods: the houses of Abraham, Isaac, and Jacob; the house of Levi; the house of Israel; and the house of Judah. Many of the origin stories for these houses were written during the monarchic period (1000–586 BCE) and provide information on ancient Israelite and Judean views of the house. Other stories focusing on foundational houses were written during and following the Babylonian exile and reflect the views of Judeans who returned from exile and sought to rebuild their homeland in what was then the Persian province of Yehud. Seeing themselves as the new Israel, the only surviving heirs to the house of Israel, these returning exiles edited and updated

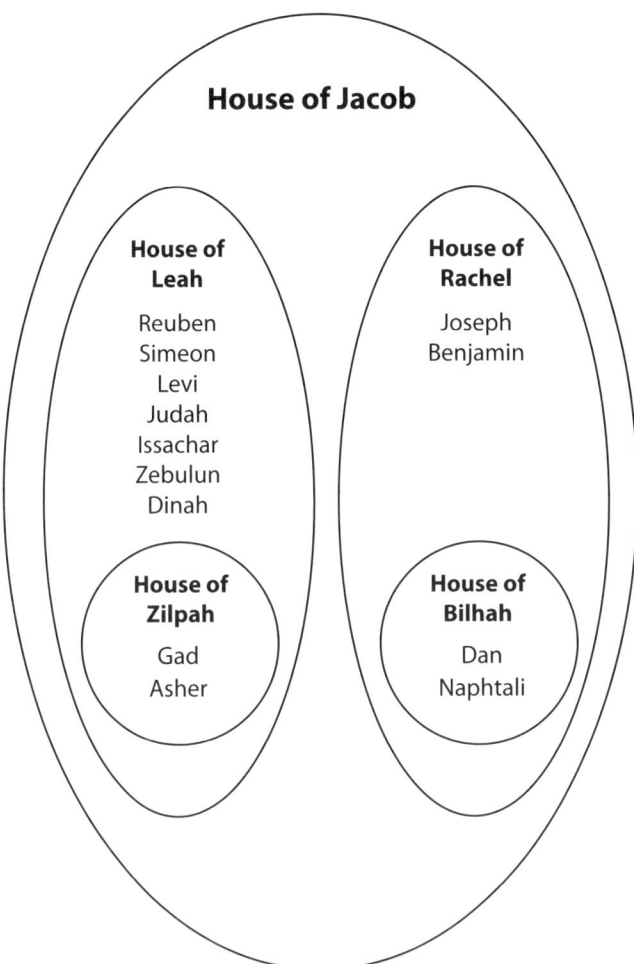

Figure 2. *The household of Jacob with maternal sub-houses, Gen 29:31–30:24; 35:16–21. Illustration created by Ondrea Keith, rendered by Bill Nelson.*

the origin stories of ancient Israel's foundational houses in order to speak to the concerns of a resettled Judah. This means that when we turn to the Bible as a primary source text on the house, we are investigating a historically layered record, and we are seeing, at times, competing views of history that are played out through differing presentations of foundational houses.

The houses described most fully in the Bible do not belong to commoners. Instead, biblical houses were named for revered paternal ancestors and contained extended families with multiple wives, tremendous generational depth, and an enduring claim to a fixed or rooted geography in what the Bible labels "The Promised Land." Abraham had three wives and eight sons. Jacob had four wives, twelve sons, and a daughter. David and Solomon had countless wives, concubines, and children. Similar complexity is found in the priestly houses of Moses and Aaron. Finally, Ezekiel presents the house of Yahweh as a polygynous household divided into two tented maternal subunits: Oholah of Samaria and Oholibah of Jerusalem (Ezek 23).[28] As the biblical authors carefully preserved, edited, and updated the origin stories of these foundational houses, each successive generation claimed a direct and legitimate genealogical pathway back to the founding father.

The Bible rarely provides us with a window into the houses of commoners; it is not a book about commoners. Occasionally, we get a glimpse of a commoner's house when that person comes into contact with one of the Bible's extraordinary individuals. When the man of god, Elijah, is told to go to a widow in Zarephath, we see her gated village and her two-story dwelling with sleeping quarters on the second floor. We note a household size of two: a mother and her son (1 Kings 17:8–24).[29] The story of Naboth the Jezreelite does not focus on his physical dwelling; instead, through King Ahab's covetous gaze, we are allowed to see the material wealth of a commoner's house, a vineyard that Naboth considers "the inheritance" of his "fathers," something he cannot sell even to a king (1 Kings 21:1–4).[30] Other brief narrative encounters with non-elite houses inform us that they had doors and roofs and a place to bake bread, as we see Lot shutting the door of his house to protect his guests who were eating unleavened bread he had prepared inside (Gen 19:1–11). In the parallel story of the Levite's concubine, we receive the added detail that houses had thresholds upon which a devastated woman could place her hands (Judg 19:27). While this is in no way an exhaustive treatment of the Bible's references to non-elite houses, the main point is that the Bible as a source on the ancient Israelite house provides its most detailed information on named, foundational houses of revered ancestors, kings, priests, and gods.

This does not mean, however, that there is no connection between the complex, elite houses of biblical ancestors and the common houses of ancient Israelites. The fact that ancient Israelites referred to all of these structures with the single word *bayit* says that they saw a connection between their own common dwellings and their kings' palaces and their gods' temples. In order for ancient Israelites and later Judeans to understand and treasure the origin stories of the houses of Abraham, Jacob, Judah, or Levi, the physical and social composition and the associated kinship terms of these houses would have to be understandable or translatable across classes.

One of the ways that the common Israelite *bayit* connects to the elite foundational houses of the Bible is through the mechanism of "nesting." The Israelite *bayit* was a nested entity such that an individual's house was understood to be part of a larger extended family household complex, which was, in turn, understood as an entity within a larger village and ultimately within a nation. In this way, a commoner's house was a microcosm of the national house. We see this in the oft-cited hierarchy of terms whereby several houses of the father (*bāttê 'āb*) or an especially large, extended-family *bêt 'āb* could become a *mišpāḥâ* or "clan." Several clans comprised a *šēbeṭ* or *maṭṭeh*, both terms usually translated as "tribe," and several tribes made up an *'am*, a "nation" or "people."[31] While there are very few texts that outline a complete hierarchy of these terms, there is a clear sense that the organizational principle governing the relationship between these kinship designations is one of nesting.[32] Smaller units, like the *bayit* or *bêt 'āb*, are nested within larger units like the *mišpāḥâ* and *'am*. Where there is ambiguity between terms, it concerns the point at which, for example, the *bêt 'āb* is large enough to merit the designation *mišpāḥâ*. Because the composition of the *bêt 'āb* changed over time, it could at its smallest be a single nuclear family and at its largest be a multi-generation, extended family including numerous nuclear cell groups.[33] The concept of nested units, even with this ambiguity, continues to explain the relationship between these terms because it is the dynamic growth and contraction of the *bêt 'āb* nested within the *mišpāḥâ* that allows for a mature, extended-family *bêt 'āb* to morph organically into a *mišpāḥâ*.[34]

More common than the hierarchy of nested terms, however, is the use of the term *bayit* by itself to represent multiple levels of social groupings. What we would call the nuclear family, the extended family, the clan, the tribe, and the nation were all appropriately labeled "houses" in biblical Hebrew. When Rebekah tells her son Jacob that she will get him Esau's best garment that is "with her in the house," she is referring to a single dwelling housing a nuclear family (Gen 27:15). When Joshua announces, "As for me and my house, we will serve Yahweh," he is likely referring to a collection of Ephraimite houses, extended families, over which he held authority (Josh 24:15).[35] When Isaiah demands, "Hear this O House of Jacob, who are called by the name of Israel," he is addressing a nation (Isa 48:1). And finally, when Solomon turns to his god in public prayer, proclaiming, "I have built you an exalted house," he is referring to a national sanctuary built for a national god (1 Kings 8:13).

Lawrence Stager has applied the concept of nested households to Jerusalem as a "regal-ritual city" wherein the palace and temple complex represented the "symbolic center of the kingdom and the cosmos."[36] He describes the concentricity of the Israelite cosmion as three-tiered based on "a series of nested households": the *bêt 'āb* at the base of the hierarchy; the king's *bayit*, which corresponded to the level of the "state" or "tribal kingdom"; and finally the *bayit* of Yahweh, "who reigns as supreme patrimonial Lord," occupying the "apex of authority in this three-tiered cosmion."[37] He concludes, "Households are nested within households up the tiers of the cosmion, each tier becoming more overarching as one moves from domestic to royal to divine levels."[38]

The concept of nesting can also be applied to the internal composition of the *bêt 'āb* itself. Several scholars have demonstrated that the house of the father, though considered "the basic unit of Israelite society," was nonetheless divisible into smaller entities that had meaningful social functions. Stager examines the biblical description of the house of Micah (Judg 17–18) and the archaeological record of contiguous dwellings around a shared courtyard within ancient Israelite villages, and in both he finds clues that suggest an extended *bêt 'āb* could contain multiple dwellings that were likewise labeled "houses" (*bāttîm*).[39] Building on the work of Stager, Susan Ackerman details the number of buildings, or *bāttîm*, that were contained within the single *bayit* of Micah as described in Judg 17–18. At least two adult men, Micah's adult son and a young Levite, have "houses" or what we might call "sub-households" within the *bayit* headed by Micah.[40] Shunya Bendor argues that within a *bêt 'āb*, each marrying son formed his own *bayit*, here understood as a nuclear family. Citing Deut 20:5–9, Bendor suggests that the actions of "building a house, planting a vineyard, and taking a wife are joined together" such that "the nuclear cell becomes a unit existing in its own right within the *bêt 'āb*." Moreover, these three actions "symbolize life at a decisive stage for a member of the *bêt 'āb* who has come to set up his own unit of existence in his *bêt 'āb*."[41] Frederick Greenspahn argues similarly that the *bêt 'āb* subdivides into the number of inheriting sons, thus, each son represents a nascent *bêt 'āb*.[42] The work of these scholars suggests that nested within an extended *bêt 'āb*, one could expect to find several smaller *bāttîm*, what I would call sub-houses.

The biblical *bayit* as a nested entity suggests that common ancient Israelites could relate to and understand the complex, polygynous structure of the Bible's royal and priestly houses. The kinship terms that are specific to a polygynous household—slave wife, concubine, son of his maidservant, the son of my mother—would make sense to people who lived in single, nuclear-family cells even if they did not have slave wives or concubines. In modern English, for example, there are a series of kinship terms that describe complex families that some of us have never experienced. Still, we all understand the meaning of terms like "stepsister," "birth mother," "egg donor," "second wife," and "ex-husband." As common citizens, we can also understand and relate to the White House that contains the Lincoln Bedroom, the Oval Office, and the West Wing, even if our own houses simply have a guestroom or pullout couch, a desk in the corner of the kitchen, and a garage. The biblical stories of foundational houses were told, retold, recorded, and preserved because they were meaningful to ancient Israelites and later Judeans. The language of the domestic household made sense and gave structure to their national, social, and religious history.

Biblical source material on foundational houses also provides a window into the perspectives or vantage points of less privileged members of a household. Because the house, unlike the lineage, contains multiple people of varying statuses, the analysis of the biblical *bayit* allows us to hear multiple perspectives on a single *bêt 'āb*, and we find that these multiple perspectives reflect internal divisions and hierarchies within a house. Anthropologists studying living societies refer to this phenomenon as paying attention to multiple ethnographic voices and strategies within a single household.[43] In biblical narratives focusing on houses, alternating characters give voice to patrilineal ideals or dogma, on the one hand, and to the disruptive and transformative actions of women, younger brothers, and slaves, on the other.

If, for example, we look at the biblical *bayit* from the perspective of the house-founding father, we find that he is centrally focused on producing and designating a male heir for the purposes of land inheritance and the continuation of his paternal name and monument on that land. Insofar as patrilineality represents a professed ideal in the biblical text, I suggest that there are a constellation of related Hebrew terms that participated in the construction of the patrilineal ideal. These include "house of the father" (*bêt 'āb*), "paternal begettings" (*tôlēdôt*), "patrimonial inheritance" (*naḥălâ*), "designated heir" (*bĕkôr*), "name" (*šēm*), "monument" (*yād*), and "seed" (*zeraʿ*).

Each of these terms represents the presumed stability and eternal nature of a foundational father's house as he passed his name, inheritance, and monument to his designated heir in an unbroken chain presented in the biblical begettings. Together these terms communicate what we might call ancient Israel's patrilineal "dogma."

Biblical narratives, however, are rarely presented from the singular vantage point of the house-founding father. They give voice to different players within the house, showing how each member viewed the household differently depending on his or her vantage point.[44] Stager, for example, notes the position of "surplus sons" in a *bêt 'āb* with a dwindling patrimonial inheritance (*naḥălâ*). He demonstrates that the Hebrew term "*nā'ar*" designated a man who had not yet and possibly would never found his own *bayit*. Stager shows how the term *nā'ar* describes men in a variety of social positions: an unmarried man who has not yet become a head of household, the soldiers who formed the core of David's personal army, and priests like Jonathan the Levite who served in the house of Micah.[45] More recently, Carolyn S. Leeb has demonstrated that a *nā'ar* was a person who stood outside the supportive network of his father's house and therefore served another house.[46] A consistent characteristic of a *nā'ar* is that he was not a head of household and therefore would view his father's house differently from a firstborn son.

Bendor also highlights the different vantage points of players within the house of the father and how Hebrew terms are keyed to changes in vantage point. Focusing on a father and his adult son in a *bêt 'āb*, Bendor notes that the unit Jacob refers to as his "*bayit*" (Gen 30:30; 34:30; 35:2), Joseph describes as his "*bêt 'āb*" (Gen 50:8).[47] This suggests that when Joseph built a house, planted a vineyard, and took a wife, he continued to be a member of his *bêt 'āb*, Jacob's *bayit*, but he was also now able to refer to his own *bayit*.[48] Niels Peter Lemche sees the same simultaneity of sons' houses within a father's house in the story of Joseph sending his brothers back to Canaan. Joseph instructs his brothers to fetch "your father and your houses" (*bāttêkem*) and bring them to settle in Egypt.[49] Finally, Carol Meyers asserts that what men in a household referred to as their *bêt 'āb*, women in the same household referred to as their *bêt 'ēm*, or "house of the mother." In her words, "viewed from within, the family household [*bêt 'āb*] had another designation: *bêt 'ēm* or 'mother's house.'"[50] I would instead suggest far greater complexity in the conceptualization of women's houses and women's vantage points within houses. Like a young man who refers to his father's house and at the same time establishes his own house nested within it, women also became members of multiple household groupings that changed over the course of their lives. A woman could refer to and reside within her "father's house" (Judg 19:2), "her mother's house" (Gen 24:28), "her husband's house" (Ruth 1:9), "her brother's house" (2 Sam 13:20), and as I argue below, her own, maternally generated "house" as a nested entity within the house of her husband. We examine all of these vantage points more fully in the chapters that follow, beginning in the next chapter with the term "house of her mother."

The Pillared House

The concepts of nesting, multiple vantage points, and dynamic growth and contraction of households find concrete articulation in the architecture of the pillared house. Archaeologists see a direct link between the biblical "house of the father" and the archaeological joint-family compound made up of multiple, often contiguous pillared houses sometimes clustered around a shared courtyard with shared subsistence resources.[51] The pillared house type has such a strong association with Israelite settlements that some scholars originally identified it as a marker of Israelite ethnicity.[52] While this view has been largely rejected, Avraham Faust and Shlomo Bunimovitz have noted that this particular type of house first appeared between 1300 and 1100 BCE in the central highlands of the land that would become ancient Israel, coinciding with the emergence of ancient Israel. It became the dominant house type during the time of the Israelite monarchy and disappeared after the sixth century BCE when Judah was conquered by Babylonia.[53] While the pillared house is not exclusively Israelite, its widespread occurrence throughout ancient Israelite sites dating to the Iron Age at the very least demonstrates that Israelites lived in this type of house. Therefore, the architecture of the pillared house represents an important index for understanding Israelite and Judean family structure.

Several recent studies of the pillared house provide important clues to the dynamic growth and contraction over time of the Israelite *bêt 'āb*. One first has to note a common geographic distinction between pillared houses in urban and rural sites. In urban sites dating to the time of the Israelite monarchy, pillared houses were in general smaller than their rural counterparts, both in square footage and in number of rooms. Most urban houses had only three rooms and square footage corresponding to a nuclear family unit, while rural houses had four and sometimes five rooms with enough square footage to accommodate a large extended family with multiple nuclear units.[54] Moreover, rural houses also contained a greater number of internal divisions within rooms, suggesting a larger number of specifically designated spaces.[55] For Faust and Bunimovitz, "the large number of rooms in rural houses should be attributed to the fact that the houses were inhabited by extended families," which "required more options for separation, segregation, and privacy, especially between the several nuclear families living in the house."[56] James W. Hardin documents the internal divisions within a particularly well-preserved strata of a pillared house in Iron Age Tel Halif.[57] He identifies five rooms, one of which is subdivided into two spaces by a line of stone cobbles. He then subdivides the room further based on artifact assemblages that suggest up to thirteen distinct "activity areas."[58] The diversity of artifacts within single rooms suggests multiple functions for a given room that might correspond to seasonal changes.[59]

A second trend in the distribution of large and small pillared houses relates to economic means. While most urban houses dating to the monarchy were small, multiple urban sites attest to the existence of a few large pillared houses built with expensive materials and containing multiple internal divisions of space.[60] Faust and Bunimovitz attribute these houses to a wealthy elite who continued to live in large extended families even while in the city. Thus, the house of the father as a multigenerational unit should not be limited chronologically to pre-monarchic Israel nor geographically to the rural highlands. Rather, during the monarchy, the *bêt 'āb* continued to be a multigenerational household for rural agriculturalists and urban elite. Moreover, the internal room divisions within the larger houses may communicate architecturally the nesting of an adult son's "house" or a mother's "house" within the house of the senior father.

Faust and Bunimovitz note that the large pillared houses with multiple internal room divisions were not uniform or chronologically stable in composition. The changing number of internal divisions within a pillared house as well as the footprint occupied by the house as a whole reflects "the life-cycle of the extended family," such that each pillared house "gives us only a snapshot of one stage in the complicated life cycle of both the house and its past inhabitants."[61] The elasticity of the house structure with walls that could come up and down during a family's lifecycle matches the elasticity of the term *bayit* and explains architecturally the accommodation of a family grouping at all stages of its growth and decline.

Finally, Stager's concept of nested households can be seen architecturally in the similar shape and layout of common pillared houses, elite palaces, and divine temples. All of these "houses" are rectangular with the entrance most often at one of the narrow ends. Each opens into a central pillared broad room with long side rooms on one or both sides. Houses, palaces, and temples were built around open courtyards. Ezekiel levels a critique against the Judean kings, whose palace was architecturally too close to the temple. In Ezekiel's view, the god of Israel was offended when the kings "placed their threshold by my threshold and their doorposts beside my doorposts, with only a wall between me and them" (Ezek 43:8). The king had made an architectural assertion that he and his god were part of a joint family compound, and Ezekiel understood and challenged that assertion.

The existence of a few large family compounds in rural village sites and in some urban sites again suggests that commoners would be able to relate to and understand the more complex structure of extended, polygynous households like those described in the Bible. Moreover, the architectural mirroring among common, royal, and divine houses supports the idea that there was an overlap of household and kinship vocabulary that members of all classes of society would understand.

House Societies

One of the ways that anthropological studies of kinship over the past fifty years can inform biblical scholarship on the house is through the concept of "house societies," first introduced by Claude Lévi-Strauss in two publications in the 1980s. Lévi-Strauss, who is known primarily for his work on "alliance theory" as a challenge to "descent theory," also notes that some societies were organized around the rubric of their indigenous term for "house."[62] Theorizing the "house" rather than the "lineage" offers an approach that is more organic to the language of particular societies. Lévi-Strauss defines the house as "a corporate body [*personne morale*] holding an estate made up of both material and immaterial wealth, which perpetuates itself through the transmission of its name, its goods, and its titles down a real or imaginary line, considered legitimate as long as this continuity can express itself in the language of kinship or affinity and, most often, of both."[63] Writing decades later, Susan D. Gillespie sees within Lévi-Strauss's work a "crystallization of the house as a long-lived property-owning social unit" and a recognition that for societies organized under the rubric of "houses," there was an understood "overlap between the house as a dwelling that shelters a social group and/or its property and the group itself."[64]

Anthropologists who are currently working with some of the ideas that Lévi-Strauss has articulated concerning house societies recognize that his work is dated in some of its universalizing tendencies. Still, many anthropologists find several benefits in focusing on a "house" rather than a "lineage," and they have developed and refined Lévi-Strauss's work. Janet Carsten and Stephen Hugh-Jones insist that "house" not replace "lineage" as a universal, timeless model, and instead argue that the term "house" must be historicized.[65] Buildings, they insist, are not static: "Architectural processes are made to coincide, in various ways, with important events and processes in the lives of their occupants and are thought of in terms of them."[66] Gillespie echoes this conviction, noting, "all of our data—ethnographic, documentary, archaeological—are historical and contingent to local situations." The house is a living entity; as such it can be "enlarged, modified, and embellished over generations."[67]

As a historical and dynamically changing entity, the house requires a processual approach. Gillespie's description of the "temporal dimension" of house societies is especially instructive for the study of the ancient Israelite *bayit*. She recommends examining "the domestic cycle of individual house groups, the life history of the structures, the continuity and changes experienced by social houses over generations, and the time depth inherent in the ideology of the house or its valued heirlooms that serves to embody a collective memory about the past, a reference to origins that often forms a salient bond uniting house members."[68] In biblical narrative, we can see how representations of the "house of Jacob," "house of Israel," or "house of David" are shaped by their evolving histories, their ideologies, and the collective memories of their origins. Changes in the shape of these foundational houses reflect historical transitions.

Current anthropological approaches to house-based societies study the house as an architectural dwelling, a social grouping of people, and a symbolic entity. As an architectural dwelling, the physical features of a house correspond to the social unit that dwells within it.[69] The archaeology of a house yields "biographies of built forms" which tell the story of a family grouping that has built, expanded, contracted, subdivided, and, most importantly, persisted over time.[70] According to Gillespie, "the physical house is more than an objectified text reflecting social and cosmic relations; it is a locus and frame for daily activities out of which meanings are constituted."[71]

Closely related to the physical structure, the house also represents "a complex idiom for social groupings" that embodies hierarchies. Far from being egalitarian, house societies understand the house as "a vehicle to naturalize rank, and as a source of symbolic power."[72] Gillespie sees hierarchies both within and between houses, and these hierarchies can become destabilized in times of political and economic change.[73] Just as a culture might present itself as a purely patrilineal society by deemphasizing or even masking bilateral kinship ties, the house can present "an outward face of unity" while internally it "represents and naturalizes hierarchy and division among its members."[74]

In concert with biblical scholars' understanding of the ancient Israelite *bayit* as a nested entity, anthropologists have noted a "concentric orientation to space" in house societies that allows the word "house" to denote a family grouping and dwelling, a political entity like a state, a king's house and dynasty, and a god's house. Gillespie sees "multiple microcosmic models ... nested one within another," evoking "one another within a proxemic structure."[75] She uses the term "scaling" to describe the process of "conceiving small or large-scale models of cultural categories" within which an individual's house can be seen as a "miniature cosmos," just as the god's cosmic abode is a larger version of the human house (151–52). "Encompassing concentricity" then links humans to multiple levels of houses such that at any level, the house is both "contained and a container" (158). At the highest level of this scaled structure, we find not only the god's house but also the symbolic houses of revered ancestors, which are projections of elite, known historical houses. Again, the idea of "scaling" between an individual's house and the symbolic house of an ancestor requires that the revered and remembered ancestral houses be in a form that is recognizable to the occupants who claim to be their descendants.

The Symbolic House

Anthropological studies of house societies prove especially helpful for our study of the biblical *bayit* in their analyses of "symbolic houses," "origin houses," and "named, noble houses." I noted above that Gillespie understands the house to have its own "ideology" and to "embody collective memory about the past."[76] Roxana Waterson notes that in some societies the word "house" could refer to an unoccupied dwelling that served as an "origin-place, ritual site, holder of ritual offices and storage-place for heirlooms."⁷⁷ During the time of the Babylonian exile, the destroyed Jerusalem temple became just such a symbolic house. The exilic prophet Ezekiel had an extended vision of the Jerusalem temple where he saw Yahweh vacate his holy abode and oversee its ritual defilement (Ezek 8–10). Ezekiel then famously envisioned the rebuilding of the temple in all its architectural and iconographic details, and he reordered the offices of priests, Levites, kings, and commoners around the central space of Yahweh's imagined house (Ezek 40–48).⁷⁸ The priestly author in the Pentateuch, who is usually dated to the time of the exile or later, was centrally focused on preserving the rites, offices, and rituals of a temple that had been destroyed.⁷⁹ The book of Ezra begins with an imperial charter for exiled Judeans, referred to as the "people" of the "God of Israel," to return to their land of origin and rebuild "the house of Yahweh," "the house of God in Jerusalem" (Ezra 1:1–5).

Like the conquered and destroyed Jerusalem temple, the "house of Israel" as a national entity ceased to exist when Assyria conquered it and deported its inhabitants in 722 BCE. Nonetheless, the prophet of the Babylonian exile known as Second Isaiah articulated a vision of the restored "Israel" within which the Judean exiles who returned from Babylonia became heirs to the "house of Israel" (Isa 46:3; 48:1). The exilic community became memory holders for the house of Yahweh and the house of Israel, and for the ritual offices and attendant rites that resided within those remembered houses.

Gillespie's treatment of "origin narratives" is especially instructive with regard to our consideration of the Bible as a primary source document on the Israelite house. She counts origin narratives as part of the "immaterial wealth" of a house that is passed from one generation to the next.⁸⁰ House members hold, remember, recite, and perform their origin narrative, which can include "elaborate accounts of the emergence and/or the arrival of predecessors; traditions of the migration and journeying of groups and individuals; tales of the founding of settlements, of houses, or of ancestral shrines; accounts of contests to establish priority, to secure the rightful transmission of ancestral relics, to assert the often disputed ordering of succession to office or, in some areas, to establish precedence in affinal relations."⁸¹ The origin house and its preserved narrative become foundational to the community of professed descendants who stake their identity on membership within the house and the ascribed right to hold and transmit the foundational narrative. The remembered origin house creates or reaffirms enduring connections among the people who preserved the origin story and the founding ancestors and land within that story. Ronald Hendel argues that for the Judean exiles in Babylonia, "the memory of Abraham induces a turn of mind and opens a possibility for overcoming a dire crisis," giving them "new hope for a return to the Promised Land."[82] R. E. Clements asserts, "The role of narrative in a community becomes an inseparable part of the self-understanding of that community, and interpretation of the narrative becomes interlocked in an awareness of its cultural and social values."[83] I would add that the memories of Abraham, Isaac, and Jacob preserved in biblical narrative are shaped by the experiences of the Judean exiles who claimed to be the direct and chosen descendants of the house of Israel and, as such, the rightful owners of the origin story.

As an origin house, the house of Israel possessed material and immaterial wealth. Anthropologists include fields, dwellings, and heirloom valuables as part of the material wealth of an origin house.[84] Rosemary A. Joyce defines heirloom valuables as "repositories of powerful histories." Some heirlooms are called "name-tag" objects because they are named as the property of a historical person.[85] Susan McKinnon adds that heirloom valuables are connected with the actions of the founding ancestors and linked to the sources of an otherworldly power.[86] Here, one cannot help but think of the "Torah of Moses," an heirloom valuable credited with divine origin—written with the finger of God—handed over on a holy mountain to a revered ancestor figure, deposited within a sacred cult object, and ultimately placed within the innermost chamber of the house of Yahweh (Exod 31:18; Deut 5:22; 10:1–5).[87] The biblical story of the return of the Judean exiles to their homeland in Judah describes "Ezra the scribe" bringing back with him "the book of the law of Moses which the Lord had given to Israel" for a public reading (Neh 8:1–4). Karel van der Toorn refers to this "Torah" as the "icon of Israel," arguing that it was revered and deployed in ways analogous to a cult statue.[88] The Bible in all stages of its oral and written development can be regarded as the heirloom valuable of the house of Israel. Those who claimed to be a part of the house of Israel also claimed the right to tell and perform its origin story. They asserted the right to possess and preserve the origin story as their own.

Origin houses also contained immaterial wealth, and much of what gets labeled immaterial wealth falls within the constellation of Hebrew terms that I have associated with the professed patrilineal ideal: names, genealogies, and monuments. Names are an important category of immaterial wealth held within a house and transferred selectively from one generation to the next. Names were considered the "property of the estate"; they represented "signs of rights in the estate granted to junior members."[89] McKinnon, whose research focuses on the people of the Tanimbar Islands, notes the hierarchy that existed between "named noble houses" and "unnamed commoner houses," all of which were part of a single "house complex."[90] Possession of a name gives a house an air of permanence, "an enduring structural identity." Named houses possess a concentration of heirloom valuables that they have "immobilized" and fixed within their centered space. Unnamed houses, on the other hand, are characterized by impermanence; their identities are "shifting" and "ephemeral," and their valuables are "dispersed, mobile and transient."[91]

Genealogies, what we have called the *tôlēdôt*, are another item of immaterial wealth. In addition to having names, origin houses lay claim to genealogies that extend back ten to thirty generations.[92] The genealogies help the current occupants of a named house to trace their origins back to a founding couple in a direct and unmediated way.[93] In fact, McKinnon argues that one of the factors that distinguishes a named noble house from unnamed, commoner houses is the perception of their "differential ability to maintain enduring pathways" from present inhabitants to founding ancestors.[94]

The Bible in its received form is the origin story, the named heirloom valuable of a group of descendants, the Judeans, who trace their ancestry back to the "house of Israel" in a direct and unmediated way. At the same time, the Bible preserves within its own metanarrative multiple stories of origin dating to much earlier, pre-exilic time periods, and these stories preserve the memory of different foundational houses. All of these foundational houses are peopled by men and women, young and old, inheriting and non-inheriting, biologically related and non-biologically related. The metanarrative of the Bible organizes these competing foundational houses through a concept of nesting. Hierarchies within and between houses are expressed through the gifting and withholding of names within an origin narrative and through conceptualizing one part of a house complex as central while imagining the other parts as peripheral.

Gendering the Symbolic House

Women and relationships forged through women play centrally strategic roles in the competition between houses to become the named, noble house of origin. Maternal kinship terms mark the dividing line between the central, named house of origin and the unnamed commoner houses that are cast to the side of the preserved memory that is the Bible. In the introduction, we discussed the patrilineal descent system as a professed ideal that can never fully be realized. Societies may accord increased value to kinship ties forged through men, but they nonetheless accept and depend on ties forged through women. McKinnon notes the indigenous Nuer term "children of girls," showing how this term referred to a group of people that the patrilineal descent group labeled "foreigners." These "children of girls" were actually descendants of sisters who were treated as sons, meaning sisters who did not marry out of their father's house. They brought husbands in, and their children were considered members of their mother's father's house.[95] Still, these "children of girls" had a lower social status than those sons who were related to the patriline through their fathers, and that lowered social status persisted for generations.[96] Biblically, we can examine several cases where men are linked to a powerful, royal house through their mothers who are the sisters or daughters of kings. Outsider men or men from weak paternal houses could use maternal ties to claim a place in a different paternal house.

Maori language about kinship encodes patrilineal values through masculine terms and terms that highlight male birth order. There are separate terms for descent lines of senior brothers and those of younger brothers, and there is a third, rarely used term that refers to a descent line made up solely of senior males and their descendants. This rare term, which corresponds to its very rare occurrence, is *ure tu*, which translates literally as "upright penis."[97] This is strikingly similar to the biblical *tôlēdôt*, which record a patrilineal ideal of senior men and their designated heirs (seeds) and use a language specific to male reproductive capacities.

Maori mythology, like many biblical narratives, features women and younger brothers "allied together against axiomatic male seniority." Karen Sinclair concludes that within the Maori language, kinship terminology such as "elder versus younger" and "men versus women" serves as a way of "conceptualizing the legitimate and system sustaining versus the antisocial and system threatening."[98] These observations suggest that biblical researchers should pay close attention to indigenous Hebrew expressions for connectedness, division, and hierarchy.

Within house societies, kinship ties expressed through women mark hierarchical distinctions between named noble houses and unnamed commoner houses. McKinnon observes that named noble houses have long-established rows of wife-taking houses that link them across generations through repeated marriage alliances. She emphasizes that the marriages contracted within the named noble houses are thought to link two complete houses, not simply the two people that are getting married. When connections are established between two individuals rather than two houses, they are seen as weak and chronologically shallow. Significantly, these weaker connections are described and denigrated using feminine kinship terms; the weak links among individuals are "sister" and "aunt" pathways rather than "brother" pathways.[99]

The Biblical Presentation of Maternal Sub-Houses

With this background on house societies, I want to turn to two biblical texts where a named paternal house of origin is presented in such a way that it subdivides into unequal maternally named sub-houses. The two texts focus on the origin houses of Abraham and Jacob and describe the moment of generational transfer within these paternally named houses. In each text, the house-founding father is old and dying and beginning to transfer his material and immaterial wealth to his designated heir. While the term "house of the mother" is not used in either text, the subdivision of the house of the father into hierarchically arranged and socially significant maternal entities is explicitly present. Moreover, the concept of nesting finds expression when high-status maternal houses remain nested within a named paternal house, while low-status, non-inheriting maternal houses often become satellite houses, cast aside geographically to the periphery of the Promised Land. We also see how names, paternal kinship labels, and insider genealogies create direct pathways to the founding male ancestor for sons born into high-status, paternally recognized maternal houses. At the same time, anonymity, maternally mediated kinship labels, and cast-off, dangling genealogies mark sons born into lower-status maternal houses and block their pathways to the house-founding father.

Succession in the House of Abraham: Genesis 25:1–26

The house of Abraham as remembered in Genesis is a named foundational house, and Genesis itself can be understood as its origin story, the heirloom valuable of what ultimately becomes the house of Israel. The right to tell, perform, and transmit this story is part of the immaterial wealth passed from generation to generation within this foundational house.

Genesis 25 concludes the Abraham cycle that began in Gen 11:27 and marks the beginning of the Jacob cycle that extends from Gen 25:19 to Gen 36:43.[100] Scholars have seen in this chapter a complex compositional history with some combination of J, P, and post-P redaction.[101] What seems very clear is that Gen 25 provides evidence for the fulfillment of promises made earlier in Genesis. As such, there is an "afterward" quality to the final form of Gen 25 that suggests it was redacted to tie up loose ends in the Abraham story and cast some threads forward into the Jacob story.

The chapter contains two of the eleven *tôlēdôt* references in Genesis: the begettings of Ishmael introduce a genealogical listing of his twelve sons that largely disappears from the biblical narrative, while the begettings of Isaac introduce the narrative of the birth of his twin sons. As a transitional chapter between the Abraham and Jacob cycles, Gen 25 describes the moment of generational transfer in his house, and in the narration of Abraham's death, burial, and distribution of his estate, we see the pronounced role of maternal subdivisions within his house. As a text, Gen 25 divides into three maternally organized genealogies in ascending order of status. At the beginning of chapter 25, three maternal "houses" are nested within the founding house of Abraham, and each of these maternal houses comes to represent a nation. First, we read of Keturah and her six sons and select grandsons (Gen 25:1–4). Then we read of Hagar's son Ishmael and the twelve tribes that descend from him (Gen 25:12–18). Finally, we read the brief genealogical notation of Isaac as Abraham's son at which point the text shifts from genealogies of Abraham to the narrative of Jacob's birth (Gen 25:19–26). Within and between these genealogies, we find the transference of the material and immaterial wealth of Abraham's house. The material wealth consists of land, property, and unspecified gifts; the immaterial wealth includes a divine blessing, names, titles, mediated and unmediated pathways to Abraham as the foundational ancestor, and finally the origin story itself.

In each of the three maternal genealogies, the writer deploys names and anonymity, male and female forms of the procreative verb *y-l-d*, and mediated and unmediated kinship titles to differentiate the sons' abilities to trace a pathway back to the house of Abraham. The genealogy recording the sons of Keturah names her as a wife of Abraham and then lists her six sons by name, using the female-focused procreative verb "She bore to him" (*wattēled lô*). While her sons are named, they are collectively labeled "sons of Keturah" and are never called "Abraham's sons" (Gen 25:1–4). Keturah herself has no genealogical background and no known family involved in the negotiation of her marriage with Abraham.[102] She and her sons drop into the text and just as quickly drop out.[103]

At verse 12, we read of Ishmael's begettings, and unlike the "sons of Keturah," Ishmael is called a "son of Abraham." But his pathway to Abraham is indirect and mediated through not one but two socially marked women, and, again, the verb that marks his coming into being is the female procreative verb "X bore to Y":

> These are the begettings of Ishmael [*wĕʾelleh tôlĕdōt yišmāʿē(ʾ)l*], son of Abraham,
> whom Hagar the Egyptian, Sarah's slave-girl [*šipḥat śārā*],
> bore [*yālĕdâ*] to Abraham. (Gen 25:12)[104]

These heavily mediated, maternal pathways to Abraham stand out all the more when they are compared to the labeling of Isaac in his begettings:

> These are the begettings of Isaac [*ʾelleh tôlĕdōt yiṣḥāq*], son of Abraham: Abraham begot Isaac [*ʾabrāhām hôlid ʾet-yiṣḥāq*]. (Gen 25:19)

In this *tôlĕdôt* clause, Isaac, like Ishmael, is named and labeled "Abraham's son," but he is Abraham's son without any reference to his mother.[105] His pathway to the founding ancestor is direct and presented in the ideologically valued, exclusively paternal form with the use of the male procreative verb *hôlîd*. Isaac is not a "son born to a concubine" or a son born to "Hagar the Egyptian, Sarah's slave girl." Isaac is simply "an Abraham-begotten son."[106]

At this point, it is helpful to recall McKinnon's retrieval of the Nuer term "children of girls," which she argues signified children who became part of a male-named genealogy through maternal ties.[107] We can also note Lila Abu-Lughod's observation that among the professed patrilineal Bedouin, a married couple who were closely related through maternal ties would nonetheless present their relationship in a more circuitous way in order to emphasize their paternal ties.[108] In labeling one group of sons "sons of Keturah" and "sons of concubines," the narrator of this origin story signals something similar to the status of "children of girls." Namely, the sons of Keturah together with Ishmael trace their "birth" to a foundational, named woman who is marked with a low social status. Isaac, on the other hand, traces his "begetting" directly to his house-founding father, Abraham.

Among the three genealogies we find snippets of narrative that tell us about Abraham's death, the distribution of his estate, and his burial. On each of these occasions, the text uses maternal houses to delineate hierarchically among sons. Verses 5–6 describe the distribution of Abraham's material wealth: "Abraham gave *all that he had* [*kol-'ăšer-lô*] to Isaac, but to the sons of his concubines he gave *gifts* [*mattānōt*]." So, in the reading out of Abraham's "will," so to speak, Isaac maintains a name and no mediating label while Ishmael and the sons of Keturah are grouped anonymously under the heading "sons of his concubines."[109] We do not know exactly what was implied in the giving of "gifts" to the sons of concubines, but we can be certain that these gifts were of a significantly lesser value than the "all that he had" that Isaac receives.[110] In a sense, gifts can be viewed as the kind of "impermanent" and "mobile" heirloom valuable that characterizes unnamed commoner houses. This seems all the more likely when we examine the second part of the material wealth: land. We read in verse 6 that while Abraham was still alive, he sent "the sons of his concubines" "from upon Isaac, his son,"[111] "eastward toward the east country." Thus Isaac's inheritance is the fixed and permanent land, the only geographic continuation of the house of Abraham. The other sons carry their very mobile "gifts" to the fringes just outside the land; their houses will "fall by the side." In fact, the text explicitly uses the language of sidelining when it describes Ishmael as "settling down alongside [*'al-pĕnê*] all his brothers" (Gen 25:18).[112] So in addition to having heavily mediated and socially degraded maternal paths to the house of the father, these sons of concubines have a literal geographic path that they must hike from the wilderness back to the house of their father. Their maternal houses are no longer nested within the house of their father; they have been cast out such that they are now satellite houses only loosely affiliated with the house of their father. We see in later chapters that one of the marks of a lower-status son is that he is part of a satellite house of the mother rather than a paternally nested house of the mother (fig. 3).

In the narrative describing the death and burial of Abraham, the sons of Keturah disappear. "Isaac and Ishmael," listed in hierarchical order, bury Abraham together, and they are jointly labeled "his sons" (Gen 25:9). Still, the place of burial and the household composition of the burial cave again privilege Isaac. The place of burial is "the cave of Machpelah, in the field of Ephron son of Zohar the Hittite, east of Mamre, the field that Abraham purchased from the Hittites" (Gen 25:10). This wordy identification serves to remind readers that this is the very cave that Abraham purchased to

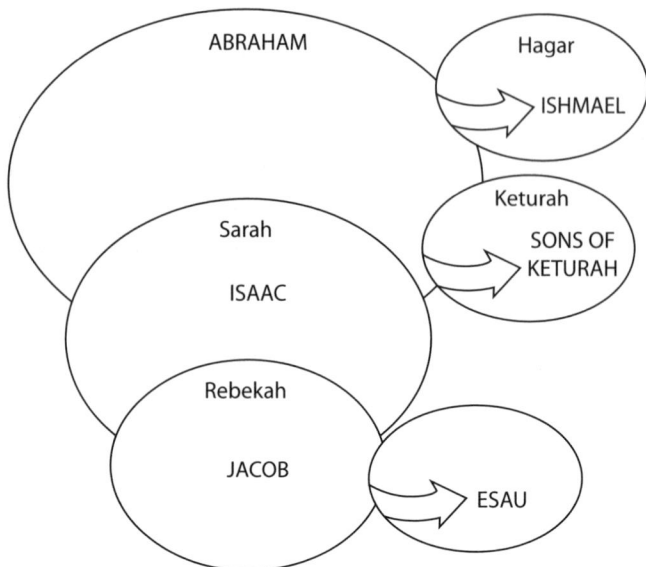

Figure 3. *The three-generation household of Abraham with Sarah's nested house and Hagar's and Keturah's satellite houses of the mother, Gen 25. Esau's house is a separate house of a non-inheriting son, Gen 33. Illustration created by Ondrea Keith, rendered by Bill Nelson.*

bury his wife Sarah, Isaac's mother (Gen 23:1–16). We then read, "There Abraham was buried, along with his wife Sarah" (Gen 25:10). The burial notice signals that the ancestral house that will continue post-death in this burial cave is the narrowed, sub-household of Abraham, which he begot through Sarah.[113]

We now turn to the immaterial wealth of the house of Abraham, and this includes the divine blessing of land, the already noted names and titles, and finally the origin story itself. After the death of Abraham, we read that "God blessed his son, Isaac, and Isaac settled in Beer-lahai-roi" (Gen 25:11). This divine blessing bestows upon Isaac his name, his unmediated path to Abraham as "his son," and something more specific than the generic "Promised Land." The place where Isaac first dwells after inheriting the house of Abraham is Beer-lahai-roi, the site of Hagar's theophany and covenant with God (Gen 16:13–14). If Hagar's descendants, the twelve tribes of Ishmael, could lay claim to any geographic site in the Promised Land, this would be it; it is the land of their maternal covenant. They have not inherited the blessings tied to the Abrahamic covenant; instead, they are men who trace their covenantal heritage to an Egyptian slave woman, Hagar, and this text makes it clear that Hagar's covenant does not include land, even a land that she named. Ishmael's sons are "sons of a slave girl." Their apical ancestor is a woman. Geographically, they fall to the side of the foundational origin house.[114]

Maternal sub-houses within the house of Abraham ultimately signify nations that are hierarchically arranged through the status of their maternal ancestors. Hagar's son Ishmael becomes a people called the Ishmaelites, associated biblically with Arabs who exist in the wilderness on the "fringes" of settled land (Gen 16:12; 37:25; Ps 83:6; 1 Chron 27:30). Among Keturah's named sons, Midian stands out as another desert nation on the southern fringes of the Promised Land that has ongoing interactions with the people of Israel.[115] Isaac alone becomes the ancestor of the nation of Israel; he "begets" that nation. We see his chosen, central, foundational status most clearly in the transference of the final item of Abraham's immaterial wealth: the origin story itself. Whereas Ishmael's begettings introduce a genealogical list of sons who are cast aside and disappear from the text, Isaac's begettings introduce a narrative that continues the Abraham story.

In this final composite conclusion to the Abraham cycle, postexilic redactors present Isaac as the Abraham-begotten son who has inherited the right to tell, perform, and preserve this story. Keturah's label as a concubine serves as a way of classifying connected but lesser nations. Hagar, who was a "slave girl" and a "maidservant" in Gen 16 and 21, adds to her list of labels "concubine." Her divinely bestowed covenant, experienced through a theophany at Beer-lahai-roi, is clarified as exclusive of any land claims. Isaac is the Abraham-begotten son and through Jacob becomes the ancestor of the Israelites. His story is preserved as part of the Torah, the heirloom valuable of descendants who call themselves "the sons of Israel."

Succession in the House of Jacob: Genesis 37–50

The Joseph story (Gen 37–50) offers one of the most sustained narratives through which we can identify the professed patrilineal household of Jacob subdivided and hierarchically arranged into maternally marked units. Joseph's narrative is introduced in the same way that Jacob's narrative was introduced, with a *tôlēdôt* clause. This clause links Joseph's story redactionally to the preceding tale of his father, and in this linkage we see the idealized presentation of the house of the father as continuous, eternal, rooted to a single land, and passing directly from father to designated son: "Jacob dwelt in the land of his father's sojournings, in the land of Canaan. These are the begettings of Jacob [*ēlleh tôlēdôt yaʿăqōb*]: Joseph" (Gen 37: 1–2a).[116] Two men are named in this generational transition: Jacob and Joseph. Jacob is tied backward in time "to the land of his father's sojournings." At the same time, his story extends forward in time with his own "begettings," the *tôlēdôt yaʿăqōb*. And even though *tôlēdôt* is plural, we immediately find ourselves focused on a single named son, Joseph. Just as Isaac's story became the continuation of his father Abraham's story, Joseph's story becomes the continuation of his father Jacob's story.

After the *tôlēdôt* of Jacob, we immediately find a narrative that subdivides his house along maternal lines and elevates one maternal house over the others. The narrative begins with Joseph playing the tattletale on an unnamed set of brothers that the text labels "the sons of Bilhah and Zilpah, his father's wives" (Gen 37:2b). These are, of course, the maidservant wives given to Jacob by Rachel and Leah in order to secure a greater number of children.[117] Labeling the young men this way serves to accentuate the distance, the non-relationship between Joseph and these sons of Jacob by maidservants. They are not "his brothers"; they are not "sons of his father." Instead, the narrator describes their link to Jacob's house through maternally mediated pathways, the less valued, peripheral means through which to claim belonging within a named foundational house. Like the grouping of the "sons of Keturah" and Ishmael together under the label "sons of concubines" in Gen 25:6, these unnamed sons of two different mothers are lumped together as a single maternally marked unit. Joseph's delivery of a "bad report" on them to "their father" further emphasizes the dividing line between Joseph and the unnamed "sons of Bilhah and Zilpah."[118]

Joseph's adolescent dream about his family bowing down to him provides another maternally defined window into the house of Jacob, this time viewed from the vantage point of an aspiring male heir. At the time of his dream, Joseph's "house of the father," the house of Jacob, comprises two primary wives, two secondary wives, twelve sons, and one named daughter (Gen 29:31–30:24; 35:16–26).[119] The death and burial of Rachel, Joseph's mother, has already been recorded (Gen 35:16–21). In his dream, Joseph sees "the sun, the moon, and eleven stars bowing down to me" (Gen 37:9). His father then asks, "Shall we indeed come, I and your mother and your brothers and bow down to you?" (Gen 37:10). Absent from this vision is his half-sister Dinah and his father's other wives. Joseph's dream envisions only those members of his *bêt 'āb* that would need to recognize his achieved status as *bĕkôr:* his half- and full brothers. The only mother who would move forward as part of the transferred house of Jacob is Rachel, and she, like Sarah before her, will be a part of her son's inherited house even in death.[120]

In the well-known story that follows, Joseph's half-brothers toss him in a pit, and he ends up sold into slavery in Egypt, leaving his father, Jacob, bereft of his favored son.[121] Again, in a composite narrative, we find the descendants of Keturah and Hagar managing together to transport Joseph to Egypt as a slave. In the first part of this text, Joseph's brothers sell him to the Midianites. In the second part of the text, the Midianites somehow morph into Ishmaelites, who in turn sell Joseph to Potiphar, Pharaoh's officer (Gen 37:25–28, 36; 39:1). In this spliced set of verses, we have the re-emergence of the "sons of his concubines" from Gen 25, the Ishmaelites and the Midianites. Those who were "sent away" from the Promised Land, disinherited in Abraham's house, become the unwitting accomplices to the sons of Jacob as they "cast out" a rival, favored brother from their father's household.

In several episodes of Joseph in Egypt, he is labeled in ways that single him out as Rachel's son. When Joseph enters the house of Potiphar, the narrator notes that Joseph was "handsome and good looking" (*yĕpê-tō'ar wîpê mar'eh*) as a way of explaining the sexual overtures from Potiphar's wife (Gen 39:6). At the same time, however, this physical description of Joseph replicates the earlier physical praise of his mother as "beautiful and good looking" (*yĕpat-tō'ar wîpat mar'eh*) (Gen 29:17).[122] Through shared beauty, the text signals that Joseph is his mother's son.

Later in the story, when Joseph has achieved a position of power in Pharaoh's court as the overseer of grain distribution in a time of famine, he meets his brothers again. Jacob had heard that there was grain in Egypt, and he decides to send his sons there to bring the grain back. The text, however, indicates that Jacob did not send Benjamin, Joseph's full brother: "So ten of Joseph's brothers went down to buy grain in Egypt. But Jacob did not send Joseph's brother Benjamin with his brothers, for he feared that harm might come to him" (Gen 42:3–4). While the text does not distinguish Benjamin with a label—they are all "brothers" (*'aḥim*)—Benjamin is singled out with a name, and as readers we know that he is the only other son of Rachel, Joseph's uterine brother.

When Joseph pretends not to recognize his brothers and accuses them of being spies, they identify themselves in terms of the house of their father. They are "sons of one man"; then they add, "We, your servants, are twelve brothers, the sons of a certain man in the land of Canaan; the youngest, however, is now with our father, and one is no more" (Gen 42:11, 13). While this self-identification groups the twelve men together as "brothers" and "sons of one man," it singles out two absent brothers who happen to be sons of the same mother, the favored wife.

Joseph's focus is immediately on his uterine brother, Benjamin, and he devises a plan to insure that Benjamin will be brought to him. He keeps one of the ten brothers, Simeon, a son of Leah, in prison and demands the delivery of Benjamin as the terms for Simeon's release. Upon the brothers' return to Jacob, they tell their father that they must deliver Benjamin to "the lord of the land" in order to regain Simeon. In Jacob's response, we see that his focus is immediately on Benjamin, to the near exclusion of his other sons: "My son [Benjamin] shall not go down with you, for his brother is dead, and *he alone* is left" (Gen 42:38). What he means here is that "he alone is left among the sons of my favored, loved wife." The loss of Simeon occasions no words of mourning and no plan of rescue.

Later in the narrative, the famine becomes so severe that Jacob relents and allows his sons to take Benjamin with them in order to secure more grain. Jacob's parting petitionary prayer again elevates the value of one son over another through naming, "May El Shaddai grant you mercy [*raḥămîm*] before the man, so that he may send back *your other brother and Benjamin*" (Gen 43:14; emphasis added). Simeon becomes the unnamed in this prayer. The emotions that Jacob directs exclusively to Benjamin are womb-centered emotions (*raḥămîm*); one womb ties Jacob's two loved sons together, that of Rachel. The word *raḥămîm*, usually translated "mercy" or "compassion," is semantically related to *reḥem* meaning "womb."[123]

Jacob's prayer demonstrates that it is possible for a father to live in and head a household containing multiple maternal subunits while viewing it in terms of a particular favored mother's house. Joseph's dream and the narrative presentation of Jacob's lived old age reality both view Jacob's house through a hierarchical ranking of houses of the mother. Certain sons remain unnamed and maternally devalued as "sons of Bilhah and Zilpah." The imprisonment of another son, Simeon, the son of Leah, occasions no displays of mourning. Only the two sons born to Jacob through Rachel are repeatedly named and receive the father's emotional energy. Within the house of Jacob, the house of Rachel occupies the privileged position.

Once the brothers arrive back in Egypt, Joseph arranges for a feast, but he keeps his identity secret. His brothers are brought into his home, and when Joseph returns and sees Benjamin, the text signals the uterine family explicitly with a maternally specific kinship label: "Then he [Joseph] looked up and saw *Benjamin, his brother, the son of his mother* [*'et-binyāmîn 'āḥîb ben-'immô*], and said, 'Is this your youngest brother, of whom you spoke to me? God be gracious to you, my son!'" (Gen 43:29). This Benjamin-focused blessing offered by Joseph upon Benjamin's safe arrival in Egypt parallels Jacob's prayer offered at the time of his departure. Both are asking God to keep what remains of the house of Rachel intact. Like Jacob, Joseph feels womb-based emotion for his uterine brother; he is "so overcome with affection [*raḥămāyw*] for his brother" that he has to leave the room and weep (Gen 43:30). As Phyllis Trible has noted, it is precisely the moment that Joseph sees "the son of his mother" that he experiences the womb-based emotion of *raḥămîm*.[124]

Throughout the rest of the story, Benjamin continues to be elevated in status by Joseph and his half-brothers. Joseph honors Benjamin when he serves him five times the portion given to his half-brothers at the feast in his house (Gen 43:34). He devises a plan to keep Benjamin with him in Egypt by planting his own silver cup in Benjamin's bag (Gen 44:1–2). When Joseph demands that Benjamin be left with him as his slave on account of his "theft," Judah describes the house of Jacob through the narrowed lens of his favored wife Rachel: "We have an elderly father, and a young brother, the child of his old age. His brother is dead; he alone is left *of his mother's [children]* [*lĕ'immô*], and his father loves him" (Gen 44:20).[125] Judah then quotes Jacob as saying, "You know that my wife bore me two sons; the one went out from me, and I said, Surely he has been torn to pieces; and I have not seen him since. If you take this one also from me, and harm comes to him, you will bring down my gray hairs in sorrow to Sheol" (Gen 44:27–29). Even though Rachel dies before the Joseph narrative begins, all of the emotional energy is directed toward the relationships within her house, the uterine sibling relationship between Joseph and Benjamin that finds expression in the kinship term "his brother the son of his mother" for whom Jacob and Joseph feel womb-based affection (fig. 4).

While the house of Rachel continues as a meaningful kinship unit after her death, the larger house of Jacob also finds expression. Joseph ultimately reveals his identity to his larger paternal house telling all his brothers, "I am *your brother* Joseph, whom you sold into Egypt" (Gen 45:4). He then offers to resettle the entire house of his father in Goshen: "You shall settle in the

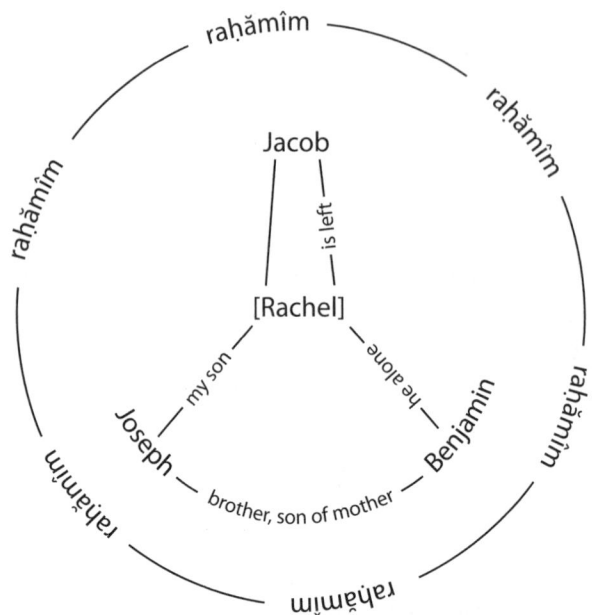

Figure 4. *The house of Rachel after her death as depicted in the story of Joseph, Gen 37, 42–45. Illustration by Bill Nelson.*

land of Goshen, and you shall be near me, you and your children and your children's children, as well as your flocks, your herds, and all that you have. I will provide for you there" (Gen 45:10–11a). While Joseph will provide for the entire house of his father, Benjamin is repeatedly singled out for special treatment (Gen 45:12, 14, 22).

The narrative description of the resettlement of the house of Jacob in the land of Goshen divides the house of Jacob into four maternally labeled sub-houses: the sons and daughter born to Leah, the sons born to her handmaid Zilpah, the sons born to Rachel, and the sons born to her handmaid Bilhah (Gen 46:8–27).[126] The whole of the Joseph narrative is a story of the house of his father, the house of Jacob, with special focus on the house of his mother, Rachel, nested within that larger entity. Joseph looks to his brother Benjamin as "his mother's son" and feels womb-based affection for him. He multiplies his food and gift portions and manipulates his half-brothers in order to secure the presence of his full brother with him in Egypt.

Maternally specific kinship terms designate a smaller group of brothers who form a subset or nested unit within the larger kin group defined by the father. The "sons of Bilhah and Zilpah," as handmaid sons, remain an unnamed and undifferentiated group throughout the narrative. "Benjamin, his brother, the son of his mother," is named and tied directly to Joseph. In the resettling of the house of Jacob, we see four maternal subunits nested within the house of Jacob, each headed by a named wife-mother. In the story of Joseph, the storyteller is aware of and comfortable with the idea that smaller maternal houses are nested within a larger paternal house and that maternal houses mark hierarchies.

Ancient Israel was a house society that organized itself into concentrically larger social groupings and geographic areas under the rubric of the single Hebrew word for house: *bayit*. The Bible and the origin stories contained within it are the heirloom valuable of ancient Israel's foundational houses. Descendants of the houses of Abraham and Jacob claim the right to possess, preserve, and tell the origin stories contained within the Bible. In the "begettings" of foundational men, we find an idealized memory of the direct and unmediated transference of material and immaterial wealth from father to designated son within the fixed geography of a named house. At the same time, the houses of ancient Israel's founding ancestors subdivided into maternally named units that had significant social ramifications for the sons nested within them. Sons who traced their genealogical pathways to the house-founding father through a wife who remained nested within her husband's house became heirs to their father's house. Sons who traced their pathways to the father through socially marked mothers whose houses had split off as satellite houses found themselves nameless and socially and geographically peripheral.

Some of the maternally specific kinship terms that we have begun to see in these two stories would have had their greatest social and political significance in polygynous households. This raises the question of the prevalence or rarity of polygynous households in ancient Israel. While the Bible records multiple wives for many of its prominent ancestors, it would have been far less common for an average ancient Israelite to live in or have direct interactions with a polygynous household. Still, several factors suggest that ancient Israelites would come into contact with families that subdivided into more than one maternal grouping. First, given the high rate of maternal death in childbirth, a man could have one child from his first wife and then lose her during the birth of a second child. He could then marry a second wife and have children by her. This would create two sets of children from two different but sequentially married wives. Second, without any of our modern advances in the treatment of infertility, an ancient Israelite man might also take a second wife or a slave wife if his first wife did not become pregnant. After taking the second wife, the first wife might ultimately bear her own child. Finally, a married man could have children with a woman who was not his wife and was not part of his household, and these children could later try to claim the status of "father's sons." In each of these cases, the existence of more than one maternal subunit within a single father's house would not signal extreme wealth or privilege. Average ancient Israelites likely lived in nuclear cells of a father, mother, and two or three children, but even those who were part of a simple family might have interactions with a prominent village man from a wealthy family who had two wives with children from each.[127] The variety of ways in which a man could have children through more than one wife indicates that maternal kinship terms would hold social currency among average ancient Israelites, and this baseline knowledge of a maternally subdivided father's house would make the stories of Abraham, Jacob, and David meaningful and enduring.[128]

2 The House of the Mother (*bêt 'ēm*)

While the term *bêt 'āb* is used extensively throughout the biblical canon and has therefore received detailed scholarly analysis, the term *bêt 'ēm*, translated literally as "house of the mother," appears only four times in the Bible (Gen 24:28; Ruth 1:8; Song 3:4; 8:2). It has received limited scholarly attention, with the work of Carol Meyers standing out as the most detailed and sustained treatment. Meyers understands the *bêt 'ēm* as an "alternate expression for the same societal unit" as the *bêt 'āb*. The difference in her view between the two terms is one of vantage point; the *bêt 'ēm*, she argues, is the way women view the *bêt 'āb* in which they live.[1] This book demonstrates that when we take into account the associated maternal kinship designations that emerge in house-of-the-mother texts, we can build a case for understanding the term *bêt 'ēm* or "house of the mother" as an indigenous Hebrew kinship designation for the "uterine family." Comprising a mother and her biological and adopted children, the house of the mother is distinct within yet supportive of the house of the father upon which it depends. In its most basic form, a *bêt 'ēm* represents a social and spatial subunit nested within the larger house of the father.[2]

The Biblical House of the Mother

Running to Her Mother's House: Rebekah

The first reference to a "house of the mother'" is found in Gen 24, the story of the betrothal of Rebekah to Abraham's chosen son Isaac. While traditional source critical analysis has assigned this chapter to the Yahwist source, numerous scholars have recognized various features that separate it from the surrounding narrative and suggest that Gen 24 postdates the Abraham and Jacob cycles.³ Alexander Rofé highlights postexilic vocabulary such as "the God of heaven and earth," "*migdānōt* (costly ornaments)," the denominative verb *b-r-k* (to kneel), and the use of the particle *'ăšer*.⁴ Rofé also argues that the theology and literary style of the narrative fits with a postexilic dating, featuring as it does a prominent role for personal prayer, lengthy dialogue, and a view against intermarriage.⁵ David Carr assigns this chapter to his "post-D hexateuchal compositional layer," which means he dates it between the seventh and sixth centuries BCE and sees it as a late addition to an existing Abraham cycle.⁶

There are additional reasons for seeing this chapter as a late addition into an established Abraham cycle. The canonical placement of the story of Rebekah's betrothal breaks a natural progression in the story of Abraham. In Gen 23, Abraham buries his wife Sarah, and in chapter 25, he takes a third wife, Keturah; dies; and is buried together in the tomb with Sarah. After his death notice and the listing of Ishmael's descendants, we find the record of Isaac's marriage to Rebekah: "These are the begettings of Isaac son of Abraham: Abraham begot Isaac. Isaac was forty years old when he took Rebekah, the daughter of Bethuel, the Aramean from Paddan-aram, the sister of Laban the Aramean, as a wife" (Gen 25:19–20). Every detail in this marriage notification replicates those in Gen 24 except for Isaac's age. This suggests that chapter 24 interrupts an otherwise smooth narrative that moves from the death of Sarah to the death of Abraham and the marriage notification of Isaac. Chapter 24 is also in conversation with existing Abrahamic genealogies in its repeated identification of Rebekah as "the daughter of Bethuel, son of Milcah whom she bore to Nahor" (Gen 24:15, 24, 47). One might ask why Rebekah's paternal grandmother is specified while her own mother is not. I would argue that the author of Gen 24 knew of the tradition of Nahor having both a wife, Milcah, and a concubine, Reumah (Gen 22:20–24), and he wanted to specify that Rebekah was born into the line that extended through a wife.⁷

The narrative of Gen 24 is the story of an aging patriarch arranging for the marriage of his son before he dies. The initial setting of the story is the paternal house of Abraham, signaled by the opening dialogue between Abraham and "the most senior servant of his house." Abraham tells his senior servant that he wishes to arrange for his son to marry a woman from his homeland, and he instructs the servant: "Place your hand on my thigh and swear by Yahweh the God of Heaven and Earth that you will not take a wife for my son from the daughters of the Canaanites amongst whom I dwell, but that you will go to my country and to my birthplace and take a wife for my son, for Isaac" (Gen 24:2–4). The marriage that Abraham proposes for his son is patrilocal because he insists that only a woman who is willing to leave her father's house and the place of her birth is worthy to be his son's wife.[8]

The servant reaches "Aram-naharaim, the city of Nahor," within two verses, and providentially Rebekah appears at the well to draw water. The narrator immediately marks her as the divinely chosen wife for Isaac; she is Rebekah, "who was born to Bethuel, son of Milcah, wife of Nahor, brother of Abraham" (Gen 24:15).[9] The narrator is careful to trace Rebekah's genealogical pathway through paternal links to Abraham. Rebekah is part of the same extended *bêt 'āb* as Abraham, the house of Terah. The narrator also identifies Rebekah as marriageable, noting "she was a young woman [*bětûlâ*] whom no man had known" (Gen 24:16).[10] After Rebekah has provided water for the servant and his camels, the servant places a gold ring and gold bracelets on her and asks her whose daughter she is and whether there is any room "in your father's house" for his company of travelers to spend the night. Rebekah reiterates what readers have already learned: she is "the daughter of Bethuel, son of Milcah whom she bore to Nahor" (Gen 24:24). The servant bows down and offers a prayer of thanksgiving for guiding his way to this woman.

The language of the "father's house" and paternally specific kinship relationships dominate the entire first half of Gen 24. Abraham, his senior servant, and the narrator all understand this proposed patrilocal marriage of Isaac within the purview of the house of his father. The chapter begins with a reference to Abraham and the senior servant of his *bayit* and a discussion of an appropriate wife for his son Isaac. The marriage Abraham proposes for Isaac is articulated as endogamous and patrilocal. Abraham presents himself as the negotiator of such a marriage. The servant swears loyalty to Abraham and his house by placing his hand on Abraham's "thigh," a euphemism for the male reproductive organ, the house-begetting organ.[11] The narrator then introduces Rebekah with a paternal genealogy, and the servant asks if he might spend the night in Rebekah's *bêt 'āb*. When she indicates he may, the servant thanks Yahweh for bringing him to "the house of the brothers of my master" (*bêt 'ăḥê 'ădōnî*) (Gen 24:27).

In verse 28, however, Rebekah "runs" and "tells her mother's house [*wattaggēd lěbêt 'immāh*] all these things."[12] The matters that she presumably communicates to her mother's house include that a visitor has arrived; that he has given her gold jewelry; that he prays to Yahweh, the same god that her household serves; and that he is the servant of Abraham. Immediately following the reference to "her mother's house," the narrator identifies Rebekah's brother in a direct, unmediated way: "Now Rebekah had a brother, and his name was Laban, and Laban ran to the man outside by the well" (Gen 24:29). Laban is not identified as "Bethuel's son," and he is not located with reference to the house of his father. Instead, he is named, tied directly to Rebekah as "her brother," and located in the "house of her mother." All of these details suggest that the shift to the mother's house entails a shift in the key relationships; we are now focusing on Rebekah, her mother, and her brother.

We also have at least a hint that the relationship between brother and sister has economic underpinnings. The servant had gifted Rebekah with jewelry that the text describes in terms of its weight rather than beauty: "a gold nose ring weighing half a shekel, and two bracelets for her arms weighing ten gold shekels" (Gen 24:22). The narrator then connects Laban's haste in running out to greet the visitor to his seeing the gold jewelry that Rebekah wears: "At the moment he saw the ring and the bracelets upon the arms of his sister and when he heard the words of Rebekah his sister saying, 'Thus the man said to me,' he came to the man who was standing by his camels near the well" (Gen 24:30).[13] The linking of the jewelry to Laban's haste suggests that the economic value of the jewelry precipitates Laban's hospitality.

Unfortunately, the text does not provide full information on Rebekah's mother's house, making it difficult to determine whether Laban is a full or half-brother to Rebekah. We do not have a complete genealogy for Bethuel; his wife is unnamed and there is no mention of a concubine. Still, three textual details strongly suggest that Laban and Rebekah were full siblings: first, Laban is found in a dwelling that is called Rebekah's "mother's house"; second, Laban is introduced as "Rebekah's brother" rather than as "Bethuel's son"; and third, Laban is repeatedly paired with Rebekah's mother in joint actions and decisions. The term "house of her mother," therefore, co-emerges with an unmediated reference to Rebekah's brother, who is repeatedly paired with her mother.[14]

In the verses that follow, Laban's actions predominate and show that he is the authoritative figure within Rebekah's *bêt 'ēm*. He insists that the servant not remain outside because "I myself have opened the house [to you]" (*wĕ'ānōkî pinnîtî habbayit*) (Gen 24:31). The emphatic use of the first-person pronoun stresses Laban's position as the one who has the right to invite guests into his *bêt 'ēm*. His role as the consummate host continues as the servant enters the house and unloads his camels, and Laban provides him with straw and water for the camels and more water to wash his feet and those of his men, and places food before him. When the servant relates his mission, repeating all the details that we as readers already know, he stresses Abraham's wealth and Isaac's status as the son who has received "all that he has" (Gen 24:34–36).[15] At the end of the servant's tale, he addresses a plural audience: "So now, if you [pl.] will act faithfully and truthfully toward my master, tell me, and if not, tell me, so that I might turn to the right or to the left" (Gen 24:49). The plurality that answers him is somewhat unexpected: "Laban *and Bethuel* answered saying, 'The matter comes forth from Yahweh, we cannot speak to you evil or good. See, Rebekah is before you, take [her] and go so that she might become the wife of the son of your master as Yahweh has spoken'" (Gen 24:50–51; emphasis added). The sudden appearance of Bethuel in the narrative and his literary subordination to Laban have occasioned much scholarly debate. If Bethuel is alive and present within this house, why is it called Rebekah's "mother's house," and why is Bethuel not acting in a more authoritative role? Why is Bethuel's name listed after that of his son Laban? The fact that Bethuel is not mentioned again and that Laban and Rebekah's mother dominate the rest of the narrative has only added to the confusion.

The explanations commentators have provided for this singular reference to Bethuel show that they accept the professed preference for patrilineality in the Bible as a reflection of reality. Commentators share the assumption that if Bethuel is alive and present in the house, the house should be called "her father's house," and he should be playing the authoritative role. With this in mind, Claus Westermann suggests that Bethuel must have been dead at this time, and therefore the reference to Bethuel in verse 50 should be removed as a late addition or emended to read "Laban and *his household.*"[16] Roland de Vaux likewise proposes that Laban was a stand-in for his dead father.[17] E. A. Speiser first explains Rebekah's running to "her mother's house" as a phrase that "can only mean that Bethuel is dead."[18] This explains for Speiser Laban's dominant role and serves as his justification for removing the reference to "and Bethuel" from verse 50, arguing that the verse "cannot be original."[19] Nahum Sarna accepts the reference to Bethuel as original but then downplays the significance of Rebekah running "to her mother's house." Sarna suggests, "In this society a girl would ordinarily refer to her home as her mother's house."[20] He then notes that Bethuel's appearance late in the narrative, subsumed under his son, is "strange" but allows for the possibility that brothers played important roles in their sisters' marriages.[21] Naomi Steinberg explains Bethuel's absence in the beginning of the narrative by suggesting that he may have had other wives and was residing with one of them at the time. In her words, "Laban acts as the family representative in the absence of his father."[22] Each of the commentators finds the passive presence of Bethuel in a space labeled "her mother's house" problematic. The identification of Laban as "Rebekah's brother" rather than "Bethuel's son," together with his dominant role in the household, exacerbates the perceived problem.[23]

Ingo Kottsieper has argued that the passive presence of the father in a space labeled "her mother's house" does not present a problem. He claims correctly that the marriage of a daughter was of less interest to a father than it was to her brothers, especially her uterine brothers.[24] I would add that if the house of the mother was a subunit nested within the house of the father, his largely passive presence in her space makes sense. Once we have examined all of the texts that feature the *bêt 'ēm*, we will see a repeated pattern of passive or absent fathers in spaces and social groupings that are maternally labeled.

Moreover, if we look at other biblical family narratives, we find that new characters like Bethuel often appear in ways that seem sudden or jarring to our modern reading sensibilities. When we read these stories more closely, however, we see that new members of a family are introduced into the narrative at precisely the moment when the social context signals a need for that specific category of kin. For example, we learn of Moses's older sister at precisely the moment when he has been set adrift on the river and needs a rescuer.[25] In another story, we learn for the first time that Laban has sons at a point when there is a perceived threat to the *naḥălâ*, the paternal inheritance, within the house of Laban (Gen 31:1). Finally, we learn that Job has a wife only after he has lost all his children and sits on a dung heap covered in boils. This low point in Job's story of loss seems to signal the narrative need for a wife who will add one final insult (Job 2:9–10). Here in Gen 24, Bethuel appears at the precise moment when his verbal assent to the marriage is required.

Once the narrative setting shifts to "her mother's house," Rebekah, "her brother and her mother" dominate the action and dialogue. After Laban and Bethuel offer their consent to the marriage, the servant takes out "vessels of silver and vessels of gold and garments" and gives them to Rebekah. He then offers "costly gifts" (*migdānōt*) to "her brother and her mother" (Gen 24: 53).[26] After sharing a meal and spending a night in the mother's house, the servant requests that he be allowed to return to his master with Rebekah. Again it is Rebekah's "brother and her mother" who request that Rebekah be allowed to remain with them for a few days. Finally, it is the same labeled pair—"her brother and her mother"—that serve as the antecedent to a series of actions: they receive the servant's request that he be allowed to leave without delay, they send for Rebekah, they ask if she is willing to go with the servant, they provide Rebekah and her wet nurse with a sendoff, and they pronounce upon Rebekah a marriage blessing (Gen 24:55–60). The blessing again emphasizes the sibling over the daughter relationship; Rebekah is sent forth as "a sister": "Our sister, may you become thousands of multitudes, and may your descendants possess the gates of those who hate them" (Gen 24:60).

The occurrence of the term *bêt 'ēm* in Gen 24 provides important information concerning the vantage point, composition, and function of this entity. The story is largely uninterested in the house of Bethuel and therefore provides no information about possible additional wives or children. This makes it difficult based on this text alone to show a clear distinction between the composition of the house of Bethuel and what I am arguing is a subunit within it, "the house of the mother." Nonetheless, this text provides our first set of data. The "house of the mother" is introduced from the vantage point of a young, marriageable daughter. It is the young Rebekah who "runs and tells her mother's house" of the arrival of a visitor. In terms of composition, the first person associated and named within Rebekah's *bêt 'ēm* is Laban, specifically introduced as "Rebekah's brother." Others present in the house include a passive, nearly silent Bethuel; Rebekah's unnamed but very active mother; and Rebekah's wet nurse. I argue that Rebekah, "her brother and her mother," and her wet nurse form a uterine family unit, a "mother's house," within the larger household of Bethuel. Even if Bethuel had no additional wives, his larger household complex could include his mother, his brothers, his unmarried sisters, his male slaves, and dependent workers. None of these additional family members would be part of Rebekah's *bêt 'ēm* (fig. 5).

Turning now from composition to social function, Rebekah's *bêt 'ēm* serves as the site of her marriage negotiations.[27] It is a physical dwelling

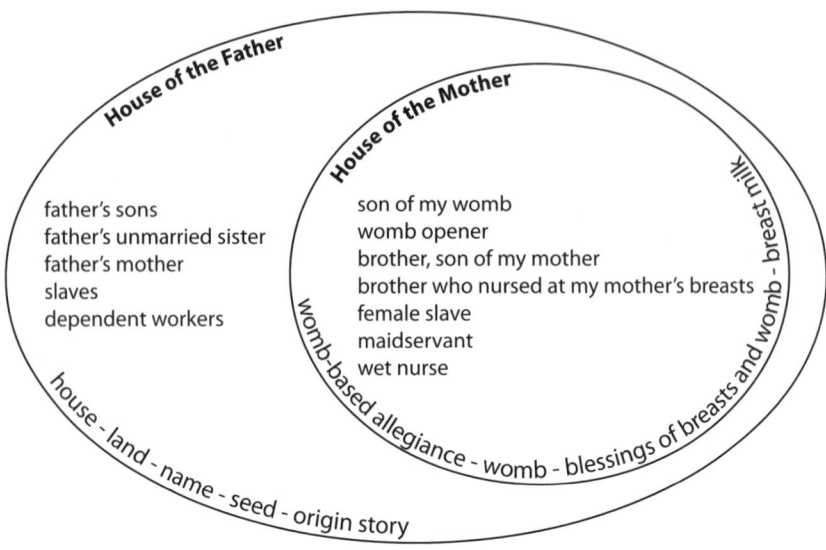

Figure 5. *The house of the mother as a nested unit within a monogamous household, e.g., Gen 24. Illustration created by Ondrea Keith, rendered by Bill Nelson.*

where Abraham's servant can enter and tell his story, offer his marriage proposal, receive the family's acceptance of that proposal, bestow marriage gifts, share a meal, and spend the night. The dominant figure within Rebekah's *bêt 'ēm* is her brother Laban. He is party to every action that occurs within the *bêt 'ēm*: he opens the house to the stranger, hosts the dinner, accepts the marriage proposal, receives gifts, and pronounces the marriage blessing.[28] Bethuel first enters the narrative as the named head of Rebekah's father's house; Rebekah identifies herself as "the daughter of Bethuel" when the servant asks about space in "her father's house." Once Rebekah has run to "her mother's house," by contrast, Bethuel appears in a single verse, listed after his son Laban, where he joins Laban in offering consent to the marriage. He has authority, but it is clearly ancillary to that of Laban. Rebekah's mother has a far greater and more active role in the betrothal event than that of Bethuel. Two other categories of people are mentioned as part of Rebekah's *bêt 'ēm*, her wet nurse (*mēniqtāh*) and her maidservants (*na'ărōtêhā*), all of whom travel together with Rebekah to the land of Canaan. The type of marriage negotiated for the daughter is patrilocal. Thus, the term *bêt 'ēm* appears and finds meaning from the vantage point of a young, marriageable daughter. It is the site of marriage negotiations for that daughter who will ultimately marry out of her natal home and reside with her husband. The key players within the marriage negotiations are the young girl's brother, followed by her mother. Her father is largely silent, and when he does appear, his authority in the marriage negotiations is subsumed under that of his son.

Returning to the Mother's House: Orpah and Ruth

The story in the book of Ruth is one of a family's loss and restoration as well as one of two women's quest for survival. Like Gen 24, there are a variety of opinions concerning the dating of this book.[29] I agree with Kirstin Nielsen's assessment that the function of the book of Ruth is to acknowledge, address, and attempt to ameliorate the problem of David's Moabite roots. Its historical context, therefore, has to be a time period when the Davidic dynasty was under threat.[30] Unfortunately, this could be any time from the actual reign of David through the postexilic effort to reinstate the monarchy under Zerubbabel.

While it is difficult to pin down exact dates for either Gen 24 or the book of Ruth, I argue that both narratives postdate the stories of the eponymous figures to whom they relate. The story of Rebekah's betrothal works with the details of two established literary cycles, those of Abraham and of Jacob. Likewise, the story of Ruth and Naomi adds to and comments on an existing David narrative. This is the logic behind the Christian Old Testament's canonical placement of the book of Ruth as a précis to the David story, and the same logic applies to the redactional insertion of Gen 24 as a précis to the Jacob story.[31] Even for Rebekah, whose paternal genealogy is ideal, the narrator has to show that her father came from a high-status mother. Ruth, the Moabite great grandmother of King David, requires more extensive treatment. On the one hand, the book of Ruth builds Ruth up through its presentation of her impeccable conduct. On the other hand, as we see in chapter 6, the narrator ultimately replaces Ruth as the mother of Obed with the Judahite Naomi. This does not bring us any closer to precisely dating the book, but if the book of Ruth is in conversation with an existing David narrative, a late seventh-century date seems the earliest possibility.

As in the story of Rebekah's betrothal, the book of Ruth begins with a fully intact Judahite family listed in terms that evoke the *bêt 'āb:* "In the days when judges judged, there was a famine in the land, and a man from

Bethlehem of Judah went to live in the fields of Moab, he, his wife and his two sons." A nuclear cell, likely of a larger *bêt 'āb* in Bethlehem, splits off on its own in order to survive a famine. The father of this nuclear cell, Elimelech, dies in Moab, and his two sons take Moabite wives. Then, the two sons die, leaving the mother, Naomi, without her two sons or husband; the house into which she married, the house of her husband, has ceased to exist. Likewise, for her two daughters-in-law, Ruth and Orpah, the house into which they have married has been "blotted out," much as the name of the deceased husband, "Mahlon," forecasted.[32]

Having heard that the famine has let up in her homeland and having few options in Moab, Naomi decides to return to Judah together with her two daughters-in-law. On the way to Judah, however, Naomi turns to her daughters-in-law and says: "Go, return, each of you *to the house of her mother* [*lĕbêt 'immāh*]. May Yahweh deal faithfully with you as you have with the dead and with me. May Yahweh grant that you find a resting place, each of you in *the house of her husband* [*bêt 'îšāh*]. When she kissed them, they raised their voices and wept" (Ruth 1:8–9). This text shares with Gen 24 a history of commentary that attempts to dismiss, emend, or undervalue the significance of the reference to the *bêt 'ēm*. André LaCocque finds the term "surprising" but explains its use here and in Song of Songs with his own argument that both books were written by women.[33] Victor Matthews gives an emotional explanation, suggesting that the house of the mother was a place women "would associate with comfort and all things familiar."[34] Edward Campbell documents a full history of commentators understanding the mother's house in emotional terms: "Naomi thinks in distress of her own motherhood"; "a mother knows best how to comfort"; the phrase "mother's house" is "a more delicate and feminine expression, thus suitable for women's speech."[35] Campbell opts to retain "mother's house" and was one of the first scholars to note correctly, based on the four references to the mother's house in the Bible, that the *bêt 'ēm* "was the locus for matters pertinent to marriage, especially for discussion and planning for marriage."[36] Tamara Cohn Eskenazi and Tikva Frymer-Kensky come close to a view that I would support when they suggest that the *bêt 'ēm* was a "conceptual unit" referring to "the mother's jurisdiction."[37]

Comparing this reference to the *bêt 'ēm* with that found in Gen 24, the vantage point on the house of the mother is once again that of a marriageable woman. Neither Ruth nor Orpah had children from their first husbands, so now widowed, Naomi hopes each can remarry. The place that they must return to in order that each one may find a "resting place" in the "house of her husband" (*bêt 'îšāh*) is "the house of her mother" (*bêt 'immāh*).[38] Once again, the *bêt 'ēm* is associated with negotiating a marriage for a daughter, and the type of marriage envisioned is patrilocal. Naomi's plan is for Ruth and Orpah to return to their mothers' houses long enough to have new marriages negotiated; then they could leave again to live in their new husbands' houses.[39]

As we know from the story of Ruth, Orpah decides to return to her mother's house, and Ruth chooses to remain with Naomi. Unfortunately, we do not have the "Book of Orpah," so we do not have a story about Orpah's return to the house of her mother. As such, this reference to "her mother's house" does not provide us with information concerning the composition and physical dwelling space of Orpah's *bêt 'ēm*. We only know that the house of the mother is a place that Naomi associates with marriage negotiations.

Leading Her Lover into the House of Her Mother: The Female Speaker in Song of Songs

The Song of Songs is a collection of erotic love poetry that is exchanged between a woman and her beloved. While there is no clear narrative progression to this collection, the woman and her lover long for each other and consistently try but fail to meet in various secluded places. For most of the book, the lovers are anonymous; still, the only named male in the book is King Solomon, and the collection begins with the identification "The Song of Songs, which is Solomon's." Rather than being literally about Solomon, however, the anonymous speakers seem to use Solomon and his palace as inspiration for their fantasies. While the poetry may be early, the current collection is considered one of the latest books of the Bible.[40] Moreover, as in the two previous house-of-the-mother narratives, the Song as a whole seems to amplify and comment on certain aspects of an existing Solomonic story.

The Song of Songs contains two of the four references to the house of the mother in the Bible, and as Phyllis Trible has noted, the word "mother" occurs seven times in Song of Songs while the word "father" does not appear at all. Similarly, while the "house of the mother" occurs twice, the "house of the father" is not mentioned.[41] We encounter the female speaker in the Song as part of a family that consists of her mother and uterine brothers, whom she refers to as "my mother's sons" (Song 1:6). She is also closely and repeatedly associated with a group of women called "the Daughters of Jerusalem."[42] Both references to the *bêt 'ēm* in the Song show that it is a physical space, and the second reference adds details that indicate it is a space where a daughter can imagine finding her uterine brother (Song 3:4; 8:1–2). In fact, the woman's uterine brothers frame the book as a whole; their admonishments concerning their sister's chastity appear in Song 1:6 and 8:8–9.

This brings us to the question of marriage and whether these two references to the *bêt 'ēm* feature discussions of marriage. Clearly, the book's focus is not marriage; still, it does contain several allusions to marriage and betrothal. The female lover is called "my sister, my bride," or simply "my bride" (Song 4:8, 9, 10, 11, 12; 5:1).[43] The female speaker calls attention to King Solomon's crown, with which his mother crowned him "on the day of his wedding" (Song 3:11). The male speaker sometimes compares himself to Solomon. For example, in Song 6:8–9, the male lover seems to refer to Solomon when he speaks of one in Jerusalem who has "sixty queens and eighty concubines, and maidens without number," yet among these, he claims that his one lover is "perfect" and "flawless," praised by the very same queens, concubines, and maidens. Finally, in Song 8:8, the brothers refer to the day of their sister's betrothal.

We find the first reference to the *bêt 'ēm* in Song 3:4. The young woman lies in bed and longs for her lover. She then arises and goes into the city streets whereupon, after passing some city patrolmen, she finds him: "I found him whom my soul loves. / I seized hold of him and would not release him / until I had brought him to the house of my mother [*bêt 'immî*], / into the chamber of her who conceived me [*ḥeder hôrātî*]." The second reference is similar in that the woman longs to bring her lover into a private place:

> Oh that you were like a brother to me,
> one who had nursed at my mother's breasts!
> I would find you outside and kiss you,
> and no one would bother me.
> I would lead you and bring you to the house of my mother,
> Into the chamber of her who conceived me.
>
> *Mî yittenkā kě'āḥ lî*
> *yônēq šědê 'immî*
> *'emṣā'ăkā baḥuṣ*

ešāqěkā gam lō'-yābûzû lî:
'enhāgăkā 'ăbî'ăkā 'el-bêt 'immî
tělammědēnî [MT; my translation for the final line follows the LXX "*eis tamieion tēs sullabousēs me*"]. (Song 8:1–2a)[44]

In both references the woman speaks of her mother's house as a private space where she can take her lover in order to engage in sexual activity.[45]

The vantage point on the *bêt 'ēm* in these texts is the same as the previous two, that of a marriageable woman. The female speaker in the Song is a young woman who has not yet been "spoken for" (Song 8:8). In both cases, the *bêt 'ēm* is a physical place where she longs to take her lover for a private tryst. As in Gen 24, here in the Song, the woman associates her mother's house with her brother and her mother. Her brother is specifically described as "one who had nursed at my mother's breasts." This added clarification suggests that the reference is to a full or uterine brother, one born of the same mother.[46] This conclusion is supported by the two other references to the female speaker's brothers in the book. In chapter 1, the woman proclaims, "I am black and beautiful," and she then explains her situation:

> Do not stare at me because I am blackened,
> Because the sun has scorched me.
> My mother's sons [*běnê 'immî*] became angry with me
> And made me the keeper of the vineyards.
> My own vineyard I have not kept. (Song 1:6)

Here again, as in the case of Joseph with Benjamin (Gen 43:29), the reference to brothers as "my mother's sons" clarifies them as uterine brothers.[47] Moreover, the young woman's uterine brothers seem to be angry with her because she has flaunted her beauty and not "kept her vineyard." The brothers are presented as those who have authority over her with regard to her chastity and her labor for the household. The other reference to the woman's brothers is in the final chapter where the "mother's sons" of chapter 1 are the presumed speakers of Song 8:8–9:

> We have a little sister, and she has no breasts.
> What shall we do for our sister on the day when she is spoken for?
> If she is a wall, we will build upon her a battlement of silver;
> But if she is a door, we will enclose her with boards of cedar.[48]

The young woman responds flippantly as she does in chapter 1 to her mother's sons, "I was a wall, and my breasts were like towers; then I was in his eyes as one who brings peace" (Song 8:10). Both of these references to the young woman's brothers place them in a position of authority over her, even if she chooses to challenge that authority. Moreover, in both cases, the brothers show concern for protecting the chastity of their sister.[49] The two explicit references to a brother or brothers specify a uterine brother, and we can assume that the speakers of Song 8:8–9 are the mother's sons spoken of in Song 1:6.

The Song of Songs presents the *bêt 'ēm* from the vantage point of a young, marriageable daughter who associates the space with her mother and uterine brother. She envisions the space as private and therefore an ideal place to bring her lover. Rather than explicit negotiations for a particular marriage, the book alludes to betrothals, brides, and wedding days in multiple places. The speaker's father is absent from the book.

The Daughter of Leah: Dinah

The story of the marriage negotiations for Dinah and Shechem found in Gen 34 does not include an explicit reference to Dinah's *bêt 'ēm*; however, the text provides several clues that we are dealing with issues understood to fall within the purview of the *bêt 'ēm*. Dinah's story begins by identifying her through a direct pathway to the house of her mother: "Now Dinah, the daughter of Leah, whom she had borne to Jacob, went out to visit the women of the land" (Gen 34:1).[50] It is unusual to identify a person through her mother, so the fact that this narrative opens with a maternal genealogy suggests that we are dealing with an event where the house of Leah will prove central, just as in the story of Joseph, the house of Rachel was central.[51] It is also significant that Dinah's pathway to her father in this opening verse is mediated through her mother.

Dinah's excursion to meet the women of the land results in her being raped by the foreigner, Shechem, in an act that the biblical narrative labels "an outrage" (*něbālâ*) (Gen 34:7).[52] As the narrator tells the story of the rape and the ensuing interaction between Shechem and Jacob, he repeatedly refers to Dinah through her paternal house as "Jacob's daughter" (Gen 34:3, 5, 7).[53] Just as Abraham's servant asked Rebekah if there was any room in "your father's house" when he wished to arrange a marriage, so too Shechem and Hamor start with Jacob, the father of Dinah. Shechem requests that his father, Hamor, approach Dinah's father, Jacob. When Jacob hears Hamor's proposal, however, he chooses to keep his peace about the issue with Shechem because "his sons were with his cattle in the field" (Gen 34:3–6). He waits until his sons come home and allows them to address the proposed marriage and the "outrage." In the ensuing interaction, Dinah's brothers are first labeled under the house of their father as "the sons of Jacob," and they are described as "indignant and very angry" on account of Shechem's treatment of their sister (Gen 34:7). Hamor, who first thought to approach Jacob with the proposal of marriage, ends up having to deal directly with "Jacob's sons" (Gen 34:14). What Hamor proposes is more than a simple marriage between Dinah and Shechem; he proposes an ongoing marriage treaty that involves each side giving their daughters to the other in marriage (Gen 34:8–9). The fact that Dinah is already residing in Shechem's house and the wording of the proposed marriage treaty— "give your daughters to us"—indicates that the marital practice suggested is patrilocal.[54] The marriage treaty also has economic implications. Hamor indicates that an exchange of daughters in marriage would allow for a sharing of the land, the property within the land, and the trading rights on the land (Gen 34:10). In a sense, Hamor is suggesting an ongoing relationship between his house and Jacob's house. After Shechem, portrayed as the over-eager groom, offers "ever so much bridewealth and gift" that the brothers might ask of him, Hamor and "the sons of Jacob" conduct the marriage negotiations leaving Shechem, the groom, and Jacob, the father of the bride, largely silent (Gen 34:11–17).[55] While Hamor and Shechem address Jacob and his sons with their request for Dinah to become Shechem's wife, it is the "sons of Jacob" that answer the request, deal deceitfully, and demand circumcision as a prerequisite to a broader marriage treaty.[56] The authority that the sons of Jacob assume over their sister Dinah is especially clear in their claim of her as a "daughter" (Gen 34:17).[57]

Three days after the men of Shechem undergo circumcision, the text introduces and names a subset within the collective group labeled "the sons of Jacob"—"two of the sons of Jacob, Simeon and Levi, Dinah's brothers" (šĕnê-bĕnê-ya'ăqōb šim'ôn wĕlēwî 'ăḥê dînā) (Gen 34:25). These two men are the first to be related directly to Dinah as "Dinah's brothers," and their names recall the beginning of the narrative where Dinah is introduced as a daughter of Leah. Simeon and Levi are Dinah's full brothers, born of the same mother, and the text has added the names and specification "Dinah's brothers" to make this genealogical point. Dinah's uterine brothers avenge "the outrage" committed against her by attacking the city of Shechem and killing all the males within it, including Shechem and Hamor. They then

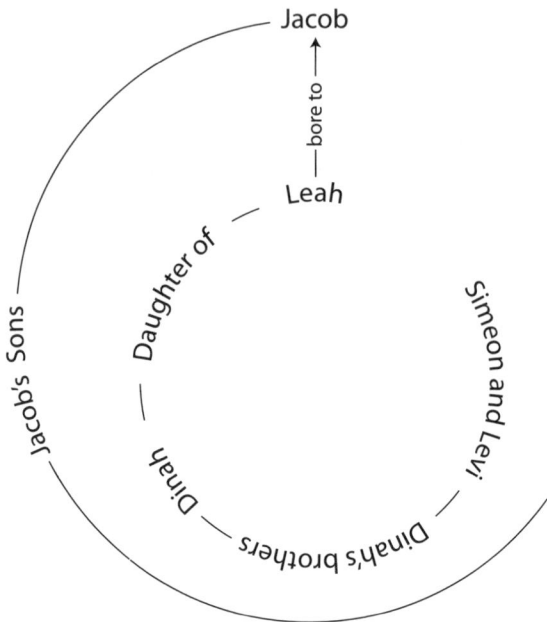

Figure 6. *The house of Leah as a nested unit within the household of Jacob, Gen 34. Illustration by Bill Nelson.*

remove Dinah from Shechem's house (Gen 34:25–26). At this point, "the sons of Jacob" as a larger group return to the narrative as those who plunder the city of Shechem (Gen 34:27–29). The term "sons of Jacob" is the broader kinship designation for Dinah's half- and full brothers, but their association is clearly with the house of their father. The narrower group, "two of the sons of Jacob, Simeon and Levi, Dinah's brothers," signals relational links through the mother (fig. 6).

Throughout this entire scene of marriage negotiations, Jacob has said nothing. When Jacob finally speaks after the mass killing of the Shechemites, his concern is not for Dinah or for the Shechemites; it is for his house. Jacob turns to Simeon and Levi and reprimands them for "bringing trouble" on him and his *bayit* by "making him odious" to the inhabitants of the land (Gen 34:30).[58] The two uterine brothers, on the other hand, seem more concerned for their mother's house, which they feel has suffered an assault. They respond unrepentantly, "Can he treat our sister as a whore?" (Gen 34:31).

The story of the deceitful marital negotiations between the houses of Jacob and Hamor shares several features with the story of Rebekah's marriage negotiations. While Rebekah runs to the house of her mother, Dinah is introduced through the house of her mother as "the daughter of Leah." The marriage proposed in both cases is patrilocal. The brides' fathers are present but remain largely silent throughout the negotiations. Both fathers yield the negotiating process to their sons. The grooms' fathers, on the other hand, are active: Abraham sends his servant, and Hamor approaches Jacob. In the Song of Songs, marriage is alluded to repeatedly in a book that never mentions a father or a father's house. Instead, the Song of Songs singles out uterine brothers, "the sons of my mother," as having protective authority over their sister. These are the brothers who will board up their sister with cedar panels on the day that she is spoken for. Dinah's story also singles out two of her uterine brothers, Simeon and Levi, as the agents of revenge in a marriage that was not properly negotiated with a groom who did not meet the brothers' standards.[59] While Dinah's story does not explicitly reference the *bêt 'ēm,* its social functions and key players are on full display. It may be that the *bêt 'ēm* as a physical space does not enter into this narrative because the marriage negotiations take place outside and the bride is already in the house of her potential husband. This text would then be an example of the *bêt 'ēm* as a kinship group with specific social functions acting outside of the physical space of the *bêt 'ēm.*

Several conclusions can be drawn from the five texts that I have surveyed. In all of the texts, we view the *bêt 'ēm* from the vantage point of a daughter in the context of discussions concerning her marriage. In each case, the marriage negotiated within the *bêt 'ēm* is one in which the daughter is expected to leave her natal home and marry into the house of her husband. In four of the five texts, the daughter's brothers assume positions of authority in the negotiations for her marriage, and two of the texts explicitly label or name uterine brothers. The *bêt 'ēm* evokes the uterine family through labeling those who reside within it as "my mother's sons" or "my brother, one who had nursed at my mother's breasts," and through describing the physical space as "the chamber of her who conceived me."

In addition to these commonalities, we find several other shared features. First, while it is difficult to date the texts where the term *bêt 'ēm* occurs, each seems to postdate and amplify the genealogy and epic story of a foundational male figure—Abraham, Jacob, David, or Solomon. A second shared feature is that intermarriage with foreigners surfaces as a primary concern in each reference. Abraham sends his servant to his home in Aram so that Isaac will not marry a Canaanite, and the story emphasizes

Rebekah's Terahite genealogy. Ruth and Orpah are both Moabite women who have married into a Judahite family. The presentation of Ruth as a devoted daughter-in-law who "cleaves" to her Judahite mother-in-law, even when Naomi insists she has no sons in her womb that Ruth might marry, clarifies and cleanses King David's genealogical association with Moab. Dinah's marriage ends in a massacre because Shechem was a foreigner, an uncircumcised Hivite, who had "defiled her." Simeon's and Levi's rejection of Dinah's marriage with a foreigner contributes to the endogamous ideology of the house of Jacob. The case of the female speaker in the Song of Songs is less clear. The reference to her as a "Shulammite" (Song 7:1 [Eng. 6:13]) may indicate that she is a Jerusalemite. On the other hand, the tense and at times adversarial relationship that she has with the "Daughters of Jerusalem" suggests that she might be an outsider to this group.[60]

Finally, the marriages discussed, negotiated, imagined, and rejected in the *bêt 'ēm* all intersect in some way with a royal house or dynasty. The woman in the Song of Songs fantasizes that she is brought into the king's chambers and judged more perfect than his queens and concubines (Song 1: 1–4; 6:8–9). The book of Ruth closes with a genealogy of King David showing that the Moabite Ruth is his great-grandmother (Ruth 4:17–22). While Jacob is not a king, he will become the eponymous ancestor to the kingdom of Israel. The story of his parentage alludes to royalty. Two of the women who figure into the story of Isaac's and Rebekah's marriage are Isaac's mother, Sarah, and Rebekah's grandmother Milcah. Their two names mean "princess" and "queen," respectively. Finally, the marriage of Dinah is explicitly royal. Shechem is "the prince of the land" that bears his name. Dinah is the only daughter of the eponymous ancestor of the kingdom of Israel. At this point in our study of maternally specific kinship terms, it is too soon to draw firm conclusions from the royal associations of the marriages that occur with reference to the *bêt 'ēm*. The most obvious explanation is that the uterine family as a kinship entity functions most prominently in elite households like those that the Bible's compilers imagined for their founding ancestors.

When Fathers Broker the Marriages of Their Daughters

We have been examining narratives that describe marriage negotiations for a daughter who would marry out of her father's household, and I have shown that this type of marriage was negotiated within the bride's *bêt 'ēm* with her brothers, not her father, playing the primary authoritative role. There are, however, biblical stories of betrothal and marriage in which it is the father of the bride rather than the brother who negotiates the terms. But these stories exhibit a structural dissimilarity to the stories mentioned above. Three prominent stories of fathers negotiating the marriages of their daughters demonstrate this dissimilarity. Laban negotiates the terms of his daughters' marriages to Jacob. Laban's wife is never mentioned (Gen 29). Reuel/Jethro initiates and plays a key role in the marriage arrangements of his daughter Zipporah to Moses, and again, Jethro's wife is never mentioned (Exod 2:15–22). Finally, Saul initiates and sets the terms for the marriages that he proposes for David and his daughters, Merab and Michal (1 Sam 18:17–30). We hear nothing of the mother(s) of Merab and Michal.[61]

These stories of father-brokered marriages share several features that are distinct from brother-brokered marriages. Each of these three fathers has multiple daughters: Laban and Saul have two named daughters; Reuel has seven daughters (Gen 29:16; Exod 2:16; 1 Sam 18:17, 20). In each of these houses of the father, there is either no male heir mentioned or there is a problem with the male heir. In the story of Laban and Jacob, there is no mention of "the sons of Laban" until years later, when Jacob attempts to leave Laban's household (Gen 31:1). Reuel/Jethro apparently has no sons. By the time Saul is negotiating David's marriage to Michal, his own son and heir, Jonathan, has "knit his soul" to that of David and made a covenant with David that involves giving David his royal robe, armor, and sword (1 Sam 18:1–4).

When a daughter's marriage is negotiated within the house of her father by her father, there are also certain shared features regarding the status of the groom. In two of these three texts, the groom is first and foremost a fugitive on the run who needs shelter and receives long-term though not permanent shelter through marrying into his wife's household.[62] Moreover, each of the three grooms is not the firstborn son of his father. Jacob fled to the house of Laban after his older brother, Esau, threatened to murder him (Gen 27:41–45). He found refuge in the house of Laban for decades. Although the text tells the story of a divinely orchestrated choice of Jacob over Esau for their father Isaac's estate, Jacob's flight, his prolonged exile, and his need to seek Esau's favor upon his return all suggest that as a second-born son, he was not in line to inherit the double portion (Gen 25:31–34; 27–33). David is the youngest of the many sons of Jesse, so he does not stand to inherit a double portion of his father's estate. In fact, he had already opted to take the well-traveled path of late-born, excess sons by joining Saul's military and entering into his personal service (1 Sam 16:11; 16–23; 18:2).[63] Moses, like Jacob, fled to Midian when he learned that Pharaoh sought to kill him (Exod 2:11–15). He too is a second-born son though his genealogy is less clear.[64] All three grooms in these father-brokered marriages marry into the houses of their fathers-in-law and enter into their service for years. Jacob and Moses tend the flocks of their fathers-in-law (Gen 30:29–43; Exod 3:1). In the multiple traditions of David's entry into Saul's household, he is consistently portrayed as serving Saul, whether as a musician, an armor bearer, or a military commander (1 Sam 16:21–23; 18–19).

This brief excursus into the conditions that might lead to a father negotiating the marriage of his daughter has demonstrated that on the level of the biblical narrative, fathers become involved when their own household would be absorbing the groom for a significant period of time. They did this in part because they lacked a proper heir themselves or because they sought the service of the son-in-law. The "house of the father" is the site of marriage negotiations for a male heir or for a daughter whose groom would marry into her household.[65] The self-interest of the house of the father in both of these cases is clear. It also seems quite logical that a father would be minimally involved in the marriage negotiations of a daughter who would marry out of his household. What remains less clear, however, is why in those cases of a daughter marrying out, the house of the mother containing mother and uterine brothers becomes centrally involved. It is not, as some have suggested, simply a matter of emotional closeness; it includes long-term reciprocal responsibilities that have economic implications.[66]

The Economics of Uterine Siblings

Modern comparative ethnographies help to shed light on some of the possible ways that the uterine family functions within patrilineal households. While there is no single model for relationships within uterine families, an examination of marriage practices in polygynous societies that practice patrilocal marriage consistently shows the importance of the uterine sibling relationship. These ethnographies provide evidence for the ongoing, economically reciprocal relationship between a daughter and her uterine brothers during and following her marriage. Securing an advantageous match for a sister provided a uterine brother with the economic resources he would need to marry well. A sister's cooperation with her uterine brother's arrangements on her behalf served as a down payment for the advocacy she might need from her brother after marrying into her husband's household.

Hilma Granqvist conducted one of these helpful ethnographic studies of marriage brokering in the early 1900s, focusing on a small Palestinian village.[67] In this village, fathers negotiated the betrothals of their sons and daughters at infancy. Most of the arranged marriages were among close kin. Granqvist recorded the betrothal history within one family in which a mother and father with a single infant daughter and no sons set a reduced amount of bridewealth for her on account of the groom's family being a close relation. Another couple, in a similar situation, had promised their infant daughter to a family as a gift. Later, when that couple produced three sons, they called off the engagement. Now that the mother needed to arrange marriages for her three sons, she needed a higher amount of bridewealth for her daughter. In her words, "I want a [good] bride price for my daughter in order to make a marriage for my sons with it."[68] In this brief story, we have our first hint at an economic relationship between the marriage of a daughter and the financial prospects of her uterine brother.

In another Palestinian village, Martha Mundy and Richard Saumarez Smith have studied the law and practice governing the *mahr*, focusing on archival materials and family histories from the late 1800s to the early 1900s. They defined the *mahr* as "the object that the groom gives the bride as a condition of the Muslim marriage contract."[69] While legally the *mahr* was a gift given to the bride, in practice the researchers documented a wide variety of ways that this gift ended up owned in the name of the bride's father, maternal uncles, and uterine brothers. One of the most frequent recipients of the *mahr* was the brother of the bride's mother. This shows that even in a professed patrilineal community where brides married out of their natal homes and lived with their husbands' families, they maintained longstanding and financially significant relationships with their uterine brothers. In this case of transferring a bride's *mahr* to a maternal uncle, the bridewealth that a senior woman's daughter received went to her brother.

Finally, in Annelies Moors's study of the transfer of gold jewelry at the time of marriage in the Palestinian village of Jabal Nablus from 1920 to 1990, she observes the common practice of young brides forfeiting their dowry to their brothers.[70] Legally, the dowry belonged to the bride, and she could take it into her new marriage and control it. In practice, brides were expected to yield the dowry to their unmarried brothers. In describing the inheritance and marriage strategies of women who routinely refrained from claiming a land inheritance or dowry that was legally theirs, Moors notes, "Women strongly identify with their natal family.... They depend on its support for their well-being.... Leaving her share in her father's estate to her brothers, a woman at once enhances her brothers' position and by implication her own, as in this way their obligations to protect and support her are reaffirmed."[71] When asked why they did not take their dowries into their marriage, most young brides indicated that their brothers had been good to them and deserved the money. The other factor, however, was that the sister's gift of her dowry secured the brothers' continued protection and support of her after the marriage. If ever the bride ran into difficulty with her husband and his family, she could count on her own brothers to negotiate on her behalf. If she insisted on taking the dowry with her, her brothers effectively owed her nothing.[72] Lila Abu-Lughod finds a similar bond between a married woman and her "natal brothers" in a Bedouin community. In this community, a married woman who lived in her husband's house retained her natal tribal affiliation throughout her life. In her married life, her brothers were expected to defend her rights and prevent any abuse.[73]

This brief examination of ethnographic studies of marriage brokering practices has suggested several patterns of relationship between a bride and her natal home, and while they are varied, one consistent feature is the economic relationship among siblings that finds expression at the time of the sister's marriage out of her father's home. There is an economic reciprocity between siblings that continues even after the sister has married out of her natal home and given birth to her own children. Bridewealth received for a sister could become the bridewealth offered when her brother married. A dowry or marriage gift that a bride chose to leave for her brothers further enhanced her brothers' financial and therefore marital prospects. And finally, a bride's generosity in yielding marital gifts to her brothers paid dividends to her in the form of continued social and possibly economic support once she had married into her husband's household.

Without the aid of modern ethnographies, the biblical evidence alone establishes that the house of the mother was a distinctly functioning kinship unit within the house of the father. Within the house of the mother, uterine brothers exercised considerable authority over their sister, particularly at the time of her marriage out of the father's house. Marriage negotiations were explicitly economic, involving an exchange of gifts and/or property.

What the modern ethnographies alert us to is the possibility of an ongoing and reciprocal economic and social relationship among uterine siblings. In the Song of Songs, the brothers and the male lover of the female protagonist imagine that the woman's marriage is in some way linked to the possession of a vineyard (Song 1:6; 8:11–12).[74] Shechem's proposed marriage to Dinah involves sharing property rights (Gen 34:9–10). Abraham's servant gives a series of marital gifts to Rebekah and her family. Rebekah receives gold jewelry and later "vessels of silver and vessels of gold and garments" (Gen 24:22, 53). The only other recipients of bridal gifts are "her brother and her mother," who receive "costly ornaments" (Gen 24:53). One question that comes up in light of the modern ethnographies is whether or not an ancient reader or hearer of this story would imagine Rebekah taking her marriage gifts with her when she traveled to Canaan. It seems highly unlikely that Abraham's servant would bring heavy vessels of gold and silver all the way to Mesopotamia only to haul them back again. It seems more reasonable to assume that Rebekah would leave these gifts with "her brother and her mother" as a kind of down-payment on her future security.

The biblical text marks the shift in Rebekah's familial ties in Gen 25:19–20 when the narrator provides a summary notation of Isaac's marriage to Rebekah. He reiterates Rebekah's paternal genealogy, presenting her as "Rebekah, the daughter of Bethuel the Aramean of Paddan-aram." He then adds her relationship to her brother: "sister of Laban the Aramaean." Tammi Schneider notes that up to the point of this marriage notation to Isaac, Rebekah has been identified through her paternal genealogy, but beginning from Gen 25:20, all future references to Rebekah's association with Paddan-aram are through her brother Laban.[75] I would argue that this shift occurs already in Gen 24:28–29, when Rebekah runs to "her mother's house" and finds "her brother Laban." Both texts indicate that the key relationship that moves forward after a daughter's marriage is the brother-sister one. Years later, when Rebekah's favored son Jacob needs a place of refuge, she can count on her brother Laban to provide it (Gen 27:41–45).

The ongoing nature of the relationship between a married woman and her uterine household is also seen in texts that describe marriages that end without children. Ruth and Orpah could expect to be taken back into their mothers' homes after their husbands died (Ruth 1:8–14). Dinah's uterine brothers, Simeon and Levi, take her back when they determine that her marriage brought dishonor (Gen 34:26). We later find Dinah grouped under the offspring of Leah when the house of Jacob relocates to Goshen

(Gen 46:15). And in chapter 4, we see that after being raped by Amnon, Tamar finds refuge for the rest of her life in the home of her uterine brother, Absalom (2 Sam 13:20).

Biblical narratives and modern ethnographic studies together provide evidence for "the house of the mother" as an indigenous, Hebrew designation for what anthropologists term "the uterine family." As we see in the stories of Jacob, his house did not simply "segment" into twelve male-headed tribes. It also divided into four politically significant and hierarchically arranged maternal units, what I would label "houses of the mother." The descendants of the sons that the text labels "the sons of Bilhah and Zilpah, his father's wives," never contend for a position in the monarchy or priesthood. The story of Joseph highlights the house of Rachel within the larger house of Jacob, foreshadowing the political dominance of Ephraim in the northern kingdom of Israel. The story of Dinah highlights the house of Leah and signals the future priestly dominance of Levi. The story of "Ruth the Moabite" addresses a problematic maternal unit in the ancestry of the house of David.

Based on the five texts analyzed in this chapter, it would seem that the house of the mother had social and economic control over the marriage brokering of a daughter who would marry out. Within the house of the mother, a girl's uterine brother(s), "the sons of her mother," exercised authority protecting the chastity of their sister, choosing an appropriate husband, setting the terms for the marriage, and receiving an economically significant portion of the marriage gifts. While the daughter clearly married out of the house of her father, she remained especially connected to "the house of her mother." If her marriage ended, she could return there and find refuge, and in times of difficulty, she could depend on her uterine brothers for support.

3 Chamber of Her Who Conceived Me (*ḥeder hôrātî*)

I have argued that the Hebrew term *bêt 'ēm* is a designation for what anthropologists call the "uterine family." Like the house of the father, it represents both a physical space and a grouping of people. As a physical space, the *bêt 'ēm* is a place one can run to, return to, and take one's lover into. Within the space of the *bêt 'ēm*, family members can talk with visitors, host a meal, offer lodging, and negotiate marriage terms. The *bêt 'ēm* can also be used as a private space where a young woman might fool around with her lover. As a grouping of people, the *bêt 'ēm* is composed in its minimal form of a mother and her biological and adopted children. It can also include maidservants, slaves, and wet nurses. The *bêt 'ēm* is distinct from yet supportive of the house of the father upon which it depends. If a mother and her children have received recognition and legitimacy within the house of her husband and their father, the *bêt 'ēm* forms a social and spatial subunit nested within the house of the father. Mothers and children who are not recognized and legitimized by the husband-father, or who are cast out by a primary wife, form maternal houses that are only loosely associated with the father. These lower-status houses of the mother are satellite houses in relationship to the house of the father; they are physically separated from the house of the father. Sons born into these low-status, satellite houses have no ascribed status in the house of their father; they must fight for any property and inheritance rights.[1]

Kinship Relatedness Expressed through Word Pairs

The house-of-the-mother texts that I covered in chapter 2 generated several syntactically related phrases and terms and, significantly, some of them are spatial and some relational. Spatially, the term *bêt 'ēm* is found in a parallelistic line with the phrase "the chamber of her who conceived me" (Song 3:4).[2] Relationally, we find that the narratives featuring the *bêt 'ēm* contain marked references to uterine brothers. Kinship terms like "house" and "brother" are notoriously vague and malleable, and therefore often require further specification. In Hebrew, this specification can take the form of a word pair. A defining feature of classical Hebrew syntax, word pairs and the parallelistic line represent an ideal structure through which to arrive at indigenous definitions of Hebrew kinship terms. In James Kugel's *The Idea of Biblical Poetry*, Kugel demonstrates that the splitting of known word pairs creates the parallelistic lines that are a signature feature of Hebrew poetry.[3] As "the basic feature of biblical songs," and much narrative as well, the parallelistic line involves "the recurrent use of a relatively short sentence-form that consists of two brief clauses." Between the two clauses, the A and B clauses, Kugel notes "a feeling of correspondence" (1–2). In attempting to account for the wide variety of ways that these two short clauses can correspond to one another, Kugel identifies the common form of relatedness wherein the B clause moves beyond the A clause "in force of specificity" such that B "particularizes," "defines," or "expands the meaning" of A (8). Thus, the B clause can at times serve as the definition of the A clause. There is, according to Kugel, an "afterwardness" to the B clause, a "seconding sequence" wherein B takes on an emphatic character. The B clause "supports A, carries it further, backs it up, completes it, goes beyond it" (8, 52). Kugel summarizes this form of parallelistic line with the statement "A, and what's more B" (58).

Adele Berlin applies psycholinguistic theory on word associations to her analysis of Hebrew word pairs. She argues that word pairs "are nothing more or less than the products of normal word associations that are made by all competent speakers."[4] This means that word pairs, whether joined or split into poetic parallelistic lines, tell us which terms native Hebrew speakers and writers associated one with another. Again, this suggests that word pairs can assist us in reaching an indigenous understanding of Hebrew kinship terms. One frequent pattern of relatedness that Berlin identifies within Hebrew word pairs is the feature of "deletion" wherein the A term names a category and the B term is a specific item within the larger category. Berlin associates the second move with "particularizing" (74). Her research also demonstrates that context played a crucial role in generating word associations. The same word could generate multiple word associations, and the context within which the speaker understood the prompting word determined which of the many possible associations would come to mind (71). We have already noted the "extreme semantic latitude" required in defining Hebrew kin terms. Words like "brother" (*'āḥ*) can mean uterine brother, half-brother, cousin, and ally.[5] Berlin's research suggests that multivalent words like "house" and "brother" required specification, and this specification often came through a narrowing of their possible meanings in the second term of a word pair.

When the woman in the Song of Songs longs to bring her lover "into the house of my mother, into the chamber of her who conceived me," the parallelistic line suggests that the "house" of the mother is defined and specified as a "chamber," a subunit of maternally designated space within a larger dwelling (Song 3:4).[6] We have already seen how a man's house could contain multiple dwellings that were also labeled "houses." We have also seen how a man's house could be subdivided into maternally named units. Turning specifically to a spatial analysis, the Bible labels certain spaces within a larger male-headed household as belonging to a wife or mother within the household. These maternal spaces can be labeled "house of the mother," "chambers," or "tents."

There are, however, several ways of reading the meaning of the parallelism in these lines from the Song of Songs. Carol Meyers has argued that the use of the spatial term "chamber" in the parallel phrase "chamber of her who conceived me" need not imply that the corresponding house of the mother was also a "spatial" designation. Instead, she argues that the term "chamber" "intensifies, focuses and clarifies the *female orientation* of its parallel."[7] This interpretation supports Meyers's understanding of the house of the mother as the same entity as the house of the father only viewed from a woman's perspective.[8] While this reading of the parallel lines is possible, an examination of spatial word pairs in parallel lines supports the interpretation of "chamber" as a spatial specification of the meaning of "house of the mother."

In one form of spatial word pairs, the A term designates a singular dwelling and the B term identifies the plural units that physically constitute the A-term dwelling. One example of this form is "tent/curtains." When Jeremiah voices the lament, "there is no one to spread my tent [*'ohŏlî*] again, and to erect my curtains [*yĕrî'ôtāy*]," we get the sense that a tent can be constructed from multiple curtains (Jer 10:20).[9] Second Isaiah evokes the same relationship of a single dwelling made up of plural parts when he calls to Daughter Zion, "Enlarge the site of your tent [*'ohŏlēk*], and let the curtains [*yĕrî'ôt*] of your habitations be stretched out" (Isa 54:2). The same relationship governs the word pair "house/chambers." In the book of Proverbs, the house is specified as a dwelling made up of multiple chambers:

> By wisdom a house [*bayit*] is built,
> and by understanding it is established;
> By knowledge the chambers [*ḥădārîm*] are filled
> with all precious and pleasant riches. (Prov 24:3–4)

We can contrast this house built through wisdom and comprising rooms filled with knowledge with the house of the adulteress, which serves as a portal to Sheol:

> Her house [*bayit*] is the way to Sheol,
> Going down to the chambers [*ḥădārîm*] of death. (Prov 7:27)

In this example, the house whose door leads to Sheol is subdivided into "chambers of death."[10] A similar type of spatial word pair is found in Jeremiah's description of a rich man's house within which we find his upper rooms:

> Woe to the one who builds his house [*bêtô*] by unrighteousness,
> And his upper rooms [*'ălîyyôtāyw*] by injustice. (Jer 22:13)

When the nouns in a spatial word pair agree in number, their relationship is either synonymous or specifying, narrowing, or intensifying. In Balaam's oracle of praise for Israel, "tents" and "encampments" are used synonymously: "How fair are your tents, O Jacob, your encampments O Israel" (Num 24:5).[11] Other examples suggest that the B term is a narrowed specification of the A term and a more valued aspect of the A term. When the psalmist declares, "O Lord, I Love the house in which you dwell, and the place of the dwelling of your glory," the attribute "glory" is a valued epithet of the deity, the divine aspect thought to be present in the temple (Ps 26:8). While in some texts the glory of Yahweh fills the temple or the tent of meeting, in others the glory is clearly associated with the Holy of Holies, the innermost sanctum of the temple. So the "place of the dwelling of your glory" intensifies and spatially narrows "the house in which you dwell." Psalm 132:7 exhibits a similar relationship: "Let us enter his tabernacles, let us bow down before his footstool." Again, the deity's footstool is the inner portion and the most valued place within the larger space labeled "his tabernacles."[12]

When we return to the word pair "house of the mother/chamber of her who conceived me," the B term seems to specify, define, and heighten the value of the A term. Where does the woman long to take her lover? She longs to bring him to her mother's house, a space that is better described as a chamber and an area that is valued for its sexual and procreative history as the site of the woman's conception. In order to support this reading of "chamber" as a descriptive specification of the house of the mother, we need to examine several narratives that describe chambered houses. We also consider maternally defined dwelling spaces more broadly.

"Into the House of My Mother, the Chamber of Her Who Conceived Me"

Numerous texts attest to the idea of dividing a man's house into maternally defined subunits labeled houses, chambers, or tents.[13] The identification of the Song with the elite house of Solomon and a broader investigation of maternally labeled spaces support reading "chamber" as defining and specifying what "the house of my mother" is in Song 3:4.

The Bible understands the word *ḥeder* as an interior room or chamber within a house. Several narrative texts show a movement inward into the space of a house, a movement that is charted from house (*bayit*) to a particular interior chamber within it. In the Joseph narrative, his brothers visit him in his *bayit*, and when he lays eyes on his uterine brother Benjamin, he retreats to an interior, private *ḥeder* to cry (Gen 43:26–30). In the story of the murder of Ishbaal, the assassins enter the *bayit* and then find Ishbaal asleep in his *ḥeder*: "Now they had come into the house [*bayit*] while he was lying on his couch in his bedchamber [*baḥădar miškābô*]" (2 Sam 4:7).[14] In the story of Amnon's rape of Tamar, Tamar first enters "the house of Amnon" and prepares cakes for him. Then Amnon sends all his attendants away and demands that Tamar "bring the food into the *ḥeder*, so that I may eat from your hand" (2 Sam 13:8–10).[15]

The Bible also seems to understand a *ḥeder* as a designated activity space within a house. It is a space for sleeping or for convalescence of a sick or old person (2 Sam 4:5; 13:6–10; 1 Kings 1:15). It is a space where one can shut the door and hide or cry (Gen 46:30; Judg 16:9; 1 Kings 22:25; 2 Kings 11:2; Isa 26:20). It is a space that can be locked (Judg 3:24; 2 Sam 13:18). It is a place where one can imagine giving voice to secrets or possibly to private, dangerous thoughts (Eccles 10:20; 2 Kings 6:12). It is a space for illicit sexual, religious, or political activity (2 Sam 13:8–10; Ezek 8:12; Song 3:4; Eccles 10:20). But, when a *ḥeder* is specifically associated with a woman, meaning it is a woman's room or a man's room that a woman has entered, it is a place the Bible associates with sexual activity (Judg 15:1; 2 Sam 13:10–14; Song 1:4; 3:4; 1 Kings 1:15).

In chapter 1, we saw how the Israelite *bayit* can be subdivided into several *bāttîm*. When the Song of Songs defines the house of the mother as a "chamber" (*ḥeder*), it indicates that the house of the mother is to be understood as a house within a house, a chamber within a larger, multi-chambered household. As a "*ḥeder* of her who conceived me," the house of the mother, like other female-labeled "chambers," is associated with sexual activity.

When the words "house" and "chamber" appear together, as in the texts cited above, they evoke a house with multiple chambers that have doors, couches, and locks. This means that the house/chamber word pair does not apply in all respects to the pillared house of the common ancient Israelite family but instead belongs to the royal, priestly, and divine houses that are described in the Bible. When the Bible refers to a house that has chambers, it is almost always describing a royal house.[16] And this makes sense given that the Song of Songs is "of Solomon," and Solomon is the imagined lover or lover's rival in several of the scenes.[17] Moreover, Jerusalem and its surroundings are the imagined locale of the structures described in the Song.[18] As love poetry attributed to Solomon, an examination of the remembered glory of his royal house is appropriate. This is especially true given that the female speaker's first articulated fantasy in the Song imagines "the king" bringing her into "his chambers," so the Song opens not only with a reference to Solomon but with a sexually charged reference to the chambers that make up his household (Song 1:4).

In 1 Kings 7, we read that Solomon built himself a house, and "his entire house" (*kol bêtô*) (1 Kings 7:1) was a large administrative complex containing multiple "houses" and "halls." His house contained the "house of the Forest of Lebanon," "the Hall of pillars," and "the Hall of the Throne." Also nested within his entire house were two dwellings specifically labeled "houses." Solomon is said to have built a *bayit* for his own dwelling space and an additional *bayit* for the daughter of Pharaoh whom he had taken in marriage (1 Kings 7:1–8). Thus, biblical writers described Solomon's palace as a house complex, referred to here as *kol bêtô*, which was in turn subdivided into smaller halls and houses (*bāttîm*), including a house for himself and a house for at least one of his wives.

In another idealized household celebrated in Ps 128, a wife is imagined as a "fruitful vine" in the "inner recesses" of her husband's house. The Psalm of ascent begins by proclaiming "Happy is each one who fears Yahweh, who walks in his ways" (Ps 128:1). Then we learn about the composition of the happy, god-fearing man's household. The male head of household addressed in this Psalm will "eat of the labor of his hands," and it will go well for him (Ps 128:2). His wife will be "like a fruitful vine *in the inner recesses of your house [bĕyarkĕtê bêtekā]*," and his children "will be like olive shoots surrounding your table" (Ps 128:3). The short poem concludes, "This is how the man who fears Yahweh will be blessed." What this poem describes is the ideal household of an agriculturalist. To be a blessed man is to eat the fruit of one's own labor and to have a house within which one's wife is producing more of his fruit.[19] Finally, for a man to be blessed he will see his fruit in the form of children like olive shoots gathering around his ample table to share in the fruit of his labor. Spatially, this image locates the wife in an interior portion of the house and associates that wifely space with sexual reproduction.[20]

These references to the house of Solomon's wife within his own larger household and to the agriculturalist's wife as a reproducing, fruitful vine in the inner recesses of his house offer at least the possibility that Song 3:4 is using the phrase "chamber of her who conceived me" to specify that the "house of her mother" was in fact a "chamber" within a larger household. Of course, the female speaker's "mother's house" is a separate entity from Solomon's "house," and both Solomon's house and that of the female speaker are imagined as elite houses within the fantasies of the Song's lovers. Moreover, many of the spaces where the lovers imagine meeting function on multiple levels as actual physical spaces and as euphemisms for the woman's body.[21] Still, the lovers' imagined sexual encounters take place in spaces that make architectural sense to their time and culture; they are elite houses and palaces with multiple chambers, fine furniture, and the food and drink of the wealthy. When the woman locates herself within her own dwelling, her "mother's house" is in the city (Song 3:1–4) and has a wall and windows with lattices (Song 2:9). She sleeps on a bed in a room that has a door with a bolt (Song 3:1; 5:2–5). This is not a commoner's house; it is a house where a woman has her own lockable chamber.[22]

"And Isaac Brought Her into the Tent of Sarah His Mother"

In addition to mothers in the Bible having houses and chambers, we also find that a house or household of a man, his *bayit*, can be subdivided into maternally designated "tents." The Hebrew word for "tent" (*'ōhel*) can be understood as a synonym for *bayit*, and like *bayit*, the Hebrew "tent" is a malleable and multivalent word.²³ Quite often in the Bible, however, tents are associated with women. Harry Hoffner suggests that the name of the first woman, Eve (*ḥawwâ*), is derived from the Hebrew *ḥawwôt* meaning "tent villages."²⁴ In the biblical usages of *ḥawwôt*, it designates villages within a male-ancestor-claimed territory. Jair, the son of Manasseh, the son of Joseph, took possession of a number of villages in Bashan previously controlled by King Og of Sihon, and he named the region *ḥawwôt yā'îr*, "the tent-villages of Jair."²⁵ According to Pierre Bonte, the Arabic word for tent is associated with women as "a symbol of feminine values" while at the same time playing "an important role in political representations and practices."²⁶ The tent is also seen as a "sanctuary and symbol of protection" in Arab society. Bonte notes, "it is the men who circulate between the tents of their mothers and wives."²⁷

The idea that the name Eve, *Ḥawwâ*, might derive from the concept of "tent" finds further support from the verb used to accomplish her creation. While the man and the creatures are "formed" (*y-ṣ-r*), the woman is "built" (*b-n-h*) from "a rib" (*ṣēlā'*) of the man: "And Yahweh Elohim *built* [*b-n-h*] the rib [*ṣēlā'*] that he had taken from the man into a woman" (Gen 2:22). Nahum Sarna identifies the term "rib" as a frequent "architectonic term in building texts."²⁸ At the moment of her creation, the man recognizes the woman as a subunit of himself: "This one at last is bone of my bones and flesh of my flesh. She shall be called woman [*'iššâ*] *for out of man* [*'îš*] *she was taken*" (Gen 2:23). The narrator then interjects his interpretation of the purpose or natural outcome of the means of the woman's creation: "Therefore a man leaves his father and his mother and cleaves to his wife, and they become one flesh" (Gen 2:24). In the phrasing "become one flesh," the narrator simultaneously suggests sexual intercourse and its product, children. Following the transgression narrative, the man gives the woman her name, *Ḥawwâ*, and the narrator explains the name as coming from the root "to live" (*ḥ-y-h*): "because she was the mother of all living" (Gen 3:20). Thus, in the creation of the very first woman, we find evidence for the confluence of several ideas. The woman is imagined physiologically to be a subunit of her husband, his rib, and the language used to describe her creation and name suggests the building of a physical dwelling place, a tent. The narrator also immediately associates her creation and her name with reproductive sexual activity.²⁹

When we examine all of the references to tents in the Bible, we find that tents are often associated with women, specifically mothers. Within a father's house, his wife or wives are frequently said to have their own "tent"; a larger paternally named house encompasses several maternal tents. Biblical narratives and poetry identify women's tents as sites of sexual activity. Like the mother's chamber in Song of Songs, a mother's tent (*'ōhel*) is often viewed from the vantage point of an adult child, where it is almost always associated with sexual activity. As we saw in the previous chapter, Abraham orchestrated Isaac's betrothal to Rebekah in Gen 24 from an entity the narrator labeled "his [Abraham's] house" (Gen 24:2). When Rebekah arrives in Canaan as a new bride, however, we read, "Isaac brought her into the tent, that of his mother Sarah [*wayĕbi'ehā yiṣḥāq hā'ōhĕlâ śārâ 'immô*]," where we learn that Isaac was comforted after the death of his mother (Gen 24:67).[30] In his mother's tent, Isaac is said to "take Rebekah as his wife and love her" (Gen 24:67). It seems likely that we are to understand this to signify the sexual consummation of their marriage, and the text locates this important transition not in the house of Abraham but in a smaller entity within that house: "her tent, that of his mother Sarah." This clearly parallels the daughter in Song of Songs, who longs to take her lover to her mother's "house," which she then specifies as "the chamber of her who conceived me" (Song 3:4). Michael M. Homan notes several places where biblical narrative and poetry associate tents, using a variety of Hebrew terms, with weddings and consummation.[31]

In two other places, adult children enter the tents of their father's wives, and the location is clearly associated with sexual activity.[32] In Gen 9, Ham comes upon his father, Noah, naked and drunk in a space best translated "her tent," presumably the tent of Ham's mother, Noah's wife (Gen 9:21). This example could easily be overlooked because the Masoretes pointed the Hebrew consonants to be read as "his tent" (*'ohŏlô*), when the *hê* at the end of the word tent would most naturally read "her tent" (*'ohŏlāh*) (Gen 9:21).[33] This would mean that the crime of Ham when he "saw his father's nakedness" in "her tent" might be that he saw his mother naked with his father in her tent or that he committed incest with his mother (Gen 9:20–27).[34] A second example is that of Absalom, who enters his father's "house" and then pitches a "tent" on the roof of that house where he sexually claims his father's concubines (2 Sam 16: 21–22). When we read that an adult child enters a maternally designated space—mother's house, chamber, or tent—it most often sets up the narrative expectation of sex.[35]

From the vantage point of outsider adults, a woman's tent is a place where one finds her children, but it can still be a place associated with sexual activity. The metaphorical woman "Daughter Zion" is pictured as having a tent within which her children dwell. As part of Yahweh's imagined punishment of his people the Judeans, he is shown taking aim at and killing "all in whom we take pride, in the tent of Daughter Zion" (Lam 2:4). As part of the restoration of Judah following the Babylonian exile, Daughter Zion is instructed to "widen the space of your tent, extend the curtains of your dwelling," so that she might make room for all her returning children (Isa 54:2).

Jael is a married woman who is envisaged as having her own tent. She is lauded as "most blessed among tent-dwelling women," and while she is "the wife of Heber the Kenite," she is said to dwell in "the tent of Jael" (Judg 4:17).[36] The general, Sisera, sees the tent of Jael as a place to hide, and Jael uses her tent to entertain Sisera privately and offer him refreshment and a place to rest.[37] Then while he sleeps, she drives a tent-associated weapon, a tent peg, through his temple in a narrative that many have shown exhibits clear sexual overtones.[38] So Jael's tent is associated with the activities of hiding, entertaining and providing meals, lodging, and sex, and as a cover for a secret assassination. All of these activities are associated with maternally defined houses and chambers as discussed above.

Several additional texts demonstrate that a tent was understood as a division of space within a house and that wives had their own tents in the house of their husband. David's oath in Ps 132:3 provides an excellent example of a tent as a subdivision of space within a house. David swears that he will not sleep in his own bed until he has built a house for Yahweh using the oath formula: "If I enter into the *tent of my house;* If I go up upon the cushion of my bed." Just as the cushion is a part of the bed, the tent is a part of the house; in this case, it likely refers to David's sleeping chamber. When Jacob flees Laban and returns from Aram with his four wives and their children, his household is subdivided into maternal tents: "Laban entered into the tent of Jacob, into the tent of Leah, and into the tent of the two maidservants, but he did not find [the household gods], so he went out from the tent of Leah and went into the tent of Rachel" (Gen 31:33). In this portion of the narrative, the household of Jacob is on the move; they are in transit. Still, in this situation of camping en route, the narrator imagines a multi-tent compound.[39] Significantly, both Leah and Rachel as primary wives have their own tent, while "the maidservants" share a tent. In chapter 1, we also noted that the resettling of the house of Jacob in the land of Goshen occurred in maternally designated units.

A comparison with the imagined household of Yahweh is instructive. In 1 Kings 6–7, Solomon builds Yahweh a "house" that is subdivided into multiple halls and rooms, though they are not referred to with the word *ḥeder*.[40] Throughout the wilderness period, Yahweh is imagined as being housed within the elaborate tent-like dwelling place called the "tabernacle." Like Jacob, Yahweh is on the move with his people, and at each stopping place, they construct the tabernacle for him; when it is time to move on, they take it down and pack it up. The tabernacle is large and elaborate enough that the text portrays curtains (*yĕrî'ôt*) and tents subdividing it into ritually restricted spaces (Exod 26:1–13; 36). The Ark of the Covenant occupies a tent within the tabernacle marked off by a screen (Exod 40:21; Num 4:5). Insofar as the households of great men were imagined as analogically related to the "house of Yahweh," it seems likely that the Israelites would imagine their patriarchs and great kings living in large tent complexes or houses that would likewise be subdivided into tents and chambers.[41] Ezekiel imagines Yahweh as a jealous husband and head of a polygynous household where his two wives, Oholah and Oholibah, occupy separate tents within the larger "house of Israel." Their names mean "her tent" and "my tent is within her," respectively (Ezek 23). Within their tents, Oholah and Oholibah have sexually entertained Assyrians and Babylonians (Ezek 23:5–7, 11–17).

When we look at the parallel phrasing of "into the house of my mother, into the chamber of her who conceived me," in light of other maternally defined chambers and tents, it becomes clear that we are to understand the house of the mother as a chamber, a subunit of space within the larger house of the father. In fact, just after the Song refers to the "chambers" of Solomon's house where the woman imagines being brought, we have her likening herself to tents and curtains:

> I am black and beautiful,
> O Daughters of Jerusalem
> Like the tents of Kedar [*kĕ'ohŏlê qēdār*],
> like the curtains of Solomon [*kîrî'ôt šĕlōmô*]. (Song 1:5)

The Bible frequently depicts wives and mothers as having their own designated spaces. As readers, we often view mothers' houses, chambers, and tents from the vantage point of an adult child who associates maternal space with sexual activity. The space is represented biblically as having the potential to be private but also as being used to entertain and provide lodging to guests.

Archaeology and the Gendering of Space

While the Bible imagines the great households of its ancestors and its god as containing multiple maternally delineated rooms, physical chambers, or screened-off tent-like spaces, the biblical representation of female space does not support the concept of a public/private dichotomy. We cannot speak of the gendered "domaining" of domestic space as female and social/public space as male. Although there are spaces labeled as belonging to a woman, the Bible does not present women as being confined to those spaces, and those spaces are not limited to private, domestic, or sexual-reproductive functions.

Archaeologists and anthropologists have thoroughly rejected the idea of discrete domestic versus public domains, and they question overly simplistic identifications of male and female space.[42] They reject the idea that women in patrilineal societies were "confined" to one section of the house or that there was a separate women's quarters, a harem of sorts. In the introduction, we have noted the critique of "domaining" within traditional anthropological studies of kinship, where the domestic sphere was treated as a separate domain from the political and social sphere. Still, several archaeologists and anthropologists have found ways to conceptualize space as gendered while not confining women to the household or to a chamber within a household.

Focusing on the archaeology of ancient households, Julia Hendon acknowledges that domestic space is not "neutral"; it is not simply a "container." She defines "dwelling areas and domestic settings" as spaces where "social relations and identities are defined and given prominence through meaningful action that draws on ideas about gender, age, and other variables."[43] Hendon then notes how archaeologists have delineated "functionally differentiated structures," and that many areas within a house "might have been more frequented by women than men" (143, 151). She hastens to add that women frequenting a certain space more than men would not imply that women were "confined" to female-delineated space. Instead, Hendon sees domestic space as "a dynamic arena in which concepts of gender are negotiated and defined through practice" (151).

Carol Meyers has also located "discrete household activities" within "gendered space" in a household.[44] Meyers first establishes that certain activities are associated with women: bread production and weaving. She then shows how archaeologists can identify discrete activity areas based on artifact assemblages related to those activities. Artifacts related to bread production, for example, are typically found in one of "the main longitudinal rooms of the dwelling"; thus we can associate that space with women's activity.[45]

Like Hendon, Meyers does not link gendered activity spaces within a larger household to women's seclusion within or confinement to the household. Instead, she provides the helpful observation that space in agrarian households could be used differently throughout the day, "sequentially or in overlapping temporal units depending on the time of day, the season of the year, and the nature of the tasks to be done."[46] Still, as I note above, Meyers rejects the idea that the biblical *bêt 'ēm* was a differentiated physical space within the house of the father because she sees it as spatially identical to the house of the father.[47]

While average ancient Israelites did not live in houses that had permanently erected architectural sleeping chambers with doors and locks, common Israelite houses nonetheless show evidence for the subdivision of space within a household complex and within a single dwelling. David J. Schloen, for example, has described the archaeological record of the "extended patrilocal joint-family household" as a contiguous set of dwellings where a senior couple lived together with two or three of their adult married sons and grandchildren. In these extended-family houses, Schloen sees "each conjugal family occupying one sleeping-room on the upper floor."[48] Aaron Brody examines precisely this type of joint-family household in the remains of three contiguous houses in Iron II Tell en-Nabeh. He argues that the three houses' shared walls and the material evidence for shared household resources suggest that these three houses formed an extended-family compound. Even though each of the three houses was relatively small and simple and could in no way be described as "elite," they jointly formed a larger household complex.[49] James Hardin, an archaeologist who focuses on pillared houses in ancient Israel, identifies "curtain walls" as "small, nonstructural walls in the pillared dwelling built between pillars or between an exterior wall and a pillar."[50] While he is referring to walls constructed of stone on the first floor, I find his phrase "curtain walls" to be helpful in a different way. It seems quite possible that woven curtains could also function as walls and could be drawn across a room at certain times of day or night to create private space, as well as space designated for a particular family member like a mother. Sleeping mats, unrolled at particular times, could also demarcate personal and private space. Elizabeth Willett's research into the pillared house shows that female-associated artifact assemblages related to bread production or weaving are often found grouped together with incense altars, female figurines, and apotropaic jewelry. She suggests that female figurines, incense burners, and apotropaic amulets served a protective function and, archaeologically, mark spaces where mothers and children slept.[51] My main point is that spaces that the Bible labels "houses," "chambers," and "tents" of mothers need not be permanently delineated structural elements of the house. If in some cases tents, screens, and curtains were the means of delineating maternal space, we would not recover that delineation archaeologically. The fact that sleeping and eating likely occurred on the second floor of the pillared house exacerbates the difficulties, because it is harder to recover archaeological evidence for room divisions and artifact assemblages for a second-story living area.[52] The archaeological evidence from the common pillared house and the joint-family compound attests to the subdivision of space even in very simple village houses. Makeshift walls, curtains, or mats may well have been a means of delineating gendered space.

The observations of Roxana Waterson, an anthropologist whose fieldwork focuses on the house society of Tana Toraha in Indonesia, demonstrate the difficulties in clearly demarcating gendered space. She notes that where gendered space within the household existed, it was "as important symbolically" as it was "physically invisible."[53] In Waterson's survey of the architecture and spatial layout of southeast Asian houses, she documents the ways in which space was "socially constructed" along spatial oppositions that included front/back, right/left, high/low, inner/outer, male/female, married/unmarried, senior/junior, close/distant kin, and kin/stranger.[54] Of course, none of these oppositions would leave coded archaeological traces. The economy of Southeast Asia, like that of ancient Israel, was "organized around the household as the basic unit of consumption and production" (170). Therefore, Waterson argues, the public/domestic dichotomy and the limiting of the political and social spheres to outside the house cannot apply to the Southeast Asian context. Rejecting the separate domain of the "domestic," she asserts that the "world of economic production, ritual, and politics" are central to the concerns and spatial organization of the house (191).

Waterson's survey of house types in Southeast Asia shows how household space was divided in a variety of ways based on gender and status. In all of the cultures she surveys, houses had designated sleeping spaces for senior couples, junior couples, and children (175–82). Fixed points in the house, like a door, a hearth, a platform, or a beam, could function as orientation points for the hierarchical and often gendered division of space (171–75).

Similarly, Carolyn Humphrey studies the organization of space within a Mongolian tent and diagrams the placement of objects within the tent. The tent was divided into upper and lower, right and left, pure and impure, male and female halves. These halves were determined in relationship to the door and the hearth.[55] The tent was also subdivided into four named areas that designated the sleeping spaces of people with specific social functions in the family. While men, women, and children could move through the tent, "they had to sit, eat and sleep in their correct places" (273). In the future, no one will be able to recover archaeologically any of these gendered and hierarchical divisions of space; thousands of years from now, the Mongolian felt tent itself will not have survived.

Biblical narratives present the "house of the mother" and tents and chambers of mothers as "activity areas" most often associated with sleeping, sex, conception, and childbirth. None of these activities would have a corresponding "artifact assemblage." Where archaeologists have been able to identify gendered space, it is gendered economic space, an "activity area" associated with women's work in the household. The reason for the difference between the Bible's presentation of gendered space and the archaeological record's limited preservation of gendered activity areas relates to the nature of the Bible as source material. The Bible records the memory of named origin houses and is centrally concerned with the continuation of a house through name and offspring. Because of this, the women's activities that the Bible is most interested in preserving are reproductive. Archaeology, on the other hand, preserves the found state of a house and its nonperishable objects. No one has "staged" the pillared houses for the archaeological record, but biblical authors have actively shaped and narrowed the memory of the foundational houses preserved in the Bible.

Maternally marked spaces in the ancient Israelite house could serve different purposes at different times of day and in relationship to different social and household functions. Maternal spaces could be private at certain times and public at others. We saw in chapter 2 that the house of the mother could serve a very public function as a space for negotiating the marriage of a daughter who would marry out of her father's household. Far from being a "harem" or "women's quarters" where wives were sequestered from the public, the house of the mother was a place where a mother and her children could entertain guests, provide a meal, and offer lodging to visitors. It was also, however, a space where a woman could pull the curtain, and in some elite houses close or even lock a door, in order to create a private space. Instead of sequestering women in interior rooms or harems, this suggests women's autonomy to claim space as their own within the household of their husbands and mark those spaces physically with a curtain or closed door.

4 My Brothers, the Sons of My Mother (*'aḥay bĕnê-'immî*)

We now shift our focus from the spatial word pair "house of the mother, chamber of her who conceived me," to the social or relational word pair "brother, son of mother." Both the spatial and relational word pairs appear within the discourse context of maternally subdivided houses, suggesting that, like the house of the father, the house of the mother was both a physical dwelling and a grouping of people. In this chapter we examine the brother/son of mother relationship in order to determine the social functions associated with this category of kin.

"My Brother, the Son of My Mother": A Relationally Specifying and Narrowing Word Pair

When we examine Hebrew word pairs that capture human relationships, we find that they follow the narrowing or particularizing pattern. In each case the A term within the word pair is a Hebrew kinship designation that is recognizably ambiguous: *bĕkôr* (usually translated "firstborn" but often better translated "designated heir"), *yôrēš* (literally "the one who inherits," often translated "heir"), *zeraʿ* ("seed" or "descendant"), *ben* ("son"), and *bayit* ("house"). If we look at the examples below, we see that in each case an ambiguous Hebrew kinship term is narrowed and specified by the B term in the word pair:

Reuben, you are my *bĕkôr*, my might,
and the first issue of my virility [*rēʾšît ʾōnî*]. (Gen 49:3)

He smote every *bĕkôr* in Egypt,
the first issue of their virility [*rēʾšît ʾônîm*] in the tents of Ham. (Ps 78:51; see also Ps 105:36)

Abraham said [to Yahweh], "What do I have? You have not given me *a descendant* [*zeraʿ*], and now any son [born in] my house will be *my heir* [*yôrēš ʾōtî*]." But Yahweh spoke to him saying, This one will not be *your heir* [*yîrāšekā*], only the one who comes forth from your loins [*yēṣēʾ mimmēʿêkā*] will *be your heir* [*yîrāšekā*]." (Gen 15:3–4)

Now Gideon had seventy sons [*bānîm*],
who came forth from his thigh [*yōṣʾê yĕrēkô*]. (Judg 8:30)

When your [David's] days are complete and you lie down with your fathers, I will raise up your seed [*zeraʿ*] after you, one that comes for from your loins [*yēṣēʾ mimmēʿêkā*], and I will establish his kingdom. (2 Sam 7:12)

In each of these examples, a broad and ambiguous kinship term for heir or descendant in the A line is narrowed and defined as the father's biological heir or descendant in the B line. Four additional examples show word pairs wherein the B term delineates a nested category within the larger A term:

The *seed of Abraham* his servant,
the sons of Jacob, his chosen ones. (Ps 105:6)

For you are our Father,
though *Abraham* does not know us
and *Israel* does not acknowledge us. (Isa 63:16a)

He rejected the *tent of Joseph*,
He did not choose the *tribe of Ephraim*. (Ps 78:67; see also Jer 7:15)

Hear this O house of Jacob [*bêt-yaʿăqōb*],
those who are called by the name Israel,
those who came forth from the loins of Judah [*ûmimmê yĕhûdâ yāṣāʾû*].
   (Isa 48:1)

In each of these examples, the A term in a word pair offers a designation for a large inclusive group: the seed of Abraham, the house of Jacob, the tent of Joseph. The B term then delineates a subgroup within the larger inclusive group. "The sons of Jacob" are one portion of the larger group that could claim to be "the seed of Abraham," and the "tribe of Ephraim" is one half of the "tent of Joseph." Similarly, "those who come forth from the loins of Judah" constitute a subgroup of the larger "house of Jacob." Each of these relational word pairs follows a pattern that moves from the broad category to the specific, from the larger social descriptor to the narrower. At the same time, the pattern captures syntactically the Hebrew kinship feature of nested categories. There is still one additional characteristic of these relational word pairs: because the B term is narrower and fewer people would fit into its defined category, it is the culturally more valued category, the category with greater emotional freight. For example, while having an heir is a shared value among the male characters in the Bible, having an heir who "came forth from his own loins" or was the "first issue of his virility" was the most prized means of securing an heir. The sons of Jacob represent the covenantally chosen portion of the seed of Abraham; Ephraim is the chosen son of Joseph. And finally, from the perspective of Second Isaiah, those who come forth from the loins of Judah are the divinely appointed, royal heirs to the larger house of Jacob.

There are several examples of this narrowing pattern in female kinship labels. In chapter 2, we saw how the ambiguous Hebrew term *bĕtûlâ* can simply mean "young woman" or "unmarried woman." It does not have to include the meaning "virgin." In the story of Isaac's betrothal to Rebekah, a parallel construction is used to specify that the label *bĕtûlâ* means "virgin." Rebekah is described as "a young woman, whom no man had known" (*bĕtûlâ wĕ'îš lō' yĕdā'ā*) (Gen 24:16).[1] The phrase "whom no man had known" not only specifies what kind of young woman the word *bĕtûlâ* refers to; it specifies it as the culturally more valued meaning of "virgin." I see a similar pattern of specification in the Song of Songs's use of the phrase "my sister, my bride" (Song 4:8, 9, 10, 11, 12; 5:1). The word "sister" can signify any number of relationships. In this poetic context, the author is specifying that the label "sister" is a term of endearment for his bride. In two places, the Bible uses a parallel construction to bring emphasis and clarity to the word "barren" (*'ăqārâ*). Sarai is described as "barren, she had no child," and Samson's mother is "barren, having born no children" (Gen 11:30; Judg 13:3). Another example may identify a mother's house as a nested entity within the larger house of the father. Proverbs 4:3 reads, "When I was a son to my father, a precious only son to my mother" (*kî-bēn hāyîtî lĕ'ābî, rak wĕyāḥîd lipnê 'immî*). This verse seems to indicate that the speaker's father had many sons, but his mother had only one. Again, the second phrase delineates a narrower and more culturally valued group or relationship.

When we turn to the relational word pairs associated with our house of the mother texts, we find that the closely associated terms "brother/son of mother" and "brother/one who had nursed at my mother's breasts" follow the same pattern. The second term is the narrower and culturally more valued. Those who could claim to be brothers of the same mother are fewer than those who could claim simply to be brothers. Biblical references to "the son of my mother" suggest that this was a person with whom one shared increased loyalty and felt heightened emotional ties. When Joseph looks up and sees "Benjamin, his brother, the son of his mother," he is so overcome with emotion that he must leave the room and cry (Gen 43:29–30). He later honors his uterine brother over his half-brothers by having Benjamin served a portion five times larger than theirs (Gen 43:34). When Joseph finally reveals his identity to all of his brothers, it is he and Benjamin who fall on each other's necks and weep (Gen 45:12–15). Turning to the Song of Songs, we remember that the female speaker refers to her uterine brothers as "my mother's sons," and she describes them as a group that claims authority over her, assigning her the job of keeping the vineyard (Song 1:6). Later, the female speaker imagines that if her lover were "like a brother, one who had nursed at my mother's breasts," she could kiss him in public and take him into the private space of her mother's house (Song 8:1–2). Finally, in Rebekah's mother's house, we find her brother Laban, likely a uterine brother, playing an authoritative role in Rebekah's marital negotiations.[2]

Biblical texts that refer explicitly to the "brother/son of mother" relationship often lament the severing of this valued bond. The Psalmist describes his desolate life, and among the many things that are going wrong he complains,

> It is on account of you that I have borne reproach,
> that I have covered my face in shame.
> I became a stranger to my brothers [*lĕ'eḥāy*],
> a foreigner to my mother's sons [*libnê 'immî*]. (Ps 69:8–9)

In another Psalm a man is rebuked for speaking deceitfully:

> You sit and speak against your brothers [*bĕ'āḥîkā*],
> You slander the son of your mother [*bĕben-'immĕkā*]. (Ps 50:20)[3]

The book of Deuteronomy contains a warning that no man should allow those who are closest to him to entice him to serve other gods. Of those people considered most closely related to any man such that they might be able to entice him away from Yahweh, "your brother, the son of your mother" is listed first:

> If your brother, the son of your mother, or your son, or your daughter, or the wife of your bosom, or your friend who is as your own soul, entices you

secretly, saying, "let us go and serve other gods,"... you shall not yield to him or listen to him. (Deut 13:6)

There are some cases where the phrase "mother's sons" might be used for rhetorical flourish without having any clear anchor in actual family ties. In Isaac's blessing of Jacob, he says,

> May you be exalted over your brothers [*lĕ'aḥeykā*],
> may your mother's sons [*bĕnê 'immekā*] bow down to you. (Gen 27:29)

Since Esau is Jacob's only brother and they share a mother, the specification of "mother's sons" seems unnecessary, but the evocation of brothers and mother's sons may have been idiomatic in blessings. Taken together, these texts that contain references to the brother/son of mother relationship indicate that a uterine brother was one with whom you shared physical affection and one you would miss more than your half-brothers if you were ever separated. Looking at the negative examples of broken relationships, we can infer that the expected relationship with a uterine brother was characterized by closeness, familiarity, a willingness to speak on behalf of one another, and a level of trust that allowed for sharing secrets. Using James Kugel's classification of "A and what's more B" (see chapter 3), the word pair "my brother, the son of my mother," seems to be saying "not just my half-brother, but my full brother."

We find the same word pair in Ugaritic literature and poetry. The Kirta Epic, for example, opens by describing the complete annihilation of Kirta's family, using the word "house" to designate family:

> Perished was the house of the king,
> Which had had seven brothers
> Eight sons of one mother.[4]
>
> *Bt [m]lk itdb*
> *dšbʻ [a]ḫm lh*
> *ṯmnt bn 'um.*[5]

Just as "eight" has one up on "seven," so do "sons of a mother" exceed in importance undifferentiated "brothers."[6] In the Baal Cycle, one of Baal's rivals, Mot, seeks revenge against Baal and demands that Baal hand over one of his "brothers" so that Mot could devour him.[7] Apparently Baal refuses, and in an effective verbal parry suggests that Mot eat his own brothers. We hear of this exchange reported by Mot:

See now, Baal gave my brothers [*aḥym*] for me to eat,
my mother's sons [*bnm 'umy*] for me to consume.[8]

Again, Mot seems to be suggesting that it is bad enough to be asked to eat your own brothers, but it is a worse insult to suggest that you eat your full brothers, the sons of your mother.

Uterine Siblings, Maternal Alliances, and Exacting Revenge

Simeon and Levi, Dinah's Brothers

In biblical narrative, uterine siblings are presented as those honor bound to avenge wrongs committed against one another. In chapter 2, we saw how the story of Dinah singles out the uterine family of Leah as an important sub-entity within the larger house of Jacob. The narrative opens by identifying Dinah as "the daughter of Leah, whom she bore to Jacob," and later uses an appositional string of terms to identify Simeon and Levi as Dinah's uterine brothers, "two of the sons of Jacob, Simeon and Levi, Dinah's brothers" (Gen 34:1, 25). While these uterine designations signal the importance of the house of Leah in this text, the larger house of Jacob is active as well. We see the relationships within the house of Jacob when Dinah is repeatedly called "Jacob's daughter" (Gen 34:3, 5, 7), and her full and half-brothers are grouped together namelessly as "Jacob's sons" or "his sons" (Gen 34:5, 7, 13, 27). The narrator and these unnamed brothers refer to Dinah as "sister" and even "daughter" (Gen 34:13, 14).[9] But the only place where we have the designation "Dinah's brothers" is in the labeling of a named sub-entity within the house of Jacob: "two of Jacob's sons, Simeon and Levi, Dinah's brothers." The narrative setting for the naming of this maternally specific subgroup is one of enacting lethal revenge for a wrong committed against a uterine sister:

> Two of the sons of Jacob, Simeon and Levi, Dinah's brothers, took their swords and came upon the city unawares, and killed all the males. They slew Hamor and his son Shechem with the sword, and took Dinah out of Shechem's house and went away. (Gen 34:25–26)

So it is Dinah's uterine brothers who feel compelled to avenge an "outrage" committed against their sister and to remove her from the house of the offender. The larger group called "Jacob's sons" is also angry when they hear of Shechem's rape of their sister, and they participate in plundering the city of Shechem, but the act of vengeance—killing all Shechemite men—is left to the uterine brothers. When Jacob confronts Simeon and Levi for the mass killing of the Shechemite men, they justify their action saying, "Can he treat our sister as a whore?" (Gen 34:31) (see fig. 6).

A similar, perceived need to exact revenge is voiced by Gideon when he captures the Midianite kings, Zebah and Zalmunah, and asks them about the men they had killed at Tabor. The kings identify the men they had killed by suggesting a paternal and royal resemblance to Gideon: "As you are, so are they, every one of them, they resembled the *sons of a king*." Gideon responds by identifying the slain men as even more closely related to him:

> They were my brothers, the sons of my mother;
> as the Lord lives, if you had saved them alive, I would not kill you.
> (Judg 8:19)

Gideon uses the maternally defined closeness that he shares with the men whom the Midianite kings had killed as reason for him to avenge their deaths by killing Zebah and Zalmunah. Whether these men were actually his full brothers is not clear; instead, the kinship designation "sons of my mother" seems to signal the requirement of exacting revenge.

The Sons of Zeruiah

The "sons of Zeruiah" represent another maternal alliance of brothers who avenge the death of one of their own. Zeruiah is identified as the mother of three sons: Joab, Abishai, and Asahel (2 Sam 17:25; 1 Chron 2:16). As readers, we first encounter this maternal unit in the aftermath of a bloody battle between the Saulides under the military command of Abner and the "servants of David" under the command of Joab (2 Sam 2:12–17). The servants of David prevail over the Saulides, and then we read, "There were three sons of Zeruiah: Joab and Abishai and Asahel" (2 Sam 2:18). Asahel decides to pursue Abner even after the battle has been won. Abner discourages him, telling him to turn back, but Asahel refuses, and Abner kills him with his spear. After hearing of the death of Asahel, Joab and Abishai, whom we know are sons of the same mother as Asahel, pursue Abner but ultimately retreat (2 Sam 2:18–32). In the next chapter, however, Joab lures Abner into a private area and stabs him to death. The reason given for this assassination is that Abner had "shed the blood of Asahel,

Joab's brother" (2 Sam 3:27), and the final summary of the event reads, "So Joab and Abishai his brother murdered Abner on account of his killing Asahel, their brother, in the battle at Gibeon" (2 Sam 3:30). The language of "shedding blood," "murder," and "brothers" all signal revenge. As in the case of Gideon, explicit maternal kinship bonds are cited as justification for brothers avenging the murder of their uterine sibling. We never learn the name of the father of the men who are "the sons of Zeruiah."[10]

Tamar, the Sister of Absalom

Another example of maternal kin and revenge within the house of the father is found in the story of Absalom avenging the rape of his uterine sister Tamar. This single-chapter story, like that of Dinah, prominently features kinship designations that signal simultaneously the divisions between house-of-the-mother and house-of-the-father relationships on the one hand and the messiness that characterizes those divisions on the other. The maternal and paternal relationships within the house of David are established in the very first verse of the narrative:

> Absalom son of David had a beautiful sister,
> and her name was Tamar,
> and Amnon son of David loved her. (2 Sam 13:1)

Absalom and Amnon are both identified with the simple paternal label "son of David." Tamar is first introduced laterally as "the sister of Absalom"; if she is part of the house of David, it is through her uterine brother Absalom. In this opening verse, which sets up the key relationships in the narrative that follows, Tamar is not identified as the "sister of Amnon" or the "daughter of David."[11] Amnon and Absalom have direct, unmediated genealogical pathways to David; their pathway to each other must be inferred. Absalom also has a direct pathway to his sister Tamar. We know from the birth notations in 2 Sam 3:2–4 that Amnon and Absalom were born to different wives within the house of David. The identification of Tamar as "the sister of Absalom" in the opening verse of her story signals the importance of the uterine sibling relationship to the story that follows. While Absalom and Amnon share only a father, Absalom and Tamar are of the house of Queen Maacah, daughter of King Talmai of Geshur, wife of David.

In the ensuing narrative, we learn that Amnon, under the counsel of Jonadab, will pretend to be sick in order to get his father, David, to send

Tamar to his bedchamber to care for him (2 Sam 13:3–6). In the next several verses, the kinship designations for Tamar shift, showing the ambiguity of the unspecified term "sister." The narrator, Jonadab, and Amnon all refer to Tamar as Amnon's "sister" (2 Sam 13:2, 5, 6). However, when Amnon speaks directly to Jonadab, he specifies her uterine sibling relationship: "I am in love with Tamar, the sister of Absalom, my brother" (2 Sam 13:4). Amnon thus claims a brotherly relationship with Absalom because they are both "sons of David," while his sibling relationship with Tamar is often mediated through Absalom.

When David becomes the actor in the narrative, we see the introduction of houses within houses. From the vantage point of David, his house contains sub-houses for each of his sons. Amnon has to ask his father, David, to send Tamar to him in his house. This request has to go through David because, as Ingo Kottsieper has noted, Amnon did not belong to Tamar's "mother's house" and therefore "did not stand in direct contact with her."[12] David dispatches Tamar to "the house of Amnon, your brother," to prepare food for him (2 Sam 13:7). Amnon's house is not Tamar's house, and it is a physical entity delineated within "the house of David." Within Amnon's house, Tamar prepares the cakes before Amnon's eyes (2 Sam 13:8–9). He then sends his attendants away and asks Tamar to come into his "chamber" (2 Sam 13:10). Once in this space, Amnon grabs hold of Tamar and says, "Lie with me *my sister*" (2 Sam 13:11). Tamar attempts to resist him saying, "No *my brother,* do not force me for such a thing is not done in Israel. Do not commit this *outrage* [*nĕbālâ*]" (2 Sam 13:12). Thus, within the house of Amnon, while both Amnon and Tamar are attempting to convince the other to do something, they refer to each other as "brother" and "sister." After Amnon has raped Tamar, his love for her turns to hate, and he no longer calls her his sister. Using the imperative, he commands her, "Get up, go." Then he calls for his attendant and demands, "send out this one from upon me [*šilḥû-nā' 'et-zō't mē'ālay haḥûṣâ*] and bolt the door behind her" (2 Sam 13:14–17). The language he uses to separate himself from Tamar replicates the language of Abraham when he "sends out" the sons of his concubines "from upon" Isaac. In other words, just as the sons of Abraham's concubines will not be a part of the house of Abraham henceforth, so also Tamar will not become a part of the house of Amnon as his wife.[13] We also note that when Amnon banishes Tamar, she, like the sons of Abraham's concubines, loses her name. While the *pi'el* of *š-l-ḥ* by itself can signify divorce,[14] and this may be one level of the intended meaning given that Tamar had raised the issue of marriage, the addition of the pronoun *mē'ālay* ("from upon me") suggests a rejection of any kinship-related responsibility for her. That is why Amnon no longer calls her "sister" and instead refers to her as "this one." In his view, she is not his responsibility, she is not his sister, and she will not be his wife. She is sent out from upon him, and the door of his house is bolted behind her.

Once outside of Amnon's house, Tamar's actions show her perceived social humiliation. She rends her garment, puts ashes on her head, and cries out (2 Sam 13:19). At this moment of total devastation, she is met by "Absalom her brother." He speaks to her, still acknowledging the sibling relationship between Tamar and Amnon: "Has Amnon *your brother* been with you? Now, my sister, keep quiet. He is *your brother*. Don't place your heart on this matter" (2 Sam 13:20). The repeated use of the kinship label "brother" in this acknowledgment of rape does not signify that the crime according to Absalom or the narrator is incest.[15] Instead, it emphasizes Amnon's breach of responsibility to his half-sister. Absalom, as her uterine brother, will accept responsibility for Tamar. He like Amnon has a house within the larger household of David, and he will give her refuge: "Tamar dwelled, a desolate woman, in the house of Absalom her brother" (2 Sam 13:20). It is likely that "Absalom's house" is the house of Queen Maacah, their mother, meaning at a time of devastating loss, Tamar, like Orpah and Dinah, returns to her mother's house (Ruth 1:8–14; Gen 34:26; 46:15).

While Absalom counsels his sister not to place her heart on the matter of her rape, the narrator informs us, "Absalom hated Amnon on account of the matter of his raping his sister Tamar" (2 Sam 13:22). Absalom keeps silent for two years and then orchestrates a gathering around a sheepshearing festival to which he invites "all the king's sons," meaning this is an event that encompasses the entire "house of David." His paternally comprehensive guest list then singles out one specific named entity within that larger household, "Amnon, my brother" (2 Sam 13:26). At the festival, Absalom has his own men kill Amnon, leaving the rest of the "sons of the king" to flee. David initially receives a report that all his sons have been killed, then he learns from Jonadab that "Amnon alone is dead." The reason he is dead, he learns, is that Absalom has avenged the rape of his uterine sister: "At the command of Absalom it was determined from the day that he raped Tamar his sister" (2 Sam 13:32).[16] This story shows the malleability and ambiguity of the kinship terms "brother" and "sister." At the same time, the story provides several well-placed clarifications that communicate the full- and half-sibling relationships within the house of David.

Several scholars have noted a strong literary connection between the story of Dinah and this one of Tamar.[17] In addition to the obvious connection of sexual violence against a sister avenged violently by brothers, commentators call attention to shared vocabulary such as the use of the *pi'el* verb *'innâ* (Gen 34:2; 2 Sam 13:14) and the description of the sexual assault as a *nĕbālâ* (Gen 34:7; 2 Sam 13:12). The two texts also exhibit a set of shared kinship assumptions and designations. Both texts begin by signaling the primacy of the uterine family for the action within the narrative while simultaneously acknowledging and naming the encompassing house of the father. Dinah's story begins, "Dinah the daughter of Leah, whom she bore to Jacob, went out." Tamar's story begins, "Absalom son of David had a beautiful sister, and her name was Tamar, and Amnon son of David loved her." These phrases provide maternally specific kinship designations even when Absalom's and Tamar's mother is not named in the story. The terms "bore to Jacob" and "son of David" are the paternal designations.

Both stories also refer to half-brothers, brothers who only share a father, as "father's sons." Dinah's half-brothers are consistently referred to as "Jacob's sons" (Gen 34:5, 7, 13), just as Amnon and Absalom are introduced as "David's sons," and later at the time of Amnon's murder, we have the references to "the king's sons" (2 Sam 13:1, 23, 27, 29, 30, 32, 33, 35, 36). In both texts, the uterine sibling relationship emerges narratively in the context of exacting revenge. When Simeon and Levi kill all the male Shechemites and remove Dinah from Shechem's house, we get the sense that from their perspective, Shechem's outrage is committed most directly against "the house of Leah," and thus it affects the honor of Simeon and Levi. We see this distinction in Jacob's response to Simeon's and Levi's rampage. He says to Simeon and Levi, "You have brought trouble on me by making me odious to the inhabitants of the land.... If they gather themselves against me and strike me down, I shall be destroyed, both I and *my house*" (Gen 34:30). Jacob's concern is for the survival of his house, which is composed of himself and "Jacob's sons." Shechem's sexual impropriety toward Dinah is a crime against the honor of the house of Jacob, but the dishonor is felt most acutely within the sub-house of Leah. Jacob's primary concern remains the long-term security for his paternally generated house. Simeon's and Levi's concern remains with the honor of their maternal house: "Can he treat our sister as a whore?"

Similarly, Amnon's crime against Tamar is felt most directly as an assault on the honor of the house of Absalom.[18] Tamar is referred to as "Absalom's sister" four times by the narrator, by Amnon, and by Jonadab (2 Sam 13:1, 4, 20). Amnon, Absalom, and Tamar do refer to each other as brother and sister, but the introductory verse together with the background genealogy from 2 Sam 3:2–4 provide the context for determining which siblings share both father and mother and which only share a father. The description of Absalom's revenge against Amnon is phrased to make the uterine sibling relationship prominent: "Let not my Lord suppose that they have killed all the young men, the king's sons, for Amnon alone is dead, for by the command of Absalom this has been determined from the day he forced his sister Tamar" (2 Sam 13:32). David like Jacob takes no action to right wrongs that have been committed against the honor of a maternal house within his household.[19] When David hears about Amnon's actions against Tamar, he is "very angry" but does nothing. By contrast, when David hears of Amnon's death from Jonadab and from "all the king's sons," he rends his garments, lays on the earth, and weeps bitterly (2 Sam 13:31, 36).[20] He mourns his son Amnon "day after day" (2 Sam 13:37). The murder of Amnon is an event that affects David and a group labeled "all the king's sons"; it is a crime against David's paternal house. The rape of Tamar, on the other hand, is an event that affects Absalom, her uterine brother, and its immediate solution—providing a place of refuge to Tamar—is found within "Absalom's house."[21] We might even assume that when "Dinah, the daughter of Leah," is removed from Shechem's house by her uterine brothers, she too will be given refuge in the house of Leah her mother, which would include Simeon and Levi (fig. 7).[22]

Jehosheba, the Sister of Ahaziah

In the story of Athaliah's murderous ascent to the throne of Judah, we have another example of a brother and sister who function as an allied pair (2 Kings 11:1–21; 2 Chron 22:10–23:21). The exact relationships among the characters in this story are not entirely clear due to some ambiguities within each text and divergences between the two accounts. Where the two texts agree, however, is that following the death of King Ahaziah of Judah, his mother, Athaliah, seeks to eliminate all the "seed" of the royal house of Judah (2 Kings 11:1; 2 Chron 22:10). Ahaziah's sister, Jehosheba/Jehoshabeath, rescues her brother's infant son Joash from Athaliah and protects her slain

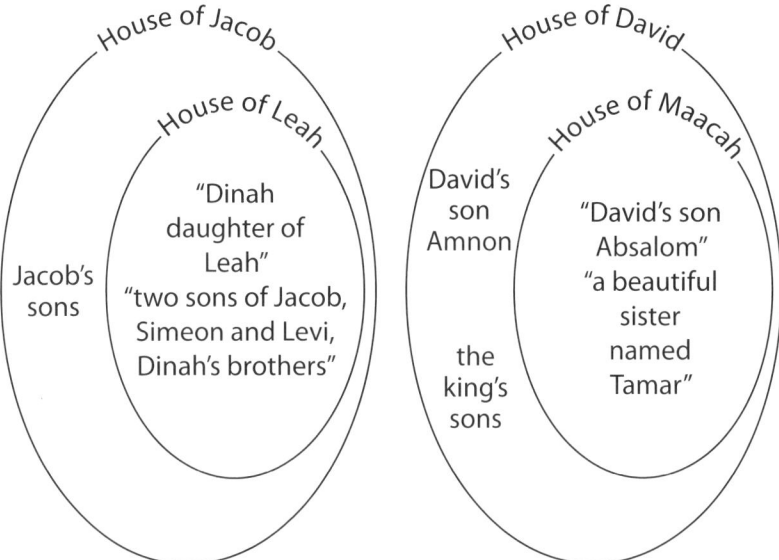

Figure 7. *Two stories of uterine siblings and revenge, Gen 34 and 2 Sam 13. Illustration created by Ondrea Keith, rendered by Bill Nelson.*

brother's son and heir for six years until he can ascend the throne. In Kings, Jehosheba is the "daughter of King Joram, sister of Ahaziah" (2 Kings 11:2), and in Chronicles Jehoshabeath is "the daughter of King Jehoram, wife of the priest Jehoiada," and "a sister of Ahaziah" (2 Chron 22:11). The King Jehoram/Joram who is mentioned is probably the Judean king, the father of Ahaziah.[23] Because Jehosheba is also called a "sister of Ahaziah," it is likely the two were uterine siblings, children of Athaliah. This means that the uterine sibling bond in this case trumped the maternal bond as a sister chose to protect her brother's son from her mother.[24]

Sons by the Same Mother as Ashurbanipal

Ugaritic and Akkadian texts also present uterine siblings as those who form alliances, providing refuge for one another and exacting revenge on behalf of one another. The Succession Treaty of Esarhaddon goes to great lengths to ensure that Ashurbanipal, Esarhaddon's designated heir, will in fact succeed him as king. The language of the treaty divides King Esarhaddon's house into two groups, a broadly defined paternal group and a narrowly defined maternal subgroup. The first group is identified using the exclusively paternal kinship labels that we have encountered in many house-of-the-father texts: "his [Ashurbanipal's] brothers, elder or younger" (*ša aḫḫīšu, rabû, ṣiḫrūtu*),[25] or "his brothers [*aḫḫīšu*], the brothers of his father [*aḫḫī abīšu*], the sons of the brothers of his father [*mārī aḫḫī abīšu*], the seed of his father's house [*zēr bīt-abīšu*]."[26] Esarhaddon considers all these paternally labeled brothers and kin as likely threats to Ashurbanipal's succession and repeatedly warns his subjects against them. Esarhaddon labels the second group "his brothers, sons by the same mother as Ashurbanipal" (*aḫḫīšu, mārī ummašu ša Aššurbanipal*), and requires that all in his kingdom "serve" and refrain from sinning against them.[27] In fact, the treaty that Esarhaddon requires his subjects and their descendants to swear allegiance to is a treaty "on behalf of Assurbanipal, the great crown prince designate *and* his brothers, sons by the same mother as Assurbanipal."[28] So while "his brothers" and "the seed of his father's house" are presented as potential threats to Ashurbanipal, "his brothers, sons by the same mother as Ashurbanipal," deserve the same honesty, service, and allegiance as Ashurbanipal himself. This suggests that when Ashurbanipal ascends to the throne, his maternal house will be elevated with him.[29] His half-brothers, the "seed of his father's house," will not be elevated and therefore represent threats.

These two groups, the broad paternally related group and the narrow maternally defined group, are hypothetically pitted against each other directly when Esarhaddon insists that if one of Ashurbanipal's "brothers" or a "seed of his father's house" comes to you and asks you to "slander his [Ashurbanipal's] brothers, sons of the same mother," and "to divide his brothers, sons of his own mother," from him, his subjects are required to report the insurrection to Ashurbanipal.[30] In Esarhaddon's succession treaty, a maternal subunit defined by Ashurbanipal's mother is nested within Esarhaddon's larger house, and the sons of this maternal unit under Esarhaddon's designated heir are elevated. The treaty uses the brother/son of mother word pair in a discourse setting of generational transfer and succession within the father's house, and it operates with the assumption that brothers of the same mother will act as allies in the house of their father.[31]

Pughat and Aqhat: Suckling of My Mother's Clan

In the Ugaritic story of Aqhat, he is identified as the divinely gifted son and heir to his father, Danel. At his birth, Aqhat receives a bow crafted by the divine craftsman Kothar-wa-Hasis. The goddess Anat covets Aqhat's bow and promises riches in return for it, but Aqhat rejects the offer. Anat then sends Yatpan, a hawk-like bird, to kill Aqhat in order to steal his bow. At the moment of Aqhat's murder, we are introduced for the first time to Aqhat's sister Pughat, and we find her in "her father's house," where she observes vultures circling overhead and weeps.[32] After Danel buries and mourns his son Aqhat, his daughter Pughat seeks his blessing before setting out to avenge the death of her brother.

At this point in the story, we know that Aqhat and Pughat share a father; she is found in Danel "her father's house," and is identified as his daughter. We can assume that they also share a mother because we only know of one wife, Danataya, for Danel. When Pughat embarks on a mission of vengeance, there is an additional hint that she is Aqhat's full sister. Pughat asks her father to let her go, declaring, "I will kill my brother's killer, put an end to whoever put an end to my mother's son."[33] This last phrase translated as "my mother's son" is 'l 'umty. The first word literally means "suckling,"[34] and according to Baruch Margalit, the second word may be either a synonym or "an alloform" of 'um, "mother."[35] Dennis Pardee translates the phrase "the (most important) child of my family,"[36] but in his notes, he seems to agree with Margalit that 'umty is a bi-form of 'um or "the word for 'tribe, clan' (< 'mother's lineage')."[37] This phrasing, "brother/suckling of my mother," closely parallels the terms juxtaposed with the "house of the mother" in Song of Songs 8:1: "like a brother, one who had nursed at my mother's breasts." While I cover the concept of "milk kinship" in chapter 6, this is a good example of a uterine sibling who is introduced with a maternally specific kinship label in a narrative context that describes avenging the death of one's uterine brother.

The Ugaritic story of King Kirta may also contain a reference to a maternal "alliance" within the house of the father. We have already mentioned how King Kirta's house was entirely destroyed: "seven brothers, eight sons of one mother."[38] The story continues, describing how his wife had died but she had left him with what Michael D. Coogan and Mark S. Smith translate as "a mother's clan" (ṯar 'um), which seems to mean a full complement of children.[39] Immediately following the term ṯar 'um, we find a listing of how various segments within this ṯar 'um had died in childbirth, by disease, or by other means.[40] The masculine noun ṯar means "avenger [of blood]" or "the closest and dearest relative who does justice."[41] The noun is derived from ṯ-'-r, which means "to avenge blood," "to stand surety for," or "to ensure honour."[42] The construct phrase ṯar 'um, therefore, could well be translated as "maternal alliance" or "allied maternal clan," namely, Kirta's deceased wife left him with enough sons to form the veritable "maternal alliance." Adding the word "alliance" to the translation, however, is for our modern benefit. For those who were part of the Ugaritic cultural sphere and later the ancient Israelite sphere, the ideas of alliance, vengeance, and closeness would be embedded within maternal kinship terms. Saying *ṯar 'um* or "sons of my mother" would immediately evoke all of these social responsibilities.

Asherah's Sons in the Baal Cycle

The Baal Cycle presents us with one final Ugaritic example of a functioning maternal alliance within a larger paternal household. Mark S. Smith has appropriately labeled the myth a royal succession narrative.[43] The story's main hero, "Baal the Conqueror," is set in opposition to a maternal alliance labeled "the sons of Asherah" as he battles adversaries in order to claim kingship in the divine family of El. El and Asherah are the senior couple in the pantheon. El is known as "the bull," "El the Compassionate," and "the creator of the gods."[44] Asherah is known as "the great lady, Athirat of the sea"; she is the "creatress of the gods." She is also El's consort, his legitimate wife, and they are the parents of "the seventy sons."[45] In the Baal Cycle, the sons of El and Asherah are consistently labeled anonymously and matronymically as "the sons of Asherah."[46] One of the key attributes of the sons in this maternal unit is their possession of royal "houses" and "courts." They stand within the house of El as sons of his consort Asherah. Their ascribed royal status is also evident when they are called Asherah's "pride of lions."[47]

When we turn to Baal, we find that every aspect of his parentage is unclear. The only absolute in his genealogical pedigree is his non-inclusion in the group labeled "Asherah's sons." We repeatedly read, "Baal has no house like the other gods, no court like Asherah's sons."[48] Baal is described in several places as a "son of El,"[49] but he is also called the "son of Dagan."[50] Smith considers Baal an outsider in the house of El, one who fights his way into this royal house to claim a house and throne for himself. His connection to El is one of "secondary divine lineage."[51] We have no information on Baal's mother; again, we only know of his definitive non-mother: Asherah.

In addition to "the sons of Asherah," Baal has two named rivals for kingship in the house of El: Yam (Sea) and Mot (Death). Their parentage is also unclear. Like Baal, they do not seem to be among the "sons of

Asherah," but they are referred to as "sons of El."[52] Baal first battles Yam and then Mot in his quest for kingship, and in each of these battles he has a fierce ally in the goddess Anat. Anat is referred to as "Maiden Anat, Mistress of Peoples." She is not a daughter of Asherah, but she is a "daughter of El."[53]

Baal's first battle is fought against Yam for "eternal kingship."[54] Kothar-wa-Hasis fashions two clubs for Baal, and he uses them to strike down Yam.[55] Anat's role in this battle, if any, is unclear. Following Baal's defeat of Yam, Anat embarks on a bloody and brutal rampage of her own against human soldiers and warriors, leaving her "up to her thighs in the warriors' gore."[56] She later takes credit for defeating Yam.[57] While the battle stories do not agree entirely on details, Anat is consistently portrayed as Baal's ally.

After defeating Yam, Baal sends for Anat to ask her to intercede on his behalf with El so that Baal might obtain El's permission to build a "house."[58] In this scene, for the first time, Anat is identified as Baal's "sister, the daughter of his father," when she approaches Baal's mountain abode. Baal then informs her of his need for a palace and again places himself in opposition to the sons of Asherah: "Baal has no house like the other gods, no court like Asherah's sons."[59] Anat agrees to intercede on Baal's behalf and refers to El as "My father El the Bull."[60] Like Pughat, who is identified as Aqhat's sister in her "father's house" at precisely the moment when her brother's death needs to be avenged, Anat is identified as Baal's sister, the daughter of his father, at a point in the narrative when Baal needs an ally and advocate. Anat proves ready to bloody her father El if necessary in order to obtain a house and court "like the sons of Asherah" for her brother Baal.[61]

In the end, Anat and Baal together decide to approach El through his consort Asherah. They travel to her palace bringing her gifts, but when Asherah sees their approach, she perceives them to be a threat and fears for the life of her own sons:

> Why has Baal the Conqueror arrived?
> Why has Maiden Anat arrived?
> Would you kill me or my sons?
> Or finish off my pride of lions?[62]

In this speech, Asherah makes it clear that neither Baal nor Anat is one of her children, and both of them as outsiders to her brood represent threats to her royally aspiring "pride of lions." Ultimately, however, Baal and Anat prevail, and Baal is granted the right to build a palace. Once he gains the right to a "house," Asherah's seventy sons begin to be referred to as Baal's "brothers," possibly signifying his increased acceptance within the larger household of El.[63]

In Baal's second battle, he challenges Mot to prove that he alone rules the gods. While the text is broken in several places, we learn that Baal descends into Mot's deathly abode, and El receives the report of Baal's death. Again, Anat surfaces as a sister-ally as she mourns his death, retrieves his body, and buries him on the heights of Zaphon, his mountain abode. Later, she confronts Mot directly demanding, "Give me my brother." When Mot refuses to relinquish his hold on Baal, Anat proceeds to split, winnow, burn, grind, and sow Mot. After dispensing with Mot, Anat seeks the help of Shapshu, the sun goddess, in order to find Baal.[64] Shapshu agrees to help Anat locate Baal the Conqueror, and when she talks to Anat, Shapshu refers to Baal as "your mother's suckling" (*l 'umtk*).[65] This is our first hint that Anat and Baal are joined not simply as outsiders to Asherah's sons but also possibly as insiders to another maternal clan. While the phrase "your mother's suckling" is clearly present in the text, the words surrounding this phrase are difficult to interpret and translate. Because of this difficulty, the maternal kinship reference in this text is often erased in translations.[66] A break in the text means that we never learn how Shapshu and Anat find Baal, but when the text resumes, Baal sits on his royal throne. He seizes Asherah's sons and tramples Mot, who ultimately declares, "Let Baal be enthroned on his royal throne."[67]

In the Baal Cycle, we have a royal household of El within which "the seventy sons of Asherah" form a maternal alliance. Each of the sons has his own house within the larger house of El. We also have several outsider children who share non-inclusion in the group labeled "sons of Asherah": Yam, Mot, Baal, and Anat. All four of these outsider gods are described as children of El. We learn that Baal and Mot do not share a mother because Mot refers to his uterine brothers, "his mother's sons," as a group that does not include Baal. Baal and Anat, on the other hand, are brought together in several ways. They are an allied team that seeks to place Baal as king over the sons of Asherah by defeating Yam and Mot and by building Baal a house and throne within the household of El. They are siblings. Baal refers to Anat as his sister when he seeks her help to establish a house for himself. Anat refers to Baal as her brother when she approaches Baal's killer, Mot, and demands, "Give me my brother." A. van Selms has noted that Baal and

Anat also share their mode of creation. They are both "brought into being" by El, an unusual verb that describes their begetting.[68] Finally, when Anat seeks to find and revive her brother Baal, Shapshu refers to Baal as her mother's suckling. Baal and Anat share a putative father in El; they share non-inclusion in Asherah's "pride"; they share a specific mode of coming into being; they are recognized as sucklings from the same maternal clan. All of these details suggest that Baal and Anat are maternal kin and possibly uterine siblings.

When the Bible labels a sibling using the brother/son of mother word pair, it is communicating a uterine sibling relationship. The relationship emerges within house-of-the-mother texts and narratives that describe maternal subunits within a larger, polygynous house of the father.[69] It is characterized by heightened emotional ties, public displays of physical affection, mutual loyalty, and a perceived duty to enact revenge on one another's behalf. If a daughter is raped, her uterine brother takes on the responsibility for avenging the rape and providing a house to his sister. Within a polygynous house of the father, sons of the same mother form a maternal alliance and support one another's aspirations to ascend to the position as heir.

5 No, Son of My Womb (*ma-bar-biṭnî*)

The relationships between a mother and her children and among children of the same mother are often characterized biblically with explicit reference to the female reproductive organs of breasts and womb. The chronological word pair "breasts and womb" encapsulates the two-stage, maternally centered process of child formation. In chapter 1, we examined the Joseph narrative, where in two places the ties that bind together the members of Rachel's house are described using the womb-related Hebrew term *raḥămîm,* usually translated "affection" (Gen 43:14, 29–30). In chapter 2, we saw that the Song of Songs associates maternal space with sex, conception, childbirth, and nursing. The reference to the house of the mother clarifies the space as the "chamber of her who conceived me," and a place where one might find a "brother, one who had nursed at my mother's breasts" (Song 3:4; 8:1–2). The lovers in the Song associate mothers and maternal space with childbirth as each speaks of the other's mother as the "the one who bore you" (Song 6:9; 8:5). We have also seen that maternally defined spaces in general, whether they are mothers' houses, chambers, or tents, are associated with sexual and reproductive activity. The association of maternally marked space and maternally specific kin with female reproductive organs and processes suggests a perceived physical basis for kinship ties established through the mother.

Womb-Based Allegiance (*raḥămîm*)

When Joseph saw his long-lost uterine brother Benjamin, "his brother, the son of his mother," he was overcome with emotion, a sense of connection that in Hebrew is called *raḥămîm* (Gen 43:29–30). Specifically, his *raḥămîm* toward his uterine brother "grew warm" (*nikmĕrû*) such that Joseph had to rush into another room to cry. Usually translated as "compassion" or "affection," *raḥămîm* is related semantically to *reḥem*, "womb," a masculine noun based specifically in female reproductive biology.[1] Biblical Hebrew has a second word, *beṭen*, a feminine noun that can mean "womb," "uterus," or more broadly "belly," applying anatomically to men and women.[2] In several texts, both words are used in a parallel construction, and I agree with the majority of scholars in understanding them to be interchangeable.[3] Wilfred G. E. Watson has shown that there is a very common poetic pattern where parallel lines feature word pairs that alternate grammatical gender,[4] and I note that many of the poetic texts that feature both *reḥem* and *beṭen* follow this gender-alternating pattern (Isa 46:3; Jer 1:5; Pss 22:10; 58:4; Job 3:11; 31:15).

In a now classic essay, Phyllis Trible argues that biblical authors were aware of the noun's maternal ties, and in places seem to have consciously deployed the term's womb-based semantics.[5] She identifies Joseph's experience of *raḥămîm* after beholding the son of his mother as one example of this conscious deployment.[6] There is, however, an earlier reference to *raḥămîm* in the Joseph narrative. Before Benjamin even arrives in Egypt, his father Jacob offers a prayer on his behalf, and, as discussed in chapter 1, this prayer focuses on keeping Benjamin, whom Jacob considers to be the sole remnant of the house of Rachel, safe. Speaking to his older sons, the sons of Leah and the two maidservants, Jacob petitions "El Shaddai" to provide his sons with a womb-based allegiance when they face the Egyptian official from whom they seek the return of Benjamin and the unnamed Simeon: "May El Shaddai grant you *raḥămîm* before the man, so that he may send back to you your other brother and Benjamin" (Gen 43:14).[7] This reference to *raḥămîm* in the context of a prayer allows for an ironic reading of Joseph's experience of *raḥămîm* when he beholds Benjamin. Jacob uses the word in its broader sense of "mercy" or "compassion" because he is thinking of the Egyptian official who will determine whether to free Benjamin. At most one could say that Jacob as a father inadvertently calls up a womb-based allegiance when making a desperate plea for the safe return of the only remaining son born to his beloved wife Rachel. When the Egyptian official turns out to be none other than Joseph, the long-lost first son of Rachel, his experience of *raḥămîm*, a strong womb-based allegiance, toward Benjamin recasts his father's prayer as not only ironic but prophetic. El Shaddai grants *raḥămîm* (mercy) to Joseph's half-brothers when they come before Joseph in Egypt, and in the process, he restores the bonds of *raḥămîm* (womb-based allegiance) among Joseph, Benjamin, and Jacob, who are tied to one another through the womb of Rachel (see fig. 4).

We find a kind of inverse to this story and its ironic use of *raḥămîm* in Hosea 1–2. In this book, Yahweh tells the prophet to take a wife of "whoredom" (*zĕnûnîm*) and have children of "whoredom," as a sign of the infidelity of the people of Israel to their god (Hosea 1:2). Hosea obeys, marrying Gomer, so the house of the mother that comes into being when Gomer bears three children is marked by "whoredom" rather than the love Jacob had for Rachel and the womb-based allegiance he and his god felt toward her children. All three of Gomer's children bear symbolic names, but it is her only daughter who bears a name that once again plays with the multiple layers of meaning accorded to the word *raḥămîm*. At the birth of Gomer's daughter, Yahweh tells Hosea to name her *lō' ruḥāmâ*, for "I will no longer show womb-based allegiance [*'ăraḥēm*] toward the house of Israel or forgive them" (Hos 1:6). While the daughter's name is often translated "Not Pitied," a better, if more cumbersome, translation might be "Not entitled to womb-based allegiance." This daughter conceived through whoredom will not receive the benefits of being part of a womb-based alliance. Her father does not love her mother and will not extend womb-based protections to her. Yahweh, then speaking as husband and father, threatens his wife with divorce, public sexual humiliation, banishment to the wilderness, and death (Hosea 2:3–5 [Eng. 2:1–3]). The severing of the marital bond implies that Gomer's maternal house will not be nested protectively within the house of her husband, and therefore "her children" will not receive womb-based allegiance from their father (Hosea 2:6 [Eng. 2:4]). This highly symbolic text locates the severance of womb-based allegiance in the wife's practice of whoredom and in the husband's suing for divorce. Jacob, Joseph, and Benjamin were tied to one another through a womb-based allegiance that began with Jacob's love of Rachel. In trying to communicate the severance of Yahweh's bond with and commitment to his people, the prophet Hosea uses the language of whoredom, divorce, and violence to sever God's *raḥămîm* toward a people called *lō' ruḥāmâ*.[8]

In these two examples of fathers expressing or withholding womb-based allegiance, we see that *raḥămîm* was the connective tissue that bound a father to members of a particular maternal house. In other words, Jacob asks El Shaddai to show *raḥămîm* for all his sons in order to seek the release of Benjamin, the son born of Rachel's womb. Yahweh as father withholds his *raḥămîm* from the children of Israel, symbolically represented by the daughter of Gomer, because he denies his relationship to their whoring mother.

We find the maternal experience of *raḥămîm* in the case of the two prostitutes who claimed to be mothers of the same infant boy. Like Gomer, these two women are described as "whoring women" (*nāšîm zōnôt*) who live together in the same house without a man and give birth to sons three days apart (1 Kings 3:16–18). When the infant of one mother dies, she switches the babies in order to claim the living son as her own. Solomon's famous response is to suggest that the living child be cut in half, giving one half to each mother. Immediately, the *raḥămîm* of the true mother "grew warm" (*nikmĕrû*), and she told the king not to kill the infant and instead to give him to the other mother. Through her action, Solomon is able to announce with conviction, "she is his mother" (1 Kings 3:26–27). Namely, Solomon knows that the woman who experienced *raḥămîm* such that she fought to preserve the life of the child of her womb is the true mother. Trible notes that only after the one woman experienced this womb-based emotion does the word "mother" enter the story.[9]

Mayer I. Gruber cautions against Trible's assumption that speakers of Hebrew would be aware of the etymological history of the word *raḥămîm*. In his view, they may just think "compassion" and not have any sense of the word's relationship to *reḥem* or "uterus."[10] This is undoubtedly true, but Trible does not claim that every time the word *raḥămîm* was used, its association with the womb was consciously deployed. Instead, there are certain contexts where the maternal relationship among siblings, between a mother and her child, or between a father and the children of a particular wife signals a uterine-conscious reading of *raḥămîm*. Few English speakers using the words "hysteria" and "hysterical" would be able to trace the etymology of these words through the Latin *hystericus* to the Greek *hysterikos* based in the Greek noun *hystera*, "womb." Nonetheless, when perusing recent book and movie titles, it becomes clear that several authors are consciously deploying these words' womb-based associations. Consider these recent book titles: *Creating Hysteria: Women and Multiple Personality Disorder;*[11] *The Hysterical Male: New Feminist Theory;*[12] and the improbable *Hysterical Hysterectomy*.[13] I might also note the 2012 movie "Hysteria," which is apparently about "the birth of the electromechanical vibrator."[14] These titles consciously play with the etymology of the words and their present-day meanings, and they do so knowing that most English speakers will understand the double entendre. Some biblical writers also seem to be using the word *raḥămîm* in contexts where readers or hearers would make the connection to womb-based, maternal emotions. That being said, in the vast majority of occurrences, this noun is used without any apparent awareness of its semantic connection to a mother's womb. People seek Yahweh's "compassion" in times of trouble (2 Sam 24:14 [= 1 Chron 21:13]; 1 Kings 8:50). In texts that pair divine *raḥămîm* with divine *ḥesed*, we should simply understand that Yahweh shows or refuses to show his "compassion" and "steadfast love" (Pss 25:6; 40:12 [Eng. 40:11]; 51:3 [Eng. 51:1]; 69:17 [Eng. 69:16]; 77:10 [Eng. 77:9]; 79:8; 103:4; 106:46; 119:77, 156; 145:9; Lam 3:22; Jer 16:5). In numerous other texts, the word *raḥămîm* does not evoke a womb-centered emotion (Prov 12:10; Dan 1:9; 9:9; 9:18; Neh 9:19, 27, 28, 31; 2 Chron 30:9). Trible is correct, however, to highlight select cases where poets and narrators seem to activate and consciously play with the womb-sourced aspect of the term.

Another case where *raḥămîm* is associated with uterine brothers is found in Amos 1:11. This chapter features a series of oracles against foreign nations, and Edom figures prominently as an enemy, even in the oracles against the Philistines and Tyre (Amos 1:6, 9). The oracle against Edom reads, "For three transgressions of Edom and for four, I will not revoke the punishment. Because he pursued his brother [*'āḥîw*] with the sword, and severed his *womb-based alliance* [*raḥămāyw*]" (Amos 1:11). Edom, of course, is Esau, the twin of Jacob. When Rebekah is pregnant with these twins, she learns from Yahweh that "two nations are in your womb," and after their birth, we learn very quickly that Esau is "Edom" (Gen 25:23, 30; Amos 1:11). This text in Amos seems to suggest that if anyone should have a womb-based commitment to Jacob-Israel, it would be his womb-twin Esau. In chapter 4, we discussed the many examples where the phrase "my brother, the son of my mother," is used to describe what should be a relationship of loyalty and trust; twins should form a "maternal alliance." Amos seems to work from the same assumption, but rather than refer to Edom as Jacob's "brother, the son of his mother," he refers to Edom as a brother who has corrupted his womb-based alliance.[15]

In the Baal Cycle, we find womb terminology used in a context that suggests a womb-based alliance or commitment between siblings. In the episode covered in chapter 4, Anat confronts Mot after he has killed Baal, and she demands, "Give me my brother!" This is the first and only place in the Baal Cycle where Anat refers to Baal as "my brother," and in the same episode, we find a new epithet use for Anat: *rḥm*.¹⁶ Only in this episode do we find Anat's name twice preceded by the epithet *rḥm*, which translators have rendered "*Damsel* Anat." The full text reads as follows:

> *rḥm* Anat approached him.
> Like the heart of a cow for her calf,
> like the heart of a ewe for her lamb,
> so was Anat's heart for Baal.¹⁷

The Ugaritic noun *rḥm* is translated "womb" and by metonymy "nubile girl, damsel." The verb *r-ḥ-m*, like the Hebrew, means "to have feelings or be compassionate" and is used in the Kirta Epic to describe the appropriate and expected emotions that a daughter feels concerning the impending death of her father.¹⁸ The metonymic form of this noun is found in a text that Johannes C. de Moor labels "An Incantation against Infertility," a text that opens with the line "a *rḥm* will give birth."¹⁹ In the Baal Cycle, when "*rḥm* Anat's heart" is first drawn to Baal like a mother animal's heart is drawn to her young, she demands of Mot, "Give me my brother." Mot then uses some of Anat's own metaphorical language to describe how he took Baal "like a lamb in my mouth" and destroyed him "as a kid in my crushing jaws."²⁰ In response to Mot's unremorseful account of how he had eaten her brother Baal, "*rḥm* Anat" again approaches Mot, with her heart "like the heart of a cow for her calf, like the heart of a ewe for her lamb," and this second time, we might say that the *rḥm* of Anat, her womb-centered allegiance to Baal, leads her to split, winnow, burn, pulverize, and sow Mot, her brother's killer.²¹ Finally, we can add that in the episode just following Anat's vengeful attack on Mot, Shapshu agrees to help Anat find Baal and refers to Baal "as your [Anat's] mother's suckling."²² This episode of a brother's violent death and an allied sister's revenge on account of that death features several unique vocabulary terms that are only found here in the Baal Cycle. They include Anat's calling on Baal as "my brother," the appellation of Anat as "*rḥm* Anat," the comparison of Anat's feelings for her brother Baal with the feelings a mother cow or ewe would have for her young, and, finally, the description of Baal as "the suckling of your [Anat's] mother's clan." Taken together, these details build a case for Anat and Baal being uterine siblings or at least belonging to the same maternal clan.

A final biblical example features the same clustering of terms related to female reproductive organs in order to convey the bonds of allegiance that characterize maternal kin. In Isa 49:15 Yahweh asks, "Can a woman forget her suckling [ḥătiškaḥ 'iššâ 'ûlāh], or refrain from showing womb-based commitment to the son of her womb [mēraḥēm ben-biṭnāh]?" This text features the *pi'el* verb from the root *r-ḥ-m*, rather than the noun *raḥămîm*. Isaiah seems to evoke the lifelong, unbreakable commitment that a mother makes to the child of her womb and breasts in order to describe Yahweh's eternal commitment to his people (see fig. 5).

In most cases in the Bible, *raḥămîm* is appropriately translated with the English word "compassion," and we should not ascribe to the Hebrew speaker a conscious awareness of its connection to the word for "womb." In the select cases that I have noted above, however, Trible is correct to assert that Hebrew authors consciously deployed the womb-based understanding of the word *raḥămîm*. In light of the fierce loyalty and allegiance that characterizes the relationship among children of the same mother, I would go beyond Trible's understanding of the word connoting a womb-based emotion. I would argue that in cases where the maternal relationship is consciously evoked, *raḥămîm* stands for a womb-based allegiance that a mother feels for her child, a father feels for children of a particular wife, or a brother or sister feels for the siblings born of the same mother's womb.

Blessings of Breasts and Womb

Hebrew poetry delineates a two-stage, maternally focused process of child formation using the chronological word pair "breasts and womb."[23] In some texts, the poet travels back from the time at the breast to the time in the womb, while in other texts the word pair marks a forward progression through time. In both cases, however, womb and breasts mark sequential stages in a child's physical formation. Once the child reaches an age when he or she can be weaned from the breast, his or her survival is on a more sure footing. Claus Westermann refers to the feast at the point of Isaac's weaning (Gen 21:8) as a celebration of "the close of life's first stage," "a rite of passage."[24] Mayer Gruber argues, based on several biblical references, that a child's weaning was associated with his or her ability to discern between "sweet and sour" and his or her ability to "receive instruction."[25] Vanessa Maher, an anthropologist who has researched breastfeeding practices, reports on several cultures that understand the breastfeeding stage to be the final stage in the "formation of a completed person."[26]

Several poetic texts in the Bible attest to this understanding of a two-stage process of child formation. Psalm 22 features a prayer in which the

Psalmist asks God for continued protection and closeness, and casts God in the role of midwife. Using the womb-to-breast sequence, the Psalmist understands God as the skilled hands managing pregnancy, childbirth, and early breastfeeding:

> For it was you who took me from the womb [*beṭen*]
> And placed me safely upon my mother's breasts [*šĕdê 'immî*]
> Upon you I was cast forth from the womb [*reḥem*]
> From the womb of my mother [*mibbeṭen 'immî*],
> you have been my God. (Ps 22:10–11 [Eng. 22:9–10])

The same sequencing is found in a Qumran psalm: "We are encompassed by iniquity since the womb, and since the breast by guilt."[27] Job curses the day of his birth and asks,

> Why did I not die [coming forth] from the womb [*mēreḥem*],
> Come forth from the womb [*mibbeṭen*] and expire?
> Why were there knees to receive me,
> or breasts [*šādayim*] that I might suck? (Job 3:11–12)

In an oracle of judgment, the prophet Hosea calls on Yahweh to give his rebellious people "a miscarrying womb [*reḥem maškîl*] and dry breasts [*šādayim ṣōmĕqîm*]" (Hosea 9:11–14).[28] Finally, as noted above, Second Isaiah presents Zion as the metaphorical wife of Yahweh who laments, "Yahweh has abandoned me, my Lord has forgotten me." And Yahweh responds, reassuring her, "Can a woman forget her suckling child [*'ûlāh*], or show no compassion for the child of her womb [*ben-biṭnāh*]? Even these may forget, yet I will not forget you" (Isa 49:14–15). This poem acknowledges that one might be able to find a human mother who forgets the child of her womb and breast, but the poem insists that the expected bond between mother and child is strong, enduring, and founded in maternal, reproductive biology.[29]

In Jacob's blessing of Joseph, we find the "blessings of breast and womb" as something that "El Shaddai" bestows on Joseph from the gifts available within the earthly domain. This blessing is notoriously difficult to translate, containing as it does any number of corruptions. Still, it is significant to note the combination of images that come together in order to present Joseph as the designated heir of his father, Jacob. Joseph is first linked to fertility and royalty as a "fruitful bough."[30] He is then presented as a mighty warrior with divinely backed weapons. His bow remains taut and his arms agile by virtue of the "hands of the Mighty One of Jacob, by the name of the Shepherd, the Rock of Israel." These divinely bestowed powers originate from "the God of your father" (Gen 49:22–25a), and they will help Joseph militarily against his enemies, the archers. He then receives divine blessings from the three regions of the cosmos: heaven above, the deep below, and the human sphere between:

> From the God of your Father who comes to your aid,
> and through El Shaddai who blesses you,
> Blessings from heaven above,
> Blessings of the deep stretched out below,
> Blessings of breast and womb. (Gen 49:25)

The "blessings of breast and womb" as part of what is offered within the human sphere once again recall Joseph's much-loved mother, Rachel, and the house she established based on womb-based allegiance.[31] Cohering to the concept of cognatic descent, Joseph not only receives the strength and military power that comes from his father's god; he has also received the blessing of a preferred substance through the womb and breasts of his mother.

The breasts and womb word pair brings us back to the mother's house in Song 8:1–2 where the MT and LXX versions differ slightly:

> Oh that you were a like brother to me,
> one who nursed at my mother's breasts.
> If I met you outside, I would kiss you,
> and no one would despise me.
> I would lead you and bring you into the house of my mother,
>
> MT: She will instruct me [*tĕlammĕdēnî*].
> LXX: and into the chamber of her who conceived me [*eis tamieion tēs sullabousēs me*]
>
> I would give you spiced wine to drink,
> freshly pressed from my pomegranates. (Song 8:1–2)

As noted in chapter 2, I follow many commentators and translators who opt for the Septuagint, translating "into the house of my mother, into the chamber of her who conceived me," instead of the Masoretic text's "she will instruct me." These translators cite the exact parallel in Song 3:4, and the association of mothers with sites of conception and birth in Song 6:9 and 8:5. Carol Meyers, on the other hand, sees both the ancient versions and the modern commentators' departure from the Masoretic text as emblematic of an ancient and modern male bias against giving mothers an instructive role.[32] She argues based on Woman Wisdom in Prov 1–9 and on the "woman of worth" in Prov 31, that Proverbs exhibits an "interwoven motif of woman, household and instruction." And this motif, she argues, is precisely what we find in Song 8:2 where the mother will "instruct" her daughter in her house.[33] Ariel and Chana Bloch also support reading with the MT, noting the instructive role of Naomi with regard to Ruth's sexual overtures to Boaz.[34]

While I agree that women are associated with instruction and in some places with sexual instruction of a daughter, I do not see "she will instruct me" as the most compelling reading for Song 8:2. In my view, the phrase "she will instruct me" stands out as awkward and unexpected within the context of the surrounding verses. In this highly poetic book, the phrase "she will instruct me" does not form a parallel line with "into the house of my mother," when the verses before and after take parallel form. Moreover, my examination of the biblical "house of the mother" and maternally labeled spaces more generally has shown that biblical literature most often links these sites to sex, conception, labor, and childbirth. Most significant for me, however, is that the Song as preserved in LXX features the poetic pairing of breasts and womb that we have seen in the biblical texts discussed above. In Song 8:1, we have a parallel line that refers to the mother's breasts and to the lovers' kiss:

> O that you were like a brother to me,
> One who had nursed at my mother's breasts.
> If I met you outside, I would kiss you,
> And no one would bother me.

Then, in verse 2, the female speaker's imagination takes her from outside to inside as she imagines leading her lover to a more private, interior space, and if we read with the Septuagint, we again have a parallel line:

> I would lead you and bring you into the house of my mother,
> Into the chamber of her who conceived me.

If this reading is correct, we have moved backward in time with regard to the speaker's mother; the young woman first alludes to nursing at her mother's breasts and second to her own conception in the chamber of her mother. But if we read the same set of lines from the perspective of the fantasies of the woman and her lover, we are moving forward in time as she imagines first kissing him outside and then leading him inside to the house of her mother, a site already marked by sexual activity. The woman then tells her lover that once she has guided him into this maternally marked space, which bears the memory of her own conception, she would offer him her own breasts, meaning we have moved from remembered maternal breasts to newly offered lover's breasts:

> I would allow you to drink spiced wine
> Freshly pressed from my pomegranates.

The woman also imagines the position from which she might offer her freshly pressed pomegranate juice to her lover, a position that might lead to lovemaking:

> His left hand would be under my head
> And his right hand would embrace me.

Finally, the action moves outside again where it began, as the woman calls to the daughters of Jerusalem, "Do not arouse or awaken love until it is ready."

The entire poem plays with the breasts and womb word pair, moving comfortably between the maternal formation of a child and the erotic joining of lovers. On one level, we hear of a mother's breasts and mother's sexual activity that leads to conception. On another, we listen in on a young woman's hopes of kissing her lover, leading him inside, offering him her pomegranate juice, and lying in his embrace. The use of a parallelistic line and the back-and-forth allusions to breasts and womb suggest that the mother's house in Song 8:2 should be qualified as it is in LXX as "the chamber of her who conceived me."

"No, My Son, No, Son of My Womb, No, Son of My Vows": Womb-Based Kinship

Biblical authors present the time spent in the womb as formative both physically and with regard to the personality traits of the child. The womb also served as a basis for a particular set of kinship bonds, and primary among these was the bond between a mother and her son. In Prov 31:1–9, a royal son, King Lemuel of Massa, remembers the words of his mother when she called out to him in warning, "No, my son! No, son of my womb! No, son of my vows!" (*mah-bĕrî ûmah-bar-biṭnî ûmeh bar-nĕdārāy*) (Prov 31:1–2).[35] King Lemuel's mother looks on her adult son the king and moves backward through time from the man who stands before her, to the memory of when she carried him in her womb, to the vow she uttered in hopes of conceiving him. In the sequence "my son, son of my womb, son of my vows," we recognize a telescoping string of appositional epithets and another chronologically ordered sequence that moves backward through time.[36] In the story of Hannah, we find the same sequence moving forward through time. Hannah makes a vow to Yahweh that if he grants her a son, she will dedicate him to Yahweh as a Nazirite from birth. Yahweh then remembers her, and she conceives and bears a son (1 Sam 1:11–20).[37] In the exclamation of Lemuel's mother—son, son of my womb, son of my vow—we hear the ever-increasing sense of a lifelong bond between mother and child. Like God who knew and consecrated Jeremiah for a specific future from the time before he had formed him in the womb (Jer 1:5), this mother has had great aspirations for her son since the time she uttered a vow in hopes of conceiving him.[38] This string of appositional epithets identifying King Lemuel as the son of his mother's womb also parallels God's identification of Abraham's son when he calls upon Abraham to offer his son as a burnt offering: "Take your son, your only one, the one you love, Isaac" (Gen 22:2). With each added designation, the bond between parent and child is solidified more firmly, and in the case of Lemuel's mother, a key aspect of the bond takes shape within her womb.

Biblical writers understand women's wombs "belong to God"; they are "a physical object upon which the deity acts."[39] God opens and closes wombs, bringing fertility and barrenness as he chooses. When we examine the texts that feature the Israelite god acting within women's wombs, we find that he is imagined "forming" (y-ṣ-r), "creating" (q-n-h), and "weaving or embroidering" (s-k-k and r-q-m) children in the womb (Isa 44:2, 24; 49:5; Ps 139:13, 15; Jer. 1:5). He also brings forth children from the womb (Pss 22:10 [Eng.]; 71:6). Even though God is seen as the active agent in conception, pregnancy, and birth, however, women also play active roles in the creative process. The verb q-n-h, which is used for the divine creative activity in Ps 139:13, replicates the verb Eve uses to describe her creation of the first human born through human reproductive processes: "I have produced [qānîtî] a man with the help of Yahweh" (Gen 4:1). In other words, this "helper of man" credits God as her "helper" in this new maternally focused creative process, indicating a divine-maternal cooperation in human procreation.

Still, scholars disagree on what biblical authors understood as the maternal contribution to the procreative process. Carol Delaney, for example, argues that the Bible understands the mother to contribute nothing of substance to the child. The father produces the "seed," which Delaney asserts represents his identity being passed to his son. The mother is "the one in whom the seed is planted; she nurtures and brings it forth, but is not herself the source of the seed."[40] The mother's role is limited to "giving nurture and birth," while the father is a "co-creator" with God. She concludes that the Bible understands procreation as "monogenetic."[41] Delaney's work follows and develops E. A. Speiser's assertion that "the purpose of genealogies [in the Bible] was to establish the superior strain of the line through which the biblical way of life was transmitted from generation to generation." The "purity" of the male seed was to be protected by "the quality of the container," namely the mother's womb.[42] Both of these scholars seem to accept the ideal of patrilineality presented in some biblical texts as a reflection of ancient Israelite reality, and in the process, they ignore other data present in biblical narratives that point to a mother's contribution to the substantive forming of her child.

While many biblical texts present sons as the "seeds" of their father, they do not associate paternal seed with the transmission of physical, ethnic, or character traits. Instead, a father transmits his name, his house, his land, and his monument to his seed. Throughout the ancestral narratives in Genesis, when the word "seed" designates a human offspring, it is associated with the covenantal promise transmitted from father to son (Gen 13:15, 16; 15:5, 13; 17:7, 8, 10; 21:13 [Ishmael]; 22:17; 26:3, 4, 24; 28:4, 13,14; 32:13; 35:12; 48:11). Outside of Genesis, covenantal promises continue to bind men and their seeds, alluding to the covenant of circumcision (Deut 30:6), the covenant between David and Jonathan and their seeds (1 Sam 20:42), the covenant of an eternal dynasty that Yahweh promises to David and his seed (2 Sam 7:12), and the commandments and "name" associated with covenantal observance among the seeds of the house of Jacob (Isa 48:17–19).[43] The covenantal promises bestow on a son a father's material and immaterial wealth—"a great name," a "blessing," "land," and "protection"—all of which are values within an idealized patrilineality. Therefore, while the word "seed" is important to the ideal of patrilineality, it is not used in reference to the transmission of physical or character traits from father to child (see fig. 5).

Delaney and Speiser overemphasize the importance of the male seed in the biblical understanding of procreation, and fail to see those places where mothers are presented as contributing to the physical, ethnic, or character composition of their children. Naomi Steinberg is correct in her assertion that a mother's ethnicity determined whether her son became his father's designated heir. In Genesis, a man's mother and wife had to come from the line of Terah in order for him to receive the covenantal blessing.[44] Coming from the line of Terah does not simply mean that these women were good quality "containers"; they contributed something of themselves and their Terahite ethnicity to the child who was eventually named heir.[45]

Several biblical texts provide evidence for the Hebrew understanding of cognatic descent. In the story of Jacob's and Esau's birth, for example, each twin is tied to one parent based on his physical appearance: the hairy Esau is tied to the masculinity of his father, Isaac, while the smooth Jacob is tied to the femininity of his mother, Rebekah (Gen 25:25–26; 27:11).[46] Joseph seems to have inherited physical beauty from his mother.[47] Several texts, both literal and metaphorical, locate the formation of negative character traits within a mother's womb. Job complains concerning the wicked: "They conceive trouble and give birth to evil; their womb fashions deceit" (Job 15:35). The psalmist laments, "Look, I was brought forth in iniquity, and in sin did my mother conceive me" (Ps 51:5), and the Qumran psalm cited above asserts humans are "encompassed by iniquity since birth and since the breast by guilt."[48] None of these texts insists that evil, guilt, iniquity, and deceit are the only possible products fashioned in the space of the womb, but they connect the traits of a mother to the child she births. They locate the formation of character traits in the female-focused reproductive process that moves from conception to pregnancy to birth.

Additional texts present the mother as the source of negative personality traits in the child, but they do not identify the womb as the site of transmission for these traits. These mothers are thought to teach iniquity rather than having it fashioned in their wombs. The metaphorical Mother Jerusalem, for example, is described as learning husband- and children-loathing from her Hittite mother (Ezek 16:44–47). Uterine sisters Oholah and Oholibah are introduced as "two women, the daughters of one mother," in a text that describes how each led a life of whoredom from her youth (Ezek 23:2). Saul curses his son Jonathan for colluding with David, saying, "You son of a perverse, rebellious woman! Do I not know that you have chosen the son of Jesse to your own shame, and to the shame of your mother's nakedness?" (1 Sam 20:30). In this text, Saul traces Jonathan's traitorous behavior against him to the rebellious nature of his mother. Again, there is no specific mention of the womb. Finally, Ahaziah's reign is introduced as follows: "Ahaziah was forty-two years old when he began to reign; he reigned one year in

Jerusalem. His mother's name was Athaliah, a granddaughter of Omri. He also walked in the ways of the house of Ahab, for his mother was his counselor in doing wickedly" (2 Chron 22:2–3). In both sets of texts—womb-focused and mother-focused—we find a transmission of traits from mother to child, sometimes occurring within the womb and sometimes occurring under the mother's active instruction. While none makes the transmission of traits from mother to child through the womb explicit, together they suggest that a mother's womb was more than a container for a man's trait-bearing seed.

Biblical Hebrew understands a mother to contribute to the physical, ethnic, and character makeup of her child from the time spent in the womb and at the breasts to the time spent under her active tutelage. A mother's womb served as the basis for a lifelong bond between mother and child and among siblings who came forth from the same womb. This womb-based connection could be expressed through the word *raḥămîm*, meaning a womb-centered allegiance that involved lifelong mutual protection. The formation of the child was a two-staged, maternally focused process encapsulated in the Hebrew word pair "breasts and womb." Used chronologically moving forward or backward, biblical authors imagined a child's physical, character, and emotional development to begin at conception, continue during the time in the womb, and find completion through breastfeeding.

6 Like a Brother to Me, One Who Had Nursed at My Mother's Breasts (*kĕ'āḥ lî yônēq šĕdê 'immî*)

The Hebrew kinship designation "O that you were like a brother to me, one who had nursed at my mother's breasts" (Song 8:1) shows an awareness of the concept of milk kinship. This verse and other biblical narratives that contain references to breastfeeding attest to the understanding that a mother or wet nurse transmitted her ethnicity and status (royal or priestly) to her suckling through the act of breastfeeding. Specifically, biblical birth narratives of foundational male figures include breastfeeding episodes in order to bolster the hero's royal or priestly credentials and to establish his insider ethnicity. The broader ancient Near Eastern literary corpus, again focusing on the birth narratives of foundational royal men and gods, supports the idea that breast milk was understood as a substance that transmitted royalty and sometimes divinity from mother or wet nurse to suckling. Children who nursed from the same mother had a relationship similar to that of uterine siblings. They had heightened emotional ties, a strong sense of allegiance, and the perceived responsibility to enact vengeance on one another's behalf.[1]

The Social and Ritual Implications of "Milk Kinship"

English speakers are accustomed to speaking about kinship relatedness in terms of "shared blood." We use phrases like "blood relatives" and "royal blood" to communicate group identity and in some cases status differentiation. Biblical scholars quite naturally have used the language of blood relatedness to describe relationships within the house of the father.[2] Recently, however, anthropologists focusing on kinship studies have questioned the universal application of the metaphor of blood as a substance that establishes kinship relatedness. Adam Kuper, for example, argues that the notion of blood relatedness is culturally constrained, a uniquely European concept that finds its fullest articulation within British imperialism, an era that coincides with the development of the field of anthropology in Europe.[3] Likewise, Edouard Conte, who examines concepts of relatedness within Arab cultures, posits that the notion of kinship being determined by blood is a particularly Western phenomenon and does not fit the self-understanding of Arabs.[4] He argues that classical Arab physicians deal little with blood and do not see blood as passing on hereditary attributes. If we examine indigenous Hebrew terms for kinship relatedness, we have to admit that the Hebrew word for blood, *dam*, is rarely if ever used as a substance that establishes a kinship relationship between people.[5] Instead, the most common substances that biblical authors use to describe relatedness are "seed" (*zeraʿ*), denoting semen and by extension the lineal relationship between fathers and their descendants, and "bone and flesh" (*ʿeṣem ûbaśār*), a more ambiguous and malleable term for kinship relatedness that is discussed in chapter 8.[6] While "seed" and "bone and flesh" are the most common substance-based metaphors for kinship relatedness in the Bible, the reference to a "brother who had nursed at my mother's breasts," together with anthropological studies of milk kinship, suggest that biblical scholars need to examine and test the hypothesis that ancient Israelites understood breast milk and breastfeeding to establish kinship bonds.

In a 1992 volume entitled *The Anthropology of Breast-Feeding: Natural Law or Social Construct*, Vanessa Maher notes the pronounced "social dimension" to breastfeeding in a wide variety of cultures. She asserts, "Breastfeeding, like female sexuality and childbirth, is the subject of considerable cultural elaboration in most societies."[7] The act of breastfeeding was first and foremost an act understood to inculcate in the child culturally defined personal boundaries and to transmit maternal traits from mother or wet nurse to child (28–29). In male-privileging societies, the recognized power of breast milk to transmit traits from mother to child resulted in laws that gave the father control over who provided breast milk to his child and for how long (21–25). None of the cultures studied in this edited volume viewed breast milk simply in terms of nutrition.[8]

Returning to Edouard Conte's 2003 study of Arab conceptualizations of kinship, he acknowledges that Arab texts present kinship bonds in terms of a shared substance. The substance, however, is not blood (*dam*) but meat or flesh (*lahma*). While blood imagery is used at times, it "has no claim to precedence."[9] Similar to the Hebrew understanding of blood, Arabic texts use the term "blood" in contexts of vengeance where the "killer of a kinsman 'cuts the blood' (*yaqta'u al-dam*) and thereby 'cuts (the bond of) the womb' (*yaqta'u [silat] al-rahim*), a term semantically closer to 'kinship' than *dam*" (17). Conte notes that hereditary attributes in Arab texts have both masculine and feminine channels of transmission. On the masculine side, there is a "perceived resemblance between males" in a family. On the feminine side, the "acquisition of traits, morphological or psychological," is understood to occur "through the mother's or wet nurse's milk" (17). His examination of Islamic legal texts shows how "doctors of Law ... broke down kinship into three component aspects": *nasab* (descent), *musahara* (affinity), and *ridha'a*, which Conte identifies as "suckling and the relations derived therefrom" (20). The generic word for kinship in Arabic is *qaraba*, meaning "proximity" or "propinquity," and Conte shows how this word can be associated with notions of agnatic descent (*nasab*). At the same time, however, he points to a related term, *qurba*, which is commonly used in parallel with *rahim* (uterus), as a way to designate kinship in its "broadest sense" (20). Thus, Conte finds in Arabic writings an understanding of kinship based on breast milk, flesh, and "bonds of the womb" that are broken when one spills the blood of a kinsman.

In a 1999 study focusing on Islamic views of breastfeeding, Avner Giladi finds that breast milk in Islamic societies establishes kinship ties with clear social implications.[10] The Qur'an mentions "milk mothers" and "milk sisters" among a list of those women sexually prohibited to a man on account of incest.[11] The Haddith literature on this Qur'anic text is in agreement that breast milk forges a kinship bond that impedes marriage. Interpretations only vary on how much shared breast milk sufficiently establishes such a kinship bond, with opinions ranging from a single drop to two full years of nursing.[12]

While marital and sexual ties were prohibited to milk siblings, social access between the sexes became freer for those who had nursed at the same breast. For example, a Muslim woman could meet her milk brother unveiled, and a wet nurse would have free, familial access to a male child she nursed for his entire life. Finally, the symbolic nursing of an adult male provided him with social access to the women of the household.[13] Each of these examples shows that breast milk established a kinship tie that had a lifelong social impact on a child.

In a 2004 study of the literature of the Irish and the Abkhazians of premodern Eurasia, Peter Parkes examines the role of shared breast milk in establishing a foster kin relationship between children and their wet nurses and also among "co-nursers" or "milk-siblings."[14] In his study, Parkes documents an understanding of fosterage established through shared breast milk. Among the Abkhazians, suckling at the same breast established "consanguineal" relationships (590). Parkes traces the roots of this view of breast milk to Aristotle and Galen, both of whom considered breast milk "a purified refinement of a woman's uterine blood" (590).[15] Shared breast milk among "milk brothers" and "milk sons" resulted in ties that lasted a lifetime. Indeed, the bond fused through breast milk could entail lifelong protection and the prosecuting of internecine feuds on behalf of "milk-brothers" and "milk-sons" (591).[16] Similar to the findings of Giladi, Parkes notes that among the Abkhazian people, "milk kinship" could be established among adults through "symbolic suckling at the breast" and that relationships thus formed involved identical moral obligations and impediments to marriage as those created through infant fosterage.[17]

Within old Irish literature, Parkes finds the sentiment that foster brothers who shared the same breast milk had a closer relationship and a greater sense of loyalty to each other than they did to their biological brothers who did not share the same breast milk. Among the Irish sources that he cites are William Good's "Descriptions and Customs of the Wild Irish," where we find the following sentiment: "All who have suck'd the same breasts are very kind and loving, and confide more in each other than if they were natural brothers, so that they will have an aversion even to their own brothers for the sake of these."[18] A very similar belief is recorded in Fynes Moryson's "Itinerary": "The foster-brothers—I mean the children of the nurse and strangers that have sucked her milk—love one another better than natural brothers, and hate them in respect of the other . . . and some oppose their own brothers to death that they might save their foster brothers from dangers thereof."[19]

Susan Montague, an anthropologist whose fieldwork has focused on the Trobriand Island people, describes an experience she had when she told a group of Trobriand women that Westerners understood relatedness in terms of "shared blood." The women, she remembers, rolled on the ground laughing until one was able to tell her, "No! People are related through mother's milk!" To the women in this group, the truth of this statement was obvious.[20] Montague soon discovered that according to the Trobriand understanding, breast milk enters the bloodstream of a child through digestion, making a child's blood "compositionally identical to that of the woman whose breast milk it consumes."[21]

The constitution of a mother's breast milk has special importance for the ritual status of Trobriand boys because it transmits particular traits to the child. Trobriand mothers adhere to certain diets in order to contribute to the intended social identity and magical capabilities of their child. Trobriand boys are raised to be able to perform particular kinds of magic that are related to their class or tier, and each type of magic is associated with one of four birds. Therefore, in order to raise a boy who is able to perform the magic appropriate to him, his mother must avoid consuming the class of bird specific to her son's magic, eating only the other three types of birds. This is because breast milk is thought to transmit the foodstuffs that the mother has consumed. Moreover, a woman's breast milk is thought to contain traces of everything she has ever eaten, including her own mother's milk. This means that multiple generations of maternal dietary requirements result in the appropriate composition of breast milk for any child.[22]

Cultures as diverse in time and place as the Trobriand Islanders, the Abkhazians of central Eurasia, the Irish, and the Arabs share a belief that breast milk forges kinship bonds that are as strong and sometimes stronger than biological relationships. In several of the examples, breast milk is the substantive conduit through which specific traits of the mother or wet nurse are transferred to the infant. In the Trobriand case, magical powers of select birds reach the child through the controlled diet of the mother and maternal grandmother. Biological or milk siblings who nurse from the same mother or wet nurse establish bonds that imply intensified pacts of loyalty, and adults can form loyalty pacts through symbolic breastfeeding. None of these observations in and of themselves proves that breast milk had similar valence in the biblical narrative, but they point to a blind spot in modern biblical scholars' treatment of kinship and suggest that we investigate the cultural valence of breast milk in the Bible and the larger corpus of ancient Near Eastern literature.

Nursing at the Breasts of Goddesses: Ancient Near Eastern Presentations of Breastfeeding

The literature of the ancient Near East attests to an understanding of breast milk as a kinship-forging substance that confers on male children royal, divine, and often priestly status. In ancient Near Eastern literature, in order to bolster their royal legitimacy, divine and human kings are presented as those who have nursed at the breasts of goddesses. In the foundational narratives of ancient Near Eastern kings, we find the recurring claim that royal heirs nursed at the breasts of goddesses who are imagined in both human and animal forms.[23] Among the human kings whose royal biographies include a breastfeeding notation, we find Yassub, the son and heir of the Ugaritic King Kirta, and Ashurbanipal, the designated heir of the Assyrian King Esarhaddon. In both cases these royal heirs are able to claim semi-divine status by virtue of having nursed at the breasts of goddesses.[24] Before he is even born, El predicts that Kirta's son Yassub will "nurse on the milk of Astarte, suck the breasts of Maiden Anat, the two wet nurses of the gods."[25] The identity of the first goddess is unclear, and some scholars read Astarte as Asherah.[26] Susan Ackerman sees Yassub's mother serving as "the earthly surrogate" for the divine Asherah, whose status as the queen mother of the pantheon imbues both mother and child with royalty.[27] Regardless of the identity of the first goddess, the narrative claim to have nursed at the breasts of goddesses bolsters Yassub's status as the royal heir.

Assyrian King Ashurbanipal is said to have nursed at the breasts of Ishtar, here called the "Queen of Nineveh." Her animal traits are apparent in the four teats she offers to Ashurbanipal:

> You were a child, Assurbanipal,
> when I left you with the Queen of Nineveh;
> you were a baby, Assurbanipal,
> when you sat on the lap of the Queen of Nineveh!
> Her four teats were placed in your mouth:
> Two you would suckle and two you would milk before you![28]

For both of these human kings, divine breast milk serves as the conduit for bestowing divine traits. In the case of Ashurbanipal, we can add that he was a king whose succession was anything but guaranteed. We saw in chapter 4 that the treaty that names Ashurbanipal as Esarhaddon's successor takes pains to reduce potential threats to his rule from competing royal sons. The treaty repeatedly calls on the oath-takers, "You shall not depose him [Ashurbanipal] nor seat (any) one of his brothers, elder or younger, on the throne of Assyria instead of him."[29] In the royal prayer to Nabu, where this breastfeeding notation is found, Ashurbanipal repeatedly entreats Nabu not to leave him among his "detractors."³⁰ Thus, the claim to have sucked at the breasts of a goddess may well have been part of a larger effort to bolster Ashurbanipal's claim to the throne over the claims of his brothers.³¹

The epic hero Gilgamesh presents the most explicit mixing of the divine and human in that he was a king born of a human father, Lugalbanda, and a divine mother, Ninsun. Mathematical logic would suggest that Gilgamesh would emerge from the womb half-human and half-divine. Instead, he ends up being declared "two thirds god and one third human."³² Perhaps he achieved this extra dose of divinity through nursing: "Wild bull of Lugalbanda, Gilgamesh, perfect of strength, suckling of the exalted cow [*ēniq arḫi ṣirti*], Wild-Cow Ninsun!"³³ Here again the divine mother and wet nurse has bovine traits, and the wild cow bears and nurses a son who is then lauded as the wild bull. Gilgamesh's rival and equal, Enkidu, is likewise a mix of types. Described as a wild beast man, he is born of a gazelle and a wild donkey, and "wild [asses] reared [him] with their milk."³⁴ Enkidu's wildness, therefore, begins at conception with two animal parents and finds its completion when Enkidu nurses at the teats of wild asses. The mix of human and divine parentage found in Gilgamesh also describes the birth of the Ugaritic pair of gods known as Shahar and Shalim (dawn and dusk). These gods were the result of a union of the god El with two human women, and they are said to "nurse the nipples of Asherah's breasts."³⁵ In this case, the divinity of Shahar and Shalim begins with their divine father and is completed at the breast of a divine wet nurse, Asherah.

Even fully divine figures add to their royal credentials by claiming to have nursed at the breasts of goddesses. The Babylonian god Marduk fights to become "king of the gods" in the Babylonian creation story known as *Enuma Elish*. This story provides Marduk with a complete birth narrative, named parents, and status-conferring, divine breast milk. His birth story reads as follows: "In the chamber of the destinies, the room of the archetypes, The wisest of the wise, the sage of the gods, Bēl was conceived. In Apsu was Marduk born, In pure Apsu was Marduk born. Ea his father begat him, Damkina his mother bore him. He sucked the breasts of goddesses, A nurse reared him and filled him with terror."³⁶ Royal male figures, whether human or divine, claim elevated divine status through the literary trope of nursing at the breasts of goddesses. Breast milk in these narratives is understood as the substance that transmits royalty and an elevated divinity to the suckling.

Jerusalem and the Biblical Metaphor of Nursing

While the Bible does not depict kings nursing at the breasts of goddesses, we find several postexilic prophetic texts that depict Jerusalem metaphorically as a redeemed woman who sucks the milk of nations and as a mother who gives birth to the nation of Israel and breastfeeds the returning exiles. In Isa 60, the prophet uses breastfeeding as a literary trope designed to show the transformation of the city of Jerusalem from a woman abandoned by her god to one who is "majestic" forever. The chapter begins with the prophet calling to Jerusalem, "Arise, shine, for your light has come, and the glory of Yahweh has risen upon you" (Isa 60:1). Jerusalem's transformation involves the rebuilding of the temple and the restarting of the sacrificial cult; it includes the return of the exiles (Isa 60:4–7, 13–14). Finally, Isaiah imagines Jerusalem's restoration in royal terms, where kings and nations bring her tribute and bow at her feet (Isa 60:8–14). The prophet then attributes the transformation of Jerusalem from abandoned to populated, from hated to majestic, to Yahweh's redemptive power and to the status-conferring properties of royal breast milk (Isa 60:15–16). In this imagining, however, those who give suck are masculine:

> "You [Jerusalem] shall suck [*y-n-q*] the milk of nations,
> you shall suck the breasts of kings,
> and you shall know that I, the Lord, am your savior and your redeemer,
> the Mighty One of Jacob." (Isa 60:16)

When Zion sucks the milk of nations and the breasts of kings, she acquires their traits and status, becoming royal and majestic herself.[37] In Isa 49, it is the exiles returning back from Babylonia who are made royal through breastfeeding with both kings and princesses serving as their wet nurses:

> Kings will be your wet nurses [*'ōmnayik*],
> and their princesses will give you suck [*mêniqōtayik*]. (Isa 49:23)[38]

The result of this combined ingestion of royal breast milk is that the exiles will become like royals with those very same kings and princesses bowing down to them and licking the dust off their feet. In this text, Isaiah poetically evokes a metaphorical transfer of the trait of royalty through breast milk.

Isaiah 66 describes Jerusalem as a mother giving birth fast without labor pains like the Hebrew women were said to have done in Egypt: "Before she was in labor, she gave birth; before her pain came upon her she delivered a son" (Isa 66:7; see also Exod 1:19). She births an entire nation in a day: "Who has ever heard of such a thing? Who has seen such things? Shall a land be born in one day?" (Isa 66:8). After she gives birth, the prophet-poet calls on the newly reborn nation of returned exiles to rejoice with Jerusalem "that you may suck and be satisfied from the breast of her consolations, that you may drink deeply with delight from the abundance of her glory" (Isa 66:11). Isaiah 66 continues imagining both God and Jerusalem in feminine terms:

> For thus says Yahweh, see, I will extend fullness to her like a river,
> and the glory of the nations like an overflowing stream;
> and you [*pl*] shall suck [*y-n-q*], you shall be carried upon [her] hip,
> and take delight upon her knees.
> As one whom his mother comforts, so I will comfort you;
> you shall be comforted in Jerusalem. (Isa 66:12–13)[39]

Here, one might imagine that the exiles return to their homeland carrying the foreign stain of Babylonia. Only through a rebirth by their capital city and through ingesting the milk of Jerusalem's breasts can they regain their ethnic status as the new Israelites marked by "glory," a repeated epithet of Yahweh's royal power. Yahweh and Jerusalem will co-parent the new Israel; she will give suck and carry, and he will comfort.[40] Zion's sons will be brought back to her with silver and gold. Yahweh has glorified her, foreigners will rebuild her walls, and kings will minister to her (Isa 60:9–10). In each of these postexilic imaginings, the rebuilding of a people and a nation involves sucking at the breasts of royalty, and for the returning exiles, it is the milk of their capital city that will complete their rebirth as Israelites dwelling in their homeland.[41]

The Kinship Valence of the Nursing Reference in Song of Songs 8:1–2

In Song 8:1–2, the female speaker imagines the relationship that she would have with a brother whom she further specifies as "one who had nursed at my mother's breasts." The female speaker's imagined relationship with her milk brother matches the described relationship between Joseph and "Benjamin, his brother, the son of his mother." Both relationships are emotionally deep, physically affectionate, and explicitly rooted in a shared tie to the same mother. The milk brother relationship described in Song 8:1 is an imagined relationship; the woman fantasizes that if her lover were her milk brother, several things would become possible.[42] She insists that if he were a brother who had nursed at her mother's breasts, she could kiss him in public and no one would censure the activity. This suggests that public displays of physical affection between milk siblings were an accepted societal norm.[43] She also claims that if he were a brother who had nursed at her mother's breasts, she could take him to her "mother's house" and no one would prevent this private tryst. The fantasy element of this imagining becomes clear when we consider the incest prohibition that would prevent brothers and sisters from having sex. The female speaker in this Song clearly wants to use the societal access granted to a milk brother in order to circumvent the rules. The house of the mother, as a kinship designation and physical space specific to the mother, is precisely the location we would expect to find uterine and milk siblings residing together.[44] The female lover wishes her beloved were a milk sibling because, just as we saw in the much later Muslim social conventions, a milk sibling is one with whom she can imagine sharing the intimate space of the mother's house without supervision or censure.

We saw in chapter 4 that the uterine sibling relationship captured in the kinship term "my brother, the son of my mother," also created the social expectation to act as allies within the house of the father and to enact revenge whenever a wrong was committed against one member of a uterine pair or grouping. The Song's reference to a milk brother does not include alliance and enacting revenge. We did note, however, that the Ugaritic term *'l 'umty*, "suckling of my mother's clan," is used when Pughat seeks to avenge her uterine brother's killing and when Anat embarks on a search for her recently revived and avenged brother Baal. In order to determine whether the Bible also associated shared breast milk sourcing with alliance and revenge, we need to examine narratives that feature breastfeeding episodes.

Four biblical narratives feature human women who breastfeed foundational male figures. The story of Hannah nursing Samuel provides evidence for the understanding of breast milk as a substance that establishes the ritual status of one who is to be a "Nazirite from birth." As such Hannah's story is best understood in conversation with the law of the Nazirite in Num 6 and the parallel story of the birth of Samson in Judg 13. The remaining three narratives that feature breastfeeding mothers are considered as a group because they each feature what is on the surface a preposterous story of breastfeeding that can only make sense if one understands breast milk as a substance that confers tribal identity and royal or priestly status. These three stories are Sarah's nursing of Isaac, Moses's mother's nursing of Moses, and Naomi's nursing of Obed.

Hannah and Samuel: Breast Milk as a Conduit for the Ritual Status of a Nazirite

Hannah's story begins on the occasion of a pilgrimage festival meal at the temple in Shiloh, when her husband Elkanah inadvertently slights Hannah by offering his fertile wife Peninnah and each of her sons and daughters a portion of the sacrifice and offering Hannah some sort of preferred or prized portion meant to bring her honor.[45] Her special portion represents Elkanah's love for her but also his pity that "Yahweh had closed her womb" (1 Sam 1:4–5). Hannah could rightly see this meal apportionment as a foreshadowing of the division of Elkanah's estate at his death. Peninnah and her many sons would receive multiple portions by right while Hannah's portion would be doled out based on pity. The ritual meal serves to accentuate her lack of children and her concomitant lack of a secure place in Elkanah's household.[46]

In her desperation, Hannah prays to the Lord and weeps bitterly: "She vowed a vow [*neder*], saying O Lord of Hosts, if you truly see the affliction of your maidservant and if you will indeed remember, not forget, your maidservant, and you give your maidservant a male child, then I will dedicate him to Yahweh all the days of his life, and no razor shall touch his head [*ûmôrâ lōʾ-yaʿăleh ʿal-rōʾšô*]" (1 Sam 1:11). The vocabulary of this verse is identical to that in the stipulations found in the law of the Nazirite in Num 6 where a person is required "to vow a vow" (*lindōr neder*) and then adopt a state of holiness for a specified period of time, separating him- or herself from "wine or strong drink" (*yayīn wĕšēkār*) and refraining from shaving or cutting one's hair (*taʿar lōʾ-yaʿăbōr ʿal-rōšô*) (Num 6:1–5). While Num 6 likely postdates the story of Samuel's birth in 1 Sam 1–2, the Samuel text shows an awareness of the requirements placed on a Nazirite. These requirements are then recorded and preserved in the legal material in Numbers. Using the vocabulary that signals the requirements of a Nazirite, the birth story of Samuel suggests that Hannah will dedicate him to the temple as a Nazirite.[47] The Septuagint moves beyond suggestion to the explicit, having Hannah say, "Then I shall set him before you as a Nazirite until the day of his death, and wine and strong drink he will not drink, and a razor will not touch his head."[48]

In order to understand the significance of an infant being set aside as a "Nazirite from birth," we need to read Hannah's story together with the story of Samson's mother. The story of Samson's mother describes the prescribed maternal diet for a mother carrying a Nazirite, while the story of Hannah adds details concerning breastfeeding a Nazirite infant. Both stories provide evidence for the belief that a gestating and nursing mother had to adhere to the ritually prescribed diet of her Nazirite son.

Several scholars have noted that in the story of Samson's birth, it is his mother who is first required to adhere to the ritually prescribed diet of a Nazirite.[49] An angel of Yahweh announces the impending pregnancy and birth of a child who will be set apart as a Nazirite from birth and commands that the mother observe the diet of a Nazirite during the time of her pregnancy. Again, the narrative cites the language of Num 6:1–5 explicitly: "Although you are barren, having borne no children, you are pregnant and will bear a son. Now be careful not to drink wine or strong drink [*yayin wĕšēkār*] or to eat anything unclean, for you shall conceive and bear a son. No razor is to come on his head, for the boy shall be a Nazirite to God from birth" (Judg 13:3b–5a). The text repeats the restrictions on the mother's diet twice more (Judg 13:7, 14).[50] The mother is to adopt this diet during pregnancy, providing the fetal Samson with food appropriate to his Nazirite needs. There is no time limit prescribed for the mother's special diet. It is possible that the restrictions only apply up to the time of birth, but it could also extend through the period of nursing. The ritual requirement that a mother abstain from eating the foods prohibited to her unborn son bears striking similarity to the Trobriand case, where the mother and maternal grandmother had to avoid eating the flesh of the bird associated with the son's (and grandson's) magic. If Samson is to be ritually set apart, he apparently must emerge from the womb not having received any alcohol or unclean foods in the womb through his mother. It would follow logically that the mother would be required to observe the dietary restrictions through the period of nursing as well, but the text remains silent on this issue.

Hannah receives no divine instructions concerning her diet while pregnant, but the narrative goes to great lengths to show that she did in fact observe the diet of a Nazirite prior to conception and during pregnancy. When Hannah prays for a son at the temple of Yahweh, the text reports that Eli the priest observed her lips moving but did not hear her words. He therefore concludes that she must be "a drunk" (*šikkōrâ*). He reprimands her saying, "How long will you make yourself drunk? Put away your wine" (1 Sam 1:13–14). Through this curious accusation, the narrator provides Hannah's character with the opportunity to defend herself by asserting in language that draws on the law of the Nazirite preserved in Num 6, "No, my Lord, I am a woman with a troubled spirit, I have drunk neither wine nor strong drink [*yayīn wĕšēkār*]" (1 Sam 1:15).[51] As Ackerman notes, a pilgrimage festival would be precisely the time when people would drink liberally.[52] Hannah's assertion that she has drunk nothing is an especially important clarification, given the ambiguity of 1 Sam 1:9, which reports that just prior to offering her prayer, "Hannah arose after eating in Shiloh and after drinking" (1 Sam 1:9).[53] If this verse allows the reader to presume that Hannah partook of strong drink in the course of the sacrificial meal, Eli's questioning of her allows her to state emphatically to a priest in the Shiloh temple where the ark of Yahweh resides, "I have drunk neither wine nor strong drink."[54]

Hannah's prayer is granted when Yahweh "remembered her," and she conceives and bears a son. Unlike the story of Samson, the story of Samuel narrates the infancy of Samuel to the point of his weaning, making Hannah's nursing of Samuel explicit. We first hear of her nursing on the occasion of the following year's visit to the temple in Shiloh. Hannah, who by then has given birth to Samuel, tells her husband Elkanah that she will not go up to the temple with him, instead saying, "As soon as the child is weaned, I will bring him that he may appear before Yahweh and dwell there forever" (1 Sam 1:22).[55] The next verse reiterates Hannah's nursing of Samuel: "And Elkanah said to his wife, 'Do what is good in your eyes. Stay until you wean him so that Yahweh may establish his word.' So the woman remained and nursed her son until she weaned him" (1 Sam 1:23).

At the point of weaning, Hannah fulfills her vow and brings Samuel to the temple together with an offering of a three-year-old bull, an ephah of flour, and a skin of wine (1 Sam 1:24). In a sense, Hannah's work of conceiving, gestating, bearing, and nursing Samuel is complete, such that she can present Samuel at the temple as a fully formed human being and a fully compliant Nazirite. At that point, when she brings "a skin of wine" to the temple, the narrator does not find it necessary to specify whether she drank any or not; her ritual preparation of her son is complete.[56]

The story of Samuel's birth is careful to present Hannah as one who has observed the ritually prescribed dietary restrictions of a Nazirite from the time just preceding Samuel's conception through the point of weaning. Hannah and Samson's mother did not become Nazirites themselves. Instead, the narratives of Samson and Samuel show an understanding that what mothers eat is transmitted to their children in the womb and at the breast. The womb and breasts transmit to the child nourishment, but more important is the ritual specificity of the mother's diet that sets her child apart from conception through weaning. In order for the two boys to be "Nazirites from birth," their mothers observe one portion of the Nazirite requirements, the portion that ties them substantively to their sons.

Isaac and Sarah

Sarah was at least ninety years old when "Yahweh visited Sarah as he had said and Yahweh did to Sarah as he had promised. Sarah conceived and bore a son to Abraham in his old age" (Gen 21:1–2). As one would expect at this advanced age, "the way of women had ceased for Sarah" (Gen 18:11). The birth itself is clearly presented as a divinely initiated miracle that provides Abraham with the promised heir through his primary wife (Gen 17:15–19). Sarah's amazement over the birth of Isaac is articulated when she wonders aloud,

> Who would ever have said to Abraham
> that Sarah would nurse children!
> And now, I have borne him a son in his old age.

> *Mî millēl lĕʾabrāhām*
> *hênîqâ bānîm śārâ*
> *kî-yāladtî bēn lizqunāyw.* (Gen 21:7)

Who indeed would have thought Sarah would nurse children at age ninety? We can understand why the child of the promise had to come from Sarah and not Hagar, and therefore we can understand the need for her miraculous conception and birthing of Isaac. But what is the reason for including this brief verse that suggests Sarah is also the one who nursed him? The text continues and describes how Isaac grew up and "was weaned" (*wayyiggāmal*) and that Abraham celebrated the day of his weaning with a "great feast" (Gen 21: 8). What is the significance of further stretching credulity by insisting that not only did Sarah bear Isaac but she nursed him to the point of weaning, normally three years?[57]

Two factors become important in providing an answer to this question: the status and ethnicity of Sarah and the existence and foreignness of Hagar in her household. The Bible does not provide Sarah with a full genealogy, but she is Abraham's wife from the homeland in "Ur of Chaldeans" (Gen 11:29; 12:5), and in one text Abraham insists, "She is indeed my sister, the daughter of my father but not the daughter of my mother; and she became my wife" (Gen 20:12; see also 12:19). So Sarah is presented as closely related to Abraham, coming from the homeland in Haran, and likely of the Genesis-preferred Terahite stock.[58]

In addition to her appropriate insider ethnicity, Sarah's character is presented biblically with numerous allusions to royalty. Her covenantal name, Sarah, means "princess," and the name of her close relative, Milcah, means "queen."[59] When Sarah receives her divine name change, she also receives a royal blessing: "As for Sarai, your wife, you shall no longer call her by the name Sarai, for Sarah is her name. I will bless her and give you a son from her, and she will become nations, kings of nations shall come forth from her" (Gen 17:15–16). Sarah's name change and royal blessing match that of Abraham, who is renamed and then told that as part of God's covenant with him, "kings shall come from you" (Gen 17:6).

This brings us to the consideration of the role of Hagar in the narrative that suggests Sarah's nursing of Isaac to the point of weaning. Because Sarah had a younger, fertile, Egyptian slave woman in her household at the time of Isaac's birth, one might assume that Hagar would become Isaac's wet nurse. Indeed, if breast milk were simply a substance of nourishment, Hagar would be an ideal solution to the problem of a ninety-year-old mother who needs to provide for her infant. Had the text said nothing about the nursing and weaning of Isaac, readers might have come to the conclusion on their own that Hagar, the Egyptian slave woman, must have nursed Isaac.

Mayer I. Gruber has shown that throughout the ancient Near East, procuring a wet nurse was the prerogative of wealthy, elite women.[60] Sarah is presented as the wife of a wealthy sheik, "rich in cattle, in silver, in gold" (Gen 13:2), an elite woman who owns her own slave woman, and a woman whose name and covenantal promise suggest royalty.[61] If Sarah had insisted that Hagar serve as wet nurse to her son, Isaac, the move would be consistent with presenting Sarah as an elite woman of status.[62] If, however, we consider the possibility that breast milk was understood as a substance that conferred ethnicity and status, then the audacious claim that a ninety-year-old Sarah not only conceived and bore Isaac but breastfed him to the point of weaning takes on added significance.

Historically, source critics have been nearly unanimous in marking a source division here, at this breastfeeding notation, between verses 7 and 8 of chapter 21. The first seven verses are clearly tied to the priestly articulation of the Abrahamic covenant in Gen 17 in that they recollect and fulfill the promises made in Gen 17.[63] Verses 8–21, which narrate the expulsion of

Ishmael, on the other hand, read as an independent narrative with no tie to Gen 17.[64] The single detail within verses 1–7 that does not have a direct tie back to language and promises made in Gen 17 is Sarah's marveling, "Who would have said to Abraham that Sarah would nurse children."[65]

This source division is important because it suggests that when Gen 21:1–5 was brought together with Gen 21:8–21, a redactor noted and sought to clarify the ambiguity concerning who had nursed Isaac. In verse 8, the verb for "to wean" is passive: "The child grew and was weaned [*wayyiggāmal*]; and Abraham made a great feast on the day that Isaac was weaned [*higgāmēl*]." This verse leaves open the possibility that Hagar, the young Egyptian slave woman of Sarah, served as wet nurse to Isaac. In fact, because of Sarah's pronounced elite status, the most likely assumption on the part of the reader would be that Hagar had served as Isaac's wet nurse. This in turn explains why Sarah waited until the weaning feast to expel Hagar and her son. As soon as Hagar's services to Isaac were complete, Sarah removed her from the household.

In the redacted, canonical version of Gen 21, Isaac's weaning feast marks Sarah's completion of the nursing period. If through nursing Isaac is understood to receive an ethnic- and status-conferring substance, then his weaning marks the completion of his formation as a Terahite boy with royal potential. On the occasion of his weaning feast, Abraham recognizes Isaac as a completed human being and a viable heir. The very real danger of infant mortality has been averted. With the survival of her young son on secure footing, Sarah looks upon "the son of Hagar the Egyptian whom she had born to Abraham" (Gen 21:9), and as the phrasing suggests, she simultaneously perceives the foreignness of Ishmael's mother and the insider legitimacy of his father. This inside-outsider first son is found "playing" with Isaac, and Sarah takes decisive steps to remove "the son of this slave woman" from her house, fearing that he would inherit along with "my son Isaac" (Gen 21:9–10). In terms of direct and indirect pathways to the foundational male, Isaac is called "his [Abraham's] son Isaac" three times (Gen 21:3, 4, 5). Abraham names him, circumcises him, and throws him a feast. Isaac's name appears or is alluded to nine times in the chapter. Ishmael, on the other hand, is never named in Gen 21, which is after all the story of his expulsion and his maternal covenant.[66] While he is acknowledged as Abraham's "son" and "seed" (Gen 21:11, 13), he is cumbersomely labeled "the son of Hagar the Egyptian, whom she had borne to him [Abraham]," "the son of this/the slave woman," and "the boy/youth"

(Gen 21:9, 10, 12, 13, 14). The covenant that will make Ishmael into a great nation is a maternal covenant in which he remains nameless as "the boy" (Gen 21:15–21). On a redactional level, verse 7 clarifies that Isaac is the chosen, insider son who will inherit the promises of the Abrahamic covenant. He is not nursed by an Egyptian slave woman but is instead nursed by his mother, an insider woman of status.⁶⁷

Moses and His Mother

The birth story of Moses bears all the hallmarks of miracle and legend that marked the birth of Isaac. Moses is born under a pharaonic edict that calls for the death of "every boy that is born to the Hebrews" (Exod 1:22). His mother attempts to preserve his life by placing him in a basket and setting him afloat on the Nile in the hopes that he will be rescued and raised by someone else. As providence would have it, none other than Pharaoh's daughter rescues him. At this point, we learn that Moses has a sister, and it is possible to say that she acts as "a suckling of his mother," or "one who had nursed at his mother's breasts," because she acts as his ally and ensures that he grows up as her own milk sibling. Moses's sister asks Pharaoh's daughter, "Shall I go and call for you a wet nurse [*'iššâ mêneqet*] from among the Hebrew women so that she might nurse [*y-n-q*] the boy for you?" (Exod 2:7). Pharaoh's daughter agrees, and Moses's mother takes the child away and nurses the child until he has "grown up."⁶⁸ At that point she returns Moses to Pharaoh's daughter, and he becomes "her son" (Exod 2:2–10). This ruse of presenting Moses's own mother as a potential wet nurse such that she not only keeps and raises her son but is paid to do so is commonly understood as part of the literary trope of mocking the Egyptians.⁶⁹ The role of breastfeeding in this narrative, however, bears striking similarities to Isaac's birth and breastfeeding story.

Moses's mother, though unnamed in this narrative, is introduced first by her tribal affiliation; she and her husband are both of the priestly tribe of Levi. Their tribal affiliation headlines Moses's birth narrative: "A man went forth from the house of Levi and took [as a wife] a daughter of Levi" (Exod. 2:1).⁷⁰ The life story of Moses is punctuated repeatedly with questions concerning his Hebrew identity. He is raised by an Egyptian princess and given an Egyptian name. He marries a Midianite woman and enters her father's household for a number of years.⁷¹ It is possible that he was not circumcised at eight days and had to undergo the procedure before returning to Egypt to act as deliverer of the Hebrews (Exod 4:24–26).[72] He marries a Cushite woman causing consternation for his brother and sister (Num 12:1–3). He never sets foot in the Promised Land of Israel (Deut 34:4). The infancy story of the breastfeeding of Moses by his Levite mother is best understood against this backdrop of questions concerning his ethnic identity.[73]

What we learn from Moses's birth story is that this foundational figure of the Israelite priesthood was conceived by a Levite father and a Levite mother. Like Isaac, he is doubly marked with the ethnicity appropriate to his later eponym. The story of Moses's mother securing the paid position as wet nurse to her own child is as preposterous as Sarah nursing a child from the age of ninety to ninety-three. Without this story, however, readers would likely assume that Pharaoh's daughter would have enlisted the help of one of her own slaves or palace wet nurses in order to feed the baby Moses.[74] In fact, when Pharaoh's daughter discovers the infant, she refrains from going to him herself and instead dispatches one of her attendants to lift him from the water (Exod 2:5). Surely she had internal palace resources for nursing Moses. Therefore, the story of Moses's mother nursing him is more than a clever ruse; it is a necessary component to the legitimatizing of Moses as a deliverer of the Hebrews and eponymous ancestor of priests. Moses is not only conceived and carried within the womb of a Levite woman; his ethnic and status formation is completed through his ingesting of her breast milk, the same milk that his protective sister had likely ingested. One might go so far as to say that he is raised in his "mother's house," because Moses's mother "took the child" and then "brought him back" to Pharaoh's daughter once he was weaned (Exod 2:9–10).[75]

The narrative that follows Moses's transfer back to the house of Pharaoh demonstrates the substantive efficacy of the Hebrew, Levitical breast milk that completed his forming. Just after Pharaoh's daughter takes the boy as "her son" and gives him the Egyptian name "Moses,"[76] we read: "And it happened at that time when Moses had grown up that he went out to his brothers [*'eḥāyw*] and saw their forced labor, and he saw an Egyptian man beating a Hebrew man, one from among his brothers [*mēʾeḥāyw*]. And he looked here and there, and when he saw that there was no one, he smote the Egyptian and hid him in the sand" (Exod 2:11–12). This killing, which results in the second pharaonic death threat pronounced against Moses, marks him as the Hebrew and the Levite that his mother raised him to be in her womb, in her house, and at her breast. He clearly recognizes who "his brothers" are, and he acts in solidarity with them. The text is not clear on whether his Hebrew brothers also recognize him as one of their own. What is clear is that they do not want Moses to act as "ruler and judge" over them (Exod 2:13–14). Just as the story of Isaac's weaning is followed by a story that announces and defends his ethnic identity against an outsider Egyptian, so too is the story of Moses's weaning followed by a narrative in which he demonstrates his Hebrew ethnicity against an outsider Egyptian.

An additional redaction of Moses's birth story is found in Moses's genealogy in Exod 6, where Moses's parents are named Amram and Jochebed (Exod 6:20). In Exod 2:1, Moses's mother is labeled a "daughter of Levi," which could be read to mean that she was an actual daughter of Levi or that she, like her husband, was simply of the house of Levi. The Exod 6:20 notation adds the genealogical information that Jochebed was Amram's "father's sister," placing Jochebed in the generation above her husband and one below Levi, clearing up any potential ambiguity.[77] If we read Exod 6 as a later redactional postscript to an existing Exod 2 narrative, the naming of Moses's mother, providing her with a genealogy, and placing her as a first-generation descendant of Levi elevates her status and heightens the endogamous nature of his parents' marriage. Isaac traces his parentage to the single homeland Terahite clan; Moses traces his parentage to a single and prominent Levitical clan.

Naomi and Obed

Like the stories of Sarah and Moses's mother, the story of Naomi begins with her tribal identification and ends with the birth of a male heir, "a son to Naomi." The book of Ruth opens by identifying "a certain man from Bethlehem of Judah" who "went to dwell in the fields of Moab, he, his wife and his two sons. The name of the man was Elimelech, the name of his wife was Naomi, and the names of his two sons were Mahlon and Chilion. They were Ephrathites from Bethlehem in Judah, and they came to the fields of Moab and dwelt there" (Ruth 1:1–2). This family narrative not only mentions the mother but provides her name and includes her under the tribal identification, "Ephrathites from Bethlehem in Judah." Like Sarah and Moses's mother, she is a woman with an appropriate insider tribal heritage.

One of the overarching themes of the book of Ruth is Ruth's foreignness. She is repeatedly called "Ruth the Moabite."[78] Before being brought into the Judean homeland, Ruth swears an oath of loyalty to her mother-in-law, Naomi, giving her famous "Entreat me not to leave you" speech (Ruth 1:16–17). While this speech can be read as a kind of loyalty oath based on Ruth's emotional attachment to her mother-in-law, it can also be understood as a necessary step that Ruth must take prior to her entry into Naomi's village in Judah.[79] Her foreignness is an issue, and prior to their return, they partially resolve the issue through this oath of allegiance.[80]

The book of Ruth is not simply the birth story of Obed; it is the birth story of King David, two generations removed.[81] I agree with Kirstin Nielsen's reading of the book as a whole as being written "in a given political situation where David's origins were under discussion and where there was a need for a defense of his family."[82] There is no birth story for David in the book of Samuel; instead, the generation for which we receive a birth story is precisely the one where King David has questionable foreign influence.[83]

The book of Ruth centers on Naomi's need to find acceptance in the village of her dead husband, and ultimately to find security for her old age there, by marrying Ruth into her husband's clan. Naomi's acceptance and security in Judah will become Ruth's, and so Ruth acts as a willing partner in Naomi's plans. Boaz, the Judean next-of-kin, acts as "the redeemer" (*gōʾēl*) and redeems the property of Naomi's dead husband and takes Ruth as his wife (Ruth 4:3–11). The culmination of the book celebrates the birth of Obed, a son who will bring security to both women, and a son who is immediately identified as the grandfather of King David (Ruth 4:13–22).

The birth story of Obed resembles those of Isaac and Moses for the simple reason that we once again have an outlandish story of breastfeeding in the context of a narrative about a foundational royal figure who could be viewed as tainted by foreignness. Obed's conception is the result of both human manipulation and divine intervention. Naomi, Ruth, and Boaz have worked the tribal system in a variety of ways in the fields, on the threshing floor, and at the city gate in order to achieve the result of this marriage—a son. At the same time, Yahweh is the one who grants the conception: "So Boaz took Ruth, and she became his wife, and he came into her, and Yahweh granted her a pregnancy, and she bore a son" (Ruth 4:13). The women of the village respond to the birth with praise for Boaz, Naomi, and Ruth, and then we read: "Naomi took the child and placed him at her breast [*wattēšītēhû bĕḥēqāh*], and she became his wet nurse [*ōmenet*], and the village women called out his name, saying, 'A son has been born to Naomi.' And they [the same village women] called his name Obed; he is the father of Jesse, the father of David" (Ruth 4:16–17). This is the first example where the birth mother is not the one who breastfeeds the foundational son, and, significantly, the birth mother is Moabite. Naomi, who like Sarah is post-menopausal, is presented as one who can act as wet nurse to Ruth's son.[84] Translations and commentaries often obscure the breastfeeding in this text, preferring to understand Naomi as a kind of foster mother or doting grandmother. Nielsen, for example, translates Ruth 4:16, "And Naomi took the boy and put him in her arms, and she cared for him like a mother."[85] Victor Matthews and André LaCocque both follow the NRSV translation that preserves the Hebrew word for "breast" but refrains from translating *ŏmenet* as "wet nurse."[86] The NRSV translation reads, "Then Naomi took the child and laid him in her bosom and became his nurse." Athalya Brenner emphasizes the maternal role of Naomi, noting that she becomes Obed's "nurse or adoptive mother," and the boy is referred to as "her son," but she does not analyze the significance of nursing language here.[87]

The difference in translations depends largely on the words *ŏmenet* from the root *'-m-n* and *ḥêq*. LaCocque has correctly noted that the term *ŏmēn* "is not limited to suckling."[88] I would agree and suggest that *ŏmēn* has greater semantic range than the other Hebrew term for wet nurse, *mêneqet*, "the one who gives suck," since the latter is only applied to women and the former is applied to both men and women.[89] Still, there is sufficient evidence for understanding *ŏmēn*, even in its masculine form, to have a base meaning rooted in the idea of breastfeeding. The feminine noun *ŏmenet* is used only twice, once to refer to Naomi and once to refer to the wet nurse of Mephibosheth (Ruth 4:16; 2 Sam 4:4). When it refers to men, it can simply mean "guardian," as in 2 Kings 10:1 where Jehu sends a letter to "the commanders in Jezreel, the elders, and to the guardians [*ŏmnîm*] of the sons of Ahab." In several other cases, however, the reference to a man as an *ŏmēn* does not preclude the understanding of wet nurse. Isaiah's metaphorical use of the term places it in poetic parallelism with *mêneqet*:

> Kings will be your wet nurses [*ŏmnayik*],
> and their princesses will give you suck [*mêniqōtayik*]. (Isa 49:23)

A similar metaphorical application of the term "wet nurse" to a man is found when Moses applies the word to himself. Moses is angry with Yahweh on account of the excessive burden he carries in leading a rebellious people out of Egypt, and he laments his station in life using a series of female-identified terms: "Did I conceive [*hārîtî*] this entire people, give birth to him [*yĕlidtîhû*], that you would say to me 'carry him at your breast [*bĕḥêqekā*] as a wet nurse [*ŏmēn*] carries a suckling [*yōnēq*] all the way to the land that you swore to their fathers?'" (Num 11:12).[90] The man who received his ethnic identity in part through the Hebrew Levitical breast milk of his mother can now imagine himself offering that milk-sourced identity to a rebellious people who refuse to acknowledge their national deity, Yahweh. We also find the entire female-focused process of child formation presented in this text, where Moses conceives, gives birth, carries, and breastfeeds a rebellious people who are referred to metaphorically as a "suckling." The combination of the nouns 'ōmēn (wet nurse, guardian) and ḥêq (breast, bosom) is exactly what we find describing Naomi in Ruth 4:16.

Like Moses, Mordecai is a man who is labeled an 'ōmēn in a literary context that suggests the transmission of ethnicity. Mordecai becomes Esther's 'ōmēn when her mother and father die. While English translations translate the term "guardian," "foster father," or "adoptive father" (Esther 2:7),[91] Mordecai plays the role of both mother and father to Esther. The term 'ōmēn is introduced in a way that links Esther's hidden Jewish identity, her awareness of "her birthplace and her people," to the time she spent under Mordecai's "guardianship" (bĕ'ōmnâ) (Esther 2:20). Moreover, the narrative that introduces Mordecai's role as an 'ōmēn who establishes the Jewish identity of his adoptive daughter Esther begins, as do our other breastfeeding narratives, by providing Mordecai's complete genealogical credentials. He is identified as coming from the royal tribe, clan, and father's house of Saul: "In the fortress of Shushan lived a Jew by the name of Mordecai, son of Jair son of Shimei son of Kish, a Benjaminite" (Esther 2:5). So even without an explicit reference to breastfeeding, we have the related idea that Mordecai has acted in a role that confers upon Esther her Jewish identity and her royal potential, and like Moses, she will be called upon to protect her own people against a foreign threat while residing as a dependent in the home of a foreign ruler. The young Moses and the young Esther will both draw on the fortitude of their ethnic identity to stand up for their people against a foreign ruler.[92]

The range of uses for the masculine and feminine forms of 'ōmēn suggest that this was a term one could use to signify a woman who literally served as a wet nurse or a man who served metaphorically as a wet nurse. It could also be used for men who served as guardians of minor royal sons. In light of Sarah, we could certainly read Naomi's act of taking her grandson Obed to her breast and becoming his wet nurse as a literal indication that she became his wet nurse. The symbolic breastfeeding that we find in the Islamic and Irish texts, however, offers the possibility that Naomi's breastfeeding could be read in a similarly symbolic fashion. The act of Naomi taking her grandson to her breast as a wet nurse would then convey a transference of her Judean ethnicity to this child of a Moabite mother.[93]

The noun ḥêq also has a broader range of meanings than the most common Hebrew word for breast, šad. BDB defines the word as "bosom," an English word rarely used today.[94] Surveying its varied contextual uses in the Bible, the word ḥêq could appropriately be rendered "chest (of a man)," "breast (of a woman)," "embrace (a person to one's chest or breast)," and "lap."[95] It is most often used for an embrace as in "the wife or husband of your embrace" (Deut 13:6; 28:54, 56; 2 Sam 12:3, 8; 1 Kings 1:2; Micah 7:5; Prov 5:20). This is the meaning when Sarai gives Hagar into Abram's "embrace" (Gen 16:5). One can also carry something or place something at one's breast or chest (1 Kings 17:19; Isa 40:11; Pss 35:13; 74:11; Prov 6:27; 21:14; Lam 2:12). The ḥêq can mean the part of one's garment that covers the chest or breast (Exod 4:6; Prov 17:23). In several texts the ḥêq is the bodily site (breast or lap) that takes in punishment or rebuke (Isa 65:6; Jer 32:18; Pss 79:12; 89:50; Job 19:27; Eccles 7:9). In the case of Ruth 4:16–17 and Num 11:12, ḥêq occurs together with the word ʾōmēn/ʾōmenet in the context of the birth of an infant. Numbers 11:12 describes the infant as "a suckling."[96] We have the same confluence of circumstances in the famous story of two prostitutes who give birth to boys. The mother of the dead infant steals the living infant and "lays him at her breast [ḥêqāh]," and she lays her dead son "at the breast" of the other prostitute (1 Kings 3:20). In this text, we have the image of a nursing infant sleeping at the breast of his mother. The story could have been written such that the mother of the dead child steals the living infant from her mother's chamber, bed, or arms. Instead, the storyteller chose to describe how the prostitute steals and lays claim to the living infant by "laying the child at her breast," an action that signifies her claim to him as her "son." The same combination of sucklings and the ḥêq of their mothers occurs in Lam 2:11–12. Because this text is set in war-ravaged Jerusalem, instead of nursing or sleeping peacefully at the ḥêq of their mothers, the sucklings (ʿôlēl wĕyônēq) are faint and "pour out their spirits on the ḥêq of their mothers."[97] The verb "pour out" seems consciously chosen as the reverse of what would happen in less disastrous times when a mother's milk would pour from her breast to her suckling infant. The word ḥêq, therefore, can designate a man's chest, a woman's breast, or a person's lap. When a text describes a newborn infant or suckling placed at the ḥêq of a mother or of a man imagining himself in maternal terms, the most appropriate translation is "breast" with the associated meanings of holding close and nursing.[98]

We see the maternity of Naomi paired with the paternity of Boaz in the use of names, kinship labels, and mediated and unmediated pathways to foundational men in the last ten verses of the book of Ruth. Throughout, the narrator has repeatedly reminded us that she is "Ruth the Moabite." But once this outsider Ruth has given birth to the insider, foundational male figure, her name disappears entirely from the story. Moreover, the kinship label that replaces her name is one that ties her directly to Naomi rather than to the son she has just birthed; she is a "daughter-in-law" to Naomi who is more valuable to Naomi "than seven sons" (Ruth 4:15). While the name "Ruth" disappears, Naomi's name is repeated three times in the five verses that describe the birth of Obed. First, "Naomi" took the boy and "placed him at her breast and became his wet nurse." Then, the women proclaim, "a son is born to Naomi" (*yullad-bēn lĕnāʿomî*) (Ruth 4:16–17).[99] This *puʿal* form "*yūllad l-*" is used in fourteen other biblical texts, and in each case it describes a biological son or sons born to a man by a woman (Gen 4:26; 10:21, 25; 35:26; 41:50; 46:22, 27; 2 Sam 21:20; Isa 9:6; Jer 20:15; Ps 87:4, 5–6; 1 Chron 1:19). This verse in Ruth seems to imply that Ruth bore this son to her mother-in-law and to her mother-in-law's people. Therefore, when Naomi places him on her breast and becomes his wet nurse, we should understand this to mean that Obed has become a "suckling of Naomi's clan."[100] Naomi's taking the infant to her breast is the symbolic, ritual action required to confer upon Obed unquestionable Judean ethnicity.[101]

Once Obed has become the son of Naomi, he finds a place in the *tôlēdôt* of Perez, son of Judah. A book that began with the paternal genealogy of Elimelek of Bethlehem in Judah closes with the begettings of all the Judean men in the line of David.[102] Ten generations, ten paternal *hôlid*'s, bring us from Perez through Boaz to David. Ruth may have sworn loyalty to Naomi, to her people the Judahites, and to their god, Yahweh, but she remains "Ruth the Moabite." As part of the book's overall effort to acknowledge and correct David's Moabite ancestry, a drastic breastfeeding intervention is staged in which an aging Judahite grandmother becomes Obed's wet nurse. This is why in the sequencing of the culminating chapter of the book, we find that only after the breastfeeding notation does Obed find a name and a place in the *tôlēdôt* that lead to King David.[103]

Hebrew narrative provides evidence for the understanding of breastfeeding as a practice that conferred on sons tribal identity, royal or priestly status, and in some cases ritual purity. In ancient Near Eastern myths and in the postexilic writings of Second and Third Isaiah, breast milk is a substance that transmits royalty and/or divinity from the wet nurse to the suckling. Human and divine princes are said to suck the breasts of goddesses, an act that prefigures their ascension to kingship. Returning exiles sucked at the breasts of their capital city, Jerusalem, and accrued the royal traits of majesty and splendor. Jerusalem herself sucks the breasts of kings and becomes royal once again. Breastfeeding narratives figure into the birth stories of three foundational male figures—Isaac, Moses, and Obed (David)—and one ritually set-apart priest, Samuel.[104] In the case of Isaac, the suggestion that he was nursed by his mother, Sarah, raises his status as the chosen heir. Unlike Ishmael, Isaac is conceived after Abraham had been circumcised, meaning he is conceived within the Abrahamic covenant. Unlike Ishmael, Isaac is born to a primary wife who hailed from the Mesopotamian homeland, a woman whose name and covenantal promise suggest royalty. Because Sarah's name means "princess," and she is told "kings of people shall come forth from her," she is able to transmit royalty to her son Isaac through her womb and at her breasts. The stature of Moses, the law giver, the founding ancestor of the levitical priesthood, and the paradigmatic prophet, is likewise raised when we learn that he was carried in the womb of a daughter of Levi and nursed at her breasts and raised in her house until the point of weaning. For Obed, the son of a Moabite and the great-grandfather of King David, symbolic nursing at the breasts of his Judean grandmother clarify his insider Judean ethnicity. Finally, Hannah's adherence to the dietary restrictions of a Nazirite during her pregnancy and breastfeeding marks her son Samuel as a fully compliant Nazirite, set apart from conception and dedicated to the temple at the point of his weaning. Biblical writers present the formation of the child as a two-stage process that begins in the mother's womb and culminates at her breasts or at the breasts of a wet nurse. The Hebrew word pair breasts and womb is shorthand for substantive transmission of traits from a mother to the "son of her womb," to the suckling that she picks up and carries at her breasts. Through her breasts and womb, a mother establishes the bonds of loyalty within her own maternal clan; she creates an allied group of children who trace their relationship to each other through her. They become "brothers, sons of the same mother," and "siblings who nursed at the same breasts."

7 The One Who Opens the Womb (*peṭer reḥem*)

Ten years after Sarai and Abram had arrived in the Promised Land, and ten years after Abram had been promised that he would become a "great nation," Sarai turns to her husband and says, "You see now, Yahweh has prevented me from bearing a child, please, go in to my slave girl [*šipḥātî*], perhaps I will be built up through her" (Gen 16:2). These are, in fact, the first words we hear directly from Sarai in the Bible, and as such should be understood as "revelatory" with regard to Sarai's character.[1] They are words that contemporary scholars have struggled to translate.[2] The verb form *'ibbāneh*, which I have translated "be built up," is most readily understood as the *nip'al* imperfect of *b-n-h* (build). A second understanding of the same verb, however, takes *'ibbāneh* to be a denominative verb from the noun *ben* meaning "perhaps I will have a son through her." The Hebrew verb *bānâ* is used to denote "the 'building' of a family, people, dynasty, or individual, and to describe the creation of the world in theological contexts." The words *bēn* and *bat*, "son" and "daughter," are considered by some to be "derivatives" of build. The cognate verbs in Ugaritic and Akkadian, *bny* and *banû*, respectively, mean "to build," "to engender," as in a father engendering a son, and "to create."[3] Translating Gen 16:2 as "perhaps I will have a son through her" certainly fits well with the text as we have it since Sarai did hope to have a son through her slave girl Hagar. The problem with this translation, however, is that it limits the possible aspirations of Sarai in her decision to give her slave girl to Abram as a wife. Yes, Sarai wants to have a son, but she wants to have a son so that she can be built up in the house of her husband.[4]

What did it mean when a wife wished to be "built up"? Later in Genesis, we read that Rachel shared the same aspirations when, in a very similar situation, she says to her husband Jacob, "Look, here is my maidservant ['ămātî] Bilhah. Go in to her so that she might bear a son upon my knees and I also might be built up ['ibbāneh] through her" (Gen 30:3). The "I also" or "even I" (gam-'ānōkî) in this verse refers back to Leah, who has already been built up through the birth of four sons (Gen 29:31–35). Commentators routinely focus on the emotional aspects of Sarai's and Rachel's desires for a child. They have described Sarai's barrenness as "a misfortune of overwhelming proportions"[5] and "a great sorrow."[6] The verb "to be built up," however, communicates much more than maternal emotions; it signifies Sarai's and Rachel's desire to inaugurate their own "house" within the house of their husbands through bearing a son.[7] We see that a wife's need for a son was distinct from yet supportive of her husband's need for an heir, and biblical Hebrew recognizes these separate needs by having different terms for the firstborn of a father, "the first fruit of his vigor" (rēʾšît 'ōn), and the firstborn of a mother, "the one who opens the womb" (peṭer reḥem). The birth of a son should not be viewed simply as fulfilling some primal maternal need; again we are not talking only about emotions.[8] Instead, the child who opens his mother's womb establishes her house within the larger household of her husband. He "builds up" his mother by raising her status in comparison to that of the other women in the household of her husband and by providing her with prestige among the community of women in her husband's village.[9] The womb-opening son builds up his mother because through him, she will secure economic maintenance for life and social prestige among women in her house and village.[10] Finally, within a polygynous house of the father, womb openers as a group are aspiring heirs; they compete one with the other, pitting one maternal house against another within the larger house of the father.

Being "Built Up" in the House of Abraham

Several biblical examples demonstrate that the aspirations of a wife in having a son were distinct from and yet supportive of the aspirations that a husband had in securing a male heir. Throughout the Hebrew Bible, we find the articulation of a paternal ideal in which a man's procurement of a male heir was associated with building up his own house. Through his son, a father maintained his name, house, and monument, and found a place in the *tôlēdôt* (paternal begettings) of his house's origin story. One of the clearest examples of this is Yahweh's promise to make David's name great by making "a house" for him. The house spoken of in this text was clearly a continuing dynasty of David's "seeds," or "descendants" (*zeraʿ*), which would come forth from his "own loins" (2 Sam 7:11–12). A man's not having descendants in the Bible was likened to having "no name," "no monument," or being "blotted out."[11] The name of Ruth's husband, Mahlon, who died without sons, may well carry the symbolic meaning of "infertile" and by extension "blotted out."[12] When Boaz agrees to redeem Elimelech's property and marry "Ruth the Moabite, wife of Mahlon," he does so in order "to raise up the name of the dead in his inheritance, that the name of the dead may not be cut off from his brothers and from the gate of his place" (Ruth 4:10). On that occasion, "all the men at the gate, the elders," pronounce a blessing on Boaz, and through the language of this blessing, we gain a view into the value and purpose of marriage expressed through men's eyes:

> May the Lord make the woman, who is coming into your house,
> like Rachel and Leah, who together built up the house of Israel.
> May you be strong in Ephrathah and be called by name in Bethlehem;
> And may your house be like the house of Perez whom Tamar bore to Judah,
> because of the descendant (seed) that Yahweh will give you by this young woman.

> *yittēn yhwh ʾet-hāʾiššâ habbāʾâ ʾel-bêtekā*
> *kĕrāḥēl ûkĕlēʾâ ʾăšer bānû šĕtêhem ʾet-bêt yiśrāʾēl*
> *waʿăśê-ḥayil bĕʾeprātâ ûqĕrāʾ-šēm bĕbêt lāḥem*
> *wîhî bêtkā kĕbêt pereṣ ʾăšer-yālĕdâ tāmār lîhûdâ*
> *min-hazzeraʿ ʾăšer yittēn yhwh lĕkā min-hannaʿărâ hazzōt.* (Ruth 4:11–12)

From this blessing we learn that a man looks to marriage in order to produce "seeds" that will build up "his house" and perpetuate "his name." Once again, we find the mixing of house-building and childbearing. This, however, is not a house-of-the-mother text; it does not describe how Ruth will be built up, nor how Rachel, Leah, or Tamar were built up. This is a house-of-the-father text; it expresses the hope that Mahlon's (or more likely Elimelech's) house will be built up through Boaz and Ruth in the same way that the house of Jacob (Israel) and later that of Judah were built up through sons born to their wives.[13]

When we turn to the house that Abram hoped to establish or build up, his paternal anxieties are most clearly articulated in Gen 15. At this point in his story, Yahweh had already promised Abram that he would become "a great nation" (Gen 12:2). In Gen 15, Abram has a vision of Yahweh in which Yahweh reassures him that his "reward would be very great" (Gen 15:1).

Abram, in a rare moment of complaint, challenges his god saying, "My lord Yahweh what will you give me? I walk about childless, and the heir of my household is Eliezer of Damascus" (Gen 15:2). He continues, "You have given me no seed [*zeraʿ*], and a house slave will be my heir [*yôrēš ʾōtî*]" (Gen 15:3). Yahweh then reassures Abram by telling him that his heir would be a biological son, "one who comes forth from your loins" (*yēṣēʾ mimmēʿĕkā*) (Gen 15:4). The entire conversation of Gen 15 is concerned with securing the house of the father headed by Abram; the language of seed and coming forth from the loins is anchored in male reproductive capacities. Sarai is not mentioned. The chapter focuses on the land inheritance that will be received by Abram's male heirs, who will number greater than the stars in the heavens. The covenant specifically promises, "To your seeds [*lĕzarʿăkā*] I give this land, from the river of Egypt to the great river, the river Euphrates" (Gen 15:18).[14] Genesis 15, therefore, is a house-of-the-father text that articulates concerns specific to a man's house: house, seed, land, and inheritance (see fig. 5).[15]

In Gen 16, Abram secures a male heir in his son Ishmael, one who came forth from his own loins. It is not until the next chapter, however, that Abram learns from God (*Elohim*) that Ishmael is not the heir to the promises that have been made. In that chapter, God ritually codifies his earlier promises of land, blessing, and sons through the cutting of a covenant, and he makes it known that these covenant promises are not only specific with regard to Abram, namely that the heir would come forth from his own loins, but also with regard to Sarai. The aged Sarai would "become nations, kings of peoples shall come forth from her" (*wĕhāyĕtâ lĕgôyim malkê ʿammîm mimmennâ yihyû*) (Gen 17:16). Whereas Gen 15 makes a promise specific to the house of the father, Gen 17 makes a promise specific to both the house of the father and the house of the mother.[16] That Abram, here renamed Abraham, already has his male heir at the time when Yahweh promises a son for Sarai (now Sarah) is clear from Abraham's response: "Oh that Ishmael might live in your sight" (Gen 17:18). Yahweh reiterates that the heir to his promise of a land inheritance is specific with regard to the house of the mother, insisting three times that the one who would inherit the covenant would be the child that Sarah would bear (Gen 17:16, 19, 21).

Sarai's different perspective on this process of securing an heir for Abram's household and covenantal promises is evident from the very first words she uttered: "perhaps I will be built up through her." Sarah was looking to establish herself, her own place in the covenantal promises. Valuable time had passed, and she had not been able to have a child. In her view,

Yahweh had prevented her from having a child, so Sarai turned to the practice of procuring an heir for the house of the father and a uterine family for herself through the surrogate services of her slave girl.[17]

Several details demonstrate that the child born from a union of Abram and Hagar would not only be an heir or firstborn for Abram but would also "build up" Sarai's status within Abram's household.[18] In Gen 16, Hagar is consistently referred to as "Sarai's slave girl" (*šipḥâ*) by Sarai, the narrator, Abram, and the angel of Yahweh (Gen 16:1, 2, 3, 5, 6, 8). Sarai is likewise referred to as Hagar's mistress or *gĕberet* (Gen 16:4, 8, 9). The title *gĕberet* and the related feminine noun *gĕbîrâ* are interesting in that they come from the essentially masculine root *g-b-r* ("to be manly").[19] This masculine root becomes the feminine noun *gĕberet* when a woman is deputized to act in a male managerial role, and this only happens when women are *gebers* over other women.[20]

Sarai's plan to be built up through Hagar, however, went awry from the moment Hagar conceived. Jacob Weingreen's translation of Gen 16:4 captures the import of the Hebrew: "and when she saw that she had conceived, her mistress *lost status* in her eyes" (Gen 16:4).[21] The hierarchy of the house is disrupted when Hagar achieved easily what had eluded Sarai for decades. This disruption is also evident in a significant shift in the possessive titles listed above. In Gen 16:3, before Hagar's pregnancy, the complete hierarchy of Abram's house is intact: "Sarai, Abram's wife, took Hagar the Egyptian, her slave girl, and gave her to Abram, her husband, as a wife." In this verse we see an explicitly marked change in status for Hagar from slave girl (*šipḥâ*) to wife (*'iššâ*), but even as a "wife," Abram continues to see Hagar as subordinate to Sarai: "your slave girl is in your power, do to her as you please" (Gen 16:6). Significantly, however, at the moment of conception, Hagar is referred to for the first time without the qualifying phrase "Sarai's slave girl": "He went into Hagar, and she conceived" (Gen 16:4). Far from being built up through Hagar, Sarai perceived that she had lost status in her husband's house and apparently lost a slave girl as well. Rather than building her mistress up, Sarai perceived that Hagar had managed to lower her. This is the kind of story that led to the proverb:

> Under three things the earth trembles; under four it cannot bear up:
> A slave when he becomes king, and a fool when he is filled with food;
> An unloved woman when she gets a husband,
> and a slave girl [*šipḥâ*] when she succeeds her mistress [*gĕbîrtāh*].
> (Prov 30:21–23)[22]

The failure of Sarai's plan is also seen through the fact that Abram, rather than Sarai, names the child. Leah and Rachel both name the children of their maidservants, and neither of their maidservants is presented as usurping their mistress's position in the house (Gen 30:1–24).

In our two parallel stories of wives who wish to be built up through their slave girl or maidservant, we find that Sarah, Rachel, Hagar, and Bilhah are all referred to with the single Hebrew term meaning "wife" (*'iššâ*) (Gen 16:1, 3; 29:28; 30:4). Even though they are all called wives, however, the status differentiation between them is clear. I find the work of Rubie Watson, an anthropologist who has studied status differentiation among women in patrilineal households in South China, suggestive here. She argues that economic criteria are not sufficient to distinguish among household women. If one looks solely at issues of inheritance, for example, women fall into a single category as those who do not inherit.[23] In order to ascertain the differences between women in a household, Watson suggests examining three criteria: how wives, concubines, and maids entered a household (through a marriage contract or ritual negotiated by their kin, through purchase, or through some other means); whether they retained any ties to their natal family after the marriage; and whether their entry into the husband's household created new kin ties for their husbands, brothers, and future offspring.[24] Today we might qualify Watson's description of a low-status wife as one obtained "through purchase," but her basic observation is correct: the degree to which a woman's family was involved in her marriage negotiations prior to and following her move into the household of her husband determined her status within her husband's house.[25]

Hagar entered Abram's household as a slave girl (*šipḥâ*) of Sarai. She became a wife (*'iššâ*) of Abram not through a marriage ceremony brokered by her uterine family but under the direction of her mistress, Sarai. Hagar's family of origin never enters the narrative, though it is significant that she returns to Egypt to secure a wife for her son. Thus, even though both Sarai and Hagar are referred to with the Hebrew word for wife, the manner through which Hagar entered the household and became a wife demonstrates that her status was still subordinate to Sarai. This is the root of Sarai's anger when rather than being built up through a son born to Hagar, she loses status.

Before examining how Sarai ultimately became "the mother of nations," I want to highlight several other biblical texts in which a husband's need for a son is distinct from his wife's need for a son. We have already mentioned the parallel story of Rachel, who wished to be built up in the house of Jacob through a son born to her maid Bilhah. Rachel's situation, however, is quite different from that of Sarai. Rachel's husband, Jacob, had no problem producing heirs. His first wife, Leah, manages to produce four sons in four verses (Gen 29:32–35). Jacob's name and monument are secure; he does not need a son from Rachel to build up his house. Rachel's need for a son is independent of the needs of the house of the father. According to Rachel, her very life depends on producing sons: "Give me sons, or I will die" (Gen 30:1). Jacob's cavalier response to Rachel shows that he had no anxiety related to the procurement of an heir for his house. Jacob responds to Rachel's desperation with anger, saying, "Am I in the place of God, who has withheld the fruit of the womb from you?" (Gen 30:2).

Here it is helpful to recall the similar lack of understanding attributed to Elkanah, the husband of Peninnah and Hannah (1 Sam 1). Elkanah also had secured plural male heirs to guarantee the future of his house through his fertile wife Peninnah. Therefore, when Hannah asks for a son of her own, he shows his lack of understanding for her situation when he asks her, "Am I not more to you than ten sons?" (1 Sam 1:8). While Hannah does not tell him, "No, in fact, you are not worth more to me than ten sons," her fervent, deal-making prayer to Yahweh asking for a son lets the reader know that for Hannah, a loving husband could never compensate for a wife's lack of a son (1 Sam 1:1–20).[26] Having already secured their own sons, Jacob and Elkanah seem inattentive to their barren wives' desire and need for their own sons. They do not offer prayers to Yahweh, the opener of wombs, on behalf of their wives, and they dismiss their wives' concerns.

We can contrast the lack of concern and involvement of these heir-abundant husbands to those husbands who still lacked an heir. We have already mentioned Abram's lament to God that a house-born slave would be his heir. Likewise, when Rebekah is described as barren, her husband Isaac had not yet secured an heir through any other wife. As a result, her need for her own son coincides with Isaac's need for an heir. Thus, unlike Jacob and Elkanah, Isaac concerns himself with his wife's barrenness: "Isaac pleaded with Yahweh on behalf of his wife, because she was barren; and Yahweh responded to his plea, and his wife Rebekah conceived" (Gen 25:21). Similarly, the heir-less Manoah is anything but dismissive when his long-barren wife reports a visit from an angel declaring that she would have a son (Judg 13). He demands to speak to the angel himself, and he offers a burnt offering in an effort to guarantee the outcome of this divine promise. He asks for clarification of the angel's instructions on what he and his wife are to do in order to be sure that the pregnancy will go to term and the promised son safely delivered (Judg 13:2–25).[27]

The story of Job captures the idea that a man's blessed state is expressed through a house full of children. The book opens describing Job as "blameless and upright" and "the greatest of all the people in the East," one whom Yahweh had "blessed" (Job 1:1, 3, 10). Job's blessed state consists of "seven sons and three daughters," and auspiciously numbered livestock and servants. The satan attributes Job's blessed state to the "fence" that Yahweh has placed around Job's "house" (*bayit*) (Job 1:10). Job's house is abundantly established; he is securely built up. Job's sudden and drastic transformation from a blessed to a cursed man is communicated in a way that expresses the unity of a man and his house. Job's physical house, his eldest son's dwelling, collapses on his social house, all his children: "Suddenly a great wind came across the desert, struck the four corners of the house, and it fell on the young people, and they died" (Job 1:19).[28] The biblical image of a destroyed man is a house collapsed upon the bodies of his dead children.

The Canaanite story of King Kirta features another male with a destroyed house. As mentioned in chapter 4, the story begins by relating how King Kirta's entire "house"—his wife and the "maternal clan" (*tar 'um*) that she had birthed—had been reduced to nothing. Kirta's response to this loss is to shut himself in his room and weep. The high god El then appears to Kirta in a dream and offers him riches and power to compensate for his loss. Kirta rejects the offer saying,

> Why should I want silver and gleaming gold, along with its land,
> or perpetual slaves, three horses,
> chariots in a courtyard, a slave woman's sons?
> Give me sons that I may be established,
> give me a clan that I may be magnified![29]

This story echoes that of Abraham before the birth of Ishmael, when he thought a house-born slave would be his heir (Gen 15:1–3). It also resonates with Job's restoration, which consists of a restored house and children (Job 42:10–17). Abraham's and Kirta's need for male heirs who come forth from their loins is as desperately voiced as Rachel's need for a son of her own in a paternal house that already had them.

Distinguishing the House of the Mother from the House of the Father: Ritual and Terminology

These stories show that within a household, the needs of wives and husbands at times overlapped as each desired to produce a son for the future continuance of the household. At other times, however, we see that the goals of wives and husbands were distinct. The Bible recognizes the differing needs of wives and husbands within the house of the father by using separate vocabulary for describing the child who meets the goals and needs of the father and the child who meets the goals and needs of the mother. We discussed some of these terms in chapter 4. The term *běkôr*, usually translated "firstborn," can be clarified as the firstborn biological child of a father with the paternally specific phrases "the first fruit of my vigor" (*rēšît 'ônî*) (Gen 49:3; see also Ps 78:51; cf. Ps 105:36) and one who "came forth from his thigh" (*yōṣě'ê yěrēkô*) (Judg 8:30). The Hebrew term "descendant" or "seed" can also be made paternally specific through adding the phrase "one who comes forth from your loins" (*yēṣē' mimmē'ékā*) (Gen 15:4; see also 2 Sam 7:12).

There are places, however, where the term *běkôr* is qualified by a phrase that indicates it refers to the firstborn of a mother within a polygynous household. Jon Levenson has discussed texts such as Exod 13:15, "every firstborn [*běkôr*] among my sons," and argues that they demonstrate the Bible's awareness that within a polygynous household there could be multiple "firstborns."[30] Deuteronomy 21:15–17 likewise acknowledges two types of firstborn sons when it distinguishes between the *běkôr* of the unloved wife, who is the father's firstborn, and the *běkôr* of the loved wife. Levenson then notes that biblical Hebrew has an unambiguous term for the firstborn of a woman in the Hebrew phrase, "the one who opens the womb," the *peṭer reḥem*. Surveying both biblical and Mishnaic texts on the uses of these terms, Levenson concludes that the Bible and later rabbinic law distinguished between the firstborn son of the father, who was significant in terms of inheritance, and the *peṭer reḥem*, the firstborn of the mother, who was significant in terms of requiring some form of sacrifice or redemption at the temple.[31] So, while the Hebrew term *běkôr* could refer to the firstborn of the father or the of the mother, there were also unambiguous terms for the firstborn biological son of the father and the firstborn biological son of the mother.[32]

Nicole Ruane stresses the exclusively "sacrificial contexts" where the term *peṭer reḥem* appears and notes the association of womb openers with the establishment of paternity and ownership of the child. In other words, a father establishes his paternity and ownership over a wife's womb-opening child through offering a sacrifice of redemption.[33] This establishment of paternity, however, does not need to be at the expense of the mother's ownership of that child, as Ruane asserts.[34] When a father claims ownership and paternity of a womb-opening son, the status of the son's mother is raised; her place within his household becomes secure.

The existence of a distinct term for the firstborn child of a mother speaks to biblical Hebrew's awareness that something new was brought into being when a woman gave birth to her first child. That "something new" came from the Israelite god, the opener of wombs, and therefore any womb opener required a ritual rite of redemption at his temple. The ritual presentation and redemption of a *peṭer reḥem* did not simply establish paternity, as Ruane asserts; it also marked the inauguration of a uterine family or "house of the mother." Personal names identified and celebrated womb openers. Jephthah, whose name means "he opens," is likely the firstborn son of his mother, the child who opened her womb (Judg. 11:1). Perez usurps his brother in the birth canal and is given the name "the one who broke through" or "the one who burst forth" (Gen 38:29). Later, a descendant of the usurped brother Zerah is named Petahiah, "Yahweh opens" (Neh 11:24), and the books of Ezra and Nehemiah include a Petahiah among the Levites, which suggests that this womb opener was dedicated to Yahweh's service (Ezra 10:23; Neh 9:5).[35]

In a recent study of Northwest Semitic personal names attested in epigraphic sources, Rainer Albertz makes several observations that are important to this study. First, he places a full third of all attested names in a category labeled "birth names" because they reflect the "religious experience of a mother during pregnancy, labor, or childbirth."[36] As such, he considers names to be a reflection of ancient Israelite and Judean women's "personal piety."[37] Based on biblical texts, Albertz identifies the opening of the womb as the moment of conception rather than birth (Gen 29:31; 30:22). He then examines the personal names attested in the epigraphic material and classifies ten distinct names that occur sixty-four times as names that allude to womb opening. These include several variations on *Pĕtaḥ*, which he translates "[DN] has opened [the womb]" and additional variations on *Niptaḥ*, translated "[the womb] was opened [by DN]."[38] All of these names fall into a larger category of "thanksgiving" names, whereby a mother gives thanks to a god for the conception and safe delivery of her child.

Several biblical texts then connect these womb-opening children to the inauguration of a mother's house. Psalm 113:9 juxtaposes a barren woman's procurement of children with her receipt of a "house":

> He [Yahweh] establishes [*môšîbî*] the barren woman in a house;
> making her the joyous mother of children.

Isaiah 54:1–2 also celebrates the transition of the barren one to the one who will have many children. Like Ps 113:9, the gift of children to the barren one is associated with cries of joy and a woman's own physical dwelling place:

> Sing, O barren one, who has not given birth;
> break forth into singing and cry aloud,
> you who have not been in labor!
> For the sons of the desolate one will be more
> than the sons of her that is married, says the Lord.
> Widen the place of your tent,
> Stretch out the curtains of your habitations;
> Don't hold back, lengthen your cords and secure your stakes.

The imperative verb "break forth" (*piṣḥî*) addressed to "the barren one" seems to command her womb to open, so that she can conceive, labor, and give birth. Moreover, calling her "the desolate one" (*šômēmâ*) recalls Absalom's sister Tamar who remains a *šômēmâ*, a childless woman, in her brother's house for the rest of her days (2 Sam 13:20).[39] Zion will not remain childless; her womb will open, and she will become the mother of so many children that she will have to enlarge her tent.

The opposite sentiment is also articulated when Job associates being barren with the burning of tents: "For the company of the godless is barren, and fire consumes the tents of bribery" (Job 15:34). Jeremiah imagines Yahweh allowing "Faithless Israel" to return to him as a wife and tells her:

> Again I will build you [*'ebnēk*], and you shall be built [*nibnêt*], O virgin Israel!
> Again you shall adorn yourself with timbrels,
> and shall go forth with the whirling of merrymakers." (Jer 31:4)

While this text does not connect being built up with the birth or return of children, the next verse does associate it with planting vineyards that bear fruit, and we have seen multiple examples where a woman's sexuality and childbearing potential are expressed metaphorically through the language of the vineyard.[40]

Again, the personal names that mothers bestowed on their children speak to this connection between conception and childbirth on the one hand and being built up or settled within a house or dwelling on the other. Albertz notes the Hebrew name *Běnāyāh*, literally "Yahweh builds," which occurs twenty-two times in the epigraphic material and twelve times in the Bible.[41] Additional variations on the root *b-n-h* add five additional Hebrew attestations, and names like *Banā'il* from the same root are attested in Ammonite, Aramean, and Phoenician texts. Albertz classifies these names as belonging to a series of "creation names" (e.g., *Sěbakyāhû*, "Yahweh has woven [the child in the womb]"), *'El'aśāh*, "El has made [the child]") and translates *Běnāyāhû* as "Yahweh has created [the child]." While *bānâ* can mean "to create," its primary meaning is "to build," and in light of the biblical association of childbearing and house building, I would translate the name "Yahweh has built up [the mother]." This translation places *Běnāyāhû* and its variants within a category of sentence names where the mother is the implied object. We begin with the *peṭaḥ* names discussed above, where Yahweh "opens" the womb *of the mother* to allow conception. Other names where the mother is the implied recipient of the action include a series of names where God is credited with taking away the stigma of childlessness and enacting revenge against rival wives, names that acknowledge that the mother has requested the child through oracle or vow, and names that praise God for remembering or hearing the prayer of the mother.[42] When a mother named her infant *Pěṭaḥ* or *Běnāyāhû*, she praised and gave thanks to Yahweh for opening her womb so that she could be built up in the house of her husband.

Sarai and Rachel, both barren, hoped that the son of their maids would build them up within the houses of their husbands. Sarai, however, was then promised that she herself would "become a mother of nations, kings of nations shall come forth from her" (Gen 17:16). Like the joy and singing that accompanied the birth of a son to a barren woman in Ps 113, Isa 54, and Jer 31, the birth of Isaac to Sarah is accompanied by laughter, as she says of his name Isaac, "God has made laughter for me; everyone who hears will laugh with me" (Gen 21:6). Chapters later this laughter-bringing son mourns the death of his mother and consummates his own marriage to Rebekah "in the tent of Sarah, his mother" (Gen 24:67). While Sarah was not "built up" as she had hoped via the birth of a son through Hagar, she was clearly built up through Isaac, becoming the mother of nations.

The Uterine Family as the Guarantor of Economic Maintenance and Social Prestige for a Wife in the Household of Her Husband

While the birth of a *peṭer reḥem* was accompanied by joy, it was not simply an emotional event. Producing a son secured a woman's continued existence and maintenance within the house of her husband. Biblical women consistently associate the birth of a son with life and childlessness with death. Recall Tamar's catastrophic failure in producing an heir in the household of Judah (Gen 38). Not only did she fail to produce a male heir but she was implicated in the death of two male heirs, and this resulted in her being consigned to "widowhood" in her father's house (Gen 38:7–11).[43] Just as Rachel demanded, "give me sons or I will die," Tamar's failure to produce sons resulted in her social death. The daughters of Lot also perceived that without sons, they would die. This fear led them to get their father drunk and have sex with him so that, in their words, "we might live through the seed of our father" (Gen 19:32, 34).[44] The second Tamar, the daughter of David and uterine sister of Absalom, is yet another example of a sonless yet sexually used woman who was consigned to her uterine home, where the text indicates she "remained desolate for all her days" (2 Sam 13:20).[45] Not producing a son had devastating economic and social consequences for a woman.[46]

In addition to providing security in the form of guaranteed economic maintenance, a son provided his mother with prestige within the community of women and in society as a whole.[47] The Hebrew midwives who rescued the male infants from Pharaoh's death sentence were given "houses" (*bāttîm*) as a reward for "fearing God" (Exod 1:21). Normally, the word "houses" in this text is translated as "families" or "children."[48] While children are certainly an implied part of this divine gift, the word "house" signifies more than children. The Hebrew for this verse directly parallels that of Yahweh's covenant with David. In both cases, the deity "makes" for a person "a house":

> Because the midwives feared God, he made for them houses [*wayyaʿaś lāhem bāttîm*]. (Exod. 1:21)

> And Yahweh told you that he would make for you a house [*bayit yaʿăśeh-lĕkā YHWH*]. (2 Sam 7:11)

At the very least, we need to understand that the Hebrew midwives were "built up" or "established" within Hebrew society through the divine gifting of a household for them. Because they acted on behalf of the Israelite god to save the Hebrew boys, they became established and esteemed members of the Hebrew society, built up and secure, heading a "house of the mother" of their own.[49]

Marriage blessings and celebratory songs at the time of the birth of a child show this dual function of a son: economic security and social prestige among women. The birthing war between Leah and Rachel together with their surrogate proxies, Zilpah and Bilhah, articulates the goals that women understood to be met through the birth of sons. The triumphal names given to the sons signify their mothers' hopes. Even if the names use false or folk etymologies, these etymologies reveal the social value of sons within the community of women. Leah gave each of her first four sons names that articulated her hope for social prestige in her husband's house where she was the unloved wife. The first is Reuben, which literally means "Look! A son!" Leah, however, expands on the name saying, "Yahweh looked upon my affliction. Surely now my husband will love me." The second is Simeon, "Because Yahweh heard that I am hated." The third is Levi, "This time my husband will be joined to me," and the fourth son is Judah, "I will praise Yahweh" (Gen 29:31–34). Collectively, these four sons removed the reproach of the unloved wife culminating in her words of praise. The two sons born to Rachel through her maid Bilhah signified God's attentiveness to Rachel's needs and her victory over—read raised status in relation to—her sister Leah. Rachel names her first son born through Bilhah Dan, "God has judged me and given me a son also." She names her second son through Bilhah Naphtali, "I have wrestled with my sister and prevailed" (Gen 30:6–8). The two sons born to Leah through her maid Zilpah signified her good fortune and her raised status "among women," who would surely now refer to her as "happy" (Gen 30:9–13). The names of the last two sons that Leah bore to Jacob have both economic and prestige associations. The economic associations are seen in the words "hire" or "rent" that Issachar is said to provide Leah and the "gift" that Zebulun is said to provide.[50] The prestige aspect of these last two sons is seen in Leah's claim that her husband would "honor" her on account of the six sons she had borne him (Gen 30:17–20). Faced with a sister whose uterine family numbered eight male heirs, it is not surprising that when Rachel finally bore her own son, she names him something like "Give me another one," but she adds in terms of the prestige factor that this son "has taken away my reproach."[51]

E. A. Speiser, noting that the meanings the mothers attributed to their sons' names were false etymologies, suggests understanding them as "etiologies."[52] He then, however, contrasts the etiologies provided by the mothers in Gen 29–30 with those ascribed to Jacob, the father, in Gen 49 and Deut 33. For Speiser, the contrasting etiologies represent "distinctive traditions" or separate sources.[53] I would argue instead that the etiologies in Gen 29–30, pronounced over the children by their mothers at their births, provide a window into a mother's understanding of the value of a son. Of the eleven names explained by Rachel and Leah, ten are interpreted to bring or imply something positive for the mother. When Leah gave birth to her sons, she felt looked upon and heard by God, and she expected to be loved and joined to her husband. She beheld in her sons her own good fortune and raised social and economic status. When Rachel acquired sons, she felt that she had been judged by God and found worthy, she had prevailed over her sister, and finally God had taken away the reproach of childlessness.

The etiologies provided by Jacob on his deathbed at the time when his "house" would transfer to his sons articulated a father's understanding of which sons were worthy of receiving an inheritance. Jacob's deathbed blessings represent his fatherly evaluation of his sons' worth.[54] We can see the differences between paternal and maternal values in Jacob's and Leah's interpretations of the name "Levi." For Leah, the birth of her third son represented an irrevocable "joining" of her to her husband: "Now my husband will be joined to me" (Gen 29:34). Years later, that same son for Jacob had made Jacob's "house" odious through violence, so Jacob said of him, "O my spirit, be not joined to their [Simeon's and Levi's] company" (Gen 34:30; 49:6).

We can also see a mother's association of children with economic and social prestige in the song attributed to Hannah in celebration of the birth of Samuel. This womb-opening son allows her to "deride her enemies," to shut up the mouths of "the arrogant," to break the "bows of the mighty" (1 Sam 2:1–4).[55] If there is any doubt that we ought to read Peninnah, Hannah's rival wife, into any of these triumphal phrases, it becomes clear when Hannah celebrates with the words "the barren one has born seven and the one who had many sons is dried up" (1 Sam 2:5).[56] The birth of sons causes a change of status among women in a household and village. Sons affect the balance of power among women. This power is seen both in terms of prestige, "a seat of honor," and in terms of economic maintenance, "ceasing to be hungry" (1 Sam 2:5, 8). While Hannah's song is clearly also directed at the future hopes for her son, one cannot fail to see that on one level it is a battle song among women in a household in which the wife who was barren now claims victory over the one who had borne many sons.

A final example comes from the book of Ruth. We have already discussed the paternal blessing that Boaz received from the men at the gate concerning his "house" that would be built through Ruth. But the book of Ruth also records a maternal blessing pronounced by the women of the village over Naomi.[57] And this blessing refers to the house of the mother that will be built up for Naomi through Ruth and Obed.[58] When Ruth bears a son, the women of the village, compatriots of Naomi, understand this son to be Naomi's and give him the celebratory appellation "a son has been born to Naomi" (Ruth 4:17).[59] The women offer a series of chants and honorific names that illustrate what they understand this son to offer Naomi, and by extension Ruth (Ruth 4:13–17). The women of the community first bless Yahweh for not leaving Naomi without a redeemer, namely a living male connection to the household into which she had married (Ruth 4:14). Then, the women identify the economic value of the son Ruth bore to Naomi, saying, "He shall be a restorer of life and a nourisher of your old age" (Ruth 4:15). Naomi voices her complete loss of prestige as a woman with no husband and no sons when she insists upon her return to Bethlehem: "I went away full, but Yahweh has brought me back empty," meaning empty of sons (Ruth 1:21). Now, however, with the son that Ruth has borne "to Naomi," the women insist that Naomi's prestige exceeds that of a mother of the proverbial seven sons: "your daughter-in-law, who loves you, who is more to you than seven sons" (Ruth 4:15). The house of the mother inaugurated through the birth of Ruth's son, Obed, seems to be that of Naomi. Ruth is praised, and her place seems to be secure, but it is Naomi's economic maintenance and social prestige that has been restored through this son.[60]

In some ways, "Ruth the Moabite" serves as Naomi's surrogate just as "Hagar the Egyptian" had served as Sarah's slave girl and surrogate.[61] Both marry into the line of foundational men in the biblical tradition and have their marriages arranged by primary wives who are insiders from the biblical perspective. Both give birth to sons who are understood to belong to the primary, insider wife. Boaz was Naomi's next of kin (Ruth 2:1). The relationship between Boaz and Naomi is described using the preferred paternal pathway; he is "Naomi's kinsman on her husband's side."[62] If Naomi were younger, Boaz would have married her in order to preserve the name of Elimelech. Because she, like Sarah, was too old to bear children, she offered her daughter-in-law Ruth to him in her place. Unlike Sarah, however, Naomi is presented as one who had genuine concern for Ruth's well-being. When speaking with Ruth, Naomi refers to Boaz as "our kinsman"

(Ruth 2:20; 3:2). She also refers to Ruth as a "daughter" and prefaces her plan of marrying Ruth to Boaz with the stated commitment of providing a "house" for Ruth: "My daughter, should I not seek a house for you, that it may be well with you?" Ruth is also presented in terms that distinguish her from Hagar. Unlike "Hagar the Egyptian," who looked down on her mistress, "Ruth the Moabite" "loved" Naomi (Ruth 4:15).

Another key difference between Sarah and Naomi is that Sarah, the head wife, ultimately went on to give birth to her own son whereas Naomi did not. As such, the foreign Ruth's devotion to Naomi and to the Israelite god, and the lack of an heir born to the primary wife, placed Ruth in the Israelite genealogy as great grandmother of King David. Still, as discussed in chapter 6, Naomi is called on to serve, at least symbolically, as Obed's wet nurse in order to secure Obed's, and by extension, King David's, Judean ethnicity. Thus, while the Gospel of Matthew records the memory of Ruth and Boaz as the father and mother of Obed, the grandfather of David, they are both stand-ins for others (Matt 1:2–6). Boaz stands in for Elimelech, Naomi's dead husband, raising up "the dead man's name on his inheritance." In the genealogy, Boaz replaces Elimelech rather than Ruth's husband, Mahlon (Ruth 4:21). Ruth is the stand-in for Naomi who is not dead but post-menopausal—"do I still have sons in my womb?" (Ruth 1:11). Ruth's faithful service builds up Naomi through providing her with her own "house of the mother" and its concomitant security and prestige among women.

Womb Openers as a Mark of Strength within a Polygynous House of the Father

Womb openers established their mothers in the houses of their husbands; they built them up and secured their future. Additional sons could add to a woman's prestige and sense of security, but the place of the womb-opening son remained special. One of the places we see the special status of womb-opening sons is in royal succession fights between dynastic houses and within polygynous royal houses. Texts that narrate the struggle for succession within the house of the father draw the battle lines between mothers' houses. Sarah and Hagar each fight on behalf of their womb-opening sons, with Sarah claiming the victory: "I will not allow the son of this maidservant to inherit along with my son Isaac" (Gen 21:10). Often, one womb-opening son is pitted against a group of brothers born to different mothers from his own. Joseph's dream of ruling his brothers pits him as Rachel's womb-opening son against all the sons of his father, excluding

Benjamin, his uterine brother.[63] Abimelech was probably the womb opener of his Shechemite concubine mother, and he stages a coup against the seventy sons of his father's "wives" (Judg 8:30–31). Jephthah, whose name, "he opens," suggests that he was a womb opener, was sidelined by all his brothers, sons of his father's wife, because he was the son of a prostitute: "You shall not inherit anything in our father's house; for you are the son of another woman" (Judg 11:2). He later becomes the head of the house of Gilead. We have also seen that the seventh-century Assyrian king Esarhaddon stipulated succession within his house, anticipating divisions between maternal houses. On one side, we find "Assurbanipal, the great crown prince designate and his brothers, sons by the same mother as Assurbanipal."[64] On the opposing side, we find a grouping of Ashurbanipal's paternally related kin: "his brothers [aḫḫīšu], the brothers of his father [aḫḫī abīšu], the sons of the brothers of his father [mārī aḫḫī abīšu], the seed of his father's house [zēr bīt-abīšu]."[65] Finally, Baal fights "the sons of Asherah," all of whom have palaces, in order to become king of the gods.[66] It is not clear whether Ashurbanipal or Baal were considered womb openers, but their struggle to succeed their father is fought with reference to maternal houses.[67]

The biblical story of the "long war" between "the house of Saul and the house of David" is an excellent narrative through which to examine several of the kinship terms and relationships that we have studied in this book, including womb openers, womb sons, maternal alliances, the house of the mother, and direct and mediated pathways to the house of the father. The narrator introduces this war story using the language of competing houses: "David grew stronger and stronger while the house of Saul grew weaker and weaker" (2 Sam 3:1).[68] We then read the evidence for the assertion, "David grew stronger and stronger," and it comes in the form of a royal arsenal of six womb-opening sons:

> Sons were born to David in Hebron. Amnon, his firstborn, belonged to the Jezrealite. His second, Chileab, belonged to Abigail wife of Nabal, the Carmelite. His third [son] was Absalom, son of Maacah, daughter of Talmai, King of Geshur; and his fourth son was Adonijah, son of Haggith, his fifth was Shephatiah son of Abital, and his sixth was Ithreum, [born to] David's wife Eglah. These were born to David in Hebron. (2 Sam 3:2–5)[69]

The genealogical information provided here seems only to be interested in womb openers; if any of David's wives had second sons or daughters, this text is not interested in telling us about them. "How strong was David's house?" a reader might ask. It is six womb openers strong (fig. 8).

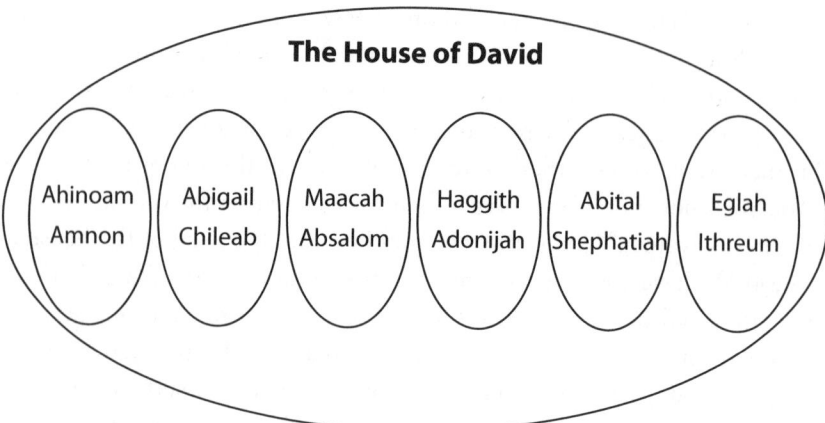

Figure 8. *David's arsenal of womb-opening sons, 2 Sam 3:2–5. Illustration created by Ondrea Keith, rendered by Bill Nelson.*

Meanwhile, the process of Saul's house "becoming weaker and weaker" involves David absorbing, neutralizing, or witnessing the elimination of every "seed" of Saul's house, beginning with Saul himself, together with his primary wife's womb-opening son. Saul's family composition is difficult to reconstruct with certainty. According to the Deuteronomistic Historian (DH), Saul and his wife Ahinoam had three sons and two daughters: Jonathan, Ishvi, and Malchishua (sons), and Merab and Michal (daughters) (1 Sam 14:49–50). The Chronicler's account attributes four sons to Saul, only two of whom appear in the DH's listing: Jonathan, Malchishua, Abinadab, and Ishbaal/Esh-baal (2 Sam 2:10; 1 Chron 8:33; 9:39). Saul's concubine Rizpah bore him two additional sons, Armoni and Mephibosheth (2 Sam 21:8). Saul's son Jonathan had one son named Mephibosheth/Meribaal (2 Sam 4:4; 1 Chron 8:34; 9:40). Saul's daughter Merab had five sons (2 Sam 21:8), and Michal had no children (2 Sam 6:23). Taken together, Saul had five sons and two daughters with Ahinoam and two sons with Rizpah (fig. 9). One helpful way to examine the near complete annihilation of the house of Saul is to use the language of direct and mediated pathways to the house of the father.[70] We recall that Abraham's sons were organized hierarchically where Isaac became the paternally claimed "Abraham-begotten son," while the "sons of his concubines" had maternally mediated kinship labels and were physically separated from the house of Abraham.[71] When we turn to the demise of the house of Saul, we can see that Saul's "seeds" are eliminated in

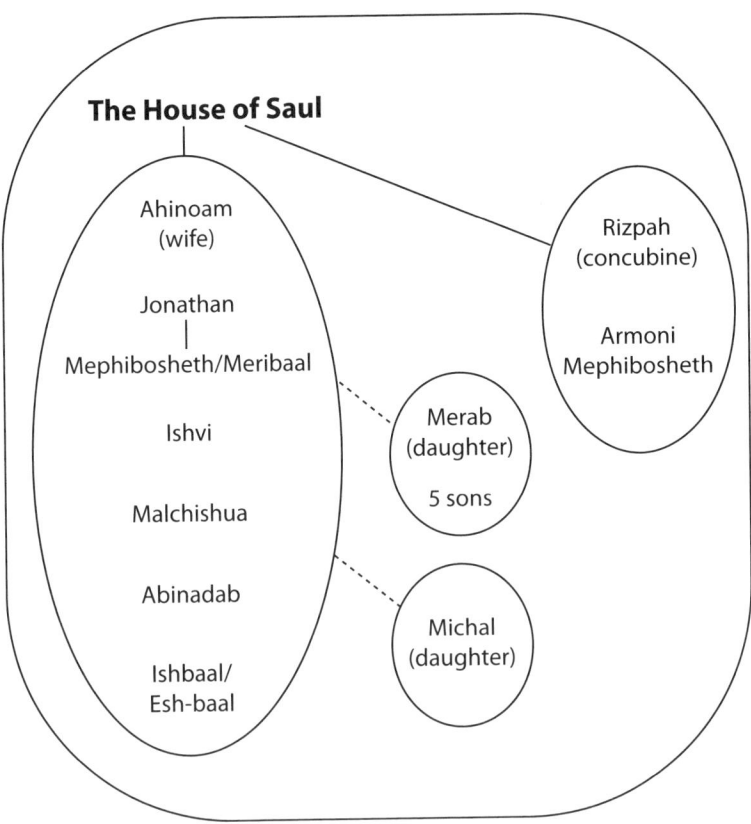

Figure 9. *The house of Saul with maternal subunits, a composite picture. Illustration created by Ondrea Keith, rendered by Bill Nelson.*

a logical order, beginning with his direct paternal heirs through his primary wife and moving only secondarily to maternally mediated kin.

The first blow against the "house of Saul" is what we might call a *tôlēdôt* blow. Saul and three of his direct lineal heirs, the sons of his loins, battle the Philistines on Mount Gilboa, and all four of them die together (1 Sam 31:1–6). The house of Ahinoam, his wife, has been reduced to one surviving son, two daughters, and one grandson by Jonathan. This is the event that precedes the announcement that Saul's house has grown weaker and weaker. Moving down Saul's paternal line, Ishbaal, his single surviving son born to his wife, inherits Saul's house (dynasty) and becomes king of Israel for two years (2 Sam 2:10).[72] With Ishbaal on the throne, the house of Saul is weak but certainly not eliminated.

This brings us to David and his role in reducing, weakening, and ultimately extinguishing the house of Saul. While David is rarely directly implicated in the death of a member of Saul's house, one of the ways we see his implied involvement is by observing the transfer of material and immaterial wealth from the house of Saul into the house of David. At the time of Saul's and Jonathan's deaths, David had already received as a gift Saul's armor, his bronze helmet, his coat of mail, and his sword (1 Sam 17: 38–39), and the robe, armor, sword, bow, and belt of Jonathan, Saul's *běkôr* and Ahinoam's womb-opening son (1 Sam 18:4). After Saul's death, an Amalekite delivers Saul's crown and armband to David (2 Sam 1:10). David's house, therefore, is not just growing stronger in terms of six, living, womb-opening sons born to wives; it is also amassing the material wealth of the house of Saul in the form of symbols of royal power.

The next piece of the house of Saul that David takes into his possession is "Michal, the daughter of Saul." After Ishbaal becomes king of Israel, David negotiates to have his wife Michal brought back to him, removing her from the house of her then husband Paltiel (2 Sam 3:12–16). In this geographic move, David absorbs Michal, "daughter of Saul," into his house and insures that she would not produce children, likely by refusing her sex (2 Sam 6:20–23). In a sense, David appropriates a "womb" of Saul's house and insures that it would not receive the gift of conception, pregnancy, and birth.[73] Shortly after the transfer of Michal, two of Ishbaal's captains murder him and bring his head to David (2 Sam 4:5–8). The narrative then shifts from Saul's four sons to his grandson, Mephibosheth, the firstborn of Jonathan. David absorbs and neutralizes Mephibosheth into his house by having him eat at his table (2 Sam 9:6–13). The tally of material wealth transferred into the house of David from the house of Saul has increased, adding the decommissioned womb of a princess, the severed head of a king, and a grandson. The maternal house of Saul's wife, Ahinoam, Saul's "*ṭar 'um*" so to speak, is now dead, snuffed out, or reduced to economic dependency at David's royal table.[74]

The last seven "seeds" of Saul have mediated, maternally marked pathways to the house of the father, but they clearly hold within them enough of the house of Saul that they require elimination. The Gibeonites ask David to hand over seven of Saul's sons in order to expiate the bloodguilt that the house of Saul had incurred against them (2 Sam 21:1–6). Once again, the number seven signifies the remaining fullness of Saul's house, which by this time comprised two weak maternal sub-houses. David hands over the two sons of Rizpah, Saul's concubine, and the five sons of Merab, Saul's older daughter (2 Sam 21:7–9). In a strong paternal house, none of these men would even be considered as potential heirs since they trace their pathways to the father through low-status wives and daughters. The Gibeonites impaled all seven of these sons of a concubine and sons of a daughter. In a final move of usurpation, David literally buries the house of Saul. He gathers the bones of Saul and Jonathan and the bones of the seven sons and grandsons that the Gibeonites had impaled and has them appropriately buried in their homeland of Benjamin (2 Sam 21:10–14).[75]

The very next chapter is David's victory song, fifty-one verses of congratulating himself as Yahweh's anointed. The song closes with David extoling Yahweh for showing steadfast love "to David and his seed forever" (2 Sam 22:50–51).[76] The house of David had grown "stronger and stronger" through the birth of six potential heirs to his throne, six womb-opening sons of wives. The house of Saul grew weaker and weaker through the methodical elimination of his maternal houses in order of their importance: the house of his wife; the house of his concubine; the houses of his daughters. Women's houses were the building blocks of men's houses. Eliminating a royal rival involved knocking down each maternal block.

No sooner does David claim victory over the house of Saul than his own house splinters into battling maternal units. DH presents this battle as the natural outgrowth of David's sin of adultery and murder in his affair with Bathsheba (2 Sam 11). The prophet Nathan had predicted as a result of this affair "the sword will never turn away from your house" (2 Sam 12:10). The battle lines of these sword fights are drawn between David's maternal houses as womb openers compete with one another to succeed David on his throne. In the first round, Amnon, the son of Ahinoam, faces off against Absalom, the son of Maacah (2 Sam 13). Absalom, David's third son and Maacah's womb opener, has Amnon, David's firstborn, murdered to avenge the rape of his sister (2 Sam 13:28–29).[77] Absalom then attempts to take David's throne by force and fails.[78] The second round of the succession fight begins when "Adonijah, son of Haggith, exalted himself saying, 'I will be king.'" The one who counters Adonijah, son of Haggith, is not Solomon but "Bathsheba, the mother of Solomon" (1 Kings 1:11; 2:13). In this final round, which ends with an heir ensconced on David's throne, the mother actually fights the battle on behalf of her son. Solomon was not a womb-opener; he was "the copy," the son who replaced the womb opener who died shortly after birth (2 Sam 12:15–19, 24).[79] When Bathsheba learns that Adonijah planned to have himself declared king, she intercedes for her son Solomon with David. She informs the aged David that if Adonijah were king, "I and my son Solomon will be counted as offenders" (1 Kings 1:21). Bathsheba's efforts succeed, and David swears to her, "Your son Solomon will reign as king after me and sit on my throne in place of me" (1 Kings 1:30).

When a biblical narrative records a woman's wish to be built up through having a son, it signifies her need for security, economic maintenance, and honor within the house of her husband. Being built up brought a woman prestige among the community of women in her husband's village. A woman's *peṭer reḥem* inaugurated her uterine family, her own generated "house" within her husband's house. Mothers celebrated womb-opening sons with praise and laughter, marked them with auspicious names, and ritually redeemed them at the temple. The special status of womb-opening sons becomes evident as they are pitted against each other during struggles for succession in elite and royal households. A mother brought her house into existence through birthing a son, she created a full maternal alliance when she birthed multiple sons, and she ascended to the status of senior mother in the paternal house when her womb-opening son defeated the sons of other wives and succeeded his father.

8 The House of the Father of His Mother (*bêt-'ăbî 'immô*)

Psalm 45, a hymn of praise in honor of an international royal wedding, offers an idealized representation of the gender-specific values expected within patrilocal marriage. In this psalm, a princess leaves the house of her father and moves into the palace of her new husband, a king. The psalm envisions the husband-king's place in his own house as permanent, extending backward in time to his foundational male ancestors and forward to his anticipated male heirs. It communicates this permanence using the language we have come to associate with idealized patrilineality: fathers, sons, land, name, memory, and ongoing generations of men:

Your sons will be in the place of your fathers,
you will make them princes over all the land.
I will bring your name to memory from generation to generation.
Therefore, the nations will praise you for eternity.

taḥat 'ăbōtêkā yihyû bānêkā
tĕšîtēmô lĕśārîm bĕkol-hā'āreṣ:
'azkîrâ šimkā bĕkol-dōr wādōr
'al-kēn 'ammîm yĕhôdukā lĕ'ōlām wā'ed. (Ps 45:17–18 [Eng. 16–17])

Thus, the man's place in his household is spoken of using terms that suggest permanence, continuity, and the passing of an inheritance to sons in the form of a remembered name and land from generation to generation.

In the advice offered to the bride, on the other hand, the language does not suggest any kind of permanence. In fact, patrilocal marriage seems to require a permanent break between the bride and her natal home:

Listen, O Daughter, and see, incline your ear.
Forget your people and the house of your father.
Then the king will desire your beauty
and because he is your lord, you will bow down to him.

*šimʿî-bat ûrěʾî wěhaṭṭî ʾoznēk
wěšikḥî ʿammēk ûbêt ʾābîk:
wěyitʾāw hammelek yopyēk
kî-hûʾ ʾădōnayik wěhištaḥăwî-lô.* (Ps 45:11–12 [Eng. 10–11])

This verse seems to suggest a permanent break between a daughter and her natal family when she marries out of her father's house. It contrasts the eternal recalling and lauding of the name of the husband's house with the imposed forgetting of the house of the father of the bride. In this royal wedding song, the bride's value in her husband's home rests in her beauty and her submissiveness. Like the wife who is described as a "fruitful vine in the inner recesses" of her husband's "house" (Ps 128:3),[1] this wife is envisioned as a transplant into her husband's palace, and the sons she will bear will establish her husband.

While psalms like these idealize the permanent break between a bride and her father's house, this chapter examines the narratives of Jacob, Abimelech, and Absalom in order to demonstrate that a wife often maintained lifelong ties to the house of her father. Far from forgetting the house of her father, a wife depended on the members of her father's house to advance her position in her husband's house. Her father's house could provide a safety net and support base for her adult children and could be instrumental in supporting her son's bid for succession in his father's house. What holds the stories of Jacob, Abimelech, and Absalom together is the shared references to a kinship unit called "the house of the father of the mother."

After Jacob stole his older brother's blessing from his blind father, his mother and coconspirator informed him that Esau planned to kill him. In order to protect her favored son, Rebekah told Jacob that he had to "flee at once to my brother Laban in Haran" and stay there until Esau's anger had abated (Gen 27:41–45). Rebekah then manipulated Isaac into sending Jacob away on the pretense of finding him a wife from their homeland. At Rebekah's urging, the aged Isaac called Jacob to him and ordered him: "Arise, go to Paddan-aram to the *house of Bethuel, your mother's father;* and take as wife from there one of the *daughters of Laban, your mother's brother*" (Gen 28:2). In Abimelech's story, we learn that after the death of his father

Gideon/Jerubbaal, "Abimelech, son of Jerubbaal, went to Shechem, to the *brothers of his mother,* and spoke to them and to all the families of *the house of the father of his mother*" (Judg 9:1). Abimelech, unlike the seventy sons of Gideon who were born to "his wives," was born to his father's concubine in Shechem (Judg 8:31). Finally, we read that Absalom, after arranging the murder of his older brother and King David's presumptive heir Amnon, "fled" to "Talmai son of Ammihud, king of Geshur" (2 Sam 13:37). While the term "house of the father of his mother" is not used here, we know from previous genealogical notations that this house is the house of the father of Absalom's mother, Queen Maacah (2 Sam 3:3).

The narrative contexts within which these references to "the house of the father of your mother" emerge involve a struggle for succession within the father's house between a younger son and his brothers. In the case of Abimelech and Absalom, the rival brothers are characterized as belonging to different uterine families or mother's houses within the house of their father. Both may well be the *peṭer reḥem* of their mothers. In the case of Jacob, the rival brothers are uterine siblings in a monogamous household, but they are presented such that each is aligned with one parent: Jacob is linked directly and repeatedly to his mother, Rebekah, while his twin brother Esau is tied to his father, Isaac. In each of the three narratives, the house of the father of one's mother provides refuge and protection to the fleeing son, who is related to them only through a daughter who has married out. The house of the father of the mother also provides the fleeing son with a livelihood or sustenance while residing away from his father's homeland. Finally, the members of the house of the father of one's mother supply money and people that strengthen the fleeing son, enabling him to return to his father's house and launch a credible campaign for succession within the house of his father.

Narratives that feature the house of the father of the mother provide evidence for the enduring quality of the relationship between a woman who marries out of her natal home and the brothers who remain within that home. These stories also demonstrate that the status of a mother in her husband's house is related to the power of and continued relationship with her father's house. A mother's strong bond with her father's house can then contribute to the status and success of her son in the house of his father.

Ideologically, the house of the father of the mother is a place a nephew resides during a time of crisis in his own father's house. It is his second best option when direct ascent into the position of heir in his father's house is not possible. In order for a son to become heir and establish a house of his own within the house of his father, he must ultimately break with his mother's father's house, meaning the sojourn in the house of the father of one's mother must be temporary and purposeful. Jacob and Absalom successfully leave the house of the father of their mother; Abimelech fails to make that break and, as a result, fails to become heir in his father's house.

Jacob and Laban

One of the four explicit references to the term "house of the mother" refers to the house of Rebekah's mother, where we find Rebekah's brother Laban, her unnamed mother, her father Bethuel, and her wet nurse (Gen 24:28–61). While Bethuel plays only a minor role in this narrative, we know something about the status of his house from the genealogies of the house of Terah. Bethuel is the son of Nahor, who is one of the three sons of Terah. We know that Bethuel's mother is named Milcah and that she is a wife, not a concubine, of Nahor (Gen 11:27–29; 22:20–23). We do not receive a name for Bethuel's wife, and if Bethuel had a concubine or another wife, the text is not interested in that detail. However, the repeated grouping of Rebekah with "her brother and her mother" in "her mother's house" signals a uterine family unit within which Laban and Rebekah are full siblings. Laban's authoritative role in the house of Rebekah's mother suggests that he is the son who will secure his mother's future if he inherits his father's house (Gen 24:28–32).[2] Decades later, when Rebekah's son Jacob flees his brother Esau, this house we knew from Gen 24:28 as "the house of her mother" has become "the house of Bethuel," a house where Rebekah's brother Laban is now in charge and a house Rebekah imagines as a refuge for her favored son.

Jacob and Esau are not only uterine siblings but twins that have shared their time in the womb, meaning we should expect them to form a maternal alliance.[3] However, we no sooner hear of their conception than we learn of their division. They fight and struggle in the womb, and Jacob emerges from the birth canal grasping onto the heel of his older brother Esau in what appears to be his first move toward usurping him (Gen 25:21–26). The division between the brothers is also marked through parental pairing: "Isaac loved Esau because he ate game, but Rebekah loved Jacob" (Gen 25:28). Kinship labels tie Jacob in a direct, unmediated pathway to his mother as "her son" (Gen 27:6, 17), and Esau to his father as "his son" (Gen 27:5).[4] Rebekah never refers to Esau as her "son"; only the narrator identifies him that way. In fact, Rebekah's path to Esau is mediated through Jacob when she refers to him as "Jacob's brother."[5] The physical description and life pursuits of the two men also align them to different parents and their corresponding genders and households. Esau is hairy, a trait the ancient world associated with masculinity, and he is a "skillful hunter and man of the fields" (Gen 25:27).[6] Jacob, however, is "smooth" like a woman, "a quiet man, dwelling in tents" (Gen 25:27; 27:11). As we saw in our discussion of gendered spaces, this reference to "dwelling in tents" may well align him with his mother.

We also find the pairing of Jacob and Rebekah versus Esau and Isaac in terms of personality traits. In chapters 5 and 6 we established that personality traits could be transferred from mother to child through her womb and breast milk. The shared personality traits of Esau and his father and of Jacob and his mother provide an ancient representation of what we would label cognatic kinship. Turning first to the household traits that mark Jacob, we have to begin with the house of Bethuel and his unnamed wife that produced Laban and Rebekah, and, through Rebekah, Jacob. Each of these figures is characterized by cleverness and trickery.[7] Jacob's emergence from the birth canal grasping his brother's heel already marks him as "clever" like the serpent in Genesis.[8] Jacob first tricks Esau into selling his birthright (Gen 25:29–34). Then, Rebekah and Jacob conspire together to trick Isaac and Esau so that Isaac mistakenly gives his blessing to Jacob instead of Esau (Gen 27). Rebekah then tricks Isaac into sending Jacob away to protect him from Esau (Gen 27:41–46). Laban tricks Jacob into marrying his older daughter Leah, and then insists that Jacob work an additional seven years for Rachel (Gen 29:21–30). Jacob tricks Laban out of his best livestock and escapes with his wives, children, and livestock to return to his father's house (Gen 30:29–43).[9] Finally, Rachel, in a move that marks her as the daughter who will carry on the family traits, steals and successfully hides Laban's household gods (Gen 31:19–35). The "house" that Bethuel's wife bore to him is a house marked by cleverness and trickery.

If there is a "house of Isaac" to which we can link Esau, it would be a house characterized by gullibility, misunderstanding, and a lack of direct contact with the Israelite god. As a boy, Isaac, ignorant of the conversation Abraham had had with his god, asks his father on the way to the mountain, "Look, the fire and the wood; but where is the lamb for a burnt offering?" (Gen 22:7). As a blind old man, Isaac reaches out and touches Jacob's pelt-covered arms and says, "The voice is Jacob's voice, but the hands are the hands of Esau," and he gives Jacob the blessing intended for Esau (Gen 27:22–23). Even though Isaac is the one who prayed to his god that his wife would become pregnant, he is not included in the divine revelation to Rebekah that the younger twin would be the stronger (Gen 25: 21–23). Esau, like his father, is gullible. He sells his birthright for a bowl of "red, red stuff"; he misses his opportunity to murder his tricky, usurping brother; and he ultimately yields the land of the covenantal promise to Jacob (Gen 25:29–34; 27:41–28:9; 33:15–20). He misunderstands his mother's aversion to his Canaanite wives and takes an Ishmaelite wife (Gen 28:6–9). Emotionally, Isaac and Esau are tied by their reactions to the trickery of the stolen blessing. The Hebrew phrasing that describes Esau's reaction to the trick consciously echoes the phrasing of Isaac's reaction. Isaac "trembled a great trembling exceedingly" (*wayyeḥĕrad yiṣḥāq ḥărādâ gĕdōlâ 'ad-mĕ'ōd*), and Esau "cried out a great and bitter cry exceedingly" (*wayyiṣ'aq ṣĕāqâ gĕdōlâ ûmārâ 'ad-mĕ'ōd*) (Gen 27:33–34).[10] Physical traits, life pursuits, and personality all conspire to pair Esau with Isaac and Jacob with Rebekah.

We now turn to the narrative that includes the reference to "the house of Bethuel, your mother's brother." After tricking Esau out of his father's blessing, Jacob learns from his mother's eavesdropping that Esau plans to kill him. Rebekah immediately seeks to protect Jacob, telling him "flee to Laban my brother in Haran." She is so fully implicated in the tricking of her husband regarding the blessing that she cannot tell Isaac the truth about Esau's murderous intentions. She must trick him yet again by telling him she cannot abide any more Hittite wives in the household, and Isaac must therefore send Jacob back to the homeland to take a wife. Isaac, as gullible and obedient as ever, calls Jacob to him, blesses him yet again, and tells him,

> Arise, go to Paddan-aram to the house of Bethuel, your mother's father, and take as a wife from there one of the *daughters of Laban, your mother's brother.*
>
> *qûm lēk paddenâ 'ărām bêtâ bĕtû'ēl 'ăbî 'immekā*
> *wĕqaḥ-lĕkā miššām 'iššâ mibbĕnôt lābān 'ăḥî 'immekā.* (Gen 28:2)[11]

The house of the father of Jacob's mother enters his narrative when his life is in danger and when his father's house is at a point of generational transfer.

Jacob flees, and once he arrives in Paddan-aram and meets Rachel, the language of "mother's brother" continues to dominate the narrative:

Now when Jacob saw Rachel the daughter of Laban, *his mother's brother*, and the sheep of Laban, *his mother's brother*, Jacob went up and rolled the stone from the well's mouth and watered the flock of Laban, *his mother's brother*. (Gen 29:10)[12]

Jacob then kisses Rachel and weeps. In previous narratives that we have examined, kissing and weeping is associated with uterine siblings. The woman speaker in the Song of Songs wished that her lover were like a milk brother, so she could kiss him in public. Joseph, upon seeing "Benjamin, his mother's son," had to leave the room to weep. Later, when he finally revealed to all his brothers who he truly was, he "fell upon his brother Benjamin's neck and wept; and Benjamin wept upon his neck. And he kissed all his brothers and wept upon them" (Gen 45:14–15a). In Jacob's case, he is kissing and weeping over a cousin related to him through his mother, one of the same maternal clan. Jacob then identifies himself as a "kinsman [literally brother] of her father" (*'ăḥî 'ābîhâ*) and as "the son of Rebekah" (*ben-ribqâ*) (Gen 29:12). This latter designation is especially significant. Up to this point in the narrative, the only time Jacob has been called Isaac's "son" is when Jacob is deceiving Isaac by pretending to be Esau (Gen 27:18–29). Here, when he speaks the truth, he identifies himself as "Rebekah's son," and we know that he is her son in both character and disposition.

When Rachel learns Jacob's identity, she "runs to her father," and the entity where Jacob ultimately receives welcome is "the house of Laban" (Gen 29:12–13). In the parallel story of Rebekah meeting the servant of Abraham at the well, she "runs to her mother's house" (Gen 24:28). The transformation of "the house of Bethuel" with the sub-house of Rebekah's mother within it to "the house of Laban" signifies that Laban succeeded his father as head of household upon Bethuel's death. As he ascended to the position of heir, his mother, if still alive, would ascend with him, becoming the senior woman in the house of her son with authority over his wife. The house of Laban, therefore, is the continuing entity of both the house of Bethuel and the house of Rebekah's and Laban's mother.

When Jacob meets Laban, the language of maternal kinship defines their relationship. Laban recognizes Jacob as "the son of his sister" (*ben-'ăḥōtô*) and greets him with hugs and kisses. Jacob's connection to Laban through his sister merits the assignation of shared "bone and flesh" as Laban declares, "Surely you are my bone and my flesh" (*'ak 'aṣmî ûbĕśārî 'āttâ*) (Gen 29:13–14). The added declarative "surely!" (*'ak*) may well suggest that

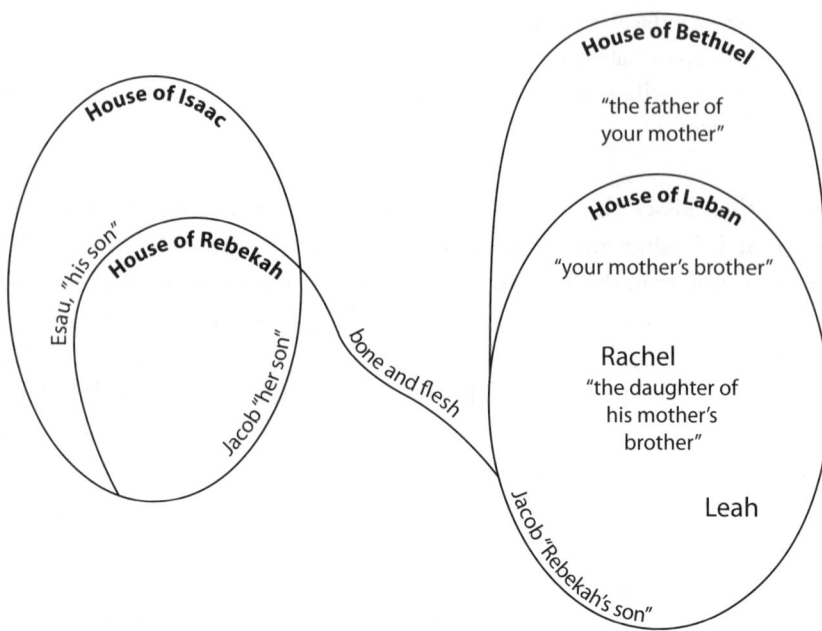

Figure 10. *The house of the father of Jacob's mother, Gen 28:1–5; 29:4–14.* Illustration created by Ondrea Keith, rendered by Bill Nelson.

Laban, looking closely at Jacob as he embraces him, recognizes a physical resemblance between Jacob and his sister Rebekah (fig. 10).[13]

Ultimately, Jacob resides in "the house of Laban" for twenty years. From one perspective, Laban provides Jacob with refuge from his murderous brother, and in return Jacob serves Laban, managing his flocks, such that Laban's house becomes wealthy. Laban also provides Jacob with his two daughters as wives, and those two daughters and their two maidservants provide Jacob with eleven sons and a daughter while residing in Paddan-aram. Jacob is well on his way to building his own house, but the house he is building is set to become a generational continuation of the house of Laban, not the house of Isaac.

At this point, it might be helpful to discuss the role of "Yahweh" in the story of Rebekah, Jacob, and Laban. It was Yahweh who first created the strong tie between Rebekah and her younger son Jacob when he revealed to Rebekah alone, while she was pregnant, that her younger son would be stronger and would be served by the older son (Gen 25:23). In Jacob's deception of his elderly father Isaac, the one statement he utters that could be considered true is when he tells his father that he was able to find the game and prepare it quickly "because Yahweh your god granted me success" (Gen 27:20). When Jacob journeys to Paddan-aram, Yahweh appears to him at Bethel and identifies himself as "Yahweh, the god of Abraham your father and the god of Isaac." Again, the absence of the label "father" that ties Jacob to Isaac is significant here; the text does not say, "the god of Isaac, *your father.*" Jacob then receives the covenantal promise of land, blessing, and divine presence: "I am with you and will keep you wherever you go" (Gen 28: 15). Once in Paddan-aram, Yahweh opens the wombs of Jacob's wives in turn, allowing his children to be born.[14] Finally, when Jacob decides to break from Laban's house and return to his homeland, Laban reveals that he, like his sister Rebekah before him, has learned through "divination" that Yahweh has blessed him on account of Jacob (Gen 30:27). The god of one's father plays a critical role in determining the son who will ascend to the position of heir, and the Israelite god has shown that he can work through mothers to insure the Yahweh-loved son inherits his father's house.[15]

The origin story of Jacob can be divided into two parentally aligned periods. As we have just outlined, from the time of conception through the establishment of his own house through fathering sons, Jacob is maternally aligned. During his childhood, he is aligned with his mother; during his twenty-year sojourn in Laban's house, the language of the maternal kinship dominates; Jacob lives in the house of the father of his mother. In this first half of Jacob's story, Rebekah is labeled Jacob's "mother" four times, while only once is she labeled the mother of "Jacob and Esau."[16] To Laban, Jacob is his "brother," "the son of his sister," "Rebekah's son," his own "bone and flesh." To Jacob, Laban is "his mother's brother." Laban's house is "the house of Bethuel, the father of your mother." Rachel is "the daughter of Laban, his mother's brother." Even the sheep belong to "Laban, his mother's brother." Through omission of kinship designations, Jacob becomes the non-son of Isaac. The only time Jacob has claimed to be a son of Isaac has been in deception. Jacob has been absorbed into Laban's household; he has married his daughters and enriched his flocks. If Jacob has begun to establish his own house, it is a sub-house within the house of Laban, his mother's brother.

In Gen 31, the kinship language abruptly shifts from the house of the father of your mother to the competing interests of Jacob's father's house, Jacob's own house, and Laban's house. Jacob is moving into the second period of his life, when he will earn the right to align himself with his father. The shift to paternally aligned language occurs when Jacob receives his Abrahamic call: "Return to the land of your fathers, to your birthplace, and I will be with you" (Gen 31:3).[17] Just as the land of Jacob's fathers re-enters the narrative, we learn of some hitherto unknown "sons of Laban," and they fear that "Jacob has taken all that was *our father's*" (Gen 31:1).[18] In several of the narratives that we have already covered, paternal kinship designations—"David's son" (2 Sam 13:1), "the king's sons" (2 Sam 13: 23, 27, 29, 30, 32), "Jacob's sons" (Gen 34:7, 13), "sons of Jerubbaal" (Judg 9:2)—refer to a collective of half-brothers that stands in tension with a son or subset of sons from a particular mother. In a sense, the introduction of "Laban's sons" at a moment when the wealth of the father's house is at stake identifies Jacob as the son of an outsider mother. Jacob had been treated as an adoptive son of Laban, absorbed into Laban's house. Now that he is being called back to the land of his fathers, the language of the narrative begins to identify him as an outsider son in the house of Laban.

After receiving his call to return to the land of his fathers, Jacob speaks to Rachel and Leah about leaving Haran. At this point, Jacob no longer refers to Laban as "my mother's brother"; he is "*your* father," and Jacob contrasts him with "the God of *my* father."[19] Rachel and Leah promptly assess the situation and conclude that there is no future for them in their "father's house"; their future lies with Jacob and his father's house (Gen 31:14–16). Jacob then makes the Abrahamic move from Haran to Canaan, and in so doing claims his father, Isaac, for the first time. Jacob gathers his wives, his children, his flocks, and all his possessions, and they mount camels and go "to the land of Canaan to his father Isaac" (Gen 31:18).[20] This is the first time that the narrative joins Isaac to Jacob as "his father" in a context where Jacob's heart is true.

In the verses that follow, multiple paternal references to Isaac are found in rapid succession. At the same time, Laban's house has become an entity separated from Jacob. When Laban overtakes Jacob's caravan, he acknowledges that he has had a visitation from "the god of *your father*," and he recognizes that Jacob had gone away because "you longed greatly for *your father's house*" (Gen 31:30). At the same time, Laban continues to see Jacob's emerging "house" as a subunit of his own when he insists, "The daughters are my daughters, the sons are my sons, the flocks are my flocks, and all that you see is mine!" (Gen 31:43). This line spoken so desperately by Laban recalls the much happier time of their meeting when Jacob joyfully recognized the daughters, the sheep, and the flocks as belonging to "Laban, his mother's brother" (Gen 29:10).

Ultimately, Jacob and Laban form a covenant allowing them to separate on good terms, a covenant that acknowledges the separate paternal status of Jacob's house. The language of this covenant ties Jacob to Laban through their more distant paternal links rather than through their closer maternal links. They swear on "the God of Abraham and the God of Nahor—the god of their father." This oath ties the two men together through the culturally preferred patrilineal pathways, that is, through Terah, the paternal ancestor they share. It also elevates the genealogical standing of Jacob to a generational level equal to that of Laban. He is no longer Laban's sister's son, a nephew. He and Laban are both Terah's great grandsons. Jacob alone assents to his side of the covenant by swearing on "the Fear of his father Isaac" (Gen 31:53).[21] The two share a sacrificial meal, and then Laban returns to his home (Gen 31:54–55). Nowhere in chapter 31 is Rebekah mentioned. She and her father's house have already played their crucial role, protecting and preparing her son to return as heir in his father's house.[22]

Abimelech and the Shechemite Concubine

The story of Abimelech is appropriately considered a royal "succession narrative" despite its presence in the book of Judges rather than Samuel or Kings. Abimelech is presented as the son of Gideon, also known as Jerubbaal, the judge best remembered for his resolute refusal of the mantle of dynastic kingship.[23] When the people approached judge Gideon and pleaded with him, saying, "Rule over us, you and your son and your grandson also," Gideon replied with a characteristically Deuteronomistic speech: "I will not rule over you, and my son will not rule over you; Yahweh will rule over you" (Judg 8:22–23). Several scholars, however, have noted details in the text that suggest that Gideon's refusal of dynastic rule might not have been so adamant.[24] He established a religious shrine of some nature in his hometown of Ophrah (Judg 6:25–27). He funded the building of the shrine through a voluntary gold tax (Judg 8:24–27). He begot seventy-one sons, and fortunately the text adds by way of explanation, he had "many wives." Finally, the text singles out one son by name, Abimelech, which translates as "My father is king" (Judg 8:31).[25] Building shrines, taxation, many wives, and royal names all suggest that there may have been something monarchic in Gideon's rule as judge.[26]

The dynastic, monarchic intent of Gideon's leadership is also suggested by the struggle for succession that ensued following his death. In introducing this struggle, the Deuteronomistic Historian distinguishes Abimelech from the rest of Gideon's sons through reference to his mother. The text reads, "Now Gideon had seventy sons, who came forth from his loins, for he had many wives. And his concubine [*ûpîlagšô*], who was in Shechem, she also bore him a son, and he called his name Abimelech" (Judg 8:30–31). On a narrative level, Abimelech is marked first by the disjunctive *vav* that introduces his mother and by the labeling of his mother as a "concubine" rather than a "wife."[27] This concubine is further distinguished from those labeled "wives" by placing her in a foreign geographical location: "she was in Shechem" (Judg 8:31). This means that Abimelech's mother's house was not nested spatially within the house of his father; it was a satellite house that Gideon visited. Already in the introduction to the succession narrative, the seventy unnamed sons are anchored within their natal *bêt 'āb* as sons of wives and products of their father's loins. The one named son is tied to his foreign mother's house and socially denigrated by her status as a nonresident concubine.

I cover the phenomenon of low-status wives and their sons more fully below, but it may be helpful now to examine the phenomenon of houses of the mother that are not nested within the house of the father. Because a low-status mother's relationship to the father of her children is tenuous, weak, or sometimes nonexistent, the house she brings into being when she bears children is often not nested within the house of her husband or the father of her children if she is not married. Consequently, her children's place within their father's house is not guaranteed. If a mother is a slave, concubine, or prostitute, the house she establishes through her children may be a subunit of the house of her father, or it could be an independent, woman-headed house. The house that Hagar established through the birth of Ishmael began as a subunit of the house of Abraham under the authority of Sarah, the head wife. Once Sarah cast Hagar out of Abraham's house, however, Hagar was forced to establish her own mother-headed house in her Egyptian homeland. At best, the house of Hagar could be seen as a satellite house of Abraham, and Ishmael's participation in the burial of his father supports this understanding. At worst, the house of Hagar in Egypt is a cast-off, disgraced, woman-headed house with no legitimate ties to the house of the father. The disinheriting of Ishmael at Abraham's death supports this reading.[28] Another example of a non-nested, female-headed mother's house is found in the story of the two prostitute mothers who fight over the one living infant in 1 Kings 3. These mothers share a single house without "a male" present, meaning their children will grow up without the benefits of a house of the father. The house of Rahab the prostitute seems to be a nested unit within the house of her father because her house includes her father, her mother, and her brothers and possibly sisters. The text does not indicate that she had children, but if she did, they would grow up as part of her house nested within the house of her father (Josh 6: 17, 22–25).[29]

Abimelech's tenuous status within the house of his father is evident at the moment of Gideon/Jerubbaal's death, when Abimelech retreats to "the house of the father of his mother." His mother's house in Shechem was either a nested unit within her father's house or an independent, woman-headed house. At the moment of generational transfer within the house of his father, Abimelech turns to the house of the father of his mother in the hopes that the members of this house will support his bid to become heir in his father's house:

> Abimelech the son of Jerubbaal went to Shechem, to *the brothers of his mother* [ăḥê 'immô]. And he spoke to them and to *all the families in the house of the father of his mother* [kol-mišpaḥat bêt-ăbî 'immô]. (Judg 9:1)

While there, he speaks with the Shechemite leaders of the house of the father of his mother and suggests to them that it would be in their best interest to have him rule over them instead of the seventy "sons of Jerubbaal"—because he was "one of them." In his attempt to convince them, Abimelech uses the same kinship terminology that marked him as an outsider within the house of Gideon and as part of the house of his mother, to present himself as an insider to his maternal kin and to win their hearts and loyalty. He asks, "What is better for you that seventy men, all of the sons of Jerubbaal, rule over you, or that one man rule over you, and remember that I am of your bone and your flesh" (Judg 9:2). This statement recalls Jacob's meeting with Laban where he presents himself as "Rebekah's son" rather than "Isaac's son," and Laban recognizes him as a "brother," "my bone and my flesh." Abimelech identifies "the seventy" as "sons of Jerubbaal" and identifies himself not as a son of Jerubbaal but as one who shares the same "bone and flesh" as the Shechemite lords.[30] The "hearts" of Abimelech's maternal kin ('ăḥê-'immô), we discover, "inclined toward Abimelech" because as he had suggested and they have now accepted, "he is our brother" ('āḥînû hû') (Judg 9:3). The son with a very tenuous status within the house of his father secures the status of a brother, one of the same bone and flesh, within "the house of the father of his mother."[31]

The Deuteronomistic overlay of this narrative provides a consistent negative evaluation of the machinations of the house of the father of Abimelech's mother. Of course, the purpose of DH was not to provide an overview of Israelite kinship structures. Rather, DH used literary and theological techniques to show how Yahweh identified his chosen heir.[32] In the time of the judges, the Deuteronomistic heir was not the one who stood in dynastic succession to his father. Instead, the chosen one in Judges was consistently the one upon whom the spirit of Yahweh rushed in such a way that he was able to deliver a military victory. Still, when DH chose to discredit Abimelech through references to the foreign, concubine status of his mother and through the location of her house within the house of her father in Shechem, we learn a great deal about cultural values tied to the status of one's mother and to the geographic location of one's mother's house.

DH's negative evaluation of Abimelech's plan for usurping the throne is seen first in the financial backing provided by his mother's clan, which DH reported came from "the temple of Ba'al Berith" (Judg 9:4). DH then reported that Abimelech used this Baal-tainted money "to hire worthless and reckless fellows" as a mercenary force.[33] With this unimpressive entourage, the son of a foreign concubine returned to his *bêt 'āb* to stake his claim. Without wasting any time, he "killed his brothers, the sons of Jerubbaal, seventy men, on one stone" (Judg 9:5). At the beginning of this narrative, we had seventy legitimate sons of the father and one disjunctive son of a concubine. Now, the nonresident son of a concubine, backed by the funding of Baal-Berith, murders the unnamed seventy on one rock. As it turns out, the "seventy" is actually sixty-nine, because Jotham, the youngest son of Gideon/Jerubbaal survives, signaling the beginning of a succession struggle between the legitimate heir of the house of the father and the illegitimate son of a concubine.[34] We get a sense of how the struggle will end when Abimelech again retreats to the house of the father of his mother. It is in Shechem that he is crowned king; he rules his mother's clan. The location of his crowning is a foreign shrine site, "by the oak of the pillar at Shechem" (Judg 9:6). Abimelech has gained power and authority but it is not over the house of his father.

The line of patrilineal descent is clear. Jotham is the single heir of the house of Gideon/Jerubbaal, who in turn is the heir to the house of Joash of Ophrah. The inheritance claims of Abimelech the son of a concubine are presented as foreign and illegitimate. To use Karen Sinclair's distinction between "dogma" and "myth," biblical dogma would diagram a pure patrilineal genealogy eliminating the messiness of wives, concubines, and late-born, non-inheriting sons. The narrative of Judg 9, on the other hand, shows greater tendencies toward the playfulness of myth and, as such, gives full visibility to wives, concubines, and younger sons. In order to represent visually the kinship status of Abimelech, one would have to include two classes of female-headed households: *bāttê 'ēm* headed by legitimate wives and *bāttê 'ēm* headed by concubines. The former would be nested within the *bêt 'āb*, under the protection of the Israelite national god, Yahweh. The house of the concubine mother, on the other hand, would be within the foreign jurisdiction of the Canaanite god, Baal-berith. Abimelech's pathway to the house of his father traverses the physical landscape from Shechem to Ophrah and is mediated by a low-status mother.

The focus of narrative action shifts from Abimelech to Jotham right at the point of Abimelech's crowning. In the case of Jacob's Yahweh-sponsored sojourn in the house of the father of his mother, the language shifts from maternal to paternal kinship at the moment when Jacob and his impressive entourage of wives, children, livestock, and people embark on the return journey "to the land of Canaan to his father Isaac" (Gen 31:18). In the case of Abimelech's Baal-sponsored efforts, the shift in kinship terms is markedly different. Jotham, the legitimate son of a wife, speaks to the lords of Shechem in the Deuteronomistically favored genre of parables or fables. He tells the rather transparent story of trees trying to anoint for themselves a king (Judg 9:7–15). The olive tree, the fig tree, and the vine are approached first, but their work producing valuable fruit makes them too busy and important to take on a leadership role. Finally, the trees are left with the bramble, a wild prickly bush, who is free to take the job as king. Rooted, cultivated trees are a frequent biblical metaphor for the stability, geographic fixity, and ongoing perpetuity of a royal house. Comparing "My Father is King" to bramble, a wild bush that produces a lesser quality fruit, communicates the nature of Abimelech's outsider, non-paternally-nested mother's house.[35] Jotham then refers to Abimelech not as his brother, not as his bone and his flesh, but rather as "the son of his maidservant" (*ben 'āmātô*) (Judg 9:18).[36]

The story of Abimelech and the Shechemite house of his mother does not end well. In keeping with the principle of poetic justice, Abimelech is brought down by a similarly conniving outsider whose name, "Gaal ben Ebed," means "Loathsome son of a slave" (Judg 9:26–29). From the Deuteronimistic perspective, the two good-for-nothing men have met their match in each other. Gaal ben Ebed approaches the lords of Shechem, the heads of the house of the father of Abimelech's mother. These are the same men who had so recently "inclined their hearts" to Abimelech, accepting him as of their bone and flesh, claiming him as "our brother." Gaal ben Ebed manages to plant the seeds of doubt and discontent when he asks the lords of the house of the father of Abimelech's mother, "Who is Abimelech? And who are *we* of Shechem that we should serve him?" (Judg 9:28). His questions point directly to the kin/not-kin status of one who is related to a house through his mother. Recall the sons of Laban, who suddenly appear when the wealth of their paternal house is at stake and accuse Jacob, the man related to their house through his mother, of stealing the wealth of their father. When the lords of Shechem acknowledged Abimelech as their "bone and flesh," they did so in the hopes that he would bring them security and power. He did precisely this when he chose to be crowned in Shechem and then eliminated the house of his father in Ophrah. As soon as Abimelech proved unable to serve as the Shechemites' conduit to power, however, the lords of Shechem were easily persuaded that they had nothing to do with this man—"Who is Abimelech?" According to Gaal ben Ebed, he is "the son of Jerubbaal," an outsider (Judg 9:28).

Abimelech and the house of the father of his mother are fully eliminated by the end of the narrative. Abimelech sets the people of Shechem to the torch in their city's towers (Judg 9:42–49). The illegitimate heir who was willing to commit fratricide seventy times over in the house of his father now shows himself similarly willing to do away with his maternal kin. Abimelech's own end confirms the Deuteronomist's judgment against his royal aspirations. Appropriately, it is a woman who ultimately brings down the man whose powerbase was maternally defined, and she does so by dropping a woman's tool, an upper millstone, on his head (Judg 9:53–55).[37] Throughout the story of Abimelech, the Deuteronomist's view that kingship is an affront to Yahweh is bolstered by denigrating references to the house of the mother and the house of the father of a concubine mother. Readers are left to conclude that men with royal aspirations are illegitimate sons of foreign concubines, supported by worthless, idol-worshipping mercenaries, men who are willing to murder their own bone and flesh.

Absalom and King Talmai of Geshur

When we turn to the story of Absalom, we have a changed historical context. The setting of this narrative is the United Monarchy, about 100–150 years after the presumed time of Abimelech. DH presents a "change of heart" in Yahweh with regard to kingship. King David is Yahweh's "son," his "anointed one," and his dynasty, his *bayit,* enjoys an eternal covenant with Yahweh (1 Sam 16:1, 12–13; 2 Sam 7:14; Ps 89:19–37).

Just as we could chart a neat, patrilineal genealogy of Gideon, we can present a similarly neat genealogy for the house of David, something frequently seen in Hebrew Bible textbooks: David, Solomon, Rehoboam. This patrilineal genealogy, however, is an after-the-fact construct that conceals the messiness of succession struggles, struggles within which mothers' houses played central roles. As we noted in chapter 7, David took six wives in Hebron and had six womb-opening sons with them (2 Sam 3:2). After moving his capital to Jerusalem, he took "more wives and had more sons" (2 Sam 5:13–16). Among these Jerusalem wives, the most significant was Bathsheba, the mother of Solomon, David's eventual heir. Absalom was David's third son, born from his third wife, Maacah, who is identified as the daughter of King Talmai of Geshur (2 Sam 3:3). Like Abimelech, Absalom was not the firstborn of his father, and his mother was a foreigner. Despite these similarities, however, Absalom's status was quite different from Abimelech's. Absalom's mother was a legitimate wife from a powerful royal family, and her own generated house, the house of Maacah, was nested within the house of David. The high status of Absalom's mother and the house of the father of his mother allowed Absalom to fight for a different degree of power than was available to the lower-status Abimelech.

In the succession narrative of David, Amnon was the firstborn son of David and presumptive heir to his throne. Jon D. Levenson and Baruch Halpern have provided evidence that Amnon's mother, Ahinoam, may have been Saul's former wife.[38] If this were the case, then Amnon embodies "the bone and flesh" of both the Davidide and Saulide political bases. Amnon, however, made a tactical error when he raped and discarded his half-sister Tamar, which allowed Absalom to use the rape of his uterine sister to justify seeking vengeance against Amnon. He waited two years and then orchestrated a situation where he could easily kill Amnon, avenge his sister's rape, and eliminate the heir in a single act (2 Sam 13:23–33).[39]

Fearing David's anger, Absalom, like Jacob and Abimelech, sought refuge in the house of the father of his mother where he remained for three years (2 Sam 13:37–39). Like Abimelech, Absalom used his kinship connections with the house of the mother of his father to build a support base for his bid for kingship. Interestingly, DH does not emphasize the kinship terminology or the foreignness of the house of the father of Absalom's mother: "Absalom fled and went to Talmai the son of Ammihud, king of Geshur" (2 Sam 13:37). It does not say he went to the "brothers of his mother, to the house of the father of his mother." The only way we know that Absalom fled to the house of the father of his mother is from reading the report of David's wives and heirs listed ten chapters earlier. The goal of the Deuteronomist in each narrative was to demonstrate the illegitimacy of the royal aspirations of Abimelech and Absalom. In the case of Abimelech, the status of his mother as a foreign, nonresident concubine provided the Deuteronomist with helpful material for discrediting Abimelech. While Absalom also turned to the house of the father of his mother for refuge and support, the status of his mother as a legitimate wife, and a princess residing in David's palace, worked against the DH's desire to discredit Absalom. As a result, DH only mentions Absalom's maternal kin in passing.

On a political level, a retreat to the Geshurites represented an appeal to the former supporters of King Saul. In 2 Sam 2:9, Saul's son Ishbaal claimed sovereignty over the Geshurites, so David's marriage to the daughter of the king of Geshur staked a political claim over Saulide territory. When Absalom received refuge and later won over the hearts of "all Israel," he demonstrated his ability to capitalize on the tribal fissures in order to create a "United Kingdom."[40]

Eventually, Absalom returned and dwelled for two years in his own "house" in Jerusalem (2 Sam 14:24, 28). This house, like that of Amnon, was likely a sub-house within his father's larger royal house.[41] He then set in motion his plans for usurping his father's throne. First, he sought and gained entrance and acceptance in his father's house (2 Sam 14:28–33). Then, he began acting as a judge and king, securing for himself the accouterments of kingship: horses, chariots, and a military entourage (2 Sam 15:1). Royally bedecked, he placed himself in the politically significant location of the "city gate," where he offered judgments concerning the people's lawsuits. The text then informs us that in this way Absalom "stole the hearts of all Israel" (2 Sam 14:28–15:6).[42] Two more years passed before Absalom set out for Hebron, the birthplace of his father's dynasty. He went there ostensibly to repay a vow he had made to Yahweh, but while there, he had himself declared king (2 Sam 15:7–12).[43]

When we contrast the tactical plans for usurpation that Absalom devised with those of Abimelech, we see how the status of one's mother in her husband's house defined the parameters of a son's set of possible moves within his own *bêt 'āb*. Abimelech, as the son of an outsider, nonresident concubine, was only able to seek kingship in Shechem, within the clan of his mother's father's house. And even this claim to kingship on foreign soil was only possible after Abimelech annihilated his own *bêt 'āb*. Because Absalom's maternal house was nested within the house of David, he was able to seek and receive support among "all the men of Israel": "the heart of each man of Israel went after him" (2 Sam 15:6, 13).[44] Abimelech also won over the hearts of people, but he won over the hearts of the foreign, Shechemite lords, not those of all Israel. Whereas Abimelech was crowned in the foreign shrine site at the oak of the pillar at Shechem, Absalom had himself crowned in Hebron, the birthplace of his father's dynasty and a shrine site of the Israelite national god Yahweh.[45]

The declaration of Absalom's kingship by "all Israel" in the Yahwistic shrine site of Hebron threatened David's *bayit*. He fled and vacated his house, leaving his concubines vulnerable (2 Sam 15:16). Absalom returned to the capital city of Jerusalem as king, took up residence in the vacated royal house of his father, and in the ultimate act of shaming the honor of David as head of household, he sexually used his father's concubines in a tent he pitched "in the sight of all Israel" (2 Sam 16:22).[46]

It would seem that Absalom succeeded fully. The text, however, provides several clues that his kingship would be short-lived. Just as the survival of Jotham threatened Abimelech's continued legitimacy among the Shechemites, the survival of King David threatened the legitimacy of Absalom among "all Israel." David and Absalom consulted their respective advisors and schemed against each other. Ultimately, David's men defeated Absalom and "all Israel," but Absalom managed to flee (2 Sam 18:6–9). Just as Abimelech died a humiliating death at the hands of a woman, Absalom died fleeing the scene of battle. Riding away on his mule, his head caught in the branches of an oak (2 Sam 18:9).[47] Absalom had already been described as possessing a luxuriant head of hair, so readers are left with the image of the newly anointed king hanging by his hair from a tree.[48] The one who had won the hearts of all Israel had his own heart pierced by the spear of his father's military commander.[49]

Absalom's death narrative surpasses that of Abimelech in detail and in shaming. He died hanging from a tree, something that the book of Deuteronomy associates with a cursed man (Deut 21:22–23). He received an inappropriate burial under a heap of stones, a shameful monument that would serve as a reminder of his shameful death for years to come (2 Sam 18:17–18). Similarly, the notation that he had erected for himself a *yad*, translated as "memorial" but also containing the literal meaning "hand" and the figurative meaning of "penis," refers to his having died without a son. Hanging from a tree, improperly buried, and without a son—all mark Absalom as a cursed man with no *bayit* to carry on his name.[50]

Idrimi and the Sisters of His Mother

A very similar story to Absalom's of royal retreat to the house of maternal relatives is found in the Akkadian text "The Autobiography of Idrimi." Dating to around 1500 BCE, this text, preserved on Idrimi's royal statue where he sits enthroned as "king of Alalaḫ," was discovered in the ancient city of Alalaḫ.[51] The 104 lines of text cover the front side of his statue and culminate down his cheek to his mouth, suggesting a first-person telling. The story recounts Idrimi's own struggle for succession in the house and land of his father. Because Idrimi does not fit into known lists of rulers and because his autobiography features popular folk themes, including the triumph of a younger brother over his older brothers, scholars consider the text a fiction composed considerably later than the events it describes.[52]

After identifying himself, Idrimi begins his personal narrative by describing "an act of hostility" that occurred in "the house of my father" (*bīt abīya*) in Aleppo. Because of this act of hostility, he and his "older brothers" "fled to the people of Emar, the sisters of my mother [*aḫātē ummiya*], and we settled in the city of Emar."[53] Once again, we have a younger son fleeing the house of his father during a time of crisis and taking up residence with the relatives of his mother. This time, however, these relatives are not the brothers of his mother but the sisters of his mother. Perhaps we are to understand that his mother did not have brothers, meaning Idrimi was taken into his mother's sisters' marital homes.[54] He arrives there together with his older brothers, but he immediately separates himself out from them, claiming that he alone has plans for retaking the abandoned father's house. He recognizes that his position among his mother's female relatives in Emar will always be that of "a servant to the citizens of Emar," but if he manages to retake his "father's house," he could become the "foremost heir." Idrimi understands the limits to the power he can amass through maternal kinship links. His mother's sisters are useful, even lifesaving, but he will never stand to inherit in the land of Emar; he cannot become "foremost heir" in the marital homes of his mother's sisters.[55]

Idrimi then sets off back to Canaan, though not directly back to his father's house. He returns as a lone warrior, taking a horse, chariot, and groom. He settles first in the town of Ammiya, a territory he claims had been under his father's control, and according to him, the citizens of Ammiya recognize him as "their lord's son" and make him "chief."⁵⁶ Recall that when Absalom returned to the kingdom of his father, he dwelt in his own house and ultimately had himself crowned in Hebron by former supporters of his father. Idrimi formed a treaty with the citizens of the villages in Ammiya, and they became his allies.

The rest of Idrimi's story reads like many narratives of establishing or reclaiming a dynasty. He speaks of his specialized knowledge in extispicy, his skills in shipbuilding, his military victories, and his success at negotiating diplomatic treaties. After defeating his many enemies, he gathers up his "brothers and comrades" and returns victorious to his royal city of Alalaḫ.⁵⁷ Only then does Idrimi "construct a house" and "make a throne like the throne of kings." He makes his brothers "like the brothers of kings" and his sons "like their sons." Like the stories of Jacob, Joseph, and Ruth, Idrimi's story ends with a restored *tôlēdôt*, so to speak. He places himself as the chosen link in an unbroken paternal line describing how he restored the cities to the condition they had been in during the time of "our fathers" and reestablished the sacrifices of "our fathers." He then looks forward in time and names his male heir, Adad-nirari.⁵⁸

In this fictionalized account of how Idrimi established his dynasty, the house of his maternal relatives was a place of refuge during a time of crisis that threatened the house of his father. It preserved his life and enabled him to return to the land of his father, stake a claim in his father's territory, build a house, establish a throne, gather his newly allied "brothers," restore the land, and reestablish sacrifices to his paternal gods. He dies leaving a designated heir, a perpetual monument, and a preserved story of origin for his dynasty, which is, of course, his house.

Bone and Flesh: Joining a Man to the House of the Father of His Mother

When we examine the language that describes the relationship between a man and the house of the father of his mother, we frequently find the terms "bone and flesh" and "inclining the heart." Laban recognizes Jacob, his sister's son, as his "bone and flesh" (Gen 29:14–15a). Abimelech presents himself to the members of the house of the father of his mother as being of the same "bone and flesh" (Judg 9:2). The Bible does not narrate the story of Absalom in the house of his maternal grandfather, King Talmai of Geshur, so we do not know if he was welcomed there as a "bone-and-flesh" relative. Nevertheless, the use of "bone and flesh" in two of our three house-of-the-father-of-the-mother texts suggests that we need to investigate this Hebrew kinship term more fully.

Biblically, we can examine four separate narratives where the language of shared bone and flesh implies kinship and its concomitant loyalty: Jacob and Laban; Abimelech and the brothers of his mother; Absalom and the men of Israel; and David and the tribe of Judah and, as I show here, David tied specifically to Amasa. In three examples, the bone-and-flesh relationship describes the relationship of a maternal uncle to his nephew. The loyalty that a person or group expresses based on shared bone and flesh is communicated with the phrase "inclining the heart" or "stealing the heart." Stated another way, a mother's son is tied to the house of her father through the language of bone and flesh and inclined hearts. Still, despite all the implied references to loyalty, the bone-and-flesh relationship of inclining hearts is unstable; it seems to depend on the usefulness of the person claiming to be kin. Hearts seem to be easily swayed for and against a bone-and-flesh relative.

In the story of Abimelech, the "brothers" of Abimelech's mother inform "the lords of Shechem" of Abimelech's royal aspirations, and "their hearts inclined toward Abimelech" (*wayyēṭ libbām 'aḥărê 'ăbîmelek*) because they recognized this "bone-and-flesh" relative as a "brother" (Judg 9:3). In the narrative describing the war between David and Absalom, they both fight for the support of "all Israel," using the language of bone and flesh and inclining hearts to convey kin-based allegiance. When David first receives the support of "all the tribes of Israel" in Hebron, they express their allegiance to him saying, "We are your bone and your flesh" (2 Sam 5:1 [cf. 1 Chron 11:1]). When Absalom later splits from David and begins to amass his own political support base, we learn that "Absalom stole the hearts of the people of Israel," such that "the heart of every man of Israel belongs to Absalom" (2 Sam 15:6, 13). After Absalom's death, David, still in exile, sends a message to his priests Zadok and Abiathar asking them to speak to the "elders of Judah," namely members of his own tribe. He wants the priests to say, "Why should you [elders of Judah] be the last to return the king to his house? The talk of all Israel has come to the king and to his house" (2 Sam 19:12 [Eng. 19:11]). David singles out the members of his own tribe from the larger house of Israel and calls them out for not showing proper allegiance. He continues, berating them, "You are my brothers!

You are my bone and my flesh! Why are you the last ones to bring back the king?" (*'aḥay 'attem 'aṣmî ûbĕśārî 'attem wĕlāmmāh tihyû 'aḥrōnîm lĕhāšîb 'et-hammelek*) (2 Sam 19:13 [Eng. 19:12]). David then narrows his focus further to one man, Amasa, one of his military commanders, and says, "Are you not my bone and my flesh? May the Lord do thus and so to me and more if you do not become the commander of my army, serving me all my days in place of Joab" (2 Sam 19:14 [Eng. 19:13]). According to the narrative preserved in 2 Samuel, Amasa and Joab are related to each other as maternal cousins; their mothers were sisters (2 Sam 17:25). 1 Chronicles adds the detail that both of their mothers were sisters of David (1 Chron 2:16). This would mean that when David wishes to shame Amasa into pledging his allegiance to David and leading the charge to bring him back to his palace, David reminds Amasa that he is Amasa's maternal uncle, using the language of shared bone and flesh. David's appeal to kin-based shared substance and its implied loyalty proves effective as "the heart of every man of Judah stretched out as [the heart of] one man," and they called for the return of David as king (2 Sam 19:15 [Eng. 19:14]).

I would suggest that the substances of kinship—bone, flesh, and heart—like those of "breasts and womb," have strong, though not exclusively, maternal connections. First, just as womb and breasts represent a two-stage maternally focused process of human formation, so too does the word pair "bone and flesh" convey a chronological sequence of physiological formation. Moreover, that sequence of formation, the divine knitting of bone and flesh, occurs within a mother's womb. In Ps 139, the Psalmist praises Yahweh as the one who "formed my inward parts and wove me in my mother's womb" (*qānîtā kilyōtāy tĕsukkĕnî bĕbeṭen 'immî*). In what is described as a "hidden" or "secret" process of infant formation, Yahweh is able to see the human skeleton or bones (*'āṣĕmî*) as he "weaves" or "embroiders" the unformed child (Ps 139:13–15). Job provides a detailed description of his own creation by God saying, "You clothed me with skin and flesh, and knit me together with bones and sinews" (*'ôr ûbāśār talbîšēnî ûba'ăṣāmôt wĕgîdîm tĕsōkĕkēnî*) (Job 10:11). We see the same chronological sequence in the famous vision of the valley of dry bones, where Yahweh recreates or revives the Judeans by taking "bones" and then adding "sinews," "flesh," and "skin." Finally, he brings the physical package to life with "breath" (Ezek 37:7–10). In sickness, decay, and death, Hebrew poets conjured images of the reverse order of creation. Lamentations reads, "He has wasted away my flesh and my skin; He has shattered my bones" (Lam 3:4; see also Job 2:5; 33:21; Ps 38:4; Prov 14:30).

The first biblical reference to the phrase "bone and flesh" already communicates the substance-based relationship that it conveys. In the Eden narrative, when the woman is "built" from the man's "rib," the man immediately recognizes her as "bone of my bones and flesh of my flesh" (Gen 2:23). The first human couple is tied together substantively, sharing the same bone and flesh. The primordial woman is "born" from the man. As soon as the couple leaves the garden, however, all future human generation occurs through biological reproduction. No other married couple is described as sharing the same bone and flesh.[59]

To be of the same bone and flesh in the Bible seems to refer to a biological relationship conceptualized as substantive. In its broadest sense, it can simply mean members of allied tribes as in 2 Sam 5:1 when all the tribes of Israel pledge their allegiance to David as their king by declaring, "We are your bone and flesh." But in the stories of Jacob and Laban, Abimelech and the brothers of his mother, and David and Amasa, shared bone and flesh links houses: a mother's generated house and the house of her father.

Son of a Slave Girl: Discrediting Heirs

Another kinship designation that has appeared in several of the texts that describe a man's struggle to become heir within his father's house is the maternal designation "son of a slave girl" and several of its variants: son of a maidservant (*ben-'āmātô*), son of his concubines (*bĕnê happîlagšîm*), or a son born to a whore or prostitute (*ben-'iššâ zônâ*). Once again, Hebrew poetic word pairs provide a window into the biblical understanding of kinship designations. The psalms use the word pair "servant/son of your maidservant" to express the petitioner's desire to debase himself in increasing degrees before the deity. The psalmist understands the designation "your servant" to be a humble way to identify oneself before a god, while the phrase "the son of your maidservant" lowers one's status even further. In Ps 86, for example, the speaker is surrounded by a band of ruffians and calls on Yahweh to deliver him: "Show your strength to your servant [*lĕ'abdekā*], deliver the son of your maidservant [*lĕben-'āmātekā*]" (Ps 86:16). Psalm 116 is a song of thanksgiving offered by a man who credits Yahweh with protecting and saving him. As part of repaying his debt to Yahweh, the psalmist declares, "I am your servant ['*ănî-'abdĕkā*], the son of your maidservant [*ben-'āmātekā*]" (Ps 116:16). The lowest-of-the-low status for a son of a maidservant is also seen in Exod 11:5 where Yahweh announces a death sentence for all of the firstborn males in Egypt. The text emphasizes the all-inclusive nature of this edict by marking out the highest- to the lowest-status firstborn sons. The high-status firstborn son is marked through paternity and royalty: "from the firstborn of Pharaoh who sits on his throne" (*mibbĕkôr parʿō hayyōšēb ʿal-kisʾô*). The lowest-status son is identified through maternity and women's work: "to the firstborn of the slave girl who is behind the hand mill" (*ʿad bĕkôr haššipḥâ ʾăšer ʾaḥar hārēḥāyim*) (Exod 11:5). These texts seem to suggest that if a man is a servant (*ʿebed*), his status is low, but if he is the "son of a maidservant" (*ben-ʾamâ*), his status is the lowest imaginable.

If a man was born to a low-status wife, his chances of succeeding his father and inheriting his house and name were diminished. Abimelech is introduced as the son born to his father's concubine in Shechem, and as soon as he attempts to rule his father's house by killing all but one of his father's seventy sons, his mother's status is used against him. Jotham, the one surviving son born to Gideon and one of his wives, confronts the lords of Shechem, who have supported Abimelech. He accuses them of rising up against "the house of my father," "killing his sons," and making "the son of his maidservant" (*ben-ʾămātô*) king (Judg 8:31; 9:18). In a very similar story, we find Jephthah introduced as a "Gileadite" and the "son of a whore" (*ben-ʾiššâ zônâ*) in the opening verse of his narrative. The sons of Gilead born to his wife insist, "You cannot inherit in the house of our father because you are the son of a different woman" (Judg 11:1–2).[60] Fathers also seem to despair of the idea that a son of one of their slave women or concubines would be their heir. Abram complains to his god, "My lord God, what will you give me? I continue childless, and Eliezer of Damascus will be my heir. . . . You have given me no offspring, and a house-born slave [literally 'a son of my house' (*ben-bêtî*)] will be my heir" (Gen 15:2–3). After King Kirta loses his wife and all his children, he disdains the compensation package offered to him by the high god El. Among the many things that Kirta has no use for are "a slave woman's sons."[61] Primary wives could denigrate the status of sons born to their slave women. Sarah emphasizes Hagar's status as a maidservant when she hopes to disinherit Ishmael: "Cast out this maidservant and her son, for the son of this maidservant [*ben-hāʾāmâ hazōʾt*] will not inherit with my son Isaac" (Gen 21:10). In each of these texts, the sons of low-status wives appear with their maternally denigrating labels in narratives that describe the struggle for succession and inheritance in the house of the father.

The devalued status of maternally marked sons is also expressed when biblical narratives lump the sons of low-status women together as an anonymous, mother-identified group. Abraham's sons through Keturah and Hagar are collectively referred to as "the sons of his concubines," and they are sent away from "Isaac, his son" (Gen 25:6). When Jacob presents his family to his estranged brother Esau, Rachel and Leah are presented separately with their respective children while the "slave women and their children" (*'et-haššĕpāḥôt wĕ'et-yaldêhen*) approach as a single group (Gen 33:1–6). Similarly, at the beginning of the Joseph narrative, the sons of Jacob's maidservant wives are anonymously and maternally labeled "the sons of Bilhah and Zilpah, his father's wives," in a chapter that narrates Joseph's dreams of ruling over his brothers and parents (Gen 37:2). The sons of low-status women were hated and often exiled by brothers born to wives. If the son of a slave woman wanted to ascend to the position of heir within the house of his father, he needed the support of maternal kin and he likely also needed to use violent force.

Mothers' houses mark hierarchical dividing lines within a polygynous house of the father. The womb openers of differing maternal houses compete with one another to become their father's designated heir. Among womb-opening sons, the sons of wives have greater ascribed status; they are the ideologically preferred heirs within the father's house. If a son happens to open the womb of a maidservant, concubine, or whore, he will have to fight to inherit in his father's house. In the battle between maternal houses, a son of any status might turn to the house of the father of his mother for backing, hoping that his mother's brothers might "incline their hearts" to him, recognize him as a "brother," and claim him as one who shares the same "bone and flesh."

The moment of generational transfer within the house of the father, usually at the moment of a father's death or grave illness, signaled the beginning of an often-bloody battle between sons for succession. In this conflict, younger sons of a father and sons of low-status wives had no guaranteed place; if they wanted to succeed their father, they had to fight for their position as heir in his house. We have seen that for Jacob, Abimelech, and Absalom, the house of the father of their mother proved to be a crucial staging ground for a coup attempt in the house of their father. These men enjoyed years of safety in the houses of the fathers of their mothers, and during these years of refuge, each aspiring heir acquired financial backing and support from his mother's brothers. During the flight to and residence within the house of the father of the mother, sons claimed direct and unmediated kinship to their mothers and her brothers. Jacob was "Rebekah's son." Jacob and Abimelech were of the same "bone and flesh" as their maternal uncles, who claimed them as "brothers." While residing in the house of the father of their mother, sons avoided paternal kinship labels that would tie them to the house of their father. But when each son sought to return to his father's house to launch a credible bid as heir and usurper, the kinship labels shifted from maternal to paternal. Jacob packs up his family to "return to the land of Canaan to his father Isaac." Abimelech returns to his father's house, but he never takes up residence there and is never acknowledged as king among his father's people; he remains his mother's son. Absalom returns to Hebron, the birthplace of his father's kingship, and then takes up residence in his father's palace in Jerusalem. He does not, however, become "David's son" again until his death: "O Absalom, my son, my son." Only the sons who successfully broke away from the house of the father of their mother and claimed unmediated ties to the house of their father succeeded in becoming heirs. By losing his maternal marking, Jacob is able to claim a place in the *tôlēdôt* of Abraham and Isaac; he becomes a father-begotten son. Idrimi leaves Emar, the city of his mother's sisters, and returns to the land of his father where the residents recognize him as "their lord's son," and he places himself as the restorer of "our father's" land. Abimelech fails to sever his ties to the house of the father of his mother and remains a "mother's son." Absalom manages to take his father's physical house and gain the hearts of "all Israel," but David does not name him as heir and only claims him as a son in death. In order to be successful, a son must use the house of the father of his mother as a temporary training camp, a place he will ultimately leave in order to become his father's son.

9 Like Rachel and Leah Who Together Built Up the House of Israel (*kĕrāḥēl ûkĕlē'â 'ăšer bānû šĕtêhem 'et-bêt yiśrā'ēl*)

We have examined the Bible's presentation of its origin stories through foundational houses and have shown how women and maternal kin marked social divisions within the house of the father and between houses. In each case, we have examined the houses as domestic units made up of fathers, mothers, slaves, full brothers, half-brothers, sisters, and others. In this concluding chapter, we turn from the house as a domestic unit to the house as a nation in order to highlight the symbolic role of mothers as nation builders and kingdom founders. While scholars have recognized that the domestic household of Jacob with his twelve sons became a symbol of the national house of Israel, very little scholarly attention has been devoted to the symbolic, national role of Jacob's four wives. In this chapter, we see how biblical authors used the differential status among wives and mothers to characterize the relative value of the nations tied to those mothers. Insofar as the Bible presents a picture of how Israelites and later Judeans organized the known world into genealogically related houses, wives and mothers played central, ideologically weighted roles. In the origin stories leading up to Jacob, where scholars have described the "linear genealogy" from Abraham to Isaac to Jacob, wives and mothers constitute national divisions. Once the stories turn to the generation of Jacob, where his domestic house becomes the national house of Israel, Jacob's four wives mark hierarchies among tribes. They determine which tribes will produce contenders in royal and priestly spheres and which tribes will be cast to the side of the central story of origin.

Wives in the Symbolic National House of Abraham

In the linear genealogy that takes us from Abraham to Jacob, biblical mothers represent nations, and their relative status vis-à-vis the house-founding father determines whether they become an ancestress of Israel or of a foreign nation. Any wife who is presented as an enduring sub-house nested within the house of her husband becomes a mother within Israel's national house. Ironically, as readers, we witness her success in promoting her son to the position of heir within his father's house through her disappearance in her son's narrative. The son who ascends to the position of heir becomes a "father-begotten-son" and takes his place in the exclusively male *tôlēdôt* of Israel. A son who fails to ascend to that position continues to be defined by his mother. He and his mother are severed from the house-founding father, and his pathway to the father is indirect, mediated through his mother. Again, readers can detect a mother's failure to promote her son to heir through her endurance in her son's story. Mothers define sons who fail; their adult sons continue to be "mother born" rather than "father begotten." The houses they establish are removed physically from the house of the father; they are satellite houses pushed to the fringes of the Promised Land. Geographically and ideologically, mother-born sons and their woman-founded houses are peripheral, "sent out from upon" the chosen national house of Israel.

In the narratives that cover the houses of Abraham and Isaac, insider mothers are credited with nation building and kingdom birthing, but in every case, the success of the mother in producing the heir is marked by her disappearance. In the priestly version of the Abrahamic covenant, God tells Abram that his primary wife, Sarai, will "become nations, kings of peoples shall come forth from her" (Gen 17:16). Sarai then gives birth to Isaac, who becomes the sole heir in his father's house; he receives "all that Abraham had" (Gen 25:5). The story of Isaac's boyhood includes references to his mother: Sarah "bears a son to Abraham in his old age," she nurses Isaac to the point of weaning, and she actively fights for his position as sole heir in his father's house (Gen 21:1–14). Beginning in Gen 22, Sarah disappears from her son's story. The "binding of Isaac," a sacrificial rite that marks Isaac as the chosen son of his father and his father's god, is an exclusive father-son event. In Gen 25, the chapter that narrates Isaac's ascent to the position of sole heir of Abraham's house, he is never labeled through his mother. He is "Isaac, Abraham's son. Abraham begot Isaac" (Gen 25:19).[1]

The absence of Sarah in reference to her son cannot be explained simply by noting that Sarah had died by the time the events of Gen 25 take place. At the end of the chapter when Isaac is listed as the "son of Abraham," Abraham had died as well. In these ancestral stories of Genesis, listing a son by his father's name without reference to his mother marks him as heir to his father's house.[2]

Rebekah, like Sarah, receives a nation-founding blessing. When she is sent off to marry Isaac, her brother and her mother declare, "Be the mother of thousands, of ten thousands; and may your descendants possess the gates of those who hate them" (Gen 24:60).[3] Rebekah will indeed become the mother of thousands, but her success in raising her favored son, Jacob, to the position of heir within Isaac's house is marked by her disappearance from Jacob's narrative. As we saw in chapter 8, Jacob's journey from second-born twin to chosen heir involved successfully transitioning from being the "son of Rebekah" in the "house of Bethuel your mother's father" to returning to "his father Isaac in the land of Canaan" (Gen 28:2; 29:12; 31:18). By the time Jacob had "set his face toward the hill country of Gilead," Rebekah's name had disappeared, allowing her beloved son to become the son and heir of Isaac (Gen 31:21).

We find another nation-building marriage blessing in the book of Ruth. The men at the gate in the city of Bethlehem bless Boaz saying, "May Yahweh make the woman who comes into your house like Rachel and Leah who together built up the house of Israel" (Ruth 4:11). I examine this text in detail below, but here I want to note that Ruth does indeed provide Boaz's house with a son and heir, and as soon as she gives birth to Obed, her name disappears from the text. Naomi becomes the child's insider, Judean mother. Once Obed is grown, however, Naomi too disappears as Obed takes his place in the exclusively paternal *tôlēdôt* of Perez, leading to King David.

Turning now to the outsider mothers in the houses that lead up to Jacob, we find that rather than becoming building blocks within a paternally named house, foreign mothers become the apical ancestor of the nations and kingdoms they bring into being. Far from disappearing from the origin stories of their sons, outsider mothers define their sons and the nations their sons beget. In order to portray foreign, enemy nations as excluded from Yahweh's blessings and sidelined from the Promised Land, biblical authors described those nations as descendants of low-status mothers whose houses were cast out from the house of the father.

The enemy nations of Ammon and Moab are an excellent example of biblically denigrated, mother-born nations. Together, they trace their ancestry to Lot, who is related to the house of Abraham through ideologically preferred paternal links; he is the son of Abraham's brother (Gen 11:27). When we first meet Lot, he is the presumptive heir to Abram's house. Abram's wife Sarai is barren, and so when Yahweh calls Abram to leave his homeland and his father's house, "Lot went with him" (Gen 12:1–4). When the two men reach the Promised Land, however, they become so independently wealthy that the land cannot support both of them, so Lot's "tent" split from the "tent" of Abram (Gen 13:2–13). This division of two men's households occurs through a treaty initiated by Abram who says, "Separate yourself from upon me [*mēʿālay*]" (Gen 13:9).[4] Lot chooses the plain of the Jordan River and journeys "eastward" to settle back across the Jordan (Gen 13:11). While both men are wealthy and receive a land allotment, and both men will establish houses, female gender will negatively stigmatize Lot's house from its earliest inception to its nation-founding culmination.

Lot becomes the father of two daughters. By contrast, the houses of Abraham and Isaac will each boast two sons, as will the insider houses of Joseph, Judah, Amram, and Elimelech.[5] The epoch-marking men of the Primeval History—Adam, Noah, and Terah—each beget three sons, and, of course, Jacob, the eponymous ancestor of the house of Israel, will beget twelve sons. Laban and Saul stand out as other fathers who have pairs of daughters, and neither of them begets an enduring house.

As a father, Lot fails to protect his daughters. When the men of Sodom threaten Lot's house and aim to harm his houseguests, he offers his daughters to the mob for sexual assault (Gen 19:8). Later, when the city of Sodom is threatened, Lot is forced to flee his home with his family. His two sons-in-law refuse to leave, so Lot flees with three women, his wife and his two daughters. Lot's wife becomes a pillar of salt (Gen 19:26), leaving him with only two daughters, and they take up residence in a cave (Gen 19:30).

As a man with two daughters, a dead wife, and two dead sons-in-law, living outside his homeland without the protection of kin, Lot's house resembles that of Naomi. Like Naomi, Lot will have his house restored through close family connections, but the restored house of Lot becomes a freakish inverse of the national house of Israel, the house of Jacob. Jacob marries two sisters, Leah and Rachel, and begets twelve sons and a daughter. Lot also joins with two sisters, but those sisters happen to be his daughters, and there is no negotiated marriage. Turning the tables on their father, who had been willing to offer them up as a sexual sacrifice to the men of Sodom, Lot's two daughters subject their father to a dual sexual assault or at the very least a dual sexual trick.[6] On successive nights, Lot's daughters have sex with their father while he is too drunk to know "when she lay down and when she got up" (Gen 19:33–35). The result of the two sexual encounters is "the two daughters of Lot became pregnant *from their father* [*mē'ăbîhen*]." Lot does not "beget" sons, so to speak; he inadvertently becomes the father of two sons born to his daughters. If we could apply the causative *hip'il* verb "beget" to women, these two sisters' actions would come close to meriting it.

Immediately following this announcement of twin incestuous pregnancies, we learn that "the eldest gave birth to a son and called his name Moab [*mô'āb*, literally 'from the father'], and he is the father of Moab to this day." The younger daughter also gives birth to a son, and she names her son *Ben-ammi* (literally "son of my people" or "son of my *own* people"), and he becomes the father of the Ammonites (Gen 19:30–37). In Moab's own story of origin, this name may well have been explained as meaning that the nation of Moab was a gift from God the father. In the origin story of the Ammonites, their name may well have signified their understanding of themselves as the legitimate heir or "son" of God's people.[7] The biblical authors took these known names and spun negative, mocking etiologies. Moab becomes "from the father" literally, conceived through one's drunken human father. Ammon comes to signify "son conceived though my own people," namely, through my own daughter. The origin story that biblical authors supplied for these two closely related yet vehemently hated nations is one that identifies them as "mother-born," sexually abhorrent nations.

Jacob's two sister-wives come to represent the southern kingdom of Judah and the northern kingdom of Israel. Although divided, the biblical narrative presents both kingdoms as ongoing, nested sub-houses within the larger paternally identified house of Jacob. While Lot has also become the father of two kingdoms, his two "sister-wives" are his daughters. The Bible presents the kingdoms of Ammon and Moab as closely related and jointly cursed (Deut 23:4 [Eng. 23:3]). The sons born to Lot's daughters found nations that trace their ancestry to women. There is no overarching "house of Lot" that endures, as there is a house of Israel or house of Jacob. What endures are the separate mother-born nations of Ammon and Moab.

Another set of mother-born sons and woman-founded nations comes from stories about secondary wives that are slaves, maidservants, or concubines. In chapter 1, we covered Gen 25, which narrates Abraham's death and burial and lists his sons by maternal house. In that chapter, Keturah, who was labeled a concubine wife of Abraham, becomes the ancestress of several outsider yet closely related nations. These outsider nations are collectively labeled "sons of Keturah," namely, they are presented as "mother-founded nations."[8]

Hagar, the second wife of Abraham and the "slave girl of Sarai," presents a more complex picture of a mother-founded nation. She receives a direct address from the angel of Yahweh with a covenantal promise that alludes to promises within the Abrahamic covenant: "I will so greatly multiply your offspring that they cannot be counted for multitude" (*harbâ 'arbeh 'et-zar'ēk wĕlō' yissāpēr mērōb*) (Gen 16:10).[9] She receives a divine birth announcement for her son: "You have conceived and you will bear a son, and you will call his name Ishmael for Yahweh has heard of your affliction" (Gen 16:11). While this divine visitation and special covenant could suggest an elevated status for Hagar and her son, Phyllis Trible is correct in seeing both Sarah and Hagar as women struggling to survive in a household structure that pits one against the other.[10] I read Hagar's reception of a divine covenant as marking her rather than Abram as the apical ancestor of the Ishmaelites, and in so doing, classifying the Ishmaelites as men of a maternal covenant. We see this clearly in Ps 83:6 where the Ishmaelites are labeled "Hagirites."

The narrative in Gen 16 that describes Hagar's theophany and covenant contains several details that show how this covenant serves to degrade the Ishmaelites as a nation and a people. We can first examine those parts of the Abrahamic covenant that are also present in Hagar's covenant. In a series of texts, Yahweh promises Abraham a great nation, a great name, multiple forms of blessings, descendants that cannot be counted for their multitude, and a very expansively defined parcel of land (Gen 12:1–3, 7; 13:14–17; 15:4–5, 18–21; 17:4–8; 22:17–18). Looking at the Hagirite covenant in Gen 16, we find that the only detail it replicates is the promise of fertility: "I will so greatly multiply your seed" (Gen 16:10). Absent from Hagar's covenant is "great nation," "great name," "blessings," and, most significantly, "land." The rare attribution of the word "seed" to a mother accentuates that the Ishmaelites stand in a maternal line of inheritance. The Hebrew word for "seed" (*zeraʻ*), usually translated "offspring" or "descendant," is used to describe the relationship between a father and his son and is specifically tied to covenantal inheritance.[11] When Abram receives his covenantal blessing that involves numerous seed, Yahweh promises to give his seed land (Gen 13:14–18). Hagar's covenant not only refers to Ishmael and his descendants as *her*, rather than Abram's, seed; it also explicitly denies Ishmael land: "He will be a wild ass of a man. His hand will be against everyone, and everyone's hand will be against him. *He will settle to the side of* all his brothers" (Gen 16:12).

When we turn to Gen 21, the second version of Hagar receiving a divine covenant, we find a mixed set of clues for the status of the Ishmaelites under this maternal covenant. On the one hand, in this text God recognizes Ishmael as Abraham's seed. At the same time, Ishmael continues to be the anonymous son of a maidservant: "God said to Abraham, 'As for the son of the maidservant, I will make a nation of him also because he is your seed'" (Gen 21:13). In this second version, Elohim promises Hagar that he will make Ishmael "a great nation," but land is still absent from this divine promise (Gen 21:18). We find Ishmael dwelling in "the wilderness of Paran" where his mother arranges for him to marry an Egyptian woman, one of her own people (Gen 21:20–21). God is with the boy, but he will not receive the blessings of the Abrahamic covenant. The other textual detail that emphasizes the denial of land in the Hagarite covenant is found in her naming the site of her theophany "Beer-lahai-roi."[12] As we noted in chapter 1, Beer-lahai-roi is precisely the location where Isaac takes up residence following Abraham's death and Ishmael's expulsion "eastward," where, as predicted in Gen 16, he "fell to the side of all his brothers" (Gen 16:12; 25: 6, 18). In the *tôlēdôt* of Ishmael in Gen 25, we see that the seed of "Hagar, the Egyptian, Sarai's maidservant," did indeed become "a multitude," but this multitude is not landed or Abrahamically blessed, and it is defined by a slave girl's covenant.

Wives in the Symbolic National House of Jacob-Israel

In the previous chapter, I covered the origin story of Jacob and showed how he shed his maternal identification as "Rebekah's son" when he "set his face toward the hill country of Gilead" (Gen 31:21) and began his journey back "to the land of Canaan to his father Isaac" (Gen 31:18).[13] Along his journey home, his now-sizable family traveled by maternal units, each mother lodging within her own tent (Gen 31:33–35). Rather than being a part of his mother's brother's house, Jacob had his own maternally subdivided house that he was leading back to his homeland.

The next episode in Jacob's story describes his reunion with Esau. In this encounter, the twins meet each other as national houses rather than simply as two men with families. Jacob finds his estranged brother living in "the land of Seir, the country of Edom" (Gen 32:4 [Eng. 32:3]). Esau has thus already become the nation that Yahweh foretold in his oracle to Rebekah: "Two nations are in your womb; two peoples born of you will be divided" (Gen 25:23). Jacob is at a disadvantage when he meets Esau because his house has not yet become the national "house of Israel." Jacob's transition to "Israel" will occur as part of his encounter with Esau, a story that is told with an overlay of military language, suggesting a struggle between two nations.

Upon his arrival on the outskirts of the Promised Land, still to the east of the Jordan, two "angels of God" meet Jacob, prompting him to declare the place "God's camp" (*maḥănēh 'ĕlōhîm*) and to name it "*Maḥănāyim*" (literally, two [military] encampments or divisions, a dual) (Gen 32:2–3 [Eng. 32: 1–2]). Jacob decides that his first overtures to his estranged brother should be diplomatic. He sends messengers ahead to inform Esau of his return, and those messengers then inform Jacob that Esau is coming to meet him "with four hundred men" (Gen 32:7 [Eng. 32:6]). Jacob immediately fears a military assault and counters Esau's threat of force by dividing his own "nation" (*'am*) into "two encampments" (*maḥănôt*) (Gen 32:8–9 [Eng. 32:7–8]). In this way, the "camp of God" that Jacob named *Maḥănāyim* becomes his own national camp, subdivided into two military divisions.

In his great fear of Esau, Jacob turns to his god in prayer and desperately seeks deliverance. In the wording and literary structure of this prayer, the paternal, nation-founding language of the Abrahamic covenant protectively encases maternally aligned subdivisions, which are imagined in terms both military and domestic. Jacob begins the prayer by calling on "the God of my father Abraham and the God of my father Isaac, Yahweh." He then reminds this god of his Abrahamic promise: "You are the one who said, 'return to your land, and to your birthplace, and I will do good for you'" (Gen 32:10 [Eng. 32:9]). Three verses later, a catch line repeats the "I will do good for you" promise, thus connecting the end of the prayer to the beginning. In this culminating verse, we find the second half of Jacob's Abrahamic promise: "And now you have said, 'I will surely do you good, and I will make your seed like the sand of the sea that cannot be counted because of its multitude'" (Gen 32:13 [Eng. 32:12]). Taken together, verses 10 and 13 provide a full recollection of the Abrahamic promise as it has been offered to Jacob, and this promise, as we have noted, is heavily paternal: father, land, seed.

References to nested encampments and to mothers and their sons structurally split Jacob's paternal covenant. In the middle two verses of the prayer, Jacob's concern is for the protection of his encampments and his maternal houses. He praises his god for blessing him so richly and notes that when he first crossed the Jordan as a young, fleeing man, he left with nothing more than his staff. Now he has returned with an entourage impressive enough to be divided into "two encampments" (*šĕnê maḥănôt*) (Gen 32:11 [Eng. 32:10]). He then raises his petition: "Deliver me from the hand of my brother, from the hand of Esau, for I am afraid of him lest he come and strike down each mother upon her children" (Gen 32:12 [Eng. 32:11]). In this request for divine deliverance, Jacob views his threatened *ʿam* in terms of the mothers and their children that comprise it. The two "encampments" are therefore best understood as subdivisions led by Leah and Rachel. We have already seen that women in general are associated with tents and tented subdivisions, and that Rachel, Leah, and their maidservants have traveled to Canaan in maternal tents. In this prayer, Jacob sees the mothers as the building blocks or support structure of his paternal house, and he fears that Esau will strike them down and in so doing blot out his house. He encases his fear for his maternal houses in the protective language of his paternal covenant, laying claim to its promises as heir.

Following his prayer, Jacob sends a series of gifts to Esau, and then he takes "his two wives, his two slave wives, and his eleven sons" across the Jabbok River toward Esau's homeland of Edom. Afterward Jacob spends the night "alone" (Gen 32:23–25 [Eng. 32:22–24]). It is at this point that we find the famous story of Jacob wrestling throughout the night with "a man" who is unable to prevail against him. When the man asks to leave, Jacob demands a blessing and receives his national name: "You shall no longer be called Jacob but Israel for you have striven with God and with man and have prevailed" (Gen 32:29 [Eng. 32:28]). When the "man" does not reveal his own name to Jacob, Jacob seems to identify him as "God," because he names the place "Peniel" saying, "For I have seen God face to face, yet my life is preserved" (Gen 32:31 [Eng. 32:30]). Thus, when Jacob encounters Esau, in the episode that immediately follows this one, he meets his brother as Israel; two "nations," sons of the same womb, come face to face.

Jacob "raises his eyes and sees Esau coming with four hundred men." Fearing an attack, he divides his *ʿam* into mother-units: "He divided the sons among Leah, Rachel, and the two slave wives" (Gen 33:1). Jacob then arranges the units in what appears to be a series of battle regiments, placing himself at the vanguard with his mother-units lined up behind him from least valued to most valued: "the slave wives with their sons in front, then Leah with her sons, and Rachel and Joseph last of all" (Gen 33:1–2). Once again, we see how wives mark hierarchies within the house of the father. The slave wives and their children are not only in front but they are grouped together anonymously as a single unit. Leah as the unloved wife follows, and Rachel, the loved wife with the favored son, occupies the safest, most protected position.

Despite all the military buildup to this encounter, Jacob and Esau do not fight. Instead, Esau greets Jacob in the manner we have come to expect of the uterine sibling relationship: Esau "fell on his neck and kissed him and they wept" (Gen 33:4). This is precisely the response of Joseph when he too "raises his eyes and sees Benjamin, his brother, the son of his mother," and at the moment of recognition, "he fell upon the neck of Benjamin his brother and wept, and Benjamin wept upon his neck" (Gen 43:29; 45:15). Jacob and Esau reunite as uterine siblings. After accepting a "gift" from Jacob, Esau, like Ishmael and the sons of Keturah, who also accepted gifts, journeys away from the Promised Land, from the land of his father, Isaac. He returns to "Seir," his national homeland (Gen 33:4–16).

Having separated himself from "the house of the father of his mother" and from "his brother, the son of his mother," Jacob stops in Succoth, just east of the Jordan, and for the first time we read that Jacob "built himself a house" (Gen 33:17).[14] He then crosses the River Jordan into the Promised Land, journeys on to Shechem, purchases land, and "pitched his tent." He then "erected an altar" to his nation-founding god calling it "El is the God of Israel" (Gen 33:18–20). Jacob has become the heir to the patriarchal promises of Abraham and Isaac. He has established his own house in the line of his fathers. His mother, Rebekah, has disappeared from the narrative, and Jacob's story becomes the origin story for the national house of Israel, a house subdivided into maternal encampments that contain groupings of the twelve, segmented tribes.

'ummâ: The Mother-Unit

We have seen that the wives and mothers we meet in Genesis come to represent nations, kingdoms, and military encampments. The biblical account of the history of Israel and Judah shows the foundational houses of Abraham and Jacob splitting into hierarchically arranged maternal subunits. In the case of Abraham's house, lower-status wives were cast out of his house, and they became the apical ancestors of mother-born nations, territorially peripheral to the Promised Land. Jacob's house also divided into maternal subunits, specifically into maternally defined military encampments. The national, symbolic, and military associations of maternal sub-houses provide a helpful backdrop for the analysis of one final, maternally specific Hebrew kinship term: 'ummâ.

The Hebrew term 'ummâ occurs with certainty only three times in the Hebrew Bible and is conventionally defined as a feminine noun meaning "tribe" or "people."[15] Various Hebrew dictionaries and lexica add nuance to the term, noting, for example, that it occurs in semantic parallel with *gôy* (foreign nation);[16] that it is attested in two plural forms, 'ummôt and 'ummîm;[17] and that its Semitic cognates include Ugaritic 'umt, Akkadian *ummatu*, Aramaic 'ummayyā('), and Arabic 'ummat.[18] The three accepted occurrences of the term are Gen 25:16; Num 25:15; and Ps 117:1. Additionally, we find one attestation in a Qumran text and a proposed occurrence in Isa 55:4.[19]

Akkadian *ummatum* and Ugaritic 'umt

Abraham Malamat's 1980 article titled "*Ummatum* in Old Babylonian Texts and Its Ugaritic and Biblical Counterparts" represents the most comprehensive treatment of the Hebrew term and its Semitic cognates.[20] Based on his survey of the use of the term in Old Babylonian texts from Tell Al Rimah, Malamat suggests translating the term "mother-unit," by which he means that *ummatum* was a tribal unit that traced its origins to a foundational mother. Socially, the *ummatum* functioned as a registration unit for "soldiers and laborers" (531). Malamat explains the frequent occurrence of the Akkadian *ummatum* in military contexts as having its roots in "the fact that armies in their earliest stages were formed on the basis of actual families" (528). Malamat then makes a grammatical argument for considering *ummatum* as a maternal subunit of the larger, grammatically masculine nation (*ummānu*). First, he notes that the construct form *ummat* occurs where "the *nomen rectum* that follows denotes a tribe," meaning that *ummatum* seems to signify a "tribal entity" or a grouping of "sub-tribes" (532). The *CAD* seems to follow Malamat's conclusions, defining *ummatu* as the "main contingent, unit (of an army or workforce), mainstay, principal support, main part (of something)." The detailed entry then adds that *ummatu* is a "sub-unit of the *ummānu*" and is used in construct with *ummānu*.[21] The *CAD* entry does not, however, define this tribal subunit as "maternal."

We have already covered the Ugaritic cognate *'umt*, which like *ummatum* carries maternal associations and seems to signify a maternally related kin group or clan. Malamat notes that *'umt* occurs only in epic texts and almost exclusively as part of the construct phrase *'l 'umt*, which is discussed in chapter 4.[22] I have argued that the best translation of this phrase is "suckling of my mother's clan," a translation that accurately reflects the maternal connotations in both lexical elements. Unlike *ummatum*, the Ugaritic phrase *'l 'umt* is not found in contexts of military conscription or labor units. Still, within the Aqhat and Baal epics, the phrase functions to establish familial allies over against enemies in contexts that call for violent and deadly revenge. In the Aqhat epic, Pughat refers to her dead brother Aqhat as *'l 'umty* at a point when she is demanding that her father allow her to "smite the one who smote *the suckling of my mother's clan.*" In the Baal epic, Shapshu speaks with Anat and refers to Baal as "the suckling of your [Anat's] maternal clan."[23] This conversation occurs after Anat has demanded that Mot return Baal, whom she refers to as "my brother." Throughout the Baal epic, Anat serves as Baal's political and military ally and advocate. The Akkadian and Ugaritic evidence supports an understanding of *ummatum* and *'umt* as maternal subunits of larger, grammatically masculine entities. They are both kinship terms based in family relationships that are then used to designate military or tribal units and family alliances.

Hebrew and Biblical Aramaic Attestations of the Term *'ummâ*

The conceptualization of the terms *ummatum* and *'umt* as maternally associated, tribal subunits of a larger, grammatically masculine "tribe" or "nation" fits well with the Hebrew usage of the term. We find the first biblical occurrence in one of our primary source texts for maternal subdivisions within the house of the father, Gen 25. In this text, Abraham sends away "the sons of his concubines from upon his son Isaac." He then dies and is buried by Isaac and Ishmael. The reference to *'ummâ* occurs as part of a summary notation at the end of the *tôlēdôt* of "Ishmael, Abraham's son, whom Hagar the Egyptian, Sarah's slave girl, bore to Abraham":

> These are the sons of Ishmael, and these are their names according to their settlements and their tent encampments, twelve chiefs according to their mother-units.
>
> *'ēlleh hēm bĕnê yišmā'ēl wĕ'ēlleh šĕmōtām bĕḥaṣrêhem ûbĕṭîrōtām šĕnêm-'āśār nĕśî'im lĕ'ummōtām.* (Gen 25:16)

If we understand the *lāmed* that precedes *'ummōtām* to mean "according to," then each tribal chief (*nāśî'*) is identified as part of a larger, maternally defined subunit.[24] The specific referent for "mother-units" in this verse remains unclear. It seems to suggest that Ishmael, like his father Abraham, had multiple wives, and his sons, the "chiefs," are listed according to their maternal houses.[25] This would suggest subgroupings of sons under their mothers in a way similar to what we found in the grouping of sons with their mothers in Jacob's approach to Esau.

The concept of *'ummōt* as a subdivision is also communicated spatially. The sons of Ishmael are listed by their "names" (*šĕmotām*), "settlements" (*ḥaṣrêhem*), "tent encampments" (*ṭîrotām*), and "mother-units" (*'ummōtām*). While "name" is something passed from father to son, the words *ḥāṣēr* and *ṭîrâ* can both be understood as dependent subdivisions of space within a larger masculine entity. *Ḥāṣēr* is a masculine noun meaning "settled abode, settlement, village."[26] Throughout the book of Joshua, each masculine tribe that traces its name to one of the sons of Jacob receives a land inheritance that includes these unwalled settlements as satellite dependencies of cities (Josh 13–21). The second word, *ṭîrâ*, is a feminine noun denoting an "encampment or battlement" forming an "enclosure," so it has both territorial and military associations.[27] We also may have a parallel line construction in Gen 25:16 whereby "their names" stand parallel to "twelve chiefs," and "their settlements and encampments" is parallel to "mother-units."

The second occurrence of the term *'ummâ* is found in Num 25, which narrates two interlocking stories of sexual and religious apostasy. The chapter begins with the men of Israel engaging in sexual relations with the women of Moab and subsequently yoking themselves to the Moabite god "Baal of Peor" (Num 25:1–3). Yahweh threatens the entire nation of Israel with a devastating plague unless the heads of each guilty house are impaled before him in the sun. In the midst of this episode, we find the story of an Israelite man bringing a Midianite woman into the Israelite camp "in the sight of Moses," and taking her into the tent of meeting. One righteous Phinehas, a "son of Aaron the priest," follows the couple into the tent of meeting and spears them through, killing both and stopping the plague (Num 25:4–9). Yahweh grants Phinehas a "perpetual priesthood" for his killing of the Israelite man and Midianite woman. The narrative concludes by identifying the two slain victims by name followed by a series of specifying kinship labels. The Israelite man is identified by personal name, father's name, father's house and rank, and tribe:

The name of the slain Israelite man, the one slain with the Midianite woman, was Zimri, son of Salu, chief of a house of the father belonging to the Simeonites.

wěšēm 'îš yiśrā'ēl hammukkeh 'ăšer hukkâ 'et-hammidyānît zmirî ben-sālû' něśî' bêt-'āb laššim'ōnî'. (Num 25:14)

The slain man is first identified by nationality, "Israelite." The text then uses a set of kinship labels that move outward in a chain of nested categories from individual—Zimri, identified by name—to father's house, here meaning nuclear family, identified by the father's name "Salu," to the status of Zimri's father as the chief (nāśî') of a larger extended father's house belonging to the tribe of Simeon.

The slain woman is likewise identified with a string of appositional, kinship epithets:

The name of the slain Midianite woman was Cozbi, daughter of Zur. He was the head of the mother-units of a house of the father in Midian.

wěšēm hā'iššâ hammukkâ hammidyānît kozbî bat-ṣûr rō'š 'ummôt bêt-'āb běmidyān hû'. (Num 25:15)

If this identification follows the pattern of Zimri's identification, then the fathers of both slain individuals hold leadership positions at a rank above that of the extended family unit. They hold leadership positions at a tribal level, where the tribe is imagined consisting of multiple, extended houses of the father. The Simeonites are subdivided into several extended-family houses of the father within which each would have multiple smaller nuclear houses of the father. Salu is not only the head of the father's house or nuclear cell into which Zimri was born; he is also "chief" of a larger, more extended "house of the father." The language describing the insider, "Simeonite house," does not include maternal subdivisions. Cozbi's chain of identifications ascends up to the level of nation, "Midian," and Midian is imagined as an entity subdivided into powerful houses of the father, which in turn are subdivided into 'ummôt or "mother-units." Cozbi's father is the head (rō'š) of several mother-units within an extended house of the father (= level of Simeon), in the nation of Midian (= level of Israel). Cozbi is identified a second time in Num 25:18 as "the daughter of the chief [naśî] of Midian."

The references to 'ummōt in Gen 25:16 and Num 25:15 share several features. As a kinship designation, 'ummōt occurs in a list of nested units.

The sons of Ishmael are listed by name and father's house and then by tent or unwalled settlement. Finally, each son of Ishmael is identified as a *naśî* belonging to an *'ummâ*, a chief listed by his mother-unit. Cozbi's Midianite family is likewise identified by name, father's house, and then by some larger paternally defined unit in which her father is a *rō'š* of *'ummōt*, "a head of mother-units," and later a "*naśî* of Midian." In both cases, foreign nations—Ishmaelites and Midianites—are divided into extended family or tribal units within which the head of one branch becomes the *naśî* or *rō'š* over several mother-units. Contextually, the references to *'ummōt* emerge as important designations in identifying a high-level leadership position. Baruch Levine sees the reference to *'ummōt* in both Genesis and Numbers as corresponding to "tribe" in the "projected structure of the Israelite nation." For Levine, a nation consisted of a number of *'ummōt*, and each *'ummâ* consisted of a number of paternal houses.[28]

The third biblical reference to *'ummâ* is found in Ps 117:1–2, and it is different from the first two references in several respects. This is a psalm of praise to Yahweh, so the word *'ummâ* does not identify a particular person. As a psalm, this occurrence is found within poetry, specifically within two couplets of parallelistic lines. Finally, this reference to *'ummâ* takes the masculine plural ending, reading *'ummîm*.[29] The two-verse psalm reads as follows:

> Praise Yahweh all nations,
> Laud him all the mother-units.
> For his steadfastness overpowers us,
> the faithfulness of Yahweh forever, Praise Yah.
>
> *halĕlû 'et-yhwh kol-gôyim*
> *šabbĕḥûhû kol-hā'ummîm:*
> *kî gābar 'ālênû ḥasdô*
> *we'ĕmet-yhwh lĕôlām halĕlû-yā.*

Levine explains the use of the masculine plural form on the feminine noun *'ummâ* with reference to the Aramaic *'ummayyā(')*, which he translates as "the peoples" and locates in Dan 3:4, 29 and Ezra 4:10.[30] The Aramaic *'ummâ* in the Bible is identical to biblical Hebrew, translated as "nation" and identified as "late" in usage.[31]

When we look at the Aramaic examples, we find the repeated sequence "nation, mother-unit, tongue," which seems to resemble the same telescoping string of kinship epithets that we have noted in the Hebrew uses of *'ummōt*. Dan 3:4 reads,

The herald proclaimed aloud,
"you are commanded O nations, mother-units, and tongues."

wĕkārôzā' qārē' bĕḥāyil
lĕkôn 'āmĕrîn 'amĕmayyā' 'ummayyā' wĕliššānayyā.

Likewise, in Dan 3:28, Nebuchadrezzar makes a decree in which he calls on "every nation, mother-unit, and tongue." In Gen 25:16, the "sons of Ishmael" are listed by name "according to their mother units." In Num 25:15, Zur, the father of Cozbi, was the "head of a mother-unit of a father's house in Midian." In the Aramaic examples, people are categorized first by language or local dialect then by the mother-unit within which that dialect is spoken, and finally by the nation that encompasses multiple mother-units and their respective dialects. A Qumran text reads very similarly:

> You established the nations according to their clans
> and the languages according to their mother-units.
>
> *Ysdth [h']mym lmšpḥwtyhm wlšnwt l'wmwtm.*[32]

Here again, shared language falls within a mother-unit, and *mišpāḥâ*, as a grammatically feminine subunit of *'am*, stands in parallel with *'ummâ*.

There may be one final Hebrew example in Isa 55:4, but this one is difficult to establish on account of the similarly written and sounding word "*lĕ'ōm*," or "*lĕ'ôm*," with the plural, *lĕ'ummîm*. This is a masculine noun that, like *'ummâ*, means "people," "nation," or "tribe," and also like *'ummâ* is found in poetic parallelism with the words *gôy* and *'am*.[33] This semantic closeness and homophony make it difficult to distinguish between *'ummîm* preceded by the preposition *lāmed* and *lĕ'ummîm*. In Isa 55:4 we find just this combination, making several readings possible. I would suggest the following:

> See I am making him a witness of nations,
> a prince and commander of mother-units.
>
> *hēn 'ēd lĕ'ummîm nĕtattîw*
> *nāgîd ûmĕṣawwēh lĕ'ummim.*

The first reference to *lĕ'ummîm* with the *mater* could be read as either "witness to mother-units" or, more likely in my view, a construct phrase, "witness of nations." In the second reference, *lĕ'ummîm* without the *mater*, we could either read "prince and commander of nations" or "prince and commander of mother units." In the first case, we read "prince and commander" in construct with "nations" (*lĕ'ummîm*). In the second case, which my translation follows, the *lāmed* is taken as a preposition prefixed to *'um-mîm*, meaning "prince and commander *to* or *of* mother-units." I have translated "*of* mother-units" following two texts in Chronicles where a person is "prince" of a tribal unit using the preposition *lāmed*.[34] Admittedly, it is also possible that both references are to "nations" (*lĕ'ummîm*) spelled differently, and the repeated appearance of *gôy, gôy* in the following verse would support reading *lĕ'ummîm* twice. For me, the stronger argument is the one that recognizes the pattern in poetic parallelism wherein the A-clause defines a category and the B-clause represents a subunit within the category. If this is the case, then the poem in Isa 55:4 moves from the larger, masculine nations (*lĕ'ummîm*) to the smaller, feminine mother-units (*'ummîm*).[35]

To summarize, we find a plural form of the Hebrew *'ummâ* in Gen 25:16, Num 25:15, Ps 117:1, and 4QD, and possibly in Isa 55:4. We also have the Aramaic plural in Ezra 4:10 and Dan 3:4, 29. These texts indicate that *'ummâ* was part of a social and political system of classification and identification and constituted a subunit of a larger, grammatically masculine *'am, gôy,* or *lĕ'ōm*. The term is late, found in priestly sources in the Pentateuch, in a Qumran text, and in biblical Aramaic in late biblical texts.

Jacob's Maternal Houses from Wilderness to Kingdom

The idea of a nation divided into "mother-units" finds full expression when we turn to the national house of Israel. Whether the stories are set in the time of the wilderness wanderings, the settlement of the land of Canaan, or the monarchy, maternal subdivisions within the house of Jacob continue to mark the hierarchical organizational structure of the nation. The houses of Rachel and Leah, Bilhah and Zilpah explicitly and implicitly inform the shape of the Israelite nation, kingdom, and restored remnant. Far from being an egalitarian confederation of twelve tribes, the nation of Israel was divided into hierarchically valued mother-units at all stages in its history.

The first observation to make concerning Jacob's maternal sub-houses is that none of the sons of maidservant wives became a contender for leadership in either the royal or priestly spheres. Geographically, the territory allotted to the maidservant sons "falls to the side" of the central territory of Judah, Benjamin, Ephraim, and Manasseh.[36] In the settlement of the land of Canaan, three of the four maidservant tribes—Asher, Naphtali, and Dan—occupied contiguous territories that together formed a northern cap to the territory of Israel.[37] The fourth, Gad, lay across the Jordan. The only two sons of wives whose territories were across the Jordan were Reuben and the half-tribe of Manasseh.

Even though Reuben was Jacob's firstborn, the first fruit of his vigor, the biblical narrative discredits him through the story of how Reuben jeopardized his status as *bĕkôr* when he "went and lay with Bilhah, the concubine of his father" (Gen 35:22). Two sequential stories of Jacob blessing his sons and grandsons show Reuben losing his special status. First, Jacob blesses the two sons of Joseph and seems to suggest that these grandsons will become a new set of first- and second-born sons: "Ephraim and Manasseh, they belong to me, just as Reuben and Simeon are mine" (Gen 48:5). One chapter later, when an elderly Jacob blesses his twelve sons, he recalls Reuben's act of sexual arrogance, "untamed as water, you will not show preeminence, because you went up on the bed of your father and defiled it, you went up on my couch!" (Gen 49:3–4). The Chronicler makes Joseph's sons' replacement of Reuben as firstborn explicit and links it directly to Reuben's sexual impropriety (1 Chron 5:1–2). Reuben's transgression with his father's "concubine" not only costs him the position as heir in his father's house but effectively demotes him to the status of a maidservant son. Territorially, he occupies a parcel across the Jordan with Gad, the firstborn of his mother's maidservant. In later texts, as we see below, he heads a maidservant division of tribes in literary contexts that demote him.

When we turn to the maternal houses of Rachel and Leah, we find that both priestly houses and all of ancient Israel's early designated royal houses trace their ancestry to these two wives. The Levites and the Aaronide priestly families claim ancestry from Levi of the house or *'ummâ* of Leah. At the time of the divided monarchy, the northern kingdom, known as "Israel" or "Ephraim," traced its ancestry to Rachel, and the southern kingdom of Judah traced its ancestry to Leah. The origins of ancient Israelite kingship, however, are found in the house or *'ummâ* of Rachel. From the time of the judges through the division of the monarchy under Jeroboam, we find four volatile, short-lived royal houses that endure for two generations: Gideon to Abimelech, Saul to Ishbaal, David to Solomon, and Jeroboam to Nadab. Of these four early royal houses, three trace their ancestry to Rachel, and one—that of David—to Leah (fig. 11).[38]

The stories of ancient Israel's early experiments with anointing a king over "all Israel" emerge from Rachel's house in center-north territories. Rachel, we recall, had two sons: Joseph her womb-opener and Benjamin for

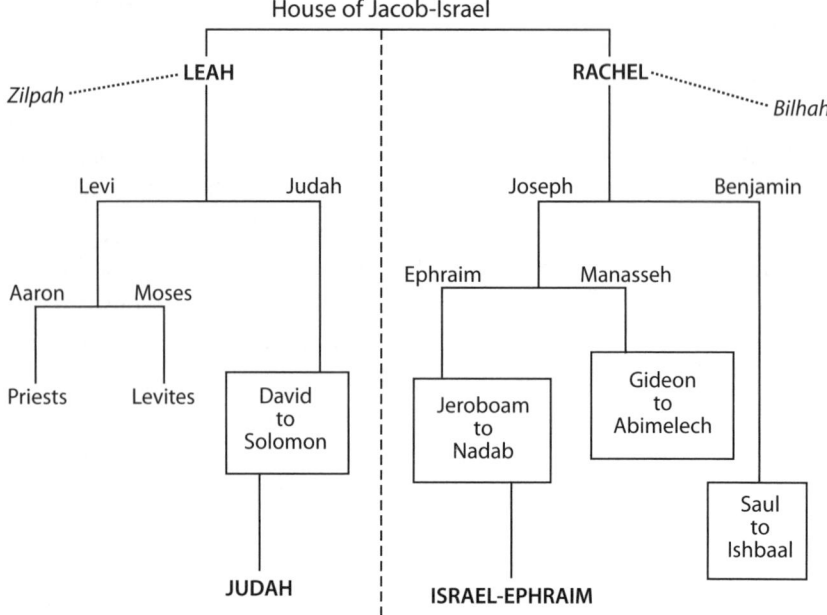

Figure 11. *The royal and priestly houses organized by maternal sub-house within the house of Jacob-Israel. Illustration created by Ondrea Keith, rendered by Bill Nelson.*

whom she died. Joseph then had Manasseh and Ephraim, both of whom were adopted as sons of Jacob, with Ephraim replacing Reuben as Jacob's *bĕkôr*. Rachel's house therefore contains Jacob's heir, Ephraim, and two additional "sons" in Manasseh and Benjamin. The first leader offered dynastic rule over all Israel is Gideon, a judge from "the weakest clan in Manasseh," whom we meet in the northern territory of Ophrah, just northeast of Bethel (Judg 6:15). After he has defeated the Midianites, the "men of Israel" say to him, "Rule over us, you, your son, and your grandson also" (Judg 8:22). While Gideon refuses their offer, his son Abimelech nonetheless claims kingship following his father's death (Judg 9:1–6).[39] So the first Israelite to be made "king" is from the tribe of Manasseh, one of the lesser members of the maternal house of Rachel, and he established kingship in Shechem.

The second man to be named king over Israel was Saul, and he is introduced with a full Benjaminite genealogy, so he too is of the house of Rachel but not of the preferred line within that maternal house (1 Sam 9:1–2). Like Gideon, Saul acknowledges his low status in the kinship structure: "Am I not a Benjaminite, from the smallest of the tribes of Israel, and is not my clan [*mišpāḥâ*] the youngest of all the clans in the tribes of Benjamin?" (1 Sam 9:20–21). Samuel anoints Saul king and then predicts that as a sign of Saul's status as Yahweh's anointed, Saul will meet two men that very day "by Rachel's tomb in the territory of Benjamin," and the men will repeat a very precise phrase that Samuel announces (1 Sam 10:1–2). The kingship of Saul, therefore, is introduced as part of the tribe of Benjamin and secured or divinely confirmed at the tomb of his maternal ancestress Rachel.

Skipping over the establishment of a southern-based monarchy under David, the next northerner to found a royal house is "Jeroboam, son of Nebat, an Ephraimite of Zeredah" (1 Kings 11:26). Finally, in Jeroboam, we have the founder of a royal house who traces his ancestry to Jacob's designated *běkôr*, the son of Rachel's womb-opening son, Joseph. Even though his dynasty, like the two previous dynasties, will only last two generations, his newly founded northern kingdom inherits the name of the house-founding ancestor, Israel, and will also be known by the name of his chosen son, Ephraim.

When we examine the advent of kingship in the south, the situation is quite different. David's genealogy and his path to kingship draw on traditions from two maternal houses. David is introduced in several stories as "the son of Jesse, the Bethlehemite" (1 Sam 16:1, 18), and as "the son of an Ephrathite of Bethlehem in Judah, named Jesse" (1 Sam 17:12). Bethlehem and Ephrathah are place names associated with the death and burial site of Rachel in the tribal territory of Benjamin (Gen 35:16–20). Judah, however, is the fourth son of Leah, Jacob's unloved wife. As noted in chapter 7, David comes to power by marrying into, absorbing, and ultimately eliminating the house of Saul. Therefore, David's royal house becomes the first to trace its genealogical ancestry to a son of Leah, but the primacy of the house of Rachel continues to be recognized through repeated allusions to key Rachel sites.

When we consider all four of ancient Israel's early experiments with dynastic kingship, Rachel's house emerges as the preeminent royal house, the king-making house. Gideon is of Manasseh; Saul is of Benjamin; Jeroboam is of Ephraim. Saul's kingship finds its divine confirmation at Rachel's tomb, the physical site of her enduring house. When the Judean David seeks kingship over all Israel, he must insinuate himself into the house of Rachel, and he does this by marrying into, absorbing, and eliminating the Benjaminite house of Saul and by locating his own ancestry at the site of Rachel's tomb.

Maternal Houses in Exilic and Postexilic Writings

One of the recurring images within exilic and postexilic writings is the hopeful vision of a restored house of Israel. When Judah, the surviving remnant of the house of Israel, imagined its return from exile, it envisioned a fully restored house where the northern kingdom of Israel was once again united with the southern kingdom of Judah. I examine three of these exilic and postexilic texts in order to show the political and even military functions ascribed to Jacob's maternal houses. The authors of each text are working with the existence of the single tribe of Judah, much reduced, and the priestly houses of Aaron and the Levites, and they are constructing an idealized memory of a united house of Israel.

The book of Ruth, as already discussed, is a Judean, pro-David composition that aims to shore up his royal pedigree.[40] With this background in mind, it is significant that the only mention of Leah outside Genesis is found in this book. In the culminating chapter of the book, where Boaz and Ruth marry and have a son, Obed, who becomes the grandfather of King David, we find a blessing spoken to Boaz on the occasion of his marriage. In this blessing, Boaz's house is placed in the royal line of Judah's house, but through its references to both Rachel and Leah, it hearkens back to the ideal of a united Israel. The blessing begins:

> May Yahweh make the woman who is coming into your house
> like Rachel and Leah, the two of whom built up the house of Israel.
>
> *yittēn yhwh ʾet-hāʾiššâ habbāʾâ ʾel-bêtekā kĕrāḥēl ûkĕlēʾâ
> ʾăšer bānû šĕtêhem ʾet-bêt yiśrāʾēl.* (Ruth 4:11)

In this blessing, two foundational wives and mothers are the building blocks of the larger, grammatically and genealogically masculine entity "the house of Israel." Rachel the younger but loved wife is listed before her older sister Leah.

In the second part of the blessing, we find three maternally focused lines. Following the listing of Rachel before Leah in verse 11, the first couplet alludes to Rachel and the second to Leah. The final line expresses the wish that Ruth, labeled "this young woman," will bear children to Boaz just as Rachel and Leah had borne children to build up Jacob's house:

> May you produce children [literally, "make strength"] in Ephrathah, and
>   bestow a name in Bethlehem.
> May your house be like the house of Perez, whom Tamar bore to Judah,

From the seed that Yahweh will give you by this young woman.

waʿăśēh-ḥayil běʾeprātâ ûqěrāʾ-šēm běbêt lāḥem
wîhî bêtkā kěbêt pereṣ ʾăšer-yālědâ tāmār lîhûdâ
min-hazzeraʿ ʾăšer yittēn yhwh lěkā min-hannaʿărâ hazzōt. (Ruth 4:11–12)

When we read the first couplet, we immediately recall that the last woman who produced a child in Ephrathah and bestowed a name in Bethlehem was Rachel, who "on the way to Ephrath, that is Bethlehem," labored and named her son "Ben-oni," meaning "son of my affliction." This son for whom Rachel died was Benjamin, Rachel's hoped-for "additional" son, a son who completed her maternal house (Gen 35:16–21).[41] So, in calling out Ephrathah and Bethlehem, this first couplet evokes a territory infused with the memory of infertility overcome at great cost to the mother, and the birth of a son whose line produced a king.

At the same time, of course, these two sites allude to David, whose father was "an Ephrathite of Bethlehem in Judah" (1 Sam 17:12). David J. Schloen notes Bethlehem's associations with the tribe of Judah in Micah 5:1 where "Bethlehem Ephrathah" is "one of the little clans of Judah" (*ṣāʿîr lihyôt běʾalpê yěhûdâ*), and in 1 Chronicles where "Ephrathah" is the name of the second wife of Caleb and the mother of Hur, who is the "father of Bethlehem."[42] In both of these examples, Bethlehem Ephrathah is a maternally defined territorial subunit of the larger tribe of Judah or clan of Caleb within the tribe of Judah. In the Micah text, Bethlehem Ephrathah is a site of a messianic prophecy for a ruler. Combining the houses of Rachel and Leah, this blessing creates a matrix of allusions to infertility overcome, royal names, and messianic prophecies.

The second couplet also brings to mind details of a hard-won royal son. Tamar, the daughter-in-law of Judah, chose a course of action that involved tremendous social risk and sacrifice in order to conceive and give birth to Perez, the ancestor of King David (Gen 38). The second part of the poem therefore begins by alluding to Rachel through the reference to Ephrathah and Bethlehem and concludes with a reference to the house of Leah through the story of Judah, Tamar, and Perez. Paired memories of maternal sacrifices embedded within the houses of Rachel and Leah preface the blessing of Ruth, here referred to as "this young woman." The hope is that Ruth, a childless widow, will become a nation-building, kingdom-founding mother nested within Boaz's house.

If the book of Ruth is the birth story of the Davidic kingdom, this blessing imagines the house of David as the united house of all Israel.

While Ruth was likely written after the fall of the southern kingdom of Judah, it presents the remnant of Judah under a Davidide as a restored house of Jacob. Ruth the Moabite will build up the house of Boaz just as Rachel and Leah together built up the house of Israel.

We find a similar kind of restored house of Jacob complete with two maternal sub-houses in Ezekiel's presentation of the national house of Yahweh (Ezek 23). Like the national house of Jacob, Ezekiel imagines the symbolic house of Yahweh as a polygynous household divided into two tented subunits named for sister wives. The wives of Yahweh are uterine sisters, "two women, daughters of one mother" (Ezek 23:2–4). The older sister is named Oholah, meaning "Her Tent," and the younger sister is named Oholibah, meaning "My Tent Is Within Her." These maternal subunits have geographic and political dimensions in that the tent of Oholah is in Samaria, the capital of the northern kingdom, and the tent of Oholibah is in Jerusalem, the capital of the southern kingdom. Just as Jacob's maternal subunits are imagined as military encampments, Ezekiel describes Yahweh's tented wives acting within the military sphere, lusting after military men from Egypt, Assyria, and Babylonia (Ezek 23:5–6, 12).

While Ezekiel's allegory replicates several aspects of Jacob's household, he makes one important switch that reveals his pro-Judean bias for a restored Israel. The switch involves the geographic location of the younger, loved wife. In Jacob's household, Rachel is the younger, loved wife, and she is associated with the north through her grandson Ephraim. The unloved, older wife is Leah, and she is the progenitress of Judah and David in the south. In Ezekiel's allegory, the younger wife is Oholibah, who is associated with Jerusalem and the southern kingdom, and the older wife is Oholah or Samaria representing the northern kingdom. In Ezekiel's vision, Yahweh's greatest emotion, his most pronounced jealousy, is reserved for his younger wife, Oholibah, who occupies the southern, Leah-associated territory and kingdom. By making the southern, Judean Oholibah the younger wife for whom Yahweh the husband expresses the strongest jealousy, Ezekiel suggests that the southern kingdom has become the loved wife in the house of Israel.[43]

Finally, in the arrangement of the tribes around the tent of meeting in Num 2, we find Jacob's house subdivided militarily into four hierarchically arranged mother-units. The text describes the arrangement of the tribes around the tent of meeting as they camp and march through the wilderness, but many scholars have noted within this arrangement a "plan for military organization"[44] replete with the language of a "military camp."[45] The twelve tribes are arranged under their "standard" (*degel*) according to their "division" or "encampment" (*maḥănēh*). The arrangement of the tribes is symbolic and hierarchical, showing a "pro-Judean tendency."[46] The favored and unfavored tribes in this ordering recall Jacob's curses and blessings in Gen 49.[47] They also show an awareness of the transgressions of Reuben and Simeon that lead to their displacement by Ephraim and Manasseh.

The organizing principle for the arrangement of the tribes is geographic wherein the east constitutes the ideologically valued compass point (fig. 12). The tent of meeting faces east as will the Jerusalem temple. Moses, Aaron, and Aaron's sons "camp in front of the tabernacle on the east—in front of the tent of meeting toward the east" (Num 3:38). Judah, the royal tribe and surviving remnant, is mentioned first, and heads a delegation of three tribes in the east.[48] A three-tribe grouping headed by one of the tribes defends each compass point around the tent of meeting.[49] The east/west axis is reserved for blessed tribes who trace their ancestry to the maternal house of a wife (Leah and Rachel). The less valued north/south axis is reserved for the cursed sons of wives and sons who trace their ancestry to the maternal house of a maidservant wife (Bilhah and Zilpah).[50] The Levites occupy the tent of meeting in the center where they stand "in position, by their regiments" (Num 2:17).

Starting with the preferred east/west axis, Judah occupies the leadership position in the east, heading a regiment of his own tribe with two other Leah tribes, his younger brothers, Issachar and Zebulun (Num 2:3–9). On the west side of the axis, we find all the Rachel tribes listed in order of chosenness: Ephraim as the head of the western regiment, followed by Manasseh and Benjamin. All four of our king-making tribes are located on the east/west axis. When we turn to the less-valued north/south axis, we find all four of the maidservant sons. We also find Reuben and Simeon, the two sons of Leah that were demoted when Jacob blessed Ephraim and Manasseh and made them his sons "just like Reuben and Simeon" (Gen 48:5–6). The composition and ordering of the northern contingent clearly marks it as the Bilhah delegation. Dan, Bilhah's womb-opening son, heads this regiment, followed by Asher and Naphtali, the second sons of Zilpah and Bilhah, respectively. As the only delegation composed exclusively of maidservant sons, the northern group is the lowest or least valued according to the ideology governing this text.[51]

The grouping that presents the most interpretive challenges is the southern regiment headed by Reuben and including Simeon and Gad. We would expect Gad, the womb-opening son of Zilpah to lead this regiment.

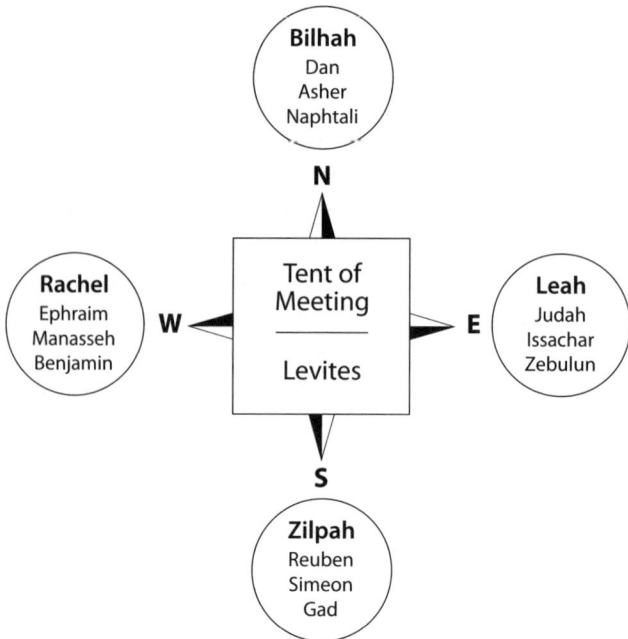

Figure 12. *The maternal ordering of the encampments, Num 2. Illustration created by Ondrea Keith, rendered by Bill Nelson.*

Instead we find Reuben, the womb-opening son of Leah. Reuben, in a sense, heads the Zilpah company, so marked by the presence of Gad.[52] Reuben is thus subsumed under the leadership of Judah as Zilpah is subsumed under the authority of Leah. We find a similar hierarchy of wife over maidservant tribes in the grouping of the western and northern regiments where Ephraim leads the Rachel regiment in the west, which in turn exercises authority and precedence over the Bilhah regiment headed by Dan in the north. As mentioned above, Reuben's sin of "going up on his father's bed" and lying with Bilhah, Rachel's maidservant, has demoted him to the status of a maidservant's son. There is a kind of poetic justice here. The son who joins himself to his father's maidservant will be joined to his father's maidservant's sons. Reuben has rendered himself fit to lead only a maidservant company (see Gen 49:3–4; 35:22).[53]

Simeon's demotion is harder to explain. He, like Reuben, is displaced by Ephraim and Manasseh. He also receives the wrath of his father when Jacob curses Simeon and Levi together for their anger (Gen 49:5–7). Since Levi is one of the most valued tribes in this text, however, it seems unlikely that the curse of Gen 49 accounts for Simeon's assignment to a maidservant regiment. In another text in Numbers, however, we find a Simeonite committing a grave sexual transgression with a Midianite in the tent of meeting (Num 25). This story may serve as an etiology for the low status and eventual disappearance of Simeon. Both Reuben and Simeon are associated with sexual sins in which they joined themselves to forbidden women. One defiles his father's couch, the other defiles his god's tent.

While Baruch Levine calls attention to the "pro-Judean" slant of this tribal organization, it is more specifically a projection of the priestly ideal of a temple-centered Judean monarchy into the formative wilderness period. The centrality of the priesthood within the tent of meeting is taken for granted, and the leadership of Aaron and Moses is signaled in Yahweh's direct communication with them about the ordering of the other, non-priestly tribes (Num 2:1). The placement of the sons of Leah and Rachel along the east-west axis communicates the reunification of the divided kingdoms of Israel and Judah. Judah's ascent to the status of royal heir is communicated through the removal of the royally associated Rachel tribes to the west; the demotion of Reuben and Simeon to the southern, maidservant regiment; and the placement of his older brother Levi in the central sacerdotal realm.[54] While no mothers are named in this text, the four wives of Jacob are very much present as "mother-units," military regiments hierarchically organized around Yahweh's tent.

Biblical authors preserved the origin stories of the foundational houses of their remembered and revered ancestors. These origin stories include pre-exilic compositions like the Abraham Cycle for the house of Abraham, the Jacob Cycle for the house of Israel, and the David story for the house of David and kingdom of Judah. They also include later exilic and postexilic additions to and amplifications on these origin stories in works like the book of Ruth, which contributes to the David story; the Song of Songs, which comments on an existing tradition of Solomon's royal house; and particular chapters like Genesis 25 that add genealogical complexity to the house of Abraham. Each of these stories function on multiple levels. At a primary level, they describe domestic households comprising a foundational male ancestor, his wife or wives, his slave wives, his children, and additional household members. At a secondary level, the Bible's foundational houses are the symbolic representations of the nation and later kingdom. On both of these levels, wives and mothers played social, political, and symbolic roles that went far beyond producing an heir for the house of the father.

One of the central findings of this book is that Israel's foundational houses, named for house-founding men like Abraham, Isaac, Jacob, and David, divided into socially significant and hierarchically arranged maternal subunits. Abraham's house as described in Genesis 25 divided into three maternal sub-houses listed in ascending order: Keturah, Hagar, and Sarah. Jacob's house was similarly divided into the smaller sub-houses of Leah, Rachel, Bilhah, and Zilpah. Finally, in David's royal house, maternal sub-houses marked violent and deadly divisions. These maternal subunits within the house of the father occupied designated physical spaces that the biblical narrative identifies through indigenous terms like "the house of the mother," "the chamber of her who conceived me," and "the tent of the mother." Maternal subunits have a corresponding set of maternally specific kinship terms that delineate the composition and social functions of maternal kin within the Bible's foundational narratives.

Our examination of the four house-of-the-mother texts together with texts that feature maternal subdivisions has generated a series of related kinship terms and produced an expanded Hebrew lexicon for kinship relationships within the house of the father. Children born of the same mother, uterine siblings, recognized their special bond with specific kinship labels: "brother, son of my mother," and "brother, one who had nursed at my mother's breasts." Uterine siblings shared a physical space called "the house of the mother" or the "tent" or "chamber" of the mother. The relationships within the house of the mother were characterized by heightened emotion, public displays of physical affection, and lifelong loyalty to one another. When a young woman married out of her natal home, she maintained a socially and economically significant relationship with her uterine brother.

Within a polygynous house of the father, uterine siblings formed a maternal alliance, protecting, providing refuge, and enacting revenge on behalf of one another. Maternal alliances formed dividing lines within the father's house whereby sons from competing maternal houses fought for the position of designated heir within the house of their father.

The English anthropological term "uterine family" is surprisingly appropriate to the Hebrew language context where maternally specific kin are labeled using terms that evoke female reproductive organs and processes: womb, conception, breasts and womb, birth, and lactation. A wife's firstborn son was referred to as her "womb-opener," and his birth was marked with a ritual presentation at the temple and sometimes with a special name that marked his status as a womb-opener. A womb-opening son also allowed a wife to claim to "be built up" within the house of her husband, to have her own "house." A mother could call upon her son as "the son of my womb" in order to emphasize her claim on him and communicate an enduring bond. The social obligations and emotions that were "housed" within the uterine family, "the house of the mother," were expressed in terms that explicitly named a shared mother, a shared womb, and shared breasts. Even the allegiance that members of a uterine family felt for one another was understood as womb based: *raḥămîm*.

Pronounced status divisions characterized the relationships among maternal house alliances. The status of the mother within the house of her husband and the status of the house of the father from which she came influenced her son's chances of becoming the designated heir within his father's house. Primary wives from royal or royally marked insider houses had the highest status. Secondary wives who were slaves, maidservants, concubines, or prostitutes bore sons who were at a distinct disadvantage within their father's house. Wives of foreign or unknown origins were similarly disadvantaged. We see this phenomenon clearly in the lines drawn between Isaac, the Abraham-begotten son, and "the sons of his concubines"; between Joseph, the womb-opening son of the loved, insider wife, and "the sons of Bilhah and Zilpah, his father's wives"; between Abimelech, the son of his father's concubine, and "the seventy sons of Jerubbaal" born to his wives; between Jephthah, the son of a whore, and the sons of Gilead's wife; and finally between Baal and "the seventy sons of Asherah." Ideologically, a womb-opening son of a high-status wife had a presumed advantage in the fight to become heir. Still, womb-opening sons of second wives, slave wives, concubines, or prostitutes could ascend to the position of heir, though they were considered upstarts who achieved their position through violence.

When a son within a maternal house became heir in his father's house, members of his mother's house were elevated along with him. We see this when an ascendant Joseph singles out Benjamin for special provisions. A son who became heir could also strengthen the house of the father of his mother. When Abimelech's maternal uncles supported his claim to kingship, they did so in hopes of elevating their own houses. Similarly, when David became king, he elevated the houses of his sisters as seen through the prominence of the "sons of Zeruiah." When a son became heir, his mother became the senior woman of the household, while his father's other wives would need to depend on her good graces in order to receive the resources of the father's house. Sarah opted to expel "this slave woman and her son" rather than share the resources of Abraham's house with Hagar and Ishmael. After Bathsheba actively participated in elevating her son Solomon to kingship, she and Solomon refused "Adonijah son of Haggith" the sexual-reproductive resources of the house of David.

If a son felt physically threatened within the house of his father, he could turn to the house of the father of his mother for refuge and protection. His mother's brothers might provide him with financial backing, reproductive resources, or physical manpower to support his return to the father's house to claim the position of heir by force. In order to claim a space within his mother's father's house, a man used maternal kinship terms to identify himself. He became "a mother's son" and claimed the status of shared "bone and flesh." Ultimately, however, in order for a man to become head of his own house, he had to break with the house of the father of his mother and lay claim to the house of his father.

In this final chapter, we have seen that the national history of the "House of Israel" is a contested history of a divided house. Maternal subunits within the house of Jacob came to define the Rachel-born northern kingdom of Israel, known as "Ephraim," and the Leah-born southern kingdom of Judah, known as the "House of David." Peripheral territories and nations traced their ancestry to foundational mothers whose houses had become satellite houses, no longer nested within the father's house. Sons who inherited the satellite houses of their mothers became "seeds of women," inheritors of a maternal covenant. Sent out from their chosen brothers in the Promised Land, unchosen sons dwelled "alongside" their brothers. Far from being reproductive "vessels" who produced male heirs to continue the *tôlēdôt* of their husbands, foundational mothers became nations, kingdoms, military units, and household alliances. Any study of the biblical house of the father and its attendant kinship structures must account for the mothers who served as its building blocks, for the breasts and wombs that defined social and political alliances within the house of the father.

Notes

Unless otherwise indicated, translations are my own.

Introduction

1. Translation from the KJV.
2. The first generation of "the man" and "his wife Eve" is also introduced through a narrative rather than a genealogy, featuring the two rival sons, Cain and Abel (Gen 4:1–16).
3. In this particular genealogy, which is conventionally assigned to the J source, the verb form for both paternal begetting and maternal bearing is the *qal* of *y-l-d*. While this form of the verb most often refers to mothers bearing children, it can describe a father begetting a child as it does here in Gen 4. The *hip'il* form of this verb, *hōlid*, which is used in the priestly genealogies, is discussed below.
4. The names of Jubal and Jabal, as well as their half-brother Tubal-Cain, may derive from the Hebrew root *y-b-l*, meaning "productive" (Walter Brueggemann, *Genesis: A Commentary for Preaching and Teaching* [Atlanta: John Knox, 1982], 65).
5. "*tôlēdôt*," BDB: 410.
6. Ronald Hendel, *Remembering Abraham: Culture, Memory, and History in the Hebrew Bible* (Oxford: Oxford University Press, 2005), 105.
7. "*yālad*," BDB: 408–9; "*y-l-d*," HALOT 2: 411–12; "*y-l-d*," DCH 4: 213–20.
8. Claus Westermann, *Genesis 1–11* (CC; Minneapolis: Fortress, 1994), 13.
9. We find the *tôlēdôt* in the Primeval History as a means of accounting for the begetting of the nations of the earth and in later texts, where "the generations" provide explanatory genealogies of ancestors in Genesis, Exodus, and Ruth. Finally, the *tôlēdôt* appear in Numbers and Chronicles as a basis for military conscription.
10. Westermann, *Genesis 1–11*, 7. Bill Arnold attributes their incorporation into Genesis to the final editor of the book because they structure the book quite intentionally into eleven panels of texts (Arnold, *Genesis* [NCBC; Cambridge: Cambridge University Press, 2009], 4–7, 85, 229).

See also Joseph Blenkinsopp, *The Pentateuch: An Introduction to the First Five Books of the Bible* (New York: Doubleday, 1992), 99–108.

11. "Reconfigured": Sarah Franklin and Susan McKinnon, eds., *Relative Values: Reconfiguring Kinship Studies* (Durham, N.C.: Duke University Press, 2001); "revived," "reformulated": Linda Stone, "Introduction: Theoretical Implications of New Directions in Anthropological Kinship," in *New Directions in Anthropological Kinship*, ed. Linda Stone (Lanham, Md.: Rowman and Littlefield, 2001), 1–2; "transformed": Louise Lamphere, "Whatever Happened to Kinship Studies? Reflections of a Feminist Anthropologist," in Stone, ed., *New Directions*, 21; "reconstituted": Michael Peletz, "Ambivalence in Kinship since the 1940s," in Franklin and McKinnon, eds., *Relative Values*, 413–14.

12. David M. Schneider, "Some Muddles in the Models: or, How the System Really Works," in *The Relevance of Models for Social Anthropology*, ed. Michael Banton (Association of Social Anthropologists of the UK and Commonwealth Monographs 1; London: Tavistock, 1965), 25–85; Schneider, *A Critique of the Study of Kinship* (Ann Arbor: University of Michigan Press, 1984).

13. For a brief summary of the history of kinship studies within anthropology and of the impact of Schneider's work, see Richard Feinberg, "Introduction: Schneider's Cultural Analysis of Kinship and Its Implications for Anthropological Relativism," in *The Cultural Analysis of Kinship: The Legacy of David M. Schneider*, ed. Richard Feinberg and Martin Ottenheimer (Urbana: University of Illinois Press, 2001), 1–31.

14. David M. Schneider, "What Is Kinship All About?" in *Kinship and Family: An Anthropological Reader*, ed. Robert Parkin and Linda Stone (Malden, Mass.: Wiley-Blackwell, 2004), 257–74; reprinted from Priscilla Reining, ed., *Kinship Studies in the Morgan Centennial Year* (Washington, D.C.: Anthropological Society of Washington, 1972), 32–63.

15. Linda Stone, "Introduction," in Parkin and Stone, eds., *Kinship and Family*, 241–42.

16. Stone, "Theoretical Implications of New Directions," 2.

17. For a brief overview of the feminist influence on reconfigured kinship studies, see Lamphere, "Whatever Happened to Kinship Studies?" 21–47; Mary Jo Maynes et al., eds., *Gender, Kinship and Power: A Comparative and Interdisciplinary History* (New York: Routledge, 1995), 10–31; and Jane Fishburne Collier and Sylvia Junko Yanigisako, eds., *Gender and Kinship: Essays toward a Unified Analysis* (Stanford, Cal.: Stanford University Press, 1987).

18. Susan McKinnon, "Domestic Exceptions: Evans-Pritchard and the Creation of Nuer Patrilineality and Equality," *Cultural Anthropology* 15 (2000): 61.

19. "An illusion": Edouard Conte, "Agnatic Illusions: The Element of Choice in Arab Kinship," in *Tribes and Power: Nationalism and Ethnicity in the Middle East*, ed. Faleh Abdul-Jabar and Hosham Dawod (London: Saqi, 2003), 16–17; "at least partly mythical": Robert Parkin, "Introduction," in Parkin and Stone, eds., *Kinship and Family*, 29; "cultural dogma": Karen Sinclair, "Mischief on the

Margins: Gender, Primogeniture, and Cognatic Descent among the Maori," in Stone, ed., *New Directions,* 157. The anthropological terms "agnatic" and "patrilineal" are used interchangeably and apply to individuals who are part of a group "constituted by their father's kin" where "elements of an individual's status are transmitted through men" (Maria Velioti-Georgopoulos, "Kinship and Descent," in *Encyclopedia of Anthropology,* ed. H. James Birx [Thousand Oaks, Cal.: SAGE Reference, 2006], 3: 1371).

20. Greg Urban, *Metaphysical Community: The Interplay of the Senses and the Intellect* (Austin: University of Texas Press, 1996), 134–35.
21. Adam Kuper argues that lineage models as a whole are "too formal and too idealist to do justice to what happens on the ground," and agrees with David Schneider that these models work primarily in the mind of the anthropologist rather than in the mind of the "supposed member of the lineage" (Kuper, "Lineage Theory: A Critical Retrospect," in Parkin and Stone, eds., *Kinship and Family,* 86–88). Eduoard Conte also advocates eliminating the use of the terms "patrilineal" and "agnatic descent," arguing that "discrete descent groups simply do not exist." Instead, he prefers to talk about "pacts," which he defines as voluntary alliances (Conte, "Agnatic Illusions," 16). Greg Urban prefers to give theoretical pride of place to a particular group's "talk" about lineages, rather than to the actual existence of lineages (Urban, *Metaphysical Community,* 135).
22. McKinnon, "Domestic Exceptions," 35–83.
23. Descent is "bilateral" or "cognatic" when characteristics and status "are transmitted through both parents and we belong to both parents' kinship groups" (Velioti-Georgopoulos, "Kinship and Descent," 3: 1371).
24. McKinnon, "Domestic Exceptions," 40.
25. McKinnon, "Domestic Exceptions," 42.
26. McKinnon, "Domestic Exceptions," 47–49, 58–61.
27. Margery Wolf, "Uterine Families and the Women's Community," in *Women and the Family in Rural Taiwan* (Stanford, Cal.: Stanford University Press, 1972), 37.
28. Lamphere, "Whatever Happened to Kinship Studies?" 23.
29. McKinnon, "Domestic Exceptions," 62.
30. Conte, "Agnatic Illusions," 15.
31. Lila Abu-Lughod, *Veiled Sentiments: Honor and Poetry in a Bedouin Society* (Berkeley: University of California Press, 1986), 51.
32. Abu-Lughod, *Veiled Sentiments,* 55.
33. Abu-Lughod, *Veiled Sentiments,* 56–57. The reason why couples chose to express their marital ties through their paternal links is that a wife who was a paternal cousin to her husband had higher status than a wife related to her husband through his mother.
34. Sinclair, "Mischief on the Margins," 156.
35. McKinnon, "Domestic Exceptions," 62–71; Lamphere, "Whatever Happened to Kinship Studies?" 23–30.
36. Abu-Lughod, *Veiled Sentiments,* 59.

37. Sinclair, "Mischief on the Margins," 156.
38. Wolf, "Uterine Families," 37.
39. McKinnon, "Domestic Exceptions," 71.
40. For an excellent overview of the past fifty years of biblical scholarship on the family in ancient Israel, with an emphasis on contributions from archaeology and sociology, see Patricia Dutcher-Walls, "The Clarity of Double Vision: Seeing the Family in Sociological and Archaeological Perspective," in *The Family in Life and in Death: The Family in Ancient Israel, Sociological and Archaeological Perspectives*, ed. Patricia Dutcher-Walls (New York: T&T Clark, 2009), 1–15. For an overview of the place of women in patrilineal ancient Israel, see Gale Yee, *Poor Banished Children of Eve: Women as Evil in the Hebrew Bible* (Minneapolis: Fortress, 2003), 34–39.
41. George E. Mendenhall, "The Hebrew Conquest of Palestine," *BA* 25 (1962): 66–87; Mary Douglas, *Purity and Danger: An Analysis of the Concepts of Pollution and Taboo* (New York: Praeger, 1966).
42. Robert Wilson, *Genealogy and History in the Biblical World* (New Haven, Conn.: Yale University Press, 1977); Hendel, *Remembering Abraham*, 36–37, 57–59, 105; Elizabeth Bloch-Smith, "Israelite Ethnicity in Iron I: Archaeology Preserves What Is Remembered and What Is Forgotten in Israel's History," *JBL* 122, no. 3 (2003): 401–3. See also Carol Meyers, *Rediscovering Eve: Ancient Israelite Women in Context* (New York: Oxford University Press, 2013), 21–22.
43. Lawrence E. Stager, "The Archaeology of the Family in Ancient Israel," *BASOR* 260 (1985): 1–35; Stager, "The Patrimonial Kingdom of Solomon," in *Symbiosis, Symbolism, and the Power of the Past: Canaan, Ancient Israel, and Their Neighbors from the Late Bronze Age through Roman Palaestina*, ed. William G. Dever and Seymour Gitin (Winona Lake, Ind.: Eisenbrauns, 2003), 63–74; David J. Schloen, *The House of the Father as Fact and Symbol: Patrimonialism in Ugarit and the Ancient Near East* (Winona Lake, Ind.: Eisenbrauns, 2001).
44. See, e.g., Hans Walter Wolff, *Anthropology of the Old Testament* (Philadelphia: Fortress, 1974); Baruch Levine, "The Clan-Based Economy of Biblical Israel," in Dever and Gitin, eds., *Symbiosis, Symbolism, and the Power of the Past*, 447–48; and H. G. M. Williamson, "The Family in Persian Period Judah: Some Textual Reflections," in Dever and Gitin, eds., *Symbiosis, Symbolism, and the Power of the Past*, 472–73.
45. "*naʿar*" and "*naʿărâ*": Stager, "The Archaeology of the Family," 25–28; Carolyn S. Leeb, *Away from the Father's House: The Social Location of* naʿar *and* naʿarah *in Ancient Israel* (JSOTSup 301; Sheffield, Eng.: Sheffield Academic Press, 2000); "*ʾāb*" and "*bat*": Johanna Stiebert, *Fathers and Daughters in the Hebrew Bible* (Oxford: Oxford University Press, 2013), 18–71; "*běkôr*": Frederick E. Greenspahn, *When Brothers Dwell Together: The Preeminence of Younger Siblings in the Hebrew Bible* (New York: Oxford University Press, 1994); "*bêt ʾāb*" and "*mišpāḥâ*": Shunya Bendor, *The Social Structure of Ancient Israel: The Institution of*

the Family (Beit 'Ab): *From the Settlement to the End of the Monarchy* (Jerusalem Biblical Studies 7; Jerusalem: Simor, 1996), 65–86; Williamson, "The Family in Persian Period Judah," 469–85; Schloen, *The House of the Father*, 147–55.

46. Urban, *Metaphysical Community*, 135, 138–39.
47. Urban, *Metaphysical Community*, 149.
48. See, most recently, Daniel E. Fleming, *The Legacy of Israel in Judah's Bible: History, Politics, and the Reinscribing of Tradition* (New York: Cambridge University Press, 2012), and David M. Carr, *Holy Resilience: The Bible's Traumatic Origins* (New Haven, Conn.: Yale University Press, 2014).
49. Elizabeth Bloch-Smith makes a similar argument concerning the role of narrative in helping a community "find meaning in times of difficult or unexpected events." Narrative, she argues, functions as "a mechanism to promote and sustain ethnic bonds through periods of 'rupture.'" She then defines periods of rupture as those situations "that call into question a group's identity" (Bloch-Smith, "Israelite Ethnicity in Iron I," 422).
50. Susan Niditch, *Underdogs and Tricksters: A Prelude to Biblical Folklore* (San Francisco: Harper and Row, 1987).
51. Arguments that defend a pre-exilic dating for the Abraham and Jacob cycles from a traditional source-critical perspective are found in Ernest Nicholson, *The Pentateuch in the Twentieth Century: The Legacy of Julius Wellhausen* (Oxford: Clarendon, 1998), 132–60, 237–48. For the pre-exilic dating of the Abraham cycle, see Hendel, *Remembering Abraham*, 31–56. The pre-exilic date and northern origin of some core of the Jacob cycle (Gen 25–35) has enjoyed broad acceptance from its early assignation as a combined JE source up through the most recent efforts to rethink the formation of the Pentateuch; see, e.g., David Carr, *The Formation of the Hebrew Bible: A New Reconstruction* (Oxford: Oxford University Press, 2011), 473–76; Konrad Schmid, *The Old Testament: A Literary History*, trans. Linda M. Maloney (Minneapolis: Fortress, 2012), 58–69; and Fleming, *The Legacy of Israel*, 74–81. On the pre-exilic dating of the story of David as found in 1 and 2 Samuel, see P. Kyle McCarter, Jr., *I Samuel: A New Translation with Introduction, Notes and Commentary* (AB 8; Garden City, N.Y.: Doubleday, 1980), 14–30.
52. Gillian Feeley-Harnik, "Naomi and Ruth: Building up the House of David," in *Text and Tradition: The Hebrew Bible and Folklore*, ed. Susan Niditch (Atlanta: Scholars Press, 1990), 164–84; Kirstin Nielsen, *Ruth: A Commentary* (OTL; Louisville: Westminster John Knox, 1997), 12–28.
53. Mary Douglas, *Jacob's Tears: The Priestly Work of Reconciliation* (Oxford: Oxford University Press, 2004); Calum Carmichael, *The Book of Numbers: A Critique of Genesis* (New Haven, Conn.: Yale University Press, 2012).
54. Focusing on biblical and Ugaritic birth stories, Ronald S. Hendel describes the relationship between the two text corpora as one generated by an oral tradition shared by neighboring cultures with a common heritage. Biblical and Ugaritic

birth stories are clearly separated by time period and geography; nonetheless, Hendel asserts, they are "multiforms of each other" (Hendel, *The Epic of the Patriarch: The Jacob Cycle and the Narrative Traditions of Canaan and Israel* [Atlanta: Scholars Press, 1987], 48).
55. Both of these texts are covered in chapter 4.
56. Ken Stone, "An Anthropological Framework for Reading," in *Sex, Honor, and Power in the Deuteronomistic History* (JSOTSup 234; Sheffield, Eng.: Sheffield Academic Press, 1996), 35. See also Robert Wilson, who argues that comparative evidence from ethnographic studies could "suggest to the interpreter more precise and potentially useful questions that might be asked of the biblical text" and "broaden the horizons of the biblical interpreter and suggest a wider range of hypotheses than the interpreter might be able to produce on the basis of the biblical text alone" (Wilson, *Prophecy and Society in Ancient Israel* [Minneapolis: Fortress, 1980], 99).
57. Stanley K. Stowers, "Theorizing the Religion of Ancient Households and Families," in *Household and Family Religion in Antiquity*, ed. John Bodel and Saul M. Olyan (Malden, Mass.: Blackwell, 2008), 8–9.
58. Stowers, "Theorizing the Religion," 7–8. See also Jonathan Z. Smith, "The End of Comparison: Redescription and Rectification," in *A Magic Still Dwells: Comparative Religion in the Postmodern Age*, ed. Kimberley C. Patton and Benjamin C. Ray (Berkeley: University of California Press, 2000), 237–41.
59. Conte, "Agnatic Illusions," 19. See also Stowers, "Theorizing the Religion." Michael Peletz addresses the shifting understanding of kinship terms under the rubric of "ambivalence." He asserts that anthropologists need to acknowledge multiple layers of "ambivalence" on the part of social actors with regard to their expressed ideals in kinship and their experienced reality with their own kin. He adds that ambivalence itself should be more "theorized," and that anthropologists should report, account for, and historicize heterogeneous data related to kinship (Peletz, "Ambivalence in Kinship," 413–43).
60. Urban, *Metaphysical Community*, 25.
61. Urban, *Metaphysical Community*, 25–26.
62. These questions are developed from Greg Urban's discourse analysis approach and from Cynthia Robin's application of that approach. See Urban, *Metaphysical Community*, 119, 122, and Robin, "Kin and Gender in Classic Maya Society: A Case Study from Yaxchilan, Mexico," in Stone, ed., *New Directions*, 212–13.

Chapter 1. House

1. Joseph Blenkinsopp, "The Family in First Temple Israel," in *Families in Ancient Israel*, ed. Leo G. Perdue et al. (Louisville: Westminster John Knox, 1997), 51.
2. Phillip J. King and Lawrence E. Stager, *Life in Biblical Israel* (Louisville: Westminster John Knox, 2002), 39.
3. King and Stager, *Life*, 39.

4. Carol Meyers, "The Family in Early Israel," in Perdue et al., eds., *Families in Ancient Israel*, 19.
5. Blenkinsopp, "The Family," 52.
6. Also known as the "four-room house" in archaeological literature. I follow Lawrence E. Stager and David J. Schloen in using the term "pillared house" because many of these houses had two, three, or five rooms, rendering the term "four-room house" inaccurate (Stager, "The Archaeology of the Family in Ancient Israel," *BASOR* 260 [1985]: 17; Schloen, *The House of the Father as Fact and Symbol: Patrimonialism in Ugarit and the Ancient Near East* [Winona Lake, Ind.: Eisenbrauns, 2001], 136–38). At the same time, Volkmar Fritz, Avraham Faust, and Shlomo Bunimovitz retain the older term "four-room house," noting that not all exemplars have pillars (Fritz, "On the Reconstruction of the Four-Room House," in *Up to the Gates of Ekron: Essays on the Archaeology and History of the Eastern Mediterranean in Honor of Seymour Gitin*, ed. Sidnie White Crawford et al. [Jerusalem: W. F. Albright Institute of Archaeological Research, 2007], 114–17; Faust and Bunimovitz, "The Four Room House: Embodying Iron Age Israelite Society," *Near Eastern Archaeology* 66 [2003]: 22–31).
7. The term *bayit*, usually in construct, occurs close to two thousand times in the Bible.
8. "The Mesha Stela" and "The Tel Dan Stela," trans. Michael D. Coogan, in *A Reader of Ancient Near Eastern Texts: Sources for the Study of the Old Testament* (New York: Oxford University Press, 2013), 76–78; "The Black Obelisk," trans. Mordecai Cogan, in *The Raging Torrent: Historical Inscriptions from Assyria and Babylonia Relating to Ancient Israel* (Jerusalem: Carta, 2008), 23.
9. See Harry Hoffner, "*bayit*," *TDOT* 2: 108; "*bayit*," *HALOT* 1: 124–25; "*bayit*," *DCH* 2: 151.
10. Roland de Vaux, *Ancient Israel: Its Life and Institutions*, trans. John McHugh (Grand Rapids, Mich.: Eerdmans, 1961), 20. There is a very similar blurring of the lines between a physical house and the social grouping or "family" that lives within it in a Mesopotamian text called the "Dialogue of Pessimism." In this text, the master declares, "I want to build a house and found a family," and the slave responds, "Found one, master, found one" ("Dialogue of Pessimism [1.155]," trans. Alasdair Livingstone, *COS* 1: 496).
11. See, e.g., Niels Peter Lemche, *Early Israel: Anthropological and Historical Studies on the Israelite Society before the Monarchy* (Leiden: E. J. Brill, 1985), 251–53; Norman K. Gottwald, *The Tribes of Yahweh: A Sociology of the Religion of Liberated Israel, 1250–1050 B.C.E.* (Maryknoll, N.Y.: Orbis, 1979), 285–90, 308–9; Abraham Malamat, *History of Biblical Israel: Major Problems and Minor Issues* (Leiden: E. J. Brill, 2001), 41–56; and Stager, "The Archaeology of the Family," 22.
12. Recent definitions of the composition of the house of the father clearly build on de Vaux's definition. See Oded Borowski, *Daily Life in Biblical Times* (Leiden: E. J. Brill, 2003), 22; Shunya Bendor, *The Social Structure of Ancient Israel: The*

Institution of the Family (Beit 'Ab): *From the Settlement to the End of the Monarchy* (Jerusalem Biblical Studies 7; Jerusalem: Simor, 1996), 48–60; and Schloen, *The House of the Father*, 150–51. A summary of the scholarly consensus on this definition of the *bêt 'āb* is found in Paula McNutt, *Reconstructing the Society of Ancient Israel* (London: Westminster John Knox, 1999), 87–94. I prefer to define the relationships within the *bêt 'āb* as "dependent" rather than biological. The issue of "common descent" and "shared blood" is complex. This book provides a detailed examination of the classical Hebrew terms employed to describe relatedness within the family.

13. De Vaux, *Ancient Israel*, 20.
14. Gottwald, *The Tribes of Yahweh*, 285.
15. King and Stager, *Life*, 39. See also Naomi Steinberg, *Kinship and Marriage in Genesis: A Household Economics Perspective* (Minneapolis: Fortress, 1993), 20–22, and Rainer Albertz, "Personal Names and Family Religion," in *Family and Household Religion in Ancient Israel and the Levant*, ed. Rainer Albertz and Rüdiger Schmitt (Winona Lake, Ind.: Eisenbrauns, 2012), 23–26.
16. King and Stager, *Life*, 40. On the Hebrew term *gērîm*, see note 21, below.
17. Frederick E. Greenspahn translates *bĕkôr* as "designated heir" rather than "firstborn son." He asserts that Israel did not practice primogeniture and instead divided a father's estate among sons, giving the *bĕkôr* a double portion. In his view, the position of *bĕkôr* was "an assigned rather than an automatic status" (Greenspahn, *When Brothers Dwell Together: The Preeminence of Younger Siblings in the Hebrew Bible* [New York: Oxford University Press, 1994], 59–69, 81–83). While I have chosen to use Greenspahn's translation, my view differs somewhat from his. The complexity of translating *bĕkôr* reflects a distinction between the ideal or norm and the practiced or special. According to the biblical ideal, a man's *bĕkôr* was his firstborn son, one who "came forth from his own loins" (e.g., Gen 15:4), as "the first fruit of his vigor" (e.g., Gen 49:3). This would be the social norm and professed ideal, a view Greenspahn rejects. In practice, as Greenspahn correctly notes, sons competed for their father's favor, and, I would add, wives strategized to influence their husband's choice, such that the *bĕkôr* became in practice an assigned or achieved status.
18. The category of "illegitimate child" is a murky one biblically. Abimelech seems to be illegitimate and non-inheriting in the house of Gideon/Jerubbaal on account of his mother being a nonresident concubine (Judg 8:29–9:6). Jephthah's brothers claim that he has no right of inheritance in his father Gilead's house because his mother is a prostitute (Judg 11:1–3).
19. Jacob in the house of Laban (Gen 29:15–30); Moses in the house of Reuel/Jethro (Exod 2:15–22); David in the house of Saul (1 Sam 18:17–29).
20. Lot in the house of Abram (Gen 12:4–5).
21. The term *gēr* is usually translated as "sojourner" (BDB: 158) or "alien" (NRSV) and can simply refer to newcomers to a land, but when a *gēr* is listed as a member of a *bayit*, he is usually found as a laborer, someone whose membership in

the household is secured through work he provides to the household. David J. Schloen identifies the "landless persons" who managed to survive as "dependent household workers," but he is referring to slaves and clients, not only *gērîm* (Schloen, *The House of the Father*, 120). When a *gēr* is in a service position within a household that is not his own, the translation "dependent worker" seems most appropriate (e.g., the *gēr* referred to in the laws concerning cessation of labor in a household on the Sabbath [Exod 20:10; 23:12], and *gērîm* who are sold or sell themselves into slavery as workers within a household that is foreign to them [Lev 25:35–55]).

22. E.g., Micah's house includes his mother (Judg 17); Solomon's house includes his mother (1 Kings 2:13–25).
23. E.g., Sarah and Hagar in the house of Abraham (Gen 16, 21); Rachel and Leah in the house of Jacob (Gen 31); the multiple wives of David (2 Sam 3:2–5).
24. E.g., Keturah in the house of Abraham (Gen 25:1–6); Rizpah in the house of Saul (2 Sam 3:7).
25. Dinah is taken back into her father's house (Gen 34:26); Tamar takes refuge in the house of her brother Absalom (2 Sam 13:20).
26. Leah and Rachel remain in their father Laban's house for decades after they marry Jacob (Gen 29–31). A married Tamar returns to her father's house to live (Gen 38:11). The Levite's concubine returns to her father's house when she is angry with her husband, and her intention seems to be to stay with her father (Judg 19:1–2).
27. Martin Noth, *Das System der zwölf Stämme Israels* (Stuttgart: Beiträge zur Wissenschaft vom Alten und Neuen Testament 4:1, 1930; repr., Darmstadt, Ger.: Wissenschaftliche Buchgesellschaft, 1966), 61–121; Gottwald, *The Tribes of Yahweh*, 345–88. See also Lemche, *Early Israel*, 202–44.
28. While the Jerusalem temple is repeatedly referred to as the "house of Yahweh," only in this text in Ezekiel is it explicitly imagined as a polygynous household. We find the word *bayit* applied to several temples in the Bible: the northern sanctuary *bêt 'ēl*, or "house of El"; "house of Dagon" (Judg 16:23–30; 1 Sam 5: 2, 5); "house of Baal" (1 Kings 16:32); "house of Nisroch" (2 Kings 19:37); "house of his gods" (Ezra 1:7).
29. See also 2 Sam 14:4–7, where the woman of Tekoa's household consists of both herself and her son.
30. See Lev 25; Num 36:7.
31. The most frequently cited example for these nested terms is Josh 7:14, 16–18.
32. H. G. M. Williamson challenges this "three-fold division" of kinship terminology from tribe to clan to house of the father, showing how often the third term is an unspecified house, as in the aforementioned example from Josh 7:14, or the third term is an individual rather than a house as in 1 Sam 10:20–21 (Williamson, "The Family in Persian Period Judah: Some Textual Reflections," in *Symbiosis, Symbolism, and the Power of the Past: Canaan, Ancient Israel, and Their Neighbors from the Late Bronze Age through Roman Palaestina*, ed. William G.

Dever and Seymour Gitin [Winona Lake, Ind.: Eisenbrauns, 2003], 473). My point is not that the terminology remains consistent but rather that the governing principle is one of nested categories of people.

33. Stager, "The Archaeology of the Family," 20–22; Schloen, *The House of the Father*, 151.
34. Shunya Bendor treats this ambiguity between *bêt 'āb* and *mišpāḥâ* at length, arguing that the relationship between the two terms is "dynamic," with no clear demarcation (Bendor, *The Social Structure*, 67–86). He then creates a model to show how a *bêt 'āb* might develop into a *mišpāḥâ* over five generations. He concludes, however, that "the model is only theoretical: in reality there is no such regularity" (71). The elasticity between the terms was already recognized by Lemche, *Early Israel*, 245–49.
35. Num 13:8 identifies "Hoshea, son of Nun," as being part of the tribe of Ephraim and later has Moses rename him "Joshua" (Num 13:16).
36. Lawrence E. Stager, "The Patrimonial Kingdom of Solomon," in Dever and Gitin, eds., *Symbiosis, Symbolism, and the Power of the Past*, 66.
37. Stager, "The Patrimonial Kingdom of Solomon," 70–71.
38. Stager, "The Patrimonial Kingdom of Solomon," 71.
39. Stager, "The Archaeology of the Family," 22. See also Susan Ackerman, "Household Religion, Family Religion, and Women's Religion in Ancient Israel," in *Household and Family Religion in Antiquity*, ed. John Bodel and Saul M. Olyan (Malden, Mass.: Blackwell, 2008), 128.
40. Ackerman, "Household Religion," 129–32. On the subdivision of the Hebrew *bayit* into multiple *bāttim* that represent chambers or halls within a larger structure, see Hoffner, "*bayit*," *TDOT* 2: 113.
41. Bendor, *The Social Structure*, 123–24. Additional biblical texts cited for the grouping of building a house, planting a vineyard, and taking a wife include Deut 28: 30; Amos 5:11; Zeph 1:13; and Isa 65:21–22.
42. Greenspahn, *When Brothers Dwell*, 50–55.
43. Linda Stone, "Introduction: Theoretical Implications of New Directions in Anthropological Kinship," in *New Directions in Anthropological Kinship*, ed. Linda Stone (Lanham, Md.: Rowman and Littlefield, 2001), 2, 17; Louise Lamphere, "Whatever Happened to Kinship Studies? Reflections of a Feminist Anthropologist," in Stone, ed., *New Directions*, 21–47; Mary Jo Maynes et al., eds., *Gender, Kinship and Power: A Comparative and Interdisciplinary History* (New York: Routledge, 1995), 1–23.
44. See Schloen, *The House of the Father*, 54.
45. Stager, "The Archaeology of the Family," 25–28.
46. Carolyn S. Leeb, *Away from the Father's House: The Social Location of the na'ar and na'arah in Ancient Israel* (JSOTSup 301; Sheffield, Eng.: Sheffield Academic Press, 2000), 42–124, 190–94.
47. Bendor, *The Social Structure*, 55. See also Lemche, *Early Israel*, 253–54.

48. Other texts that show adult sons having their own "houses" while their father was still alive include 2 Sam 13:7–8; 14:23–24; and Job 1:1–5.
49. Lemche, *Early Israel,* 254.
50. Meyers, "The Family in Early Israel," 34; Carol Meyers, "'To Her Mother's House': Considering a Counterpart to the Israelite *Bêt 'āb*," in *The Bible and the Politics of Exegesis: Essays in Honor of Norman Gottwald on His Sixty-Fifth Birthday,* ed. David Jobling, Peggy L. Day, and Gerald T. Sheppard (Cleveland: Pilgrim, 1991), 39–51, 304–7; Meyers, "Returning Home: Ruth 1:8 and the Gendering of the Book of Ruth," in *A Feminist Companion to Ruth,* ed. Athalya Brenner (1993; repr. Sheffield, Eng.: Sheffield Academic Press, 2001), 95.
51. Stager, "The Archaeology of the Family," 1–35; Schloen, *The House of the Father,* 147–50; Larry G. Herr, "The House of the Father at Iron I Tall Al-'Umayri, Jordan," in *Exploring the Long Durée: Essays in Honor of Lawrence E. Stager,* ed. J. David Schloen (Winona Lake, Ind.: Eisenbrauns, 2009), 191–98.
52. Yigal Shiloh, "The Four-Room House: Its Situation and Function in the Israelite City," *Israel Exploration Journal* 20 (1970): 180. Most scholars now recognize that the pillared house is not exclusively Israelite. See, e.g., Stager, "The Archaeology of the Family," 17; Schloen, *The House of the Father,* 137; and Fritz, "On the Reconstruction of the Four-Room House," 114–15.
53. Faust and Bunimovitz, "The Four Room House," 30. See also Avraham Faust, *Israel's Ethnogenesis: Settlement, Interaction, Expansion and Resistance* (London: Equinox, 2006), 71–78.
54. Faust and Bunimovitz, "The Four Room House," 26; James W. Hardin, *Lahav II Households and the Use of Domestic Space at Iron II Tel Halif: An Archaeology of Destruction* (Winona Lake, Ind.: Eisenbrauns, 2010), 44–48.
55. Faust and Bunimovitz, "The Four Room House," 26.
56. Faust and Bunimovitz, "The Four Room House," 26. Both David J. Schloen and Aaron Brody have questioned the assumption that smaller pillared houses were limited to a nuclear family, suggesting that we have underestimated the number of people who could live within a given space and the way that contiguous urban houses might have formed extended family units with shared resources (Schloen, *The House of the Father,* 135; Brody, "'Those Who Add House to House': Household Archaeology and the Use of Domestic Space in an Iron II Residential Compound at Tell En-Naṣbeh," in Schloen, ed., *Exploring the Long Durée,* 45–56).
57. James W. Hardin, "Understanding Domestic Space: An Example from Iron Age Tel Halif," *NEA* 67 (2004): 71–83. Tel Halif is in southern Israel at the southwestern foothills of the Judean mountains.
58. Hardin, "Understanding Domestic Space," 74–78.
59. Hardin, "Understanding Domestic Space," 75.
60. Faust and Bunimovitz, "The Four Room House," 27.
61. Faust and Bunimovitz, "The Four Room House," 26.

62. Claude Lévi-Strauss, *The Elementary Structures of Kinship: Revised Ed.*, trans. James Harle Bell, John Richard von Sturmer; ed. Rodney Needham (London: Eyre and Spottiswoode, 1969). A summary of the history of anthropological approaches to kinship moving from descent theory to alliance theory can be found in Adam Kuper, *The Reinvention of Primitive Society: Transformations of a Myth*, 2nd ed. (New York: Routledge, 2005), 163–200.
63. Claude Lévi-Strauss, *The Way of the Masks*, trans. Sylvia Modelski (Seattle: University of Washington Press, 1982), 174.
64. Susan D. Gillespie, "Beyond Kinship: An Introduction," in *Beyond Kinship: Social and Material Reproduction in House Societies*, ed. Rosemary A. Joyce and Susan D. Gillespie (Philadelphia: University of Pennsylvania Press, 2000), 8.
65. Janet Carsten and Stephen Hugh-Jones, "Introduction," in *About the House: Lévi-Strauss and Beyond*, ed. Janet Carsten and Stephen Hugh-Jones (Cambridge: Cambridge University Press, 1995), 19.
66. Carsten and Hugh-Jones, "Introduction," 39.
67. Gillespie, "Beyond Kinship," 11–13.
68. Gillespie, "Beyond Kinship," 3.
69. Carsten and Hugh-Jones, "Introduction," 20.
70. Roxana Waterson, "House, Place, and Memory in Tana Toraja (Indonesia)," in Joyce and Gillespie, eds., *Beyond Kinship*, 187.
71. Susan D. Gillespie, "Maya 'Nested Houses': The Ritual Construction of Place," in Joyce and Gillespie, eds., *Beyond Kinship*, 142.
72. Carsten and Hugh-Jones, "Introduction," 20–21.
73. Gillespie, "Beyond Kinship," 8–10.
74. Susan D. Gillespie, "Lévi-Strauss: *Maison* and *Société à Maisons*," in Joyce and Gillespie, eds., *Beyond Kinship*, 42.
75. Gillespie, "Maya 'Nested Houses,'" 139.
76. Gillespie, "Beyond Kinship," 3.
77. Roxana Waterson, "Houses and Hierarchies in Island Southeast Asia," in Carsten and Hugh-Jones, eds., *About the House*, 54.
78. See Jonathan Z. Smith, *To Take Place: Toward Theory in Ritual* (Chicago: University of Chicago Press, 1987), 47–73.
79. Joel S. Baden, *The Composition of the Pentateuch: Renewing the Documentary Hypothesis* (New Haven, Conn.: Yale University Press, 2012), 174–77; Joseph Blenkinsopp, *The Pentateuch: An Introduction to the First Five Books of the Bible* (New York: Doubleday, 1992), 50–52.
80. Gillespie, "Beyond Kinship," 12.
81. James J. Fox, *Inside Austronesian Houses: Perspectives on Domestic Designs for Living* (Canberra: Research School of Pacific Studies, Australian National University, 1993), 16, cited in Gillespie, "Beyond Kinship," 12.
82. Robert Hendel, *Remembering Abraham: Culture, Memory, and History in the Hebrew Bible* (Oxford: Oxford University Press, 2005), 32.

83. Ronald E. Clements, "Israel in Its Historical and Cultural Setting," in *The World of Ancient Israel: Sociological, Anthropological and Political Perspectives: Essays by Members of the Society for Old Testament Study*, ed. Ronald E. Clements (Cambridge: Cambridge University Press, 1989), 12.
84. Rosemary A. Joyce, "Heirlooms and Houses: Materiality and Social Memory," in Joyce and Gillespie, eds., *Beyond Kinship*, 202.
85. Joyce, "Heirlooms," 207–8.
86. Susan McKinnon, "The Tanimbarese *Tavu:* The Ideology of Growth and the Material Configurations of Houses and Hierarchy in an Indonesian Society," in Joyce and Gillespie, eds., *Beyond Kinship*, 172.
87. The term "Torah of Moses" is found in Ezra 7:6.
88. Karel van der Toorn, "The Iconic Book: Analogies between the Babylonian Cult of Image and the Veneration of the Torah," in *The Image and the Book: Iconic Cults, Aniconism, and the Rise of Book Religion in Israel and the Ancient Near East*, ed. Karel van der Toorn (Leuven, Belgium: Peeters, 1997), 229–48. For Francesca Stavrakopoulou, the Torah of Moses is "a marker of Israel's land claims" and the stone tablets are "boundary markers" (Stavrakopoulou, *Land of Our Fathers: The Roles of Ancestor Veneration in Biblical Land Claims* [New York: T&T Clark, 2010], 71–80).
89. David M. Schneider, *A Critique of the Study of Kinship* (Ann Arbor: University of Michigan Press, 1984), 21–23, cited in Joyce, "Heirlooms," 191.
90. McKinnon, "The Tanimbarese *Tavu*," 170–71.
91. McKinnon, "The Tanimbarese *Tavu*," 173.
92. Waterson, "House, Place, and Memory," 181–82.
93. McKinnon, "The Tanimbarese *Tavu*," 170–71.
94. McKinnon, "The Tanimbarese *Tavu*," 170–71; Susan McKinnon, *From a Shattered Sun: Hierarchy, Gender, and Alliance in the Tanimbar Islands* (Madison: University of Wisconsin Press, 1991), 114–27.
95. Susan McKinnon, "Domestic Exceptions: Evans-Pritchard and the Creation of Nuer Patrilineality and Equality," *Cultural Anthropology* 15 (2000): 51.
96. McKinnon, "Domestic Exceptions," 58, 63.
97. Karen Sinclair, "Mischief on the Margins: Gender, Primogeniture, and Cognatic Descent among the Maori," in Stone, ed., *New Directions*, 158.
98. Sinclair, "Mischief on the Margins," 168–70.
99. McKinnon, "The Tanimbarese Tavu," 171.
100. Gerhard von Rad suggests labeling Gen 25:19–35:29 "an Isaac story," beginning as it does with the "begettings" of Isaac and ending with his death. Also, chapter 35 records the birth of Benjamin, Jacob's twelfth son, matching the begettings of Ishmael in Gen 25:12–18 (von Rad, *Genesis: A Commentary* [OTL; Louisville: Westminster John Knox, 1973], 263).
101. See, e.g., E. A. Speiser, *Genesis: Introduction, Translation, and Notes* (AB 1; New York: Doubleday, 1964), 188–89; Samuel Rolles Driver, *The Book of Genesis*

(WC; London: Methuen, 1920), 239–45; and Claus Westermann, *Genesis 12–36* (CC; Minneapolis: Fortress, 1994), 394–402.

102. The name "Keturah" means "spices" or "incense," and several of the nations that are said to descend from her have connections to the spice trade that are documented both biblically and in cuneiform sources (Nahum Sarna, *Genesis: The Traditional Hebrew Text with the New JPS Translation* [Philadelphia: JPS, 1989], 171–72; Westermann, *Genesis 12–36*, 396).

103. The sudden appearance and disappearance of Keturah leads most commentators to conclude that Gen 25:1–4 represents an independent source incorporated into the Abraham cycle by the final redactor. Westermann, for example, shows how chapter 25 painstakingly demonstrates the fulfillment of promises made earlier in Genesis with the exception of Keturah, who is not needed to fulfill the "great nation" promise (Westermann, *Genesis 12–36*, 394–95).

104. In order to reflect the two different Hebrew words that are used for household servants or slaves, I consistently translate *šipḥâ* as "slave girl" or "slave wife" and *'āmâ* as "maidservant" or "maidservant wife." In general, these two words seem interchangeable. Female characters consistently refer to themselves as either a *šipḥâ* or an *'āmâ* when speaking to high-status men from whom they hope to get something (e.g., Hannah to God and to Eli the priest [1 Sam 1:11–16 (*'āmâ*); 1:18 (*šipḥâ*)]; Abigail to King David after her husband has offended him [1 Sam 25:24–25, 28, 31 (*'āmâ*); 25:41 (*'āmâ* and *šipḥâ*)]; the medium at Endor when speaking to Saul and hoping to preserve her life [1 Sam 28:21 (*šipḥâ*)]; the wise woman of Tekoa addressing David in order to get him to bring Absalom back [2 Sam 14:6, 15–17 (*šipḥâ* and *'āmâ*)]; Bathsheba to David when she wants Solomon named his heir [1 Kings 1:17 (*'āmâ*)]; the prostitute who comes before Solomon hoping to regain her infant son [1 Kings 3:20 (*'āmâ*)]; the Shunammite woman to Elisha [2 Kings 4:2, 16 (*šipḥâ*)]; Ruth addressing Boaz when he has allowed her to glean among his women [Ruth 2:13 (*šipḥâ*)] and when she hopes he will take her under his cloak [Ruth 3:9 (*'āmâ*)]). For discussions on the possible relationship between these two terms, see Adele Berlin, *Poetics and Interpretation of Biblical Narrative* (Sheffield, Eng.: Almond, 1983), 88–89, and Tammi J. Schneider, *Mothers of Promise: Women in the Book of Genesis* (Grand Rapids, Mich.: Baker Academic, 2008), 103–19, 126–37.

105. Phyllis Trible notes the marking of Ishmael's mother as a foreigner and slave, and denying her the title "wife" in the *tôlēdôt* of Ishmael (Trible, "Ominous Beginnings for a Promise of Blessings," in *Hagar, Sarah, and Their Children: Jewish, Christian, and Muslim Perspectives*, ed. Phyllis Trible and Letty M. Russell [Louisville: Westminster John Knox, 2006], 55–56).

106. Biblical commentators see the phrase "Abraham begot Isaac" as redundant and unnecessary, and some explain it as a possible reaction to Sarah's compromised position in the house of King Abimelech of Gerar in Gen 20 just prior to the announcement of the birth of Isaac in Gen 21 (e.g., Speiser, *Genesis*, 196;

Bill Arnold, *Genesis* [NCBC; Cambridge: Cambridge University Press, 2009], 231). I see this added phrase as necessary to show the unbroken paternal chain that links Abraham directly to Isaac without reference to a mother. Phyllis Trible is correct in noting that this "redundancy" serves to "accent only his paternal line," with the result that "Sarah, the indispensable mother is disposable" (Trible, "Ominous Beginnings," 57).

107. McKinnon, "Domestic Exceptions," 51.
108. Lila Abu-Lughod, *Veiled Sentiments: Honor and Poetry in a Bedouin Society* (Berkeley: University of California Press, 1986), 56–57.
109. Keturah's six sons and Ishmael's twelve sons represent "two confederations of tribes" that interacted with Israel through trade and had similar languages and cultures. The biblical authors expressed this cultural closeness in "familial terms" (Sarna, *Genesis*, 171; Driver, *The Book of Genesis*, 244).
110. The word used for "gifts" in this text is *mattānôt*, which usually refers to gifts offered at a temple or innate human abilities understood as gifts. Only in this text does it refer to an inheritance of some sort ("*mattānôt*," BDB: 682).
111. I provide the very literal if awkward translation "from upon Isaac" for *mēʻal yiṣḥāq* to show the inference of feared inheritance claims placed "upon" Isaac and his father's house. See also Jer 16:13, where God is threatening to "hurl" his people "from upon [*mēʻal*] this land" into another land where he will show them no favor. When Abram and Lot divide their households, Abram says to Lot, "Separate yourself from upon me [*hippāred nāʼ mēʻālāy*]" (Gen 13:9, 11), and Lot chooses the land east of the Jordan. The exact phrase, "send out from upon," is found in the story of Amnon and Tamar, where Amnon sends Tamar out from upon him after raping her (2 Sam 13:17). See chapter 4.
112. My analysis here builds on that of Naomi Steinberg, who describes Abraham's marriage to Keturah as "inferior" to his union with Sarah because "the marriage of Abraham and Keturah separates procreation from property" (Steinberg, *Kinship and Marriage in Genesis*, 85–86).
113. We never receive a death notice of Hagar or Keturah, but the banishment of Hagar from Abraham's house (Gen 21:14) suggests that she would not be buried in the cave of Machpelah. Elizabeth Bloch-Smith suggests, based on Iron Age burial practices in Israel, that "family members were interred together" and generations of one family would share a single-family tomb or cave. What is interesting to note, however, is that according to data Bloch-Smith cites, men outnumbered women in these tombs 2:1 (Bloch-Smith, "From Womb to Tomb: The Israelite Family in Death as in Life," in *The Family in Life and in Death: The Family in Ancient Israel, Sociological and Archaeological Perspectives*, ed. Patricia Dutcher-Walls [New York: T&T Clark, 2009], 123, 127). The gender imbalance that places twice as many men as women in a family tomb may suggest that not every woman in a family merited a place in the family tomb. Jacob's description of the occupants of his family tomb at the time of

his death indicates that it housed Abraham, Sarah, Isaac, Rebekah, and Leah (Gen 49:29–33). Absent from this list are all of the secondary slave wives and concubines: Hagar, Keturah, Bilhah, and Zilpah. None of these low-status wives had death or burial notices. Rachel was buried separately near Bethlehem (Gen 35:18–21). According to Francesca Stavrakopoulou, Abraham's initial purchase of the burial cave for Sarah was a move to possess "hereditary land, constructed around the territorial function of a tomb." Later generations could make land claims based on their descent from an occupant of the tomb (Stavrakopoulou, *Land of Our Fathers*, 37–53).

114. On Hagar as the founding ancestor of the Ishmaelite nation, see Thomas B. Dozeman, "The Wilderness and Salvation History in the Hagar Story," *JBL* 117, no. 1 (1998): 23–43, and my analysis in chapter 9.

115. Moses marries Zipporah, a Midianite, and Zipporah's father is a priest of Yahweh. For a concise summary of the Midianite/Kenite hypothesis for the origins of Yahwism, see Lawrence E. Stager, "Forging an Identity: The Emergence of Ancient Israel," in *The Oxford History of the Biblical World*, ed. Michael D. Coogan (New York: Oxford University Press, 1998), 105–11. On the complicated connection between Moses and the Midianites through Zipporah, see Christopher B. Hays, "'Lest Ye Perish in the Way': Ritual and Kinship in Exodus 4:24–26," *Hebrew Studies* 48 (2007): 39–54.

116. The literary pattern that we saw in Gen 25 is followed in the lead-up to the Joseph narrative. Isaac dies and is buried by his two sons, Esau and Jacob (Gen 35:27–29). We then read a composite collection of genealogies of Esau beginning with *wĕʾēlleh tōlĕdôt ʿēśāw* (Gen 36:1, 9). Esau and his descendants are located outside the Promised Land in the "hill country of Seir" (Gen 36:8). Because Esau and Jacob share a mother, his departure is not marked by a socially degraded, maternally mediated path to his father, Isaac.

117. Bilhah and Zilpah are referred to with the labels *šipḥâ* (slave girl) and *ʾāmâ* (maidservant).

118. According to Naomi Steinberg, this bad report is Joseph's attempt to discredit these brothers as potential heirs (Steinberg, *Kinship and Marriage*, 122–23).

119. Gen 37:35 refers to "all his [Jacob's] sons and all his daughters," trying to comfort Jacob when he thinks he has lost Joseph, suggesting that there may have been traditions of additional daughters.

120. The continuing role of Sarah in the house that Isaac inherits from Abraham is seen first in the composition of the family tomb at Machpelah where Sarah and Abraham are buried together without either of his secondary wives, which the text labels "concubines" (Gen 25:9–10). But it is also seen in Isaac's consummation of his marriage with Rebekah in "her tent, that of Sarah his mother" (Gen 24:67). Naomi Steinberg notes that Gen 37 reprises Gen 25 in its reference to the Ishmaelites and the family tomb, which becomes the burial place for all of the patriarchs and their primary wives, excluding Rachel (Steinberg, *Kinship and Marriage*, 125).

121. The text is not explicit about Benjamin's absence when Joseph is sold into slavery, but Joseph is described as the younger brother, still at home, while his other brothers tend flocks in Shechem. Therefore, it makes sense that Benjamin, the even younger brother, would also be at home.
122. This physical tie between Joseph and his mother is noted by Robert Alter, *Genesis: Translation and Commentary* (New York: Norton, 1996), 225n6.
123. "*raḥămîm*," BDB: 933; Phyllis Trible, *God and the Rhetoric of Sexuality* (Philadelphia: Fortress, 1978), 31–59.
124. Trible, *God and the Rhetoric of Sexuality*, 33.
125. A more literal translation would be "He alone is left [of those] belonging to his mother." Note that Judah refers to Joseph as "his brother," meaning "Benjamin's brother" not "our brother."
126. Steinberg, *Kinship and Marriage*, 130.
127. On average ancient Israelite household size, see Stager, "The Archaeology of the Family," 18.
128. It is very difficult to obtain reliable statistics on the percentage of polygynous families within a given ancient society. Instead, we have separate pieces of evidence that suggest that, while rare, polygyny was not limited to the extremely wealthy or to royal families. Susan McKinnon notes that among the Nuer, widows, divorced women, and otherwise unmarried women could become the concubines of poor men from outsider tribes who could not afford to pay the full bridewealth (McKinnon, "Domestic Exceptions," 60). Lila Abu-Lughod's study of the Bedouin shows that polygyny was not limited to elite or royal families (Abu-Lughod, *Veiled Sentiments*, 51–55). Margery Wolf's research of women in rural Taiwan focuses on common village dwellers and documents social hierarchies of families within these villages where prominent village men might have more than one wife (Wolf, "Uterine Families and the Women's Community," in *Women and the Family in Rural Taiwan* [Stanford, Cal.: Stanford University Press, 1972], 37). Carolyn Leeb documents a similar pattern of polygynous marriages among the poor of rural Haiti (Leeb, "Polygyny: Insights from Rural Haiti," in *Ancient Israel: The Old Testament in Its Social Context*, ed. Philip S. Esler [Minneapolis: Fortress, 2006], 50–65). While better data is still needed, it seems fair to say that polygyny is and was practiced primarily by men with means, but economic means are relative to those around them. A man need only be better off than the woman or the family of a woman he wishes to take into his house.

Chapter 2. The House of the Mother

1. Carol Meyers, "'To Her Mother's House': Considering a Counterpart to the Israelite *Bêt 'āb*," in *The Bible and the Politics of Exegesis: Essays in Honor of Norman Gottwald on His Sixty-Fifth Birthday*, ed. David Jobling, Peggy L. Day, and Gerald T. Sheppard (Cleveland: Pilgrim, 1991), 43, 50. This understanding of

the house of the mother has remained consistent in her published work up to the present. See Meyers, *Discovering Eve: Ancient Israelite Women in Context* (New York: Oxford University Press, 1988), 179–80; Meyers, "Returning Home: Ruth 1:8 and the Gendering of the Book of Ruth," in *A Feminist Companion to Ruth*, ed. Athalya Brenner (1993; repr. Sheffield, Eng.: Sheffield Academic Press, 2001), 95; Meyers, "Gender Imagery in the Song of Songs," in *A Feminist Companion to the Song of Songs*, ed. Athalya Brenner (Sheffield, Eng.: Sheffield Academic Press, 1993), 209; Meyers, "In the Household and Beyond: The Social World of Israelite Women," *Nordic Journal of Theology* 63 (2009): 19–41; and Meyers, *Rediscovering Eve: Ancient Israelite Women in Context* (New York: Oxford University Press, 2013), 112–13.

2. This chapter is a significantly revised and expanded version of my essay "The House of the Mother and the Brokering of Marriage in the Bible: Economic Reciprocity among Natal Siblings," in *In the Wake of Tikva Frymer-Kensky*, ed. Steven Holloway, JoAnn Scurlock, and Richard Beal (Piscataway, N.J.: Gorgias Press, 2009), 143–70.

3. Gerhard von Rad labels the chapter a *novelle*, recognizing that it tells a complete story and thus may form a literary unit independent in origin from the surrounding chapters. He also recognizes a long editorial history to the story and the unparalleled use of the divine epithet "Yahweh the God of heaven and earth." These considerations have caused von Rad to posit "the relatively late origin of the story," but he does not elaborate on what he means by "late." He simply concludes that it must postdate J, which he dates around 950 BCE (von Rad, *Genesis: A Commentary* [OTL; Louisville: Westminster John Knox, 1973], 253–59; his dating of J source, 25). Claus Westermann finds in Gen 24 "an old family narrative" that parallels Gen 29:1–14 and Exod 2:15–22. Westermann attributes all of these to the J source. He then adds that Gen 24 is a reworking of the Yahwist family narrative into a "guidance narrative" that postdates the J source (Westermann, *Genesis 12–36* [CC; Minneapolis: Fortress, 1994], 383–84). Wolfgang W. M. Roth attributes Gen 24 to the Yahwist, but he still sees the chapter as "the Yahwist's interpretive epilogue of his Abraham cycle" (Roth, "The Wooing of Rebecca: A Tradition-Critical Study of Gen 24," *CBQ* 34 [1972]: 179). All of these commentators share the view that Gen 24 postdates and comments on an existing Abraham cycle or tradition.

4. Alexander Rofé, "An Enquiry into the Betrothal of Rebekah," in *Die hebräische Bibel und ihre zweifache Nachgeschichte: Festschrift für Rolf Rendtorff zum 65. Geburtstag*, ed. Erhard Blum, Christian Macholz, and Ekkehard W. Stegemann (Neukirchen-Vluyn, Ger.: Neukirchener Verlag, 1990), 27–39.

5. Rofé, "An Enquiry," 29–31.

6. David Carr, *The Formation of the Hebrew Bible: A New Reconstruction* (Oxford: Oxford University Press, 2011), 280–81.

7. Tammi J. Schneider notes that the combined genealogies of Rebekah in Gen 11: 26–29 and 22:3 show that "Rebekah has both the correct father and grand-

mother" (Schneider, *Mothers of Promise: Women in the Book of Genesis* [Grand Rapids, Mich.: Baker Academic, 2008], 43). I would specify this even further: Rebekah has the right father, grandfather, and paternal grandmother (a wife, not a concubine), all of which pave her direct and legitimate pathway back to Nahor, Abraham, and the paternal house of Terah.

8. Naomi Steinberg notes that land is a repeated cause for tension in the patriarchal narratives, and because inheritance was patrilineal, the heir had to reside in his father's house (Steinberg, *Kinship and Marriage in Genesis: A Household Economics Perspective* [Minneapolis: Fortress, 1993], 24–26).

9. In two places Bethuel is not listed directly as Laban's father. In Gen 24:48, Abraham's servant refers to Rebekah as "the daughter of the brother of his master" (*bat-'ăḥî 'ădōnî*), and in Gen 29:5, Laban is referred to as a "son of Nahor" (*ben-nāḥôr*). While both of these references could indicate that Nahor was the father of Laban and Rebekah, it is more likely that the very elastic kinship terms "brother," "son," and "daughter" are used more broadly in these two texts. Rebekah and Laban are a son and daughter within the house of Nahor, which continues through Bethuel, their father.

10. The word *bĕtûlâ* is translated best "young woman," with the implication that she is likely not yet married. See John J. Schmitt, "Virgin," *ABD* 6: 853; Mieke Bal, *Death and Dissymmetry: The Politics of Coherence in the Book of Judges* (Chicago: University of Chicago Press, 1988), 46–52; and Carolyn Pressler, *The View of Women Found in the Deuteronomic Family Laws* (Berlin: Walter de Gruyter, 1993), 25–31. The appositional phrase added in Gen 24:16, "whom no man had known," specifies that this *bĕtûlâ* is also a virgin.

11. Gottfried Vanoni, "*śîm*," *TDOT* 14: 104; E. A. Speiser, *Genesis: Introduction, Translation, and Notes* (AB 1; New York: Doubleday, 1964), 178.

12. This is one of the places where Carol Meyers sees the reference to "her mother's house" as "an alternate expression for the same societal unit, and not as a function of the particular configuration of Nahor's family" (Meyers, "'To Her Mother's House,'" 43).

13. See Schneider, *Mothers of Promise*, 47.

14. The pattern replicates the genealogy from Cain to Lamech, where Lamech's wives comprise two maternal subunits within which the first son is tied to his mother, and the second child is tied to his or her full sibling (Gen 4:17–24; see introduction).

15. Nahum Sarna has noted the pronounced emphasis on Abraham's wealth throughout this chapter, citing Gen 24:10, 22, 30, 35, 36, 47, 53 (Sarna, *Genesis: The Traditional Hebrew Text with the New JPS Translation* [Philadelphia: JPS, 1989], 162n2). The note that Abraham gave "all that he had" (*kol 'ăšer lô*) to Isaac anticipates Abraham's gift of "all that he has" in Gen 25:5.

16. Westermann, *Genesis 12–36*, 382, 389.

17. Roland de Vaux, *Ancient Israel: Its Life and Institutions*, trans. John McHugh (Grand Rapids, Mich.: Eerdmans, 1961), 29–30. Other commentators that have

suggested emending the text by killing off Bethuel and excising verse 50 include von Rad, *Genesis*, 257; Bruce Vawter, *On Genesis: A New Reading* (Garden City, N.Y.: Doubleday, 1977), 272; and J. Skinner, *Genesis*, 2nd ed. (Edinburgh: T&T Clark, 1930), 344.

18. Speiser, *Genesis*, 180.
19. Speiser also suggests that after the death of his father, Laban acts as "fratriarch" and assumes authority over his sister's marriage in a way that parallels the practice reflected in the Nuzi "sistership document" (Speiser, *Genesis*, 181, 184–85). Thomas Thompson rejects Speiser's argument and specifically his use of the term "fratriarchy." Instead, Thompson sees Laban and his mother "exercising patriarchal authority" in a pattern similar to that found in Old Babylonian marriage contracts (Thompson, *The Historicity of the Patriarchal Narratives: The Quest for the Historical Abraham* [Harrisburg: Trinity, 2002], 249). Robert Alter cites and agrees with the many textual critics who understand the reference to Bethuel as a scribal or redactional insertion (Alter, *Genesis: Translation and Commentary* [New York: Norton, 1996], 120).
20. Sarna, *Genesis*, 166. See also André LaCocque, *Ruth*, trans. K. C. Hanson (CC; Minneapolis: Fortress, 2004), 44.
21. Sarna, *Genesis*, 168.
22. Steinberg, *Kinship and Marriage in Genesis*, 84.
23. This is the first of many textual examples where the presence of a maternally specific kinship term causes scholarly consternation to the degree that textual emendation and erasure is offered as one of the leading solutions.
24. Ingo Kottsieper, "'We Have a Little Sister': Aspects of the Brother-Sister Relationship in Ancient Israel," in *Families and Family Relations as Represented in Early Judaisms and Early Christianities: Texts and Fictions*, ed. Jan Willem Vas Henten and Athalya Brenner (Leiden: Deo, 2000), 69–72.
25. Exod 2:1–4. The connection between uterine siblings and rescue are discussed in chapter 4.
26. The Hebrew word translated here as "costly gifts" is *migdānōt*. Tracy Lemos has noted that this word is only used four times in the Bible, and the other three occurrences do not deal with marriage and as such do not shed light on its meaning here. She also notes the rarity of the bride, her mother, and her brother being the direct recipients of marriage gifts. Identifying the gift as "indirect dowry," she suggests that the use of the term *migdānōt* instead of the more common term *mohar* (bridewealth) "may relate somehow to who served as the recipients of this particular gift" (Lemos, *Marriage Gifts and Social Change in Ancient Palestine: 1200 BCE–200 CE* [Cambridge: Cambridge University Press, 2010], 46–47). The other occurrences of the term are in 2 Chron 21:3; 32:23 and Ezra 1:6, all postexilic texts, suggesting again a postexilic dating for Gen 24.
27. Edward Campbell, *Ruth: A New Translation with Introduction and Commentary* (AB 7; New York: Doubleday, 1975), 64; Meyers, "'To Her Mother's House,'"

45–50; Tikva Frymer-Kensky, *Reading the Women of the Bible* (New York: Schocken, 2002), 10.

28. In a group of Sumerian texts known as "The Bridal Songs of Inanna," we also find marriage negotiations taking place within the house of her mother, Ningal, with Inanna's brother Utu taking an active role. See Gwendolyn Leick, *Sex and Eroticism in Mesopotamian Literature* (London: Routledge, 1994), 74–75, and Diane Wolkstein and Samuel Noah Kramer, *Inanna: Queen of Heaven and Earth, Her Stories and Hymns from Sumer* (New York: Harper and Row, 1983), 30–32.

29. Edward Campbell places the book in the monarchic period (950–700 BCE) with a preference for the Solomonic era (Campbell, *Ruth*, 23–28). Kirstin Nielsen refrains from dating the book of Ruth, suggesting that a defense of David's origins could have been needed at several points throughout the history of the Davidic monarchy. The latest date she seems willing to entertain is late pre-exilic based on the book of Ruth's intertextual dependence on 1 Kings (Nielsen, *Ruth: A Commentary* [OTL; Louisville: Westminster John Knox, 1997], 28–29). Katharine Doob Sakenfeld accepts some of the arguments that point to late biblical Hebrew within the book of Ruth and identifies a range of possible dates from late pre-exilic to postexilic (Sakenfeld, *Ruth: Interpretation: A Bible Commentary for Teaching and Preaching* [Louisville: John Knox, 1999], 1–5). Several commentators note late biblical Hebrew, Aramaicisms, and a dependence on Deuteronomy to arrive at an early postexilic date (LaCocque, *Ruth*, 18–21; Victor Matthews, *Judges and Ruth* [NCBC; Cambridge: Cambridge University Press, 2004], 209–11; Tamara Cohn Eskenazi and Tikva Frymer-Kensky, *Ruth: The Traditional Hebrew Text with the New JPS Translation and Commentary* [Philadelphia: JPS, 2011], xvi–xix). On the difficulty and ultimate failure of efforts to date the book of Ruth, see Jack M. Sasson, *Ruth: A New Translation with a Philological Commentary and a Formalist-Folklorist Interpretation*, 2nd ed. (Sheffield, Eng.: JSOT Press, 1989), 240–52, and, most recently, Jerry A. Gladson, *A Critical and Exegetical Commentary of the Book of Ruth* (Lewiston, N.Y.: Edwin Mellen, 2013), 19–50.

30. Nielsen, *Ruth*, 99.

31. Gilian Feeley-Harnik sees the book of Ruth as central to the story of the monarchy; it "explains the birth of the Israelite monarchy out of Moab" (Feeley-Harnik, "Naomi and Ruth: Building up the House of David," in *Text and Tradition: The Hebrew Bible and Folklore*, ed. Susan Niditch [Atlanta: Scholars Press, 1990], 165).

32. Sasson, *Ruth*, 13–19.

33. LaCocque, *Ruth*, 44.

34. Matthews, *Judges and Ruth*, 220–21.

35. Campbell, *Ruth*, 64.

36. Campbell, *Ruth*, 64.

37. They also note but reject the idea that the *bêt ʾēm* may have referred to a physical dwelling within a larger house compound (Eskenazi and Frymer-Kensky, *Ruth*, 10–11).
38. There are two biblical texts that describe "problem wives" returning to "the house of the father" rather than "the house of the mother." In both of these cases, however, the wife did not return home seeking a new marriage. Judah sent his daughter-in-law Tamar back to her "father's house" to "remain a widow" after two of three sons of Judah died while being married to Tamar (Gen 38:11). The Levite's concubine, after becoming angry with her husband, left him and returned to her father's house. She did not seek a new marriage (Judg 19:2). A law concerning who may eat holy food within a priest's household indicates that a widowed priest's daughter who was childless could expect to return to her "father's house" and be fed and cared for (Lev 22:13). In none of these texts is there an expectation that the returned daughter will remarry.
39. The term *bêt ʾîšāh*, "house of her husband," is another example of how the terminology for the *bayit* shifts in accordance with the vantage point of the person within it.
40. For a summary of twentieth-century scholarship on the Song of Songs that dates the book anywhere from the Solomonic age to the late third century BCE, see Marvin Pope, *Song of Songs* (AB 7C; Garden City, N.Y.: Doubleday, 1977), 22–33. Pope ultimately seems to favor arguments dating the book to the time of Solomon (Pope, *Song of Songs*, 27, 33). Cheryl Exum documents the variety of arguments supporting a wide range of dates and ultimately concludes that knowing when the book was written would not help the reader understand the book (Exum, *Song of Songs* [OTL; Louisville: Westminster John Knox, 2005], 63–67). Marc Brettler addresses the difficulty in dating the book in "Unresolved and Unresolvable: Problems in Interpreting the Song," in *Scrolls of Love: Ruth and the Song of Songs*, ed. Peter S. Hawkins and Lesleigh Cushing Stahlberg (New York: Fordham University Press, 2006), 185–98.
41. Phyllis Trible, "Love Lyrics Redeemed," in Brenner, ed., *A Feminist Companion to the Song of Songs*, 115–16.
42. Ariel Bloch and Chana Bloch, *Song of Songs: A New Translation with Introduction and Commentary* (Berkeley: University of California Press, 1995), 3, 5–6.
43. The phrase "my sister, my bride" is an example of poetic parallelism wherein the second phrase specifies that the speaker is using the ambiguous word "sister" to designate his "bride."
44. This is the only text that I am covering in this study where I am choosing the LXX over the MT reading. In the Hebrew, Song 8:2a reads, "into the house of my mother; she [or 'you'] will instruct me." The Greek, on the other hand, reads as I have translated above, "into the house of my mother and into the chamber of the one who conceived me." I follow several commentators who favor the LXX on this verse in light of the parallel phrasing in Song 3:4 and the associa-

tion of a mother's space with conception and birth in Song 6:9 and 8:5. See, e.g., Pope, *Song of Songs*, 653; Exum, *Song of Songs*, 244; and the NRSV. I offer an additional argument in support of the LXX version in chapter 5.

45. We find the same association of a mother's house with a girl and her lover in the Egyptian poem "The Stroll," which reads in part: "My brother roils my heart with his voice, making me take ill. Though he is among the neighbors of my mother's house, I cannot go to him. Mother is good in commanding me thus: 'Avoid seeing [him]!' (Yet) my heart is vexed when he comes to mind, for love of him has captured me" ("The Stroll," in *The Song of Songs and the Ancient Egyptian Love Songs*, trans. Michael V. Fox [Madison: University of Wisconsin Press, 1985], 52, no. 32, sections A and B).

46. Marvin Pope, citing T. R. Denis Buzy, recognizes the identification of a brother as one who had "nursed at the breasts of my mother" as a way of signifying a "uterine brother" (Pope, *Song of Songs*, 656–57). I discuss this reference extensively in relation to "milk kinship" in chapter 6.

47. Pope correctly notes that this phrase, "my mother's sons," is normally found in parallel with "my brothers" and suggests that the phrase "my brothers" had been lost from this poem (Pope, *Song of Songs*, 322–23).

48. Cheryl Exum argues that the speakers of the line "we have a little sister" are not the "mother's sons" referred to in Song 1:6. Instead, she understands Song 8:8–9 to be a scenario the female speaker imagines about another woman and then contrasts it to her own situation (Exum, *Song of Songs*, 255–59). I, however, follow most commentators in understanding the speakers of the line to be the girl's brothers referred to as "my mother's sons" in Song 1:6. See Pope, *Song of Songs*, 678, and Carey Ellen Walsh, *Exquisite Desire: Religion, the Erotic, and the Song of Songs* (Minneapolis: Fortress, 2000), 168.

49. Kottsieper, "'We Have a Little Sister,'" 52.

50. Recall that the story initiating the betrothal of Isaac was headlined with his father, Abraham (Gen 24:1). Tikva Frymer-Kensky also notes the significance of headlining the narrative with a reference to Dinah's mother, understanding it to signify that the text concerns marriage because mothers in the ancient Near East were the "chief negotiators" in the marriages of their daughters (Frymer-Kensky, *Reading the Women of the Bible*, 179–80).

51. Tammi Schneider sees the identification of Dinah as "the daughter of Leah" as "parenthetical," and she indicates that Dinah is "more than simply Leah's daughter" because it is her full brothers who "take the lead to protect their sister's honor" (Schneider, *Mothers of Promise*, 138). Rather than parenthetical, I would argue that "daughter of Leah" defines the narrative that follows and forecasts the important relationships that govern the action. Dinah is not "more than simply Leah's daughter"; she is precisely Leah's daughter with all the key sibling and household relationships that the maternal kinship designation implies.

52. While there has been considerable debate concerning whether it is appropriate to label what occurred to Dinah as rape, I am convinced that the Hebrew supports a reading of forced sex on an unwilling Dinah. On the specific meaning of the *pi'el* form of the verb *'innâ*, see Ellen van Wolde, "Does *'innâ* Denote Rape? A Semantic Analysis of a Controversial Word," *VT* 52 (2002): 528–44. For arguments supporting the translation "rape," see Schneider, *Mothers of Promise*, 144–46; Yael Shemesh, "Rape Is Rape Is Rape: The Story of Dinah and Shechem (Gen 34)," *ZAW* (2007): 1–21; Pressler, *The View of Women*, 14–16; Susanne Scholz, *Rape Plots: A Feminist Cultural Study of Genesis 34* (New York: Peter Lang, 2002), 134–42; and Carolyn Blyth, *The Narrative of Rape in Genesis 34: Interpreting Dinah's Silence* (Oxford: Oxford University Press, 2010), 38–92.
53. Schneider, *Mothers of Promise*, 139.
54. Dinah's presence in Shechem's house is mentioned in Gen 34:26, when she is removed from his house after a raid.
55. The Hebrew word *mōhar*, translated as "bridewealth," refers to property transferred from the household of the husband to the kin of the bride as part of the marriage process. For an excellent and comprehensive treatment of the biblical practices related to bridewealth, see Lemos, *Marriage Gifts*, 20–61.
56. The terms "his sons" and "sons of Jacob" are used in Gen 34:5, 7, 13.
57. Dinah is the youngest child of Leah (Gen 30:21), so her older brothers refer to her as "our daughter." Joseph also greets his younger brother Benjamin as "my son" (Gen 43:29).
58. Gila Ramras-Rauch describes Jacob's silence and discomfort as "cautious" given that he has just returned to his homeland, and in the chapter previous to this, he has reconciled with his formerly hostile brother. All of this fits with my emphasis on Jacob's concern being for "his house" (Ramras-Rauch, "Fathers and Daughters: Two Biblical Narratives," in *Mappings of the Biblical Terrain: The Bible as Text*, ed. Vincent L. Tollers and John Maier [Lewisburg, Penn.: Bucknell University Press, 1990], 163).
59. The story of Tamar's failed marriage negotiations with Amnon also features a largely silent father, David, and a uterine brother, Absalom, who rescues his sister, houses her, and avenges her rape. This marriage, however, is not exactly patrilocal because the potential groom and bride share a father (2 Sam 13). I discuss this text in chapter 4.
60. Renita Weems sees "a polemical tone to the entire book," with the tense relationship between the female protagonist and the Jerusalem women being one feature of the polemic (Weems, "Song of Songs," in *The Women's Bible Commentary*, ed. Carol A. Newsom and Sharon H. Ringe [London: Society for Promoting Christian Knowledge, 1992], 159–60).
61. Samson's marriage to the Timnite woman follows a different pattern. Samson confers with "his mother and his father" about wanting to marry her (Judg 14:1–7). Later, his father alone goes down to Timnah to speak with the potential bride and to be present for the marriage feast (Judg 14:10). Samson appears to

reside with his bride after the marriage, but the text is not clear if this was a temporary or permanent arrangement. The marriage ends quickly, so we never learn where an Israelite man and his Philistine wife might have lived long-term (Judg 14:19–20).

62. This is not to imply, as others have previously, that these are examples of *"errebu* marriages." There is no evidence of a distinct type of marriage wherein a man marries permanently into the house of his father-in-law, and, indeed, each of these grooms ultimately leaves and sets up his own house. Instead, this is an example of "descent group recruitment through women," a less valued but often necessary option for some households. (The phrase "descent group recruitment through women" comes from Karen Sinclair, "Mischief on the Margins: Gender, Primogeniture, and Cognatic Descent among the Maori," in *New Directions in Anthropological Kinship*, ed. Linda Stone [Lanham, Md.: Rowman and Littlefield, 2001], 156. See my discussion of the critique of patrilineality in the introduction.) On David's status as a fugitive, see Baruch Halpern, *David's Secret Demons: Messiah, Murderer, Traitor, King* (Grand Rapids, Mich.: Eerdmans, 2001), 18–21.

63. On younger sons choosing careers in the military, government, or priesthood, see Lawrence E. Stager, "The Archaeology of the Family in Ancient Israel," *BASOR* 260 (1985): 25–28, and Carolyn S. Leeb, *Away from the Father's House: The Social Location of* naʿar *and* naʿarah *in Ancient Israel* (JSOTSup 301; Sheffield, Eng.: Sheffield Academic Press, 2000), 42–124, 190–94.

64. In Exod 2, the birth story of Moses, he is presented as the Levite couple's firstborn son who has an older sister but no brother. It is not until Exod 4:14–17 that we are introduced to Aaron, Moses' brother, and not until Exod 6:20 that Aaron is listed before Moses as the firstborn. Thus it is possible to claim Moses as a second-born son, but even if he were the firstborn son, he did not stand to inherit in his father's house because he was adopted into the family of Pharaoh.

65. The situation of the daughters of Zelophehad also fits with this pattern. Zelophehad had multiple daughters and no sons. Had he lived, he would likely have brokered at least one marriage of a son-in-law into his household. Once he died, his five daughters successfully petitioned Moses for their father's inheritance (Num 26:33; 27:1–11). Later, the stand-ins for Zelophehad's "house," who are described as "the heads of the father's houses of the sons of Gilead," demand that any marriages contracted by the daughters of Zelophehad must be marriages within the tribe of Manasseh in order to keep the property under the control of "the house of the father" (Num 36:1–12; Josh 17:3–6).

66. Kottsieper, "'We Have a Little Sister,'" 73–74.

67. Hilma Granqvist, *Marriage Conditions in a Palestinian Village* (Helsingfors, Finland: Akademische Buchhandlung, 1931).

68. Granqvist, *Marriage Conditions*, 28–29.

69. Martha Mundy and Richard Saumarez Smith, "'Al-Mahr Zaituna': Property and Family in the Hills Facing Palestine, 1880–1940," in *Family History in the*

Middle East: Household, Property, and Gender, ed. Beshara Doumani (Albany: State University of New York Press, 2003), 119. See also Susan McKinnon, *From a Shattered Sun: Hierarchy, Gender, and Alliance in the Tanimbar Islands* (Madison: University of Wisconsin Press, 1991), 200–203.

70. Annelies Moors, "Women's Gold: Shifting Styles of Embodying Family Relations," in Doumani, ed., *Family History,* 101–17.
71. Moors, "Women's Gold," 105.
72. Moors, "Women's Gold," 104–5.
73. Lila Abu-Lughod, *Veiled Sentiments: Honor and Poetry in a Bedouin Society* (Berkeley: University of California Press, 1986), 54–56. Abu-Lughod does not distinguish here between full and half-brothers. It would be interesting to know whether the obligations of full brothers to a married sister were greater than those of half-brothers. Marriage contracts from Nuzi also attest to the frequent role of a bride's brother in negotiating the terms of a marriage and receiving a portion of the marriage gifts. See Jonathan Paradise, "Marriage Contracts of Free Persons at Nuzi," *JCS* 39, no. 1 (1987): 1–36.
74. While the vineyard symbolizes the woman's sexuality, it also represents a possible marriage gift. Caleb's daughter Achsah, for example, asks her father for a field as a marital gift (Judg 1:11–15).
75. Schneider, *Mothers of Promise,* 43.

Chapter 3. Chamber of Her Who Conceived Me

1. Non-nested, satellite houses of the mother include the house of Hagar after she and Ishmael were sent away from the house of Abraham (Gen 21:8–21); the house of Gideon's concubine, Abimelech's mother (Judg 8:29–9:57); and the house of the prostitute who bore Jephthah to Gilead (Judg 11). I cover the house of Abimelech's mother in chapter 8 and the national house of Hagar in chapter 9. I cover the kinship term "son of my slave girl" in chapter 8.
2. The same parallelistic line is also found in LXX Song 8:2. See chapters 2 and 5 for further discussion of this verse.
3. James Kugel, *The Idea of Biblical Poetry: Parallelism and Its History* (Baltimore: Johns Hopkins University Press, 1998), 33.
4. Adele Berlin, *The Dynamics of Biblical Parallelism* (Bloomington: Indiana University Press, 1992), 67.
5. "'āḥ," BDB: 26; *HALOT* 1: 29; *DCH* 1: 173–78.
6. Ilana Rashkow sees the house of the mother as a spatial subunit of the house of the father, suggesting the "house of the mother" refers to "the bedroom of a woman's mother" (Rashkow, "Ruth: The Discourse of Power and the Power of Discourse," in *A Feminist Companion to Ruth,* ed. Athalya Brenner [1993; repr. Sheffield, Eng.: Sheffield Academic Press, 2001], 29n1).
7. Carol Meyers, "Returning Home: Ruth 1:8 and the Gendering of the Book of Ruth," in Brenner, ed., *A Feminist Companion to Ruth,* 104; emphasis added.

8. Carol Meyers, "'To Her Mother's House': Considering a Counterpart to the Israelite *Bêt 'āb*," in *The Bible and the Politics of Exegesis: Essays in Honor of Norman Gottwald on His Sixty-Fifth Birthday*, ed. David Jobling, Peggy L. Day, and Gerald T. Sheppard (Cleveland: Pilgrim, 1991), 43; Meyers, "Returning Home," 95–96.
9. See Exod 26 where curtains are joined together to create the tabernacle.
10. There are numerous examples of this type of word pair that moves from large spatial category to the units which make up that space. See, e.g., country/cities (Isa 1:7–9) and cities/houses (Isa 6:11).
11. There is, however, a noticeable shift in the level of reference as one moves from the A clause to the B clause in Num 24:5. The first line seems to refer to the man Jacob whose domestic house divides into four maternal tents (Gen 31:33); the second line refers to the nation Israel, whose national house divides into maternally defined encampments (Gen 32–33; Num 2; both of these texts are discussed in chapter 9). Other examples of spatial word pairs that agree in number are tents/dwellings (Jer 30:18); tabernacle/tent (Ps 78:60); tents/curtains (Jer 4: 20; 49:29; Hab 3:7; Song 1:5).
12. Even though the word "tabernacles" is plural here, it designates the singular dwelling place of the deity.
13. A man's house can also be divided into the number of "wombs" it contains, where wombs stands metonymically for women or wives. When Abraham passes his wife Sarah off as his sister, she ends up in King Abimelech's house where "Yahweh closed up completely every womb [*kol reḥem*] in Abimelech's house" (Gen 20:18).
14. The same word sequence designates the movement toward the interior of a house in Exod 7:28 [Eng. 8:3] where Pharaoh is told that frogs will enter "your house, your bedchamber, your bed."
15. Another text that shows the understanding of *ḥeder* as an interior space is Deut 32:25, which uses *ḥeder* as an antonym to *ḥûṣ* (outside).
16. Chambered houses belong to Joseph (Gen 43:30); Pharaoh (Exod 8:3; Ps 105:30); King Eglon of Moab (Judg 3:24); Ishbaal, son of King Saul (2 Sam 4:7); Amnon, son of King David (2 Sam 13:10); David (1 Kings 1:15); the king of Aram (2 Kings 6:12); Queen Athaliah (2 Kings 11:2); and Yahweh's house (Ezek 8:12). Non-royal chambered houses include those of Delilah's parents (Judg 15:1; 16:9, 12); unnamed "people" (Isa 26:20); "the bridegroom" (Joel 2:16); "the adulteress" (Prov 7:27); and a house built "through wisdom" (Prov 24:4).
17. Ariel and Chana Bloch understand King Solomon as "a central figure in the lovers' fantasies" rather than as an actual character in the poem (Bloch and Bloch, *Song of Songs: A New Translation with Introduction and Commentary* [Berkeley: University of California Press, 1995], 10–11). While I generally agree with this assertion, there are places in the poem where the female speaker's imagined lover is Solomon or is a man that in her fantasies becomes Solomon, e.g., Song 1:1–4.

18. The unnamed woman speaker in the Song is at one point called "The Shulammite," which likely means the Jerusalemite or "woman of Jerusalem" (Bloch and Bloch, *Song of Songs*, 8).
19. The association of the man with agricultural labor and the woman with reproduction is found already in the Eden narrative, where the man is made of the earth with the purpose of tilling it, and the woman is made from the man with the result that the two become one flesh (Gen 2:5–8, 21–24). These same gender-specific jobs are reasserted with the addition of "labor" in the divine punishments (Gen 3:16–19).
20. The "innermost parts" of the house, the *yarkĕtê habbayit*, are also mentioned as a place of hiding in an elite house of one who is "at ease in Zion" and "feels secure on the mountain of Samaria" (Amos 6:1, 10).
21. The Song evokes the woman's sexuality through the language of a vineyard (Song 1:6), a locked garden (Song 4:2), a mother's house or chamber (Song 3:4; 8:1–2), and a room with a locked door (Song 5:2–5).
22. Jeremiah imagines the houses of the rich in a similar way, describing them as "spacious," with "larger upper rooms" and windows, cedar paneling, and painted walls the color of vermilion (Jer 22:13–14).
23. The Hebrew for "tent" can mean a dwelling place as a whole and also a curtained-off space within a larger dwelling, especially in the case of the tabernacle and the temple ("*'ohel*," BDB: 13–14). See also Harry Hoffner, "*bayit*," *TDOT* 2: 108.
24. Hoffner, "*bayit*," *TDOT* 2: 110.
25. BDB: 295. See Num 32:41; Deut 3:14; Josh 13:30; Judg 10:3–5; 1 Kings 4:13; and 1 Chron 2:23.
26. Pierre Bonte, "Ibn Khaldun and Contemporary Anthropology: Cycles and Factional Alliances of Tribe and State in the Maghreb," in *Tribes and Power: Nationalism and Ethnicity in the Middle East*, ed. Faleh Abdul-Jabar and Hosham Dawod (London: Saqi, 2003), 63.
27. Bonte, "Ibn Khaldun," 63.
28. Nahum Sarna, *Genesis: The Traditional Hebrew Text with the New JPS Translation* (Philadelphia: JPS, 1989), 22. BDB defines *ṣēlāʻ* as 1. "*rib* of man"; 2. "*rib* of a hill"; 3. "*side chambers* or *cells*"; and 4. "*ribs* of cedar and fir, i.e. planks, boards (pl.), of temple wall" ("*ṣēlā*," BDB: 854).
29. In Job 4:19, Eliphaz compares the bodies of mortal men to their houses in terms of their shared substance: men are those who live in "houses of clay whose foundation is in the dust," and they are contrasted with angels.
30. Again, several commentators have opted to erase the maternal identification of this tent. Gerhard von Rad translates the verse, "Then Isaac brought her into the tent," and admits that he has "corrected" the verse "a great deal." His "correction" erases the phrase "Sarah, his mother" from the verse. "Stylistically," he argues, the phrase is "remarkably clumsy" (von Rad, *Genesis: A Commen-*

tary [OTL; Louisville: Westminster John Knox, 1973], 253, 259). Speiser also eliminates Sarah, translating "into *his* tent" and describing the Hebrew that includes Sarah as "grammatically unmanageable" (E. A. Speiser, *Genesis: Introduction, Translation, and Notes* [AB 1; New York: Doubleday, 1964], 178, 182). Claus Westermann retains the identification of the tent as "the tent of Sarah, his mother," but goes on to erase the reference to Sarah as "his mother" at the end of the verse, emending the text to read, "So Isaac was consoled after the death of *Abraham his father.*" His notes indicate that he views both references to "Sarah, his mother," and "his mother" as insertions, describing the first phrasing as "grammatically impossible" (Westermann, *Genesis 12–36* [CC; Minneapolis: Fortress, 1994], 381–82, 391).

31. Michael M. Homan, *To Your Tents, O Israel! Terminology, Function, Form, and Symbolism of Tents in the Hebrew Bible and the Ancient Near East* (Culture and History of the Ancient Near East 7; Leiden: E. J. Brill, 2002), 79–81, citing Gen 24:67; Song 3:7, 9; Ps 19:5–6; and Joel 2:16.

32. Homan, *To Your Tents*, 82–83.

33. My thanks to Zhao Ruoyan who, while a graduate student in Hebrew Bible at Chinese University of Hong Kong, made me aware of the issue of the Masoretic pointing of "her tent" as "his tent." There are two other places where the consonantal text is "*hlh*," but the Masoretic pointing is "his tent." In both of these cases, the tent is associated with Abram but could be read as Sarai's tent, that is, a part of the house or larger tent of Abram (Gen 12:8; 13:3).

34. On Ham's crime as maternal incest, see John Sietze Bergsma and Scott Walker Hahn, "Noah's Nakedness and the Curse on Canaan (Genesis 9:20–27)," *JBL* 124, no. 1 (2005): 25–40.

35. In Num 25:6–18, we read the story of the Israelite man found engaging in sex with a Midianite woman while in "the tent" (*haqqubbâ*), but the Hebrew word used for tent is quite uncommon.

36. This parallels Gen 24, where we have the "house of Abraham" and the "tent of Sarah."

37. As a place to offer food and lodging, the tent of Jael resembles the house of Rebekah's mother, where a meal is served and lodging is provided (Gen 24).

38. See, e.g., Susan Niditch, "Erotocism and Death in the Tale of Jael," in *Women in the Hebrew Bible: A Reader*, ed. Alice Bach (New York: Routledge, 1999), 305–16, and Ellen van Wolde, "Deborah and Ya'el in Judges 4," in *On Reading Prophetic Texts: Gender-Specific and Related Studies in Memory of Fokkelien van Dijk-Hemmes*, ed. Bob Becking and Meindert Dijkstra (Leiden: E. J. Brill, 1996), 283–90.

39. This text, however, is somewhat ambiguous. If Laban went into the tent of the two maidservants, why does he come out of the tent of Leah? The phrase "and into the tent of the two maidservants" could be a later interpolation although the motivation for it remains unclear. Are we to understand that Laban entered

a series of separate tents sequentially, or are the tents of the wives curtained subdivisions of space within the larger tent of Jacob? The most likely interpretation is that we have a clustering of wives' tents that together would be understood as the "household of Jacob" or "tents of Jacob."

40. The description of Solomon's building of the temple is found in 1 Kings 6–8. The subdivided interior spaces are called "halls" or "vestibules" (*'ûlām*), "inner sanctuary" (*děbîr*), and "side chambers" (*ṣělā'ōt sābîb*) (1 Kings 6:3, 5).

41. See Lawrence E. Stager, "The Patrimonial Kingdom of Solomon," in *Symbiosis, Symbolism, and the Power of the Past: Canaan, Ancient Israel, and Their Neighbors from the Late Bronze Age through Roman Palaestina*, ed. William G. Dever and Seymour Gitin (Winona Lake, Ind.: Eisenbrauns, 2003), 70–71.

42. Julia Hendon, "The Engendered Household," in *Women in Antiquity: Theoretical Approaches to Gender and Archaeology*, ed. Sarah Milledge Nelson (Lanham, Md.: Alta Mira, 2007), 146–50; Carol Meyers, "In the Household and Beyond: The Social World of Israelite Women," *Nordic Journal of Theology* 63 (2009): 19–20.

43. Hendon, "The Engendered Household," 155.

44. Carol Meyers, "Material Remains and Social Relations: Women's Culture in Agrarian Households of the Iron Age," in Dever and Gitin, eds., *Symbiosis, Symbolism, and the Power of the Past*, 428.

45. Meyers, "In the Household," 23–27. See also Gloria London, "Four-Room Structures at Late-Bronze/Iron I Age Hill Country Workstations," in *The Near East in the Southwest: Essays in Honor of William G. Dever*, ed. Beth Alpert Nakhai (Boston: American Schools of Oriental Research, 2003), 69–84, and James W. Hardin, *Lahav II Households and the Use of Domestic Space at Iron II Tel Halif: An Archaeology of Destruction* (Winona Lake, Ind.: Eisenbrauns, 2010), 173.

46. Meyers, "Material Remains," 428; Aaron Brody, "'Those Who Add House to House': Household Archaeology and the Use of Domestic Space in an Iron II Residential Compound at Tell En-Naṣbeh," in *Exploring the Long Durée: Essays in Honor of Lawrence E. Stager*, ed. J. David Schloen (Winona Lake, Ind.: Eisenbrauns, 2009), 45–56.

47. Meyers, "In the Household," 19–20. Meyers is responding to several commentators who have understood the "house of the mother" to be a women's quarters or harem where women were confined behind doors. See, e.g., Samuel Rolles Driver, *The Book of Genesis* (WC; London: Methuen, 1920), 235n28.

48. David J. Schloen, *The House of the Father as Fact and Symbol: Patrimonialism in Ugarit and the Ancient Near East* (Winona Lake, Ind.: Eisenbrauns, 2001), 147–48.

49. Aaron Brody, "The Archaeology of the Extended Family: A Household Compound from Iron II Tell en-Naṣbeh," in *Household Archaeology in Ancient Israel and Beyond*, ed. Assaf Yasu-Landau, Jennie R. Ebeling, and Laura B. Mazow (Leiden: E. J. Brill, 2011), 237–54.

50. Hardin, *Lahav II*, 48.

51. Elizabeth Willett, "Women and House Religion: A Discussion of the Importance of Israelite House Architecture in Understanding Women's Social, Economic and Religious Activities," *The Bible and Interpretation*, www.bibleinterp.com/articles/HouseReligion.shtml.
52. Lawrence E. Stager, "The Archaeology of the Family in Ancient Israel," *BASOR* 260 (1985): 15–17.
53. Roxana Waterson, "House, Place, and Memory in Tana Toraja (Indonesia)," in *Beyond Kinship: Social and Material Reproduction in House Societies*, ed. Rosemary A. Joyce and Susan D. Gillespie (Philadelphia: University of Pennsylvania Press, 2000), 179.
54. Roxana Waterson, *The Living House: An Anthropology of Architecture in South-East Asia* (Oxford: Oxford University Press, 1990), 168.
55. Caroline Humphrey, "Inside a Mongolian Tent," *New Society* (October 1974): 273.

Chapter 4. My Brothers, the Sons of My Mother

1. The same parallel phrase is found in Judg 21:12 and figures narratively in Judg 11:37–40.
2. While Laban is never labeled a "mother's son," meaning he is not specified as a uterine sibling, in chapter 2 I argue that the text provides many clues that indicate he was a uterine sibling.
3. The text from Job 19:17 may offer a slight variation on the word pair brother/son of mother. He bemoans, "I am repulsive to my wife, loathsome to the sons of *my womb* [*biṭnî*]." The phrase "my womb" could stand metonymically for Job's mother or wife. Because the phrase stands in parallel with "my wife," it would seem on the surface that the intended reading is "sons of my wife's womb." This, however, does not make sense in the context of the book of Job because Job's children, the sons of his wife's womb, are all dead when he utters this lament. The reference to "mother's sons" could be a case of idiomatic phrasing. See the discussion of Gen 27:29 below.
4. "Kirta," in Michael D. Coogan and Mark S. Smith, *Stories from Ancient Canaan*, 2nd ed. (Louisville: Westminster John Knox, 2012), 72.
5. *KTU* 1.14, I, 8–9. The translation "perish" is based on a reading of *itdb* as *itbd* from the root *'-b-d* (metathesis).
6. We find the same seven-to-eight word pair used biblically in poetic parallelism in Eccles 11:2 and Mic 5:4 [Eng. 5:5]. We also find numerically increasing parallelism moving from three to four in Amos's oracles against the nations in Amos 1–2 with the repeated phrase "for three transgressions of *place name* and for four, I will not revoke the punishment," and as a literary structuring device in Prov 30:15, 18, 21, 29 (see also Isa 17:6).
7. "Baal Cycle," in Coogan and Smith, *Stories from Ancient Canaan*, 150–51.
8. "Baal Cycle," in Coogan and Smith, *Stories from Ancient Canaan*, 151; *KTU* 1.6, VI, 10–11, 14–15.

9. The brothers refer to Dinah as "our daughter" in Gen 34:16. This is likely prompted by the language of the marriage treaty that Hamor has proposed: "Give your daughters to us, and take our daughters for yourselves" (Gen 34:9). It could also be that older brothers referred to a younger sister as "our daughter" when they sought to protect or exercise authority over her. Recall that when Joseph saw Benjamin, "his mother's son," he greeted him as "my son" (Gen 43:29).
10. Diana Vikander Edelman, "Zeruiah," in *Women in Scripture: A Dictionary of Named and Unnamed Women in the Hebrew Bible, the Apocryphal/Deuterocanonical Books, and the New Testament*, ed. Carol Meyers, Toni Craven, and Ross S. Kraemer (Boston: Houghton Mifflin, 2000), 168. There are, however, two unnamed references to the existence of a father. Asahel is buried in "his father's tomb in Bethlehem" (2 Sam 2:32), and after Joab murders Abner, David curses Joab and "his father's house" (2 Sam 3:29). I return to the "sons of Zeruiah" and their "bone and flesh" relationship to the house of David in chapter 8.
11. Tammi J. Schneider, *Mothers of Promise: Women in the Book of Genesis* (Grand Rapids, Mich.: Baker Academic, 2008), 139; Ken Stone, *Sex, Honor, and Power in the Deuteronomistic History* (JSOTSup 234; Sheffield, Eng.: Sheffield Academic Press, 1996), 106–7.
12. Ingo Kottsieper, "'We Have a Little Sister': Aspects of the Brother-Sister Relationship in Ancient Israel," in *Families and Family Relations as Represented in Early Judaisms and Early Christianities: Texts and Fictions*, ed. Jan Willem Vas Henten and Athalya Brenner (Leiden: Deo, 2000), 62.
13. Gen 25:6 reads "*wayĕšallĕḥēm mē'al yiṣḥāq bĕnô . . . qēdĕmâ*."
14. "*šālaḥ*," BDB: 1019; Victor H. Matthews and Don C. Benjamin, "Amnon and Tamar: A Matter of Honor (2 Sam 13:1–38)," in *Crossing Boundaries and Linking Horizons: Studies in Honor of Michael C. Astour on His 80th Birthday*, ed. Gordon Young et al. (Bethesda, Md.: Capital Decisions, 1997), 360.
15. The debate over whether Amnon's crime is rape or incest is ongoing. See, e.g., David Daube, "Absalom and the Ideal King," *VT* 47 (1998): 315; William H. Propp, "Kinship in 2 Samuel 13," *CBQ* (1993): 48–53; and P. Kyle McCarter, Jr., *II Samuel: A New Translation with Introduction, Notes, and Commentary* (AB 9; New York: Doubleday, 1984), 324.
16. In my view Amnon's crime is rape, and even though rape is not a capital offense, Absalom used the rape of Tamar as an excuse to murder Amnon. It is an understandable act of vengeance, but it does not need to adhere strictly to what we know of ancient Israelite law. Hans Wilhelm Hertzberg also sees Amnon's crime as rape rather than incest (Hertzberg, *I and II Samuel: A Commentary*, trans. John Bowden [London: SCM Press, 1964], 322–23).
17. See, e.g., Matthews and Benjamin, "Amnon and Tamar," 346–49; Kottsieper, "'We Have a Little Sister,'" 58–70; McCarter, *II Samuel*, 322; Schneider, *Mothers of Promise*, 138–47; and Stone, *Sex, Honor*, 117–19.
18. Matthews and Benjamin, "Amnon and Tamar," 359.

19. Recall that within the Song of Songs, the female speaker's uterine brothers, referred to as "my mother's sons," are the ones charged with ensuring her sexual inaccessibility (Song 1:6; 8:8–12). The woman's father is never mentioned in the Song. See also Kottsieper, "'We Have a Little Sister,'" 70.
20. Joel Rosenberg notes that even though David is largely absent in the story of Amnon and Tamar, all of the characters are ultimately labeled in ways that show their relationship to him and his royal house (Rosenberg, *King and Kin: Political Allegory in the Hebrew Bible* [Bloomington: Indiana University Press, 1986], 140–41).
21. Ingo Kottsieper notes that for the readers of the Amnon and Tamar story, "it was to be expected from a full brother of a girl, not her father, to take revenge for his sister who was raped" (Kottsieper, "'We Have a Little Sister,'" 61–62).
22. Years later, Dinah arrives in Egypt as part of the Leah contingent, and she has no offspring listed (Gen 46:15). Tamar's residence as a "desolate one" in Absalom's house suggests that she too died with no children. It is interesting to contrast Jacob's inaction and lack of emotion regarding the abduction and rape of Dinah to his pronounced mourning for Joseph and concern for Benjamin. The loss of a son is a threat to a man's house; the loss of a daughter reduces the honor and marital prospects of her uterine brothers.
23. At the same time, there is an Israelite king known by the same name, making matters confusing and historically murky. For a detailed treatment of the Bible's ideological presentation of Athaliah and her relationship to the Omride dynasty, see Patricia Dutcher-Walls, *Narrative Art, Political Rhetoric: The Case of Athaliah and Joash* (JSOTSup 209; Sheffield, Eng.: Sheffield Academic Press, 1996).
24. In Exod 2, we have another protective sister in the unnamed sister of Moses who apparently watches over her infant brother as her mother sets the baby afloat along the Nile. When Pharaoh's daughter decides to keep the child, Moses's sister secures for her mother the position as wet nurse to Moses.
25. "Esarhaddon's Succession Treaty," in *Neo-Assyrian Treaties and Loyalty Oaths*, ed. Simo Parpola and Kazuko Watanabe (SAA 2; Helsinki: Helsinki University Press, 1988), lines 55–56, 68–72.
26. "Esarhaddon's Succession Treaty," lines 113–15, 214–15, 318–20, 336–38.
27. "Esarhaddon's Succession Treaty," lines 92–100, 101–7, 170–72, 269–74, 363, 495–96, 503–4, 514–15, 632–36. In lines 632–36 uterine brothers are to be protected along with "other brothers, offspring of Esarhaddon," so in these lines the whole house of Esarhaddon is to be protected.
28. "Esarhaddon's Succession Treaty," lines 283–90.
29. Ashurbanipal's mother cannot be identified with certainty, but most scholars identify Ešarra-hammat, Esarhaddon's principal wife, as his mother (Karen Radner, "Aššūr-bâni-apli," in *The Prosopography of the Neo-Assyrian Empire*, vol. 1, part 1 A, ed. Karen Radner [Helsinki: Neo-Assyrian Text Corpus Project,

1998], 160–61). The status of Esarhaddon's mother, Naqia, was raised once he was named crown prince, and she may have received property that had belonged to the former queen mother in Sennacherib's royal house (Sarah C. Mellville, *The Role of Naqia/Zakutu in Sargonid Politics* [SAAS 9; Helsinki: Neo-Assyrian Text Corpus Project, 1999], 21).

30. "Esarhaddon's Succession Treaty," lines 336–59.
31. See the stories of Abraham's death and the Joseph story in chapter 1. I return to Esarhaddon's succession treaty in chapter 8.
32. *KTU* 1.19, I, 32–37.
33. "Aqhat," in Coogan and Smith, *Stories from Ancient Canaan*, 54, lines 34–35.
34. '-*l* as a verb means "to be suckled, to nurse, to suck"; '*l* as a noun means "offspring" or "infant" (G. del Olmo Lete and J. Sanmartín, *A Dictionary of the Ugaritic Language in the Alphabetic Tradition 2*, trans. Wilfred G. E. Watson [Leiden: E. J. Brill, 2003], 154–55, 157–58).
35. Baruch Margalit, *The Ugaritic Poem of AQHT: Text, Translation, Commentary* (Berlin: Walter de Gruyter, 1989), 450. Margalit translates the line: "For I would smite the one who smote my brother; who slew my mother's suckling" (Margalit, *The Ugaritic Poem of AQHT*, 165, lines 34–35).
36. "The 'Aqhatu Legend," trans. D. Pardee (*COS* 1: 108, 355). The Ugaritic text of this phrase is fragmented, but its two occurrences help to fill in the gaps. In its first occurrence, we find: *imḫs.mḫs.'aḫy. 'akl [m]/kl[y ']l.'umty* (*KTU* 1.19, IV, 34–35), and its second occurrence: *tmḫs.mḫs ['aḫḫ/ tkl.mkly. 'l. 'umt[h* (*KTU* 1.19, IV, 39–40).
37. "The Aqhatu Legend," trans. D. Pardee (*COS* 1: 108, 355n126). Three other translators note but decide against translating *'l 'umty* with a maternally specific kinship term that alludes to nursing. Simon B. Parker translates as "I would slay the slayer of my sibling, Finish [who] finished my brother" (Parker, "Aqhat," in *Ugaritic Narrative Poetry*, ed. Simon B. Parker, [Atlanta: Scholars Press, 1997], 77, 80nn36, 38). Nicholas Wyatt translates as "that I might smite my brother's smiter, that I may kill my sibling's killer!" (Wyatt, *Religious Texts from Ugarit* [London: Sheffield Academic Press, 2002], 309). Finally, in *Textes ougaritiques*, the translation reads, "Je frapperai celui qui a frappé mon frère, je détruirai celui qui a détruit l'enfant de ma famille," but the translation notes clarify that the final phrase actually means "l'enfant de ma famille maternelle" (A. Caquot, M. Sznycer, and A. Herdner, *Textes ougaritiques: Introduction, traduction, commentaire I* [Paris: Éditions du Cerf, 1989], 456, lines 196–97; see also lines 201–2. For the maternal family clarification, see note v on page 456). Hennie Marsman argues that the term *'umty* represents kin of the same mother (Marsman, *Women in Ugarit and Israel: Their Social and Religious Position in the Context of the Ancient Near East* [OTS, vol. 49; Atlanta: SBL, 2003], 222).
38. "Kirta," in Coogan and Smith, *Stories from Ancient Canaan*, 72, lines 7–11; *KTU* 1.14, I, 7–11.

39. "Kirta," in Coogan and Smith, *Stories from Ancient Canaan*, 72, line 15.
40. "Kirta," in Coogan and Smith, *Stories from Ancient Canaan*, 72, lines 15–20.
41. Del Olmo Lete and Sanmartín, *A Dictionary of the Ugaritic Language in the Alphabetic Tradition 2*, 891.
42. Del Olmo Lete and Sanmartín, *A Dictionary of the Ugaritic Language in the Alphabetic Tradition 2*, 891.
43. Mark S. Smith, *The Ugaritic Baal Cycle*, vol. 1 (Leiden: E. J. Brill, 1994), 87–96.
44. On the role of El in the divine family at Ugarit, see Mark S. Smith and Wayne T. Pitard, *The Ugaritic Baal Cycle Volume II: Introduction with Text, Translation, and Commentary of KTU/CAT 1.3–1.4* (Leiden: E. J. Brill, 2009), 46–47.
45. Wayne T. Pitard, "Voices from the Dust: The Tablets from Ugarit and the Bible," in *Mesopotamia and the Bible: Comparative Explorations*, ed. Mark W. Chavalas and K. Lawson Younger, Jr. (Grand Rapids, Mich.: Baker Academic, 2002), 257.
46. In one brief episode, we learn the names of two of Asherah's sons as she unsuccessfully tries to promote them to the position of king (*KTU* 1.6, I, 47–65).
47. *KTU* 1.3, V, 37. Significantly, Asherah does not reside within El's house. She has her own palace and chooses to visit El when she pleases. This likely reflects her independent status as a goddess with a cult following of her own.
48. *KTU* 1.3, IV, 47–48; 1.3, V, 38–39; 1.4, IV, 50–51.
49. *KTU* 1.3, V, 35.
50. *KTU* 1.2, I, 18–19.
51. Smith, *The Ugaritic Baal Cycle*, vol. 1, 92–93.
52. El is called Yam's father in *KTU* 1.2, I, 33, 36. Mot is referred to as "El's son" in *KTU* 1.6, II, 13.
53. Father-daughter language is used of Anat and El in *KTU* 1.3, IV, 54; 1.3 V, 27.
54. *KTU* 1.2, IV, 10.
55. *KTU* 1.2, IV, 11–30.
56. *KTU* 1.3, II, 28.
57. *KTU* 1.3, III, 38–39.
58. *KTU* 1.3, IV.
59. *KTU* 1.3, IV, 47–48.
60. *KTU* 1.3, IV, 54.
61. *KTU* 1.3, V, 1–6, 35–39.
62. *KTU* 1.4, II, 21–26.
63. *KTU* 1.5, V, 28–29; 1.5, VI, 44–47.
64. *KTU* 1.4, VII–1.6, IV.
65. *KTU* 1.6, IV, 19.
66. Michael Coogan's and Mark Smith's recent translation leaves the line out (Coogan and Smith, *Stories from Ancient Canaan*, 150, line 20). Other translations vary widely. Baruch Margalit translates, "I'll cast an eye from the dome of the earth, And I'll seek out Puissant Baal, [I'll seek] the *bulge* [?] of your 'L. UMT" (Margalit, *The Ugaritic Poem of AQHT*, 449–50). Dennis Pardee

arrives at a completely different translation: "Pour sparkling wine in your tent, Put garlands on your *kinfolk* [*'l 'umtk*], for I will go looking for Baʻalu" ("The Baʻalu Myth [1.86]," trans. D. Pardee [*COS* 1: 271]).

67. *KTU* 1.6, VI, 33.

68. A. van Selms, *Marriage and Family Life in Ugaritic Literature* (London: Luzac, 1954), 64. See *KTU* 1.3, V, 36, where El is "the king who brought him [Baal] into being [*mlk d yknnh*]."

69. The case of Jacob and Esau is an exception. We have two rival brothers who are sons of the same mother. I cover their relationship in chapters 8 and 9.

Chapter 5. No, Son of My Womb

1. See "*reḥem*" and "*raḥāmim*," BDB: 933; "*reḥem*," *HALOT* 3: 1217–18; and T. Kronholm, "*reḥem*," *TDOT* 13: 454–59. While BDB translates *raḥāmim* as "compassion," it adds parenthetically that many understand *raḥāmim* to mean "*brotherhood, brotherly feeling*, of those born from the same womb," or "a *motherly feeling*."

2. "*beṭen*," BDB: 105. See also *HALOT* 1: 121, and *DCH* 2: 141–42.

3. Hanne Loland has argued that only *beṭen* means "womb," while *reḥem* means "the process or way to birth," the "birth canal" (Loland, *Silent or Salient Gender?* [Tubingen: Mohr Siebeck, 2008], 153–60). While this chronological reading where the birth process moves from *beṭen* to *reḥem* is possible in Jer 1:5 and Ps 22:10, there are several places where a chronological reading would place *beṭen* after *reḥem*. Job 3:11–12, for example, outlines a chronological process of his birth beginning with *reḥem* and moving next to *beṭen* and then moving to the "knees" that received him, and finally to the "breasts" where he was suckled. The word *beṭen* also seems to be associated with the moment of birth in Ps 58:4 [Eng. 58:3], where "the wicked go astray from the *reḥem*, they err from the *beṭen*, speaking lies." Again here, it is hard to correlate the internal time of pregnancy, Loland's understanding of *beṭen*, with "speaking lies." Instead it seems that *beṭen* and *reḥem* can both be used to describe any time from conception to birth.

4. Wilfred G. E. Watson, "Gender-Matched Synonymous Parallelism in the OT," *JBL* 99, no. 3 (1980): 323–26.

5. Phyllis Trible, *God and the Rhetoric of Sexuality* (Minneapolis: Fortress, 1986), 31–59. Trible stops short of arguing for an etymological relationship between *raḥāmim* and *reḥem*, instead suggesting that the two terms exhibit "semantic correspondences" (56n4).

6. Trible, *God and the Rhetoric of Sexuality*, 33–34.

7. The fact that the blessing deity in this text is El Shaddai is intriguing. Several studies have raised the possibility that this divine epithet, usually translated "God Almighty," comes from an earlier tradition where it was understood as "God with Breasts" and is often associated with the blessing of fertility. See,

e.g., W. F. Albright, "The Names Shaddai and Abram," *JBL* 54 (1935): 180–87; and, more recently, David Biale, "The God with Breasts: El Shaddai in the Bible," *History of Religions* 21 (1982): 24–56, and Harriet Lutzky, "Shadday as a Goddess Epithet," *VT* 48 (1998): 15–36.

8. See H. Simian-Yofre, "*rḥm*," *TDOT* 13: 443–44.
9. Trible, *God and the Rhetoric of Sexuality*, 33. Trible points to two prophetic texts (Jer 31:15–22 and Isa 63:15–16) where the Israelite god is imagined as a mother and expresses womb-based emotion (40–53) and several places where God is said to withhold *raḥămim* from the people whom he has "formed in the womb." This again suggests that authors made connections between the emotion and the maternal reproductive organ (54–55). Simian-Yofre largely rejects any maternally specific reading of *raḥămim*, defining it as denoting "the human personality as a whole" and having a "physiological and emotional connotation" (Simian-Yofre, "*rḥm*," *TDOT* 13: 444–45). Hanne Loland rejects Trible's argument because, as noted above, she translates *reḥem* as "birth canal" or "the time or place of the birth" rather than "womb" (Loland, *Silent or Salient Gender?* 190–92).
10. Mayer I. Gruber, "The Motherhood of God in Second Isaiah," in *The Motherhood of God and Other Studies* (Atlanta: Scholars Press, 1992), 3–16, esp. 5n5.
11. Joan Acocella, *Creating Hysteria: Women and Multiple Personality Disorder* (San Francisco: Jossey-Bass, 1999).
12. Arthur Kroker and Marilouise Kroker, eds., *The Hysterical Male: New Feminist Theory* (New York: St. Martin's Press, 1991).
13. Marion Hughes, *Hysterical Hysterectomy* (2013), lulu.com.
14. *Hysteria*, a film by Tanya Wexler (Sony Pictures, 2012), www.sonyclassics.com/hysteria/.
15. Michael Fishbane proposes reading *raḥămim* in Amos 1:11 as "friends and allies" (Fishbane, "The Treaty Background of Amos 1, 11 and Related Matters," *JBL* 89 [1970]: 313–18; 91). R.B. Coote adds that in some cases, *raḥămim* could have covenant dimensions (Coote, "Amos 1, 11: RHMYW," *JBL* 90 [1971]: 206–8).
16. In Ugaritic the word *rḥm* means "womb" but can also refer by metonymy to a "nubile girl, damsel" (G. del Olmo Lete and J. Sanmartín, *A Dictionary of the Ugaritic Language in the Alphabetic Tradition 2*, trans. Wilfred G. E. Watson [Leiden: E. J. Brill, 2003], 737). There may be an example of the word *rḥm* representing a woman in the Aramaic Deir 'Allah Inscription dating to the eighth century BCE and on the Moabite Mesha Stele dating to the ninth century BCE. See JoAnn Hackett, *The Balaam Text from Deir Alla* (HSM 31; Chico, Cal.: Scholars Press, 1984), 26, line 13, and commentary on p. 70; and Kent P. Jackson and Andrew Dearman, "The Text of the Mesha Inscription," in *Studies in the Mesha Inscription and Moab*, ed. Andrew Dearman (Atlanta: Scholars Press, 1989), 94, line 17.
17. These lines occur twice; see *KTU* 1.6, II, 5–9, 27–30. In the first instance, the word *rḥm* in line 5 is restored based on it occurrence in line 27. English translation

from Michael D. Coogan and Mark S. Smith, *Stories from Ancient Canaan*, 2nd ed. (Louisville: Westminster John Knox, 2012), 147–48.
18. del Olmo Lete and Sanmartín, *A Dictionary of the Ugaritic Language in the Alphabetic Tradition 2*, 737. When Kirta is dying, he instructs his son not to weep for him but instead to "speak to your sister, I know she will *have compassion* [*rḥmt*]. She will make her cry heard in the fields." So in the context of an impending death of the father, a son is instructed to find his sister, who will mourn for her father on the basis of her *rḥm* (*KTU* 1.16, I, 33).
19. *KTU* 1.13, 2; Johannes C. de Moor, "An Incantation against Infertility (*KTU* 1,13)," *UF* 12 (1981): 305–10.
20. *KTU* 1.6, II, 12, 22–23.
21. *KTU* 1.6, II, 27–35.
22. *KTU* 1.6, IV, 19. See chapter 4.
23. Other chronologically related word pairs include "suckling/weaned child" (Isa 11:8; Joel 2:16) and "bone and flesh," which is covered in chapter 8.
24. Claus Westermann, *Genesis 12–36* (CC; Minneapolis: Fortress, 1994), 338.
25. Mayer I. Gruber, "Breast-Feeding Practices in Biblical Israel and in Old Babylonian Mesopotamia," *JANES* 19 (1989): 68–69, citing Isa 7:14–16; 28:9–10.
26. Vanessa Maher, "Breast-Feeding in Cross-Cultural Perspective: Paradoxes and Proposals," in *The Anthropology of Breast-Feeding: Natural Law or Social Construct*, ed. Vanessa Maher (Oxford: Berg, 1992), 9.
27. 4Q507, 2. See James H. Charlesworth, *The Dead Sea Scrolls: Hebrew, Aramaic, and Greek Texts with English Translations, Pseudepigraphic and Non-Masoretic Psalms and Prayers IVa* (Louisville: Westminster John Knox, 1997), 54–55.
28. We find this same pairing twice in the Gospel of Luke, where first a woman praises the mother of Jesus saying, "Blessed is the womb that bore you and the breasts that you sucked" (Luke 11:27). Then on the way to his crucifixion, Jesus tells the weeping women around him, "Daughters of Jerusalem, do not weep for me, but weep for yourselves and for your children. For the days are surely coming when they will say, 'Blessed are the barren, and the wombs that never bore, and the breasts that never nursed'" (Luke 23:28–29).
29. See Loland, *Silent or Salient Gender?* 190–91. Another biblical poem that alludes to both breast and womb while not naming either is found in Lam 2:20, where the poet looks upon the devastation of his city and the social disintegration of his people and calls upon his god to look at their misery: "Here, women eat their own fruit, their suckling babies!" A similar linkage between breast and womb is found on the Deir 'Alla inscription where the text laments, "There is not mercy when Death seizes a suckling of the womb [*'ul rḥm*]" ("Deir Alla," *COS* 2: 144, excerpts F–G).
30. The Bible frequently associates majestic trees with royalty, and so Joseph as a "fruitful bough" is an extension of a royal tree. The Davidic messiah is described as a "shoot that comes forth from the stump of Jesse." And in several places trees are associated with kingship, e.g., 2 Kings 14:9; Ezek 17.

31. This sequence of heaven above, the deep below, and the human realm last is also found in the Babylonian poem "I Will Praise the Lord of Wisdom," where the sufferer asks,

    Who can learn the will of the gods in heaven?
    Who understands the intentions of the gods of the underworld?
    Where have human beings learned the way of a god? (*COS* 1: 488)

    See also Deut 30:11–14. Mark Smith sees the word pair "breast and womb" in this text as a divine epithet for the goddess Asherah, who has disappeared from the text (Smith, "The Blessing God and Goddess: A Longitudinal View from Ugarit to 'Yahweh and . . . His Asherah' at Kuntillet 'Ajrud," in *Enigmas and Images: Studies in Honor of Tryggve N. D. Mettinger,* ed. Göran Eidevall and Blazenka Scheuer [Winona Lake, Ind.: Eisenbrauns, 2011], 210–13).

32. Carol Meyers, "Returning Home: Ruth 1:8 and the Gendering of the Book of Ruth," in *A Feminist Companion to Ruth,* ed. Athalya Brenner (1993; repr. Sheffield, Eng.: Sheffield Academic Press, 2001), 105–6.

33. Meyers, "Returning Home," 106.

34. Ariel Bloch and Chana Bloch, *Song of Songs: A New Translation with Introduction and Commentary* (Berkeley: University of California Press, 1995), 210.

35. Massa is identified as a son of Ishmael in Gen 25:14.

36. Hans Walter Wolff has shown how these appositional strings of words connoting body parts are examples of "stereometric thinking," which "pegs out the sphere of man's existence by enumerating his characteristic organs, thus circumscribing man as a whole," and "synthesizing" the "organs of the human body with their capacities and functions" (Wolff, *Anthropology of the Old Testament* [Philadelphia: Fortress, 1974], 8). Wolff borrowed the term "stereometry" from Benno Landsberger, who defined it as "the simple stringing together of pictures of unsurpassable vividness" and who considered poetic parallelism in Hebrew and Akkadian to convey "the expression of thought, which is always most precisely shaped and aims for the greatest expressiveness" (Landsberger, *The Conceptual Autonomy of the Babylonian World,* trans. Thorkild Jacobsen, Benjamin Foster, and H. von Siebenthal [Monographs on the Ancient Near East, vol. 1, fascicle 4; Malibu, Cal.: Udena, 1976], 14). Landsberger's article was first published in 1926. While Wolff's examples all refer to non-gendered, though presumed male bodies (Prov 18:15; Ps 6:2–4), I have found several places, including Prov 31:2, where stereometric thinking pegs out the existence of a mother based on references to her reproductive body parts.

37. We find a similar chronological sequence of maternally focused terms used metaphorically in the books of Hosea and Job where the prophets reach backward in time in order to undo creation and snuff out reproductive fertility. Hosea's proclamation of judgment against Ephraim announces, "Ephraim's glory shall fly away like a bird—no birth, no pregnancy, no conception!" (Hosea 9:11). Job

in the midst of his suffering cries out, "Let the day perish in which I was born, and the night that said, 'A man-child is conceived'" (Job 3:3).

38. Another maternal claim on a royal heir that takes the form of a telescoping string of appositional epithets is found in an inscription on a funerary stele of Adad-Guppi, who identifies herself as the mother of "Nabunaid, king of Babylon." She describes how she interceded on her son's behalf, "lifting her hands" to the moon god Sin so that he might elevate "Nabunaid, my only son, my offspring, beloved of his mother" to kingship ("The Adad-Guppi Autobiography," trans. Tremper Longman III [*COS* 1: 477–78]). See also C. J. Gadd, "The Harran Inscriptions of Nabonidus," *Anatolian Studies* 8 (1958): 48, column 2, line 46 (*mār ṣīt libbiya narām ummišu*).

39. Trible, *God and the Rhetoric of Sexuality*, 34–35.

40. Carol Delaney, "Cutting the Ties That Bind: The Sacrifice of Abraham and Patriarchal Kinship," in *Relative Values: Reconfiguring Kinship Studies*, ed. Sarah Franklin and Susan McKinnon (Durham, N.C.: Duke University Press, 2001), 454.

41. Delaney, "Cutting the Ties that Bind," 454. See also Nelly Furman, "His Story versus Her Story: Male Genealogy and Female Strategy in the Jacob Cycle," in *Women in the Hebrew Bible: A Reader*, ed. Alice Bach (New York: Routledge, 1999), 123.

42. E. A. Speiser, *Genesis: Introduction, Translation, and Notes* (AB 1; New York: Doubleday, 1964), 93–94.

43. See also Isa 59:21; Jer 30:10; 46:27 where "seed" is associated with covenant.

44. Naomi Steinberg, *Kinship and Marriage in Genesis: A Household Economics Perspective* (Minneapolis: Fortress, 1993), 1–11, 95–100; Tammi J. Schneider, *Mothers of Promise: Women in the Book of Genesis* (Grand Rapids, Mich.: Baker Academic, 2008), 16.

45. Nancy Jay attempts to establish a source-critical division based on the Bible's understanding of procreation. She argues that the priestly source was most concerned with a pure and eternal agnatic patriline and therefore dismisses the importance of women in perpetuating group identity. The Yahwist source, on the other hand, "tolerates cognatic descent" (Jay, *Throughout Your Generations Forever: Sacrifice, Religion, and Paternity* [Chicago: University of Chicago Press, 1992], 96, 98, 103). This source-critical division, however, misrepresents the priestly source. Even though the priestly source is the primary source for the exclusively paternal *tôlēdôt*, it is also the source that often adds maternal specificity to a patriline. See, e.g., Gen 17:15–19, which specifies that the Abrahamic covenant will be perpetuated through Sarah, not Hagar, and Exod. 6:20, which provides a name for Moses's mother and father and specifies that his mother was a first-generation daughter of Levi. The priestly creation story is also the story that imagines God creating male and female simultaneously (Gen 1:27).

46. On Esau's hair as a masculine marker that distinguishes him from his smooth brother, see Susan Niditch, *My Brother Esau Is a Hairy Man: Hair and Identity in Ancient Israel* (New York: Oxford University Press, 2008), 112–18.
47. See chapter 1.
48. 4Q 507, 2.

Chapter 6. Like a Brother to Me, One Who Had Nursed at My Mother's Breasts

1. This chapter is a revised version of my article "'Oh That You Were Like a Brother to Me, One Who Had Nursed at My Mother's Breasts': Breast Milk as a Kinship-Forging Substance," *JHS* 12, article 7 (2012): 1–41, www.jhsonline.org/Articles/article_169.pdf.
2. See, e.g., Roland de Vaux, *Ancient Israel: Its Life and Institutions*, trans. John McHugh (Grand Rapids, Mich.: Eerdmans, 1961), 20; Shunya Bendor, *The Social Structure of Ancient Israel: The Institution of the Family* (Beit 'Ab): *From the Settlement to the End of the Monarchy* (Jerusalem Biblical Studies 7; Jerusalem: Simor, 1996), 58; and Phillip J. King and Lawrence E. Stager, *Life in Biblical Israel* (Louisville: Westminster John Knox, 2002), 39.
3. Adam Kuper, "Lineage Theory: A Critical Retrospect," in *Kinship and Family: An Anthropological Reader*, ed. Robert Parkin and Linda Stone (Malden, Mass.: Wiley-Blackwell, 2004), 79–96.
4. Edouard Conte, "Agnatic Illusions: The Element of Choice in Arab Kinship," in *Tribes and Power: Nationalism and Ethnicity in the Middle East*, ed. Faleh Abdul-Jabar and Hosham Dawod (London: Saqi, 2003), 16–17.
5. Blood is primarily understood as a "basis of life" and as a substance poured out in sacrifice and shed through violence (see "*dam*," *HALOT* 1: 224–25, and B. Kedar-Kopfstein, "*dam*," *TDOT* 3: 234–50).
6. As a word describing human kinship, *zeraʽ* means male seed or semen and therefore designates the relationship between a father and his biological descendants. In three places, however, a woman's offspring is referred to as her "seed"—Eve's collective offspring in Gen 3:15, Hagar's offspring in Gen 16:10, and Rebekah's offspring in Gen 24:60 (*HALOT* 1:282; D. Preuss, "*zeraʽ*," *TDOT* 4: 144).
7. Vanessa Maher, "Breast-Feeding in Cross-Cultural Perspective: Paradoxes and Proposals," in *The Anthropology of Breast-Feeding: Natural Law or Social Construct*, ed. Vanessa Maher (Oxford: Berg, 1992), 9.
8. Similar conclusions are reached in Deborah Valenze, *Milk: A Local and Global History* (New Haven, Conn.: Yale University Press, 2011), 1–33, and Marilyn Yalom, *A History of the Breast* (New York: Knopf, 1997), specifically on male control of breastfeeding, 107.
9. Conte, "Agnatic Illusions," 17.

10. Avner Giladi, *Infants, Parents, and Wet Nurses: Medieval Islamic Views on Breast-feeding and Their Social Implications* (Leiden: E. J. Brill, 1999).
11. Sura 4, verse 23, cited in Giladi, *Infants*, 21. See also Jane Khatib-Chahidi, "Milk Kinship in Shi'ite Islamic Iran," in Maher, ed., *The Anthropology of Breast-Feeding*, 109–32.
12. Giladi, *Infants*, 30–31. Jane Khatib-Chahidi provides a full listing of the types of kinship relationships established through breast milk in Islamic Iran (Khatib-Chahidi, "Milk Kinship," 113–18).
13. Giladi, *Infants*, 27–30.
14. Peter Parkes, "Fosterage, Kinship, and Legend: When Milk Was Thicker than Blood?" *Comparative Studies in Society and History* 46 (July 2004): 587–615.
15. Aristotle, *De generatione animalium*, 4: vii, cited in Parkes, "Fosterage," 590.
16. S. D. Inal-Ipa, *The Social Reality of the Atalyk Fosterage Institution in 19th-Century Abkhazia* (Sukhum, Russia: Alashara, 1956), 80–86, 107–11; Sula Benet, *Abkhasians: The Long-Living People of the Caucasus* (New York: Holt, Rinehart and Winston, 1974), 57–58, cited in Parkes, "Fosterage," 591.
17. Peter Parkes indicates that within Abkhazian culture, "Ritual adoption by token suckling or 'breast-biting' (*ak'ukatshara*) was deployed to defuse suspicions of adultery or to create milk-kinship after blood feud" (Parkes, "Fosterage," 591). In the Succession Treaty of Esarhaddon, there is an obscure reference to men who might join together through "a mutually binding oath" with the intention of unseating the crown prince Ashurbanipal. The treaty lists several known rituals through which men could bind themselves together in a pact of loyalty. Among rituals such as "setting a table," "drinking from a cup," and "kindling fire," we find "grabbing onto the breasts [*ṣibit tulê*]" as a means through which adult men could swear loyalty to one another ("Esarhaddon's Succession Treaty," in *Neo-Assyrian Treaties and Loyalty Oaths*, ed. Simo Parpola and Kazuko Watanabe [SAA 2; Helsinki: Helsinki University Press, 1988], lines 152–61). On the idiom *ṣibit tulê*, see *CAD* Ṣ, 165–66. Wilfred G. E. Watson has argued, based on gender-matched parallelism, that Isa 28:15–18 is a biblical example of a reference to "pressing the breast" as a means through which parties cut a covenant or make a pact. Repointing *ḥōzeh*, "seer," to *ḥāzeh*, "breast," he translates verses 15 and 18: "We will cut a covenant (f) with Death (m), and with Sheol (f) we will 'press the breast' (m). . . . Cancelled is your covenant (f) with Death (m), And your pact (*ḥāzût*) (f) with Sheol (f) will not stand" (Watson, "Gender-Matched Synonymous Parallelism in the OT," *JBL* 99, no. 3 [1980]: 331).
18. William Good, "Descriptions and Customs of the Wild Irish," in William Camden, *Britannia; or, A Chorographical Description of Great Britain and Ireland*, trans. Edmund Gibbons (London, 1722), 2: 1418, cited in Parkes, "Fosterage," 589–90.
19. Fynes Moryson, *An Itinerary Written by Fynes Moryson* (London: John Beal, 1617), cited in Parkes, "Fosterage," 590.

20. Susan Montague, "The Trobriand Kinship Classification and Schneider's Cultural Relativism," in *The Cultural Analysis of Kinship: The Legacy of David M. Schneider*, ed. Richard Feinberg and Martin Ottenheimer (Urbana: University of Illinois Press, 2001), 174.
21. Montague, "Trobriand Kinship," 174.
22. Montague, "Trobriand Kinship," 169–70. Among the Malays of Southeast Asia, a mother establishes kinship bonds within her family first through her breast milk and then through her continued food preparation and serving at the family hearth (Janet Carsten, "The Substance of Kinship and the Heat of the Hearth: Feeding, Personhood, and Relatedness among Malays in Pulau Langkawi," in Parkin and Stone, eds., *Kinship and Family*, 309–27).
23. Susan Niditch, in her comparative study of the folkloric pattern governing the foundational narrative of a hero, notes one literary pattern where the hero is abandoned at birth and nursed by animals or a humble human woman (Niditch, *Underdogs and Tricksters: A Prelude to Folklore* [San Francisco: Harper and Row, 1987], 72–74, citing the comparative work of Alan Dundes, "The Hero Pattern and the Life of Jesus," in *Interpreting Folklore* [Bloomington: Indiana University Press, 1980], 232–33).
24. Peter Machinist discusses this trope in royal Assyrian narratives that describe "the king as a creature begotten, suckled, endowed with special talents by some deity or deities" (Machinist, "Kingship and Divinity in Imperial Assyria," in *Text, Artifact, Image: Revealing Ancient Israelite Religion*, ed. G. M. Beckman and T. J. Lewis [Providence, R.I.: Brown Judaic Studies, 2006], 163). A similar trope of kings suckling at the breasts of goddesses is found in Egyptian texts and iconography. Gay Robins asserts, "by the act of suckling, a goddess confirms the king as her son and thus ratifies his divinity" (Robins, *Women in Ancient Egypt* [Cambridge, Mass.: Harvard University Press, 1993], 91).
25. KTU 1:15, II, 26–27; "Kirta," in Michael D. Coogan and Mark S. Smith, *Stories from Ancient Canaan*, 2nd ed. (Louisville: Westminster John Knox, 2012), 83.
26. See, e.g., the translation by Dennis Pardee (*COS* 1: 102, 337).
27. Susan Ackerman, "The Queen Mother and the Cult in the Ancient Near East," in *Women and Goddess Traditions in Antiquity and Today*, ed. Karen L. King (Minneapolis: Fortress, 1997), 186–87.
28. "Dialogue between Assurbanipal and Nabu," trans. A. Livingstone (*COS* 1: 145, 476, rev. lines 6–8). Peter Machinist cites several additional Neo-Assyrian Sargonid kings who suck at the breasts of goddesses and concludes, "a deity, usually goddess, or deities can create or give birth to the king, can nurture him by giving him suck on her knees, can be called, thus mother and/or father, sometimes with the explicit denial of human parentage; and the king, in turn, can apparently be associated with the flesh of the gods" (Machinist, "Kingship and Divinity," 168).
29. "Esarhaddon's Succession Treaty," lines 55–56, 68–72. The length and detail of this treaty speaks to the uncertainty of support for Ashurbanipal and the genuine

fear that his rule would be challenged. Ashurbanipal's succession to his father Esarhaddon's throne is also supported by his grandmother's treaty, the "Zakutu Treaty," in which she supports "her favorite grandson, [Assurba]nipal" and warns anyone who might plot an "ugly scheme" against him ("Zakutu Treaty," in *Neo-Assyrian Treaties and Loyalty Oaths*, ed. Simo Parpola and Kazuko Watanabe [SAA 2; Helsinki: Helsinki University Press, 1988], 62, lines 9–18.)

30. "Dialogue between Assurbanipal and Nabu," trans. Alisdair Livingstone (*COS* 1: 145, 476, obv., lines 6, 22, rev., lines 3, 4, 9).

31. Shamash-Shum-Ukin was Ashurbanipal's older brother who was dispatched to Babylon in an effort to remove him as a direct threat to Ashurbanipal. He did in fact rebel against Ashurbanipal in 652 BCE in an unsuccessful military campaign that nonetheless occupied Ashurbanipal for four years. See "Chronicle 1," lines 30–38 (A. K. Grayson, *Assyrian and Babylonian Chronicles* [Winona Lake, Ind.: Eisenbrauns, 2000], 86).

32. Andrew George, *The Babylonian Gilgamesh Epic: Introduction, Critical Edition, and Cuneiform Texts I* (Oxford: Oxford University Press, 2003), 540–41, tablet 1, line 48.

33. George, *The Babylonian Gilgamesh Epic*, 540–41, tablet 2, lines 35–36.

34. George, *The Babylonian Gilgamesh Epic*, 651, tablet 8, lines 3–5. Humbaba, the forest monster, insults Enkidu by saying, "Come, Enkidu, (you) spawn of a fish, who knew not his father, hatchling of terrapin and turtle, who sucked not the milk of his mother!" (George, *The Babylonian Gilgamesh Epic*, 607, tablet 5, lines 87–88).

35. *KTU* 1.23, line 24, partially reconstructed based on parallels in 59 and 61; "The Lovely Gods," in Coogan and Smith, *Stories from Ancient Canaan*, 162, line 24. Scholars are divided on the identity of the two females impregnated by El and on the relationship between "the lovely gods" and the binomial pair Shahar and Shalim. Dennis Pardee understands the two females impregnated by El to be human and the "gracious gods" to refer to the divine pair called Shahar and Shalim ("Dawn and Dusk," trans. D. Pardee [*COS* 1: 87, 274–75, 281–82nn58, 59]). Theodore Lewis takes the two females to be goddesses, but he, like Pardee, sees "the gracious gods" to be a descriptive phrase for Shahar and Shalim (Theodore Lewis, trans., "The Birth of the Gracious Gods," in *Ugaritic Narrative Poetry*, ed. Simon B. Parker [Atlanta: Scholars Press, 1997], 209–10). Mark S. Smith distinguishes between the "the lovely gods," also translated "the goodly gods," and the divine pair Shahar and Shalim, who are introduced later in the text. Smith notes that the "goodly gods," who are described as sucking at the breasts of Asherah, are ravenous and associated with the steppe, while Shahar and Shalim are not described as ravenous and are not tied to the steppe (Smith, *Rituals and Myths of the Feast of the Goodly Gods of KTU/CAT 1.23: Royal Construction of Opposition, Intersection, Integration, and Domination* [Atlanta: SBL, 2006], 69–72). Smith also discusses the evidence concerning the humanity or divinity of the mothers and concludes that the mother of the goodly gods is the

single goddess Asherah, described with the epithet *raḥmay* (Smith, *Rituals and Myths*, 89–92).

36. Wilfred G. Lambert, trans., "Mesopotamian Creation Stories," in *Imagining Creation*, ed. Markham J. Geller and Mineke Schipper (Boston: E. J. Brill, 2008), 39, lines 79–86. The Akkadian transliteration is from Philippe Talon, *The Standard Babylonian Creation Myth: Enūma Eliš* (SAACT 4; Helsinki: Neo-Assyrian Text Corpus Project, 2005), 36, tablet 1, line 85.

37. Several New Testament texts refer to God giving Christians milk, not solid food, because they are not ready for solid food. 1 Peter 2:2 imagines a kind of spiritual breast milk that will allow the new believer to mature into full salvation: "Like newborn babies crave pure spiritual milk, so that by it you may grow up in your salvation." Perhaps the transformative nature of breast milk is so powerful that it is attributed to male kings in Isa 60 and to a male god in this New Testament text.

38. NRSV renders the first phrase "kings will be your foster fathers." JPS reads, "Kings shall tend your children." The translation of the masculine form of the Hebrew term *'ōmēn* as "wet nurse" is discussed fully below.

39. Most scholars have understood the reference to breastfeeding in this text exclusively in terms of nourishment and emotional bonding between God and Jerusalem, on the one side, and the returning exiles, on the other. For a summary of this scholarship, see Hanne Loland, *Silent or Salient Gender?* (Forschungen zum Alten Testament 2. Reihe 32; Tubingen: Mohr Siebeck, 2008), 188–90.

40. In both Isa 60 and 66, the qualities that are transferred to the exiles and to Zion respectively through breastfeeding are royal: *kābôd*, translated "glory" or "splendor," is a divine and royal attribute "embodied in the crown" (M. Weinfeld, "kabod," *TDOT* 7: 27–31); *gā'ôn* is also specifically related to Yahweh's kingship (D. Kellermann, "gā'āh," *TDOT* 2: 347–48).

41. This postexilic, biblical portrayal of the capital city, Jerusalem, as a queenly mother breastfeeding her newly reconstituted nation of exiles may find historical precedent in the Judean pillar figurines. See Chapman, "'Oh That You Were Like a Brother to Me,'" 14–17, 40–41.

42. Gianni Barbiero also sees in these verses an imagined, dreamlike quality and argues that Song 8:1–4 "describes the difficulties which society puts in the way of realizing the union of love: difficulties on the part of the family (Song 8:1–2) and on the part of society ('daughters of Jerusalem,' 8:4)" (Barbiero, *Song of Songs: A Close Reading*, trans. Michael Tait [Leiden: E. J. Brill, 2011], 423–29, 433).

43. As noted above, I agree with Marvin Pope that the specification of the brother here to designate a "uterine brother," though a milk sibling who is not a biological brother, is also possible. He argues that uterine siblings of the opposite sex would be able to show affection publicly (Pope, *Song of Songs* [AB 7C; Garden City, N.Y.: Doubleday, 1977], 657).

44. Recall the presence of Rebekah's wet nurse in the house of her mother (Gen 24:59).

45. The Hebrew *mānâ 'aḥat 'appāyim* literally means "one portion *of* (?) nose (or face)." Several alternative readings have been suggested to deal with the difficulty of the text: "double portion," "choice portion," "a portion from the face." What is clear from the context is that the portion offered to Hannah is meant to honor her and show Elkanah's love for her in spite of her lack of children (see P. Kyle McCarter, Jr., *I Samuel: A New Translation with Introduction, Notes, and Commentary* [AB 8; Garden City, N.Y.: Doubleday, 1980], 51–52, 60, and Hans Wilhelm Hertzberg, *I and II Samuel: A Commentary*, trans. John Bowden [London: SCM Press, 1964], 24).
46. According to Saul Olyan, Elkanah's distribution of this sacrifice communicates his status as one who stands between the priests and his family dependents. The order of his distribution from first wife to sons and daughters and finally to his second wife also communicates a hierarchy within his household (Olyan, *Rites and Rank: Hierarchy in Biblical Representations of Cult* [Princeton, N.J.: Princeton University Press, 2000], 11–12).
47. Becoming a "Nazirite from birth" suggests that the separate and holy status was a lifelong commitment. This differs from the priestly text found in Num 6 where the separate and holy status of a Nazirite is only temporary, enduring for the specified period of the vow. Because it was only temporary, Saul Olyan notes that the Nazirite could not make the same claims to holiness as that of a priest (Olyan, *Rites and Rank*, 61).
48. Translation from McCarter, *I Samuel*, 53–54. McCarter argues that the MT of this verse is "corrupt" and that LXX and 4QSam^a can be used to reconstruct the text to read, "Then I shall set him before you all the days of his life: Wine or strong drink he will not drink, and no razor will touch his head" (McCarter, *I Samuel*, 53–54).
49. Susan Niditch, *Judges* (OTL; Louisville: Westminster John Knox, 2008), 143; Susan Ackerman, *Warrior, Dancer, Seductress, Queen: Women in Judges and Biblical Israel* (New York: Doubleday, 1998), 113.
50. LXX Judg 13:14 has masculine verbs in place of the MT's feminine verbs, suggesting that the translator understood the last set of dietary restrictions to be for Samson not his mother.
51. For a complete treatment of the relationship between 1 Sam 1 and the law of the Nazirite as related to Hannah's diet, see Susan Ackerman, "Hannah's Tears," in *Celebrate Her for the Fruit of Her Hands: Essays in Honor of Carol L. Meyers*, ed. Susan Ackerman et al. (Winona Lake, Ind.: Eisenbrauns, 2015), 13–26.
52. Ackerman, *Warrior, Dancer, Seductress*, 113–14.
53. LXX lacks the phrase "and after drinking," but this does not seem to reflect a concern with Hannah's drinking because LXX 1 Sam 1:18 indicates that after offering her prayer, Hannah returned to her husband and "they ate and drank." For a detailed examination of the textual variations between MT, LXX, and 4QSam^a in this chapter, see McCarter, *I Samuel*, 51–58.

54. While 1 Sam 1 does not mention the presence of the ark of Yahweh in the Shiloh temple, its presence at Shiloh is something a reader would have known (1 Sam 4:3). Ackerman notes that both Samson's mother and Hannah are required to "uphold Nazirite standards of sanctity" as they seek to bear "Nazirite sons" (Ackerman, *Warrior, Dancer, Seductress,* 114).
55. LXX makes Hannah's nursing of Samuel even clearer by making the verb "wean" active rather than passive: "[I shall stay] until the child comes up, when *I have weaned* him" (LXX translation from McCarter, *I Samuel,* 55).
56. The author of the pseudepigraphal work, Pseudo-Philo, embellishes Hannah's celebratory song in 1 Sam 2 to include a reference to her breast milk. He attributes "testimonies" to Hannah's breast milk, which in turn allows her son Samuel to speak enlightening words. The song reads, "Drip, my breasts, and tell your testimonies, because you have been commanded to give milk. For he who is milked from you will be raised up, and the people will be enlightened by his word, and he will show the nations the statutes, and his horn will be exalted very high" (Pseudo-Philo 51:3, from D. J. Harrington, trans., "Pseudo-Philo," in *The Old Testament Pseudepigrapha 2* [New York: Doubleday, 1985], 365). This text reveals a clear connection between the substantive content of the breast milk and the character of the child that is nursed.
57. Textual evidence from the ancient Near East suggests that a child was nursed for between two and three years (Mayer I. Gruber, "Breast-Feeding Practices in Biblical Israel and in Old Babylonian Mesopotamia," *JANES* 19 [1989]: 62–63, 66–68; Robins, *Women in Ancient Egypt,* 88–89).
58. Naomi Steinberg provides a detailed treatment of the "patrilineal endogamy" that governs the marriage patterns in Gen 11:10–29 and notes, "All of the women within the patrilineage of Abraham are ultimately members of the patrilineage of Terah" (Steinberg, *Kinship and Marriage in Genesis: A Household Economics Perspective* [Minneapolis: Fortress, 1993], 12–14).
59. Milcah is mentioned in Gen 11:29; 22:20, 23; 24:15, 24, 47. She is the daughter of Abraham's brother and the grandmother of Rebekah. See Naomi Steinberg, "Milcah 1," in *Women in Scripture: A Dictionary of Named and Unnamed Women in the Hebrew Bible, the Apocryphal/Deuterocanonical Books, and the New Testament,* ed. Carol Meyers, Toni Craven, and Ross S. Kraemer (Boston: Houghton Mifflin, 2000), 127.
60. Gruber, "Breast-Feeding," 73–82. Gruber supports this assertion citing Mesopotamian, Egyptian, biblical, Mishnaic, and classical Greek texts.
61. We could also add that Sarah's beauty is of a royal caliber, as she attracts the attention of the Egyptian Pharaoh (Gen 12:13–14) and Abimelech, the king of Gerar (Gen 20:2).
62. The fact that Rebekah's wet nurse is provided with a name, "Deborah," and that she accompanies Rebekah as an adult to the land of Canaan (Gen 24:59), speaks to the elite status of families who could procure a wet nurse and to the enduring

nature of the relationship between a wet nurse and her charge. That the Bible would include notification of her death and burial further supports this view (Gen 35:8). Carol Meyers offers the compelling suggestion that the narrative's inclusion of the detail of Rebekah's wet nurse "may be a literary embellishment pointing to her prominence among the matriarchs" (Meyers, "Deborah 1," in Meyers, Craven, and Kraemer, eds., *Women in Scripture*, 66).

63. Note the use of the divine name, "Yahweh," in Gen 17:1 and 21:1, both introducing priestly texts. Claus Westermann explains this as P "passing on an ancient patriarchal promise that has come down in which the name of God was given as Yahweh" (Westermann, *Genesis 12–36* [CC; Minneapolis: Fortress, 1994], 257).

64. E. A. Speiser follows Samuel Rolles Driver in marking verses 1–5 as priestly and 6–21 as a product of the Elohist (Speiser, *Genesis: Introduction, Translation, and Notes* [AB 1; New York: Doubleday, 1964], 154–56; Driver, *The Book of Genesis* [WC; London: Methuen, 1920], 209–13). Gerhard von Rad marks a break after verse 7 and argues that chapter 21 as a whole "lost its own literary unity in the final redaction of the Hexateuch, for obviously three documents [J, E, P] are brought together here" (von Rad, *Genesis: A Commentary* [OTL; Louisville: Westminster John Knox, 1973], 231). Westermann sees Gen 21:1–7 as "a highly and skillfully redacted composite of J, P, and other material, not E," and verses 8–21 as the product of an "interpolator" (Westermann, *Genesis 12–36*, 330–35, 338). Nahum Sarna also marks the break after verse 7 (Sarna, *Genesis: The Traditional Hebrew Text with the New JPS Translation* [Philadelphia: JPS, 1989], 145).

65. Verses 1–7 recall the language and fulfill the promises of Gen 17 as follows: "yet I have born him a son in his old age" (Gen 21:7) fulfills God's promise from Gen 17:16, "I will give you a son by her." Sarah's reference to Abraham's "old age" (Gen 21:7) recalls Abraham's reference to both of their ages in Gen 17:17. The naming of the son Isaac and his circumcision at eight days (Gen 21: 3–4) fulfills the requirements set out in Gen 17:12, 19. Finally Sarah's reference to "laughter" (Gen 21:6) echoes Abraham's laughter at the time of the divine promise of Isaac's birth (Gen 17:17). The only detail of verses 1–7 that does not fulfill promises made in Gen 17 is the note concerning Sarah's "nursing sons." Driver suggests on separate grounds that Gen 21:7, the breastfeeding verse, is a late interpolation into P based on the use of the verb *millēl*. Driver identifies this verb as "Aramaic," linking it to Dan 6:21 and noting its use in other late texts such as Ps 106:2 and Job 8:2; 33:3 (Driver, *The Book of Genesis*, 210).

66. Sarna, *Genesis*, 145; Robert Alter, *Genesis: Translation and Commentary* (New York: Norton, 1996), 99n10.

67. The idea that Isaac's status might be lowered had he nursed at the breasts of a slave woman finds an interesting correlate in an Akkadian text that reads: "My daughter is no slave girl, I (only) placed her in the charge of PN [personal name], a slave girl of your father-in-law's house, for nursing" (*CAD* E, "*enequ*," 166).

68. The verb used here is *g-d-l* and should be understood as the point of his weaning, based on the same verb being used in conjunction with Isaac's growing up (*g-d-l*) and being weaned (*g-m-l*) in Gen 21:8. See Brevard S. Childs, *The Book of Exodus: A Critical Theological Commentary* (OTL; Louisville: Westminster John Knox Press, 1974), 7.
69. William H. Propp labels the trope "the hoodwinked foreigner" (Propp, *Exodus 1–18: A New Translation with Introduction and Commentary* [AB 2; New York: Doubleday, 1999], 154). G. W. Coats sees the wet nurse narrative as serving the literary purposes of "irony" (Coats, *Moses: Heroic Man, Man of God* [JSOTSup 57; Sheffield, Eng.: JSOT Press, 1988], 44).
70. Carol Meyers notes that the explicit mention of the ethnicity of both Moses's parents provides "the sacerdotal pedigree of Moses" (Meyers, *Exodus* [NCBC; Cambridge: Cambridge University Press, 1995], 42). Several commentators have noted that Moses's mother is identified as an actual daughter of Levi (*bat lēwî*), while the father is simply "from the house of Levi" (*mibbêt lēwî*), meaning a member of the tribe (see, e.g., Propp, *Exodus 1–18*, 148).
71. Moses was in the house of Jethro/Reuel long enough for him to marry and have at least two sons (Exod 2:21–22; 4:20; 18:2–4).
72. This text is notoriously difficult to interpret, but one of the possible readings is that Zipporah circumcises Moses and another is that she circumcises Gershom in place of Moses. Whether it was Moses, Gershom, or both that were not circumcised at the point of departure from Midian, Moses would be guilty of not following covenantal obligations.
73. Propp sees the entire narrative of Exod 1:22–2:22 as being held together by "confusion over Moses' ethnic affiliation" (Propp, *Exodus 1–18*, 146).
74. The story of Hadad, the royal heir of the house of Edom, records precisely this practice. Like Moses under threat from Pharaoh, the boy Hadad flees Joab, who seeks to kill "every male Edomite." He finds safety in the household of "Pharaoh, King of Egypt." Hadad grows up in Pharaoh's house, marries Pharaoh's sister-in-law, and has a son, Genubath, who, unlike Moses, is "weaned in Pharaoh's house" (1 Kings 11:14–22).
75. Again, as in other stories of the mother's house, there is no further mention of the father. For Propp, Exod 2:9 suggests that Moses grew up "under his mother's tutelage" (Propp, *Exodus 1–18*, 152).
76. Carol Meyers sees the intentional signaling of Moses's two ethnic identities in his name. "*Mose*" means "child of" in Egyptian, but, Meyers notes, the name is given the Hebrew etymology of "to draw" out of water; this dual signification "symbolizes the youth's membership in two communities" (Meyers, *Exodus*, 44).
77. Propp, *Exodus 1–18*, 147. Robert Wilson notes that movement of a person up in a genealogy closer to the founding ancestor "reflects the lineage's increased power" (Wilson, *Genealogy and History in the Biblical World* [New Haven, Conn.: Yale University Press, 1977], 51). In this case, Jochabed is shown to

occupy a more powerful position within the Levite genealogy than her husband. Exod 6:20 also adds Aaron as an older brother, but no sister is mentioned.
78. While Ruth is in her homeland in Moab, she is called simply "Ruth" (Ruth 1:3, 14, 16). Once she arrives in Judah, she becomes "Ruth the Moabite" (Ruth 1:22). The narrator continues to label her "Ruth the Moabite" in Ruth 2:2, 21; 4:5, 10. She is also identified as "the Moabite who came from Moab" in Ruth 2:6. At the same time, in her relationship to Boaz and Naomi, she can be simply "Ruth," often with an added familial label like "daughter" or "daughter-in-law" (Ruth 2:8, 22; 3:9; 4:13).
79. Mark S. Smith correctly notes that Ruth's pledge to Naomi forges a kinship bond between the two women that was necessary in light of the death of Ruth's husband. I disagree, however, with his assertion that Ruth ultimately becomes one of Naomi's people (Smith, "'Your People Shall Be My People': Family and Covenant in Ruth 1:16–17," *CBQ* 69 [2007]: 252–57). Instead, I see Ruth gaining a place among Naomi's people but remaining "Ruth the Moabite." The role of breastfeeding in this story supports this assertion.
80. On the role of ethnic tensions in the story of Ruth, see Eunny P. Lee, "Ruth the Moabite: Identity, Kinship and Otherness," in *Engaging the Bible in a Gendered World: An Introduction to Feminist Biblical Interpretation in Honor of Katharine Doob Sakenfeld*, ed. Linda Day and Carolyn Pressler (Louisville: Westminster John Knox, 2006), 92.
81. On the book of Ruth as the birth story of Davidic kingship, see Gillian Feeley-Harnik, "Naomi and Ruth: Building up the House of David," in *Text and Tradition: The Hebrew Bible and Folklore*, ed. Susan Niditch [Atlanta: Scholars Press, 1990), 164–84, and Edward L. Greenstein, "Reading Strategies and the Story of Ruth," in *Women in the Hebrew Bible: A Reader*, ed. Alice Bach (New York: Routledge, 1999), 211–31.
82. Kirstin Nielsen, *Ruth: A Commentary* (OTL; Louisville: Westminster John Knox, 1997), 99.
83. At a time when David is threatened by Saul, he takes his mother and father to the king of Moab for safekeeping (1 Sam 22:3–4).
84. In Ruth 1:11–13, Naomi insists that she is too old to have a husband and bear sons.
85. Nielsen, *Ruth*, 92.
86. Victor Matthews, *Judges and Ruth* (NCBC; Cambridge: Cambridge University Press, 2004), 238; André LaCocque, *Ruth*, trans. K. C. Hanson (CC; Minneapolis: Fortress, 2004), 140. Carolyn Pressler also dismisses the idea that Naomi "nursed" Obed, arguing that the phrase simply means "she cradled" Obed "like any doting grandmother" (Pressler, *Joshua, Judges, Ruth* [Louisville: Westminster John Knox, 2002], 305).
87. Athalya Brenner, "Naomi and Ruth," in *A Feminist Companion to Ruth*, ed. Athalya Brenner (1993; repr. Sheffield, Eng.: Sheffield Academic Press, 2001),

71. See also Johanna Stiebert, *Fathers and Daughters in the Hebrew Bible* (Oxford: Oxford University Press, 2013), 22.
88. LaCocque, *Ruth*, 143.
89. Moses's mother in Exod 2:7; Rebekah's nurse (Gen 24:59; 35:8); Joash's wet nurse (2 Kings 11:2; 2 Chron 22:11); female milch camels (Gen 32:16 [Eng. 32:15]).
90. This same imagery of a "nursing father" is found in the Thanksgiving Hymns (*Hodayot*) at Qumran, where the "righteous teacher" likens himself to a father and a wet nurse (Jacob Cherian, "The Moses at Qumran: The צדקה מורה as the Nursing-Father of the יחד," in *The Dead Sea Scrolls and the Qumran Community*, ed. J. H. Charlesworth [The Bible and the Dead Sea Scrolls 2; Waco, Texas: Baylor University Press, 2006], 351–62).
91. NRSV and JPS read "Mordecai adopted her."
92. We can also compare this to the story of Joseph. By the time Joseph finds himself residing in the house of the Egyptian official Potiphar, he is a young man, and his birth story had contained no references to breastfeeding. The blessing of Joseph in Gen 49:25, however, indicates that he received the blessings of "breast and womb." Given the lauded place of Rachel in Joseph's story, I read this blessing as an indication that Joseph received the appropriate ethnic formation in the womb and at the breasts of Rachel.
93. Several scholars have understood Naomi's action to signify her adoption of Obed, and G. Gerleman has said that Naomi's adoption is for the purpose of providing Obed with a Judahite mother (Gerleman, *Ruth: Das Hohelied* (Biblischer Kommentar, Altes Testament 18; Neukirchen-Vluyn, West Ger.: Neukirchener, 1965], 37–38). No scholars that I am aware of have linked symbolic breastfeeding to an adoption that is meant to provide or shore up an infant's insider ethnicity.
94. "ḥêq," BDB: 300.
95. BDB: 300–301. *DCH* 3: 216 defines the range of meanings to include "fold," "bosom" [including Num 11:12 and Ruth 4:16 here], "hollow," "inner part of the body," and "channel or rim." *TDOT* defines ḥêq as "part of chariot or altar," "bulge of a garment," "bosom, lap," and "innermost part of man" (G. André, "chêk," *TDOT* 4: 356–58). In a lengthy response to an earlier version of this chapter, Brian Peterson takes issue with my translating ḥêq as "breast," insisting that the word means "lap" or "front of the body" and "never means breast" (Peterson, "Is Breast Milk a 'Kinship-Forging Substance' in the Hebrew Bible? A Response to Cynthia Chapman," *McMaster Journal of Theology and Ministry* 14 [2012–13]: 86–87). A survey of the biblical uses of the term, however, shows several places where a more modern form of the English "bosom" would be appropriate.
96. Phyllis Trible translates Moses imagining himself as a "wet nurse" offering a "bosom" to a "suckling" (Trible, *God and the Rhetoric of Sexuality* [Philadelphia: Fortress, 1978], 68–69).

97. Lamentations 2:11 refers to two groups in sequence for whom the poet-author weeps: "the daughter of my people" and "the babes and sucklings." These are then the antecedents for those in verse 12 who "cry to their mothers," "ask for bread and wine," "faint like the wounded," and have "their life poured out on their mother's *ḥêq*."

98. In many ways, the word *ḥêq* is like the words *beṭen* and *raḥămîm*. Each of these can be applied to both men and women; a man has a "chest" and a "belly" and can feel "compassionate." Just because these body parts and body-related emotions are attributed to both men and women, however, does not mean that they cannot be used in ways that deliberately seek to evoke the maternal and the female reproductive process. On *beṭen* and *raḥămîm*, see chapter 5.

99. In all three breastfeeding narratives, naming serves as a literary cue of the chosen foundational male over and against the foreign outsider. Isaac is named repeatedly in Gen 21 while Ishmael is referred to as "the son of that slave woman." Moses is the only character named in his birth story. And here, at the birth of Obed, the foreign outsider Ruth becomes "daughter-in-law" while Naomi and Obed are named.

100. Danna Nolan Fewell and David M. Gunn see Ruth acting as a surrogate for Naomi, birthing a son for her (Fewell and Gunn, "'A Son Is Born to Naomi!': Literary Allusions and Interpretation in the Book of Ruth," in Bach, ed., *Women in the Hebrew Bible*, 238).

101. We find a somewhat analogous situation in Jacob's adoption of Joseph's two sons that were born to an Egyptian mother. We have the same passive description of their birth that eliminates any reference to their mother when Jacob says, "Now, your two sons that were born to you in the land of Egypt." We also find similar wording that lays claim to the sons as one's own through adoption: "They belong to me." And finally, just as Obed replaces two of Naomi's sons, Ephraim and Manasseh will ultimately usurp and replace two of Jacob's sons: "Ephraim and Manasseh, like Reuben and Simeon, will become mine" (Gen 48:5). The ritual means through which Ephraim and Manasseh become sons of Jacob is different from Naomi's adoption of Obed as her own through real or symbolic breastfeeding. Jacob offers Ephraim and Manasseh his deathbed blessing. See de Vaux, *Ancient Israel*, 20.

102. Greenstein, "Reading Strategies," 215.

103. In post-biblical rabbinic commentary, Naomi's breastfeeding intervention ends up being only the first step in erasing the stain of Moabite ethnicity from the genealogy of King David. *Ruth Rabbah* adds to Ruth 4:13 the note that "She [Ruth] had no ovary, so the Holy One Blessed be He, formed an ovary for her" (*Ruth Rabbah* LXXX:I IB). This means that zygote Obed came from a combination of God-formed ovary and "strong (Boaz)" Judean seed, and infant Obed ingested the Judean breast milk of his grandmother Naomi. The Moabite Ruth has truly become simply the vessel. My thanks to my stu-

dent Benjamin Morrison for first directing my attention to the detail of the god-formed ovary in this text.
104. If, as many have noted, the birth story of Samuel is actually that of Saul, then we have breastfeeding narratives figuring into the birth stories of four foundational males. This was first argued by I. Hylander, *Der literarische Samuel-Saulkomplex (I Sam. 1–15)* (Uppsala, Sweden: Almquist and Wicksell, 1932), and is now supported by, among others, Hertzberg, *I and II Samuel*, 26, and McCarter, *I Samuel*, 65–66.

Chapter 7. The One Who Opens the Womb

1. Robert Alter suggests that "in any given narrative event, and especially at the beginning of any new story, the point at which dialogue first emerges will be worthy of special attention, and in most instances, the initial words spoken by a personage will be revelatory . . . constituting an important moment in the exposition of character" (Alter, *The Art of Biblical Narrative*, 2nd ed. [New York: Basic Books, 2011], 93–94).
2. Commentators and translations that have opted to read a *nipʻal* verb from *b-n-h* include Robert Alter, *Genesis: Translation and Commentary* (New York: Norton, 1996), 67; Claus Westermann, *Genesis 12–36* (CC; Minneapolis: Fortress, 1994), 233, 239; and Naomi Steinberg, *Kinship and Marriage in Genesis: A Household Economics Perspective* (Minneapolis: Fortress, 1993), 62. Commentators that have opted to read a denominative verb from *bēn* include Nahum Sarna, *Genesis: The Traditional Hebrew Text with the New JPS Translation* (Philadelphia: JPS, 1989), 119; Gerhard von Rad, *Genesis: A Commentary* (OTL; Louisville: Westminster John Knox, 1973), 190; and E. A. Speiser, *Genesis: Introduction, Translation, and Notes* (AB 1; New York: Doubleday, 1964), 116.
3. Siegfried Wagner, "*banah*," *TDOT* 2: 166–68; "*b-n-y*," in G. del Olmo Lete and J. Sanmartín, *A Dictionary of the Ugaritic Language in the Alphabetic Tradition 1*, trans. Wilfred G. E. Watson (Leiden: E. J. Brill, 2003), 233–34; "*banû*," *CAD* B, 85–90.
4. Claus Westermann captures the sense of this verb, translating the phrase "perhaps I shall build a family from her." He then asserts that Gen 16:2 is a "verbalization of patriarchal anthropology which has continued effectively across the centuries: the life of a woman is an integral whole . . . only when she is a member of a family in which she presents her husband with children" (Westermann, *Genesis 12–36*, 233, 239). Samuel Rolles Driver translated "it may be that I shall obtain children by her" but then noted that the literal translation is "be built up from her," suggesting "the family being represented under the figure of a house" (Driver, *The Book of Genesis* [WC; London: Methuen, 1920], 180).
5. Westermann, *Genesis 12–36*, 237.
6. Von Rad, *Genesis*, 191.

7. A wife established her own house in the larger household of her husband when she bore a son. In the introduction, I noted that within "house societies," "the building of a house is only completed with the birth of children" (Janet Carsten and Stephen Hugh-Jones, "Introduction: About the House: Levi-Strauss and Beyond," in *About the House: Lévi-Strauss and Beyond*, ed. Janet Carsten and Stephen Hugh-Jones [Cambridge: Cambridge University Press, 1995], 39–40). See also Gale Yee, *Poor Banished Children of Eve: Women as Evil in the Hebrew Bible* (Minneapolis: Fortress, 2008), 38. The marriage blessing pronounced on behalf of Rebekah by her uterine family expresses a similar hope that her marriage will find its fulfillment in children: "Our sister, be the mother of thousands of ten thousands; and may your descendants possess the gate of those who hate them!" (Gen 24:60).
8. Athalya Brenner makes this point, arguing that the biblical women who gave birth to the male heroes acted in ways that provide evidence of "calculations of power politics rather than mere emotion or similar consideration" (Brenner, "Female Social Behaviour: Two Descriptive Patterns within the 'Birth of the Hero' Paradigm," *VT* 36 [1986]: 265).
9. Karel van der Toorn notes that for wives in the ancient Near East, "motherhood is prestige" (Van der Toorn, *From Her Cradle to Her Grave: The Role of Religion in the Life of the Israelite and the Babylonian Woman* [Sheffield, Eng.: JSOT Press, 1994], 77). See also Steinberg, *Kinship and Marriage*, 62–63.
10. As we saw in chapter 3, an interesting connection to the matriarchs' desire "to be built up" through having a son is found in the description of Yahweh Elohim's creation of the first woman, who is "built" from a man's "rib" and later named "Eve" (*Ḥavvah*), a name that may come etymologically from the Hebrew word for "tent villages" (*ḥavvot*): "And Yahweh Elohim *built* [*b-n-h*] the rib that he had taken from the man into a woman" (Gen 2:22). The role of the woman as the skeletal frame of her husband is also seen in Prov 12:4, "A good wife is the crown of her husband, but she who brings shame is like rottenness in his bones."
11. David's son Absalom was said to have set up a pillar in his own name explaining, "I have no son to keep my name in remembrance" (2 Sam 18:18). A curse in the prophetic book of Nahum is pronounced presumably against the unnamed king of Assyria: "The Lord has given a commandment about you: 'No more shall your name be perpetuated'" (Nah 1:14). LXX Job 2:9 has Job's wife equating the death of his sons and daughters with his "memorial" being "abolished."
12. Jack M. Sasson, *Ruth: A New Translation with a Philological Commentary and a Formalist-Folklorist Interpretation*, 2nd ed. (Sheffield, Eng.: JSOT Press, 1989), 18–19.
13. I return to this blessing in chapter 9 in order to show how it presents Rachel and Leah as kingdom and nation builders nested within the larger house of Israel.
14. On the important connections between descendants and land, see H. C. Brichto, "Kin, Cult, Land and Afterlife: A Biblical Complex," *Hebrew Union College Annual* 44 (1973): 1–54.

15. Absent from this list of house-of-the-father concerns is the word "name." Genesis 15 has traditionally been labeled a Yahwist text, and as we see below, the priestly version of the covenant in Gen 17 includes the establishing and perpetuation of Abraham's name. Concerning Abram's quest for an heir, Naomi Steinberg has traced the sequence of strategies that Abram employs. He first considers adopting his nephew Lot and then considers adopting a non-kinsman, Eliezer. Finally, in Gen 15, he learns that only his own biological son would be his heir (Steinberg, *Kinship and Marriage*, 56–61).
16. This is another example where the priestly author of Gen 17 is the one who adds maternal specificity. See also Exod 6:20 and Num 26:59, both priestly texts, where genealogical specificity is added to the information concerning Moses's mother provided in Exod 2:1.
17. There are only two biblical examples of this practice, Gen 16:4 and 30:3. We find versions of this practice in the Code of Hammurabi no. 144–48 and in the Nuzi archives. See the discussion in Speiser, *Genesis*, 120, and Westermann, *Genesis 12–36*, 239.
18. Tammi J. Schneider, *Mothers of Promise: Women in the Book of Genesis* (Grand Rapids, Mich.: Baker Academic, 2008), 27.
19. BDB translates the verb *g-b-r* as "be strong, mighty; prevail" (147) and the masculine noun *geber* as "man." The two feminine nouns *gĕberet* and *gĕbîrâ* are both translated "lady, queen," while *gĕbîrâ* can also mean "queen mother" and *gĕberet* can mean "mistress over servants" (BDB: 150). Given the royal associations of Sarah, whose name means "princess" and who brings forth "kings of peoples," I see these two feminine nouns functioning almost identically.
20. Westermann defines *šipḥâ* as one who is subordinate to a *gĕberet;* she is the "personal servant of the wife whose power of disposition over her is restricted to this; the girl stands in a relationship of personal trust to her" (Westermann, *Genesis 12–36*, 238).
21. Jacob Weingreen, "The Case of the Blasphemer (Leviticus XXIV 10ff)," *VT* 22 (1972): 119; emphasis added.
22. Claus Westermann notes the same poetic pairing of *šipḥâ* and *gĕberet* in Ps 123:2 and Isa 24:2; both texts confirm the authority of a *gĕberet* over a *šipḥâ* (Westermann, *Genesis 12–36*, 238).
23. Biblically, we do have the exceptional cases of Job's three daughters (Job 42:15) where their receipt of an inheritance may signify Job's extraordinary wealth, and the case of Zelophehad's daughters, who had to fight for an inheritance in the absence of sons (Num 27:1–11).
24. Rubie Watson, "Wives, Concubines, and Maids: Servitude and Kinship in the Hong Kong Region, 1900–1940," in *Marriage and Inequality in Chinese Society*, ed. Rubie S. Watson and Patricia Buckely Ebrey (Berkeley: University of California Press, 1991), 223.
25. The notion that a bride's transfer into the household of her husband could be reduced to a simple economic transaction whereby the groom or his family

"purchased" the bride is overly simplistic. The practice of exchanging gifts or property at the time of marriage changed over time and was flexible within specific time periods. See Tracy Lemos, *Marriage Gifts and Social Change in Ancient Palestine: 1200 BCE–200 CE* (Cambridge: Cambridge University Press, 2010), 20–61.

26. King Lemuel's mother recalls a very similar deal-making prayer that she offered in order to give birth to him when she addresses him as an adult saying, "No my son, no son of my womb, no son of my vows" (Prov 31:1–2).
27. Manoah ultimately becomes the father of Samson.
28. Eliphaz, the first of Job's friends to comment on his loss, also conflates Job, Job's physical body, and Job's house when he notes that God finds faults even with angels, and therefore, "how much more, those who dwell in houses of clay, whose foundations are upon the dust." Ultimately they are destroyed and perish, "their tent cord is plucked up within them" (Job 4:19–21).
29. "Kirta," in Michael D. Coogan and Mark S. Smith, *Stories from Ancient Canaan*, 2nd ed. (Louisville: Westminster John Knox, 2012), 73–74, column 2, lines 1–5; *KTU* 1.14, II, 1–5. On the importance of sons and heirs to their fathers in the Ugaritic epics of Kirta and Aqhat, see Ronald S. Hendel, *The Epic of the Patriarch: The Jacob Cycle and the Narrative Traditions of Canaan and Israel* (Atlanta: Scholars Press, 1987), 48–59.
30. Jon Levenson, *Death and Resurrection of the Beloved Son: The Transformation of Child Sacrifice in Judaism and Christianity* (New Haven, Conn.: Yale University Press, 1993), 46–47, 55–57.
31. Levenson, *Death and Resurrection*, 46–47, 55–57; Jeffrey Tigay, *Deuteronomy* (JPS Torah Commentary; Philadelphia: JPS, 1996), 195–96.
32. See Frederick E. Greenspahn, *When Brothers Dwell Together: The Preeminence of Younger Siblings in the Hebrew Bible* (New York: Oxford University Press, 1994), 65–69, where he notes that the male counterpart to the maternally specific *peṭer reḥem* was not *bĕkôr* but rather *rēʾšît ʾōn*, "the first fruits of a man's vigor." The nesting of a mother's single child, her *peṭer reḥem*, within a father's house that contained many sons can also be seen in Prov 4:3: "When I was a son to my father, tender, and the only son [*yāḥîd*] to my mother."
33. Nicole Ruane, *Sacrifice and Gender in Biblical Law* (Cambridge: Cambridge University Press, 2013), 201–2.
34. Ruane, *Sacrifice and Gender*, 202, 212.
35. See the dedication of Samuel and Samson, both womb openers, as Nazirites from birth. I have found no information on what happened when the child who opened the womb was a daughter. The birth of a daughter would certainly not be sufficient to "build up" a wife in the house of her husband. The question is whether or not a daughter would be considered a *peṭer reḥem*. The differing time periods of ritual impurity following the birth of a son or a daughter (Lev 12) would indicate that a womb-opening daughter might require a different type of ritual redemption.

36. Rainer Albertz, "Personal Names and Family Religion," in *Family and Household Religion in Ancient Israel and the Levant*, ed. Rainer Albertz and Rüdiger Schmitt (Winona Lake, Ind.: Eisenbrauns, 2012), 248, 252.
37. Albertz, "Personal Names," 248.
38. Albertz, "Personal Names," 276, 586–87. "DN" stands for "divine name."
39. In Isa 62:4–5, the word *šômēmâ* seems to signify a woman who is abandoned by her husband or a man who has sexually used her and left her unmarried.
40. The clearest examples are Song 1:6; 8:11–12; Ps 138:3; and Ezek 19:10–14.
41. Albertz, "Personal Names," 278, 587–88.
42. Albertz, "Personal Names," 270–74. Albertz includes another name that I might translate differently from him. Albertz translates the name *'Adāyāhû*, which is attested in seventeen instances as "Yahweh has adorned [the child]" (280). In light of Jer 31:4 where Yahweh again builds up his wife "Faithless Israel," and she responds by "adorning herself with timbrels," I suggest that *'Adāyāhû* could just as easily mean "Yahweh has adorned [the mother with the birth of this child]."
43. For a married, childless woman, living in the house of her father was an extreme social burden and disgrace, what Susan Niditch has called "a social anomaly" (Niditch, "The Wronged Woman Righted: An Analysis of Genesis 38," *Harvard Theological Review* 72 [1979]: 144–46).
44. Steinberg notes that Lot's daughters do not seem concerned with preserving their father's line; rather, they are willing to "go against all taboos" in order to secure "their own social standing" (Steinberg, *Kinship and Marriage,* 72–73). I cover the story of Lot's daughters in chapter 9.
45. The fear of remaining "desolate" in the house of her mother for the rest of her days may well be why Ruth chose not to return to her mother's house when her own marriage ended without a son (Ruth 1:7–18). The report that "Michal, daughter of Saul, had no child till the day of her death" suggests that her barrenness was either a punishment from God or, more likely, a punishment from her husband.
46. In Nuzi marriage contracts, a wife's inability to produce an heir allowed her husband to procure a second wife. See Jonathan Paradise, "Marriage Contracts of Free Persons at Nuzi," *JCS* 39, no. 1 (1987): 1–36.
47. Van der Toorn, *From Her Cradle to Her Grave*, 77; Yee, *Poor Banished Children*, 38.
48. E.g., NRSV and NIV. The NKJV, ASV, and JPS translate correctly, in my view, as "households."
49. See Shalom Paul, "Exodus 1:21 'To Found a Family': A Biblical and Akkadian Idiom," *Maarav* 8 (1992): 139–42.
50. While several translations render the word *zēbed* "dowry," Tracy Lemos argues compellingly for the broader rendering of "gift," noting that the word is a *hapax legomena* and that a sixth son born well into a marriage is unlikely to constitute a "dowry" (Lemos, *Marriage Gifts*, 50–51).

51. A literal translation of Joseph's name would read, "May he add another [son]" (Gen 30:24).
52. Speiser, *Genesis*, 231–32.
53. Speiser, *Genesis*, 232.
54. Greenspahn, *When Brothers Dwell*, 59–69, 81–83.
55. The song or psalm of Hannah is likely a separate composition from the story of Samuel's birth that precedes it. While McCarter sees it as a late insertion into the Samuel corpus, he does not see it as a late composition. In his view, the psalm exhibits traits of early Israelite poetry. Placing this psalm on Hannah's lips, therefore, represents its "secondary context," but a context still appropriate to the theme of the barren woman who finally bears a son. See P. Kyle McCarter, Jr., *I Samuel: A New Translation with Introduction, Notes, and Commentary* (AB 8; Garden City, N.Y.: Doubleday, 1980), 74–76.
56. Seven sons signify a full complement. Job in his blessed state has seven sons and three daughters (Job 1:2). The village women compliment Naomi by declaring that her daughter-in-law, Ruth, is more valuable to her than seven sons (Ruth 4:15). The judge Gideon and King Ahab both had seventy sons (Judg 8:30; 2 Kings 10:1). The goddess Asherah had seventy sons. In some Ugaritic texts, this ideal number of sons is expressed in the parallel lines "seven, and what's more eight," so when Kirta's house was in a blessed state, it contained "seven brothers, eight sons of a mother." In his restored house, his new wife Hurriya bears him "seven sons and daughters, produces eight" ("Kirta," in Coogan and Smith, *Stories from Ancient Canaan*, 72, lines 7–9; 83, lines 21–25). The "seven and what's more eight" sequence may be behind the presentation of David as the eighth son of Jesse and Yahweh's anointed king (1 Sam 16:6–13). I have translated the Hebrew word *umlālâ* as "dried up" rather than the more typical "forlorn" or "languishing." Biblically, *umlālâ* is consistently associated with dried up fertility in crops, flocks, and marine life. By extension, *umlālâ* seems to refer to the empty devastation of a city following war (Isa 16:8; 19:8; 24:4, 7; 33:9; Jer 14:2; Hosea 4:3; Joel 1:10, 12; Nah 1:4). A very close parallel to Hannah's song that uses the word *umlālâ* is found in Jer 15:5–12 where Yahweh brings judgment against Jerusalem using a series of maternal images. First, he addresses Jerusalem as a rejected and punished woman whom no one will pity (Jer 15:5–7). Then, he singles out the widows and mothers with language that recalls Hannah's song: "Their widows have become more numerous than the sands of the sea. I have brought against them, upon the mothers of youths, a noonday destroyer. I have caused agitation and terror to fall suddenly upon her. The one who bore seven is dried up [*umlālâ*]. Her spirit is breathed out" (Jer 15:9a). And finally, Jeremiah concludes, addressing his own mother: "Woe is me, my mother, because you bore me, a man of dispute and a man of strife to all the land" (Jer 15:10a).
57. On the role of these "neighborhood women" in forming "informal family networks," or "intergroup relationships," see Carol Meyers, "Women of the Neigh-

borhood (Ruth 4:17): Informal Female Networks in Ancient Israel," in *A Feminist Companion to Ruth and Esther*, ed. Athalya Brenner (Sheffield, Eng.: Sheffield Academic Press, 1999), 110–27.

58. Adele Berlin considers Naomi as the book of Ruth's "central character" in that all other characters in the book are described by their relationship to her (Berlin, *Poetics and Interpretation of Biblical Narrative* [Sheffield, Eng.: Almond, 1983], 82–84).

59. Edward Greenstein notes that Obed is also legitimately conceived. He was not conceived on the threshing floor but rather after the properly negotiated "quasi-levirate" marriage (Edward L. Greenstein, "Reading Strategies and the Story of Ruth," in *Women in the Hebrew Bible: A Reader*, ed. Alice Bach [New York: Routledge, 1999], 214).

60. André LaCocque, "Subverting the Biblical World: Sociology and Politics in the Book of Ruth," in *Scrolls of Love: Ruth and the Song of Songs*, ed. Peter S. Hawkins and Leslie Cushing Stahlberg (New York: Fordham University Press, 2006), 20–26; Athalya Brenner, *The Israelite Woman: Social Role and Literary Type in Biblical Narrative* (Sheffield, Eng.: JSOT Press, 1994), 96–97; Danna Nolan Fewell and David M. Gunn, "'A Son Is Born to Naomi!': Literary Allusions and Interpretation in the Book of Ruth," *JSOT* 40 (1988): 99–108.

61. Athalya Brenner has identified a "structural analogy" between the Naomi-Ruth story and the Sarah-Hagar story. Like Sarah, Naomi is the "senior partner" and Ruth is "the younger and subordinate." The analogy also encompasses the insider ethnicity of Sarah and Naomi and the foreigner status of Hagar and Ruth (Brenner, "Female Social Behaviour," 266). See also Judith E. McKinlay, "A Son Is Born to Naomi: A Harvest for Israel," in Brenner, ed., *Feminist Companion to Ruth and Esther*, 155–56.

62. See Berlin, *Poetics and Interpretation*, 84.

63. While the dream portrays all eleven brothers bowing down to Joseph, the narrative repeatedly shows Jacob and Joseph singling out Benjamin as part of Rachel's maternal house. See chapter 1.

64. "Esarhaddon's Succession Treaty," lines 283–90.

65. "Esarhaddon's Succession Treaty," lines 113–15, 214–15, 318–20, 336–38.

66. See chapter 4.

67. Another royal house where maternal sub-houses may have influenced the pattern of succession was that of Josiah. Following Josiah's death in a battle with Pharaoh Neco of Egypt, the Judean "people of the land" anointed his son Jehoahaz to succeed him. Jehoahaz's mother was Hamutal (2 Kings 23:30–31). Just three months later, Pharaoh Neco removed Jehoahaz and installed Jehoiakim (= Eliakim), another son of Josiah, on the throne. Jehoiakim was from a different mother's house within the house of Josiah, that of Zebidah (2 Kings 23:33–36). It is possible that Pharaoh Neco played into known family rivalries among maternal houses when he chose a son of a rival mother to succeed Jehoahaz, the king chosen by the people. Neco may have thought he could secure

greater loyalty by elevating a son from a lower-status or disgraced maternal house. Jehoiakim stayed on the throne long enough to be succeeded by his own son, Jehoiachin, but when Nebuchadrezzar deported Jehoiachin to Babylon, he turned to the pre-Egyptian house of Hamutal within Josiah's house to find his puppet king, Zedekiah (= Mattaniah) (2 Kings 24:8, 17–18). Again, if the maternal sub-house of Zebidah had gained ascendancy under Egyptian influence, it behooved the new imperial power to elevate a son from the rival maternal sub-house of Hamutal. The fact that this is the maternal house from which the "people of the land" had chosen Josiah's first heir might have given Zedekiah greater credibility. The Babylonian Chronicles record Nebuchadrezzar's attack against "the city of Judah" where "he captured the city and he seized its king." The text then notes, "A king of his own choice he appointed in the city" ("Chronicle 5," in A. K. Grayson, *Assyrian and Babylonian Chronicles* [Winona Lake, Ind.: Eisenbrauns, 2000], 102, lines 11–13). Jeremiah, who ends up forcibly taken into exile in Egypt and who counseled Babylonian exiles to "pray for the peace of your city," had a particularly negative view of the Egyptian-appointed Jehoiakim, son of Zebidah (Jer 22:13–14; 36:24). Those exiled to Babylonia, including the prophet Ezekiel, had a positive and hopeful view of Jehoiachin, which may simply be due to his surviving and experiencing exile with them while other descendants of Josiah had not (See Ezek 1:2; 2 Kings 25:27–30).

68. Jon Berquist notes with regard to this text, "This was not a family feud; this was a political battle for the leadership of a nation. National leadership and national identity were expressed in terms of households of Saul and David" (Berquist, *Controlling Corporeality: The Body and the Household in Ancient Israel* [New Brunswick, N.J.: Rutgers University Press, 2002], 49). On the connection between David's coronation, house building, and the birth of sons, see Baruch Halpern, *David's Secret Demons: Messiah, Murderer, Traitor, King* (Grand Rapids, Mich.: Eerdmans, 2001), 32.

69. It is possible that some of these sons were not womb openers. If Ahinoam is the same Ahinoam that had been Saul's wife, then Amnon is the first child she bore to David but not her womb opener. Likewise, Abigail had been married to Nabal, so she may have had children prior to her marriage to David (see Jon D. Levenson and Baruch Halpern, "The Political Import of David's Marriages," *JBL* 99, no. 4 [1980]: 516). In this genealogical list, however, the text seems most interested in communicating the strength of David's house through presumed womb-opening sons. Gillian Feeley-Harnik sees men's work in the Bible to be "focused mainly on building up lines of first-born sons," while women work to "undercut primogeniture or repair recurrent and disastrous attacks on firstborn males" (Feeley-Harnik, "Naomi and Ruth: Building up the House of David," in *Text and Tradition: The Hebrew Bible and Folklore,* ed. Susan Niditch [Atlanta: Scholars Press, 1990], 177).

70. The Chronicler indicates that the line of Saul continued through his grandson, Meribaal (= Mephibosheth) (1 Chron 8:34–40; 9:40–44).

71. See chapter 1 for discussion of Gen 25.
72. Baruch Halpern notes that the Samuel narrative locates Ishbaal's royal court in Mahanaim in the Transjordan, which suggests he never actually ruled Israel proper in the Cisjordan (Halpern, *David's Secret Demons*, 27). Saul's second son, Ishvi, noted in Saul's genealogy in 1 Sam 14:49–50, disappears from the narrative, suggesting that he may have died young.
73. On the tension between the house of Saul as represented by Michal and the kingship of David, see Alter, *The Art of Biblical Narrative*, 143–58, and J. Cheryl Exum, *Fragmented Women: Feminist (Sub)versions of Biblical Narratives* (JSOT Sup 163; Sheffield, Eng.: Sheffield Academic Press, 1993), 24–25, 49.
74. The Ugaritic phrase *ṭar 'um* means "maternal clan" or "maternal alliance" within a father's house. Kirta's first wife produced for him a *ṭar 'um*, meaning multiple children. All of these children, "seven brothers, eight sons of one mother," died leaving Kirta's "house" utterly destroyed. See discussion of this text in chapter 4.
75. By burying Saul and his sons, David also takes on the role of the faithful son and deserving heir of Saul. His marriage to Michal is aimed at communicating the same type of connection: he was a loyal son within Saul's house, and now he is the royal heir to Saul's eliminated house.
76. While the house of David is the unquestioned victor over the house of Saul, David himself begins to show military weakness, an ominous sign for his royal house. We see this weakness when Abishai, the son of David's sister Zeruiah, replaces the war weary David as the killer of Philistines (2 Sam 21:15–17) and David's servants likewise become the killers of four Philistine giants (2 Sam 21: 18–22).
77. If David's wife Ahinoam was the previous wife of Saul, the murder of Amnon actually continues the extinguishing of Saul's house, not because Amnon was thought of as Saul's son but because he was born to a woman marked by the house and seed of Saul. This would also mean that Amnon was not a womb-opener. The first round of this competition among sons skips Chileab, son of Abigail, David's second son. Chileab was likely never seen as a contender for the throne in that he was listed as belonging to "Abigail, wife of Nabal, the Carmelite." In other words, his mother is also tainted with a negative former husband. Chronicles attempts to clean up or fix the Davidic genealogy by listing the second son as "Daniel, by Abigail the Carmelite," eliminating the label "wife of Nabal."
78. I cover Absalom's revolt in chapter 8.
79. Just as David's son Chileab was marked by the former husband of his mother as the son of "Abigail, the wife of Nabal, the Carmelite," the son David conceived with Bathsheba through adultery is marked by her husband: "Yahweh struck the child that the *wife of Uriah* bore to David" (2 Sam 12:15). After grieving the loss of this Uriah-tainted son, the story continues, "Then David consoled *his wife Bathsheba*, and went to her and lay with her, and she conceived and bore a son, and he named him Solomon, and Yahweh loved him" (2 Sam 12:24).

Chapter 8. The House of the Father of His Mother

1. See discussion of this psalm in chapter 3.
2. The pairing of Rebekah's mother and her brother Laban is found in Gen 24:53, 55, 56–61.
3. Recall that Amos 1:11 articulates just such an expectation. Note, however, that within a monogamous household, the rivalry among children is within the uterine family unit rather than between mothers' houses. In addition to this case of Jacob and Esau, see also the household of Adam and Eve, where uterine brothers Cain and Abel fought (Gen 4:1–8), and the house of Amram and Jochebed, where Aaron and Miriam challenged Moses's leadership (Num 12: 1–16; 26:59). The wise woman of Tekoa presents herself as another mother of two sons, where one son kills the other (2 Sam 14:4–7). In none of these households is there a competing mother's house against whom these uterine siblings might unite.
4. On the pairing of the two brothers with a corresponding parent, see Susan Niditch, *My Brother Esau Is a Hairy Man: Hair and Identity in Ancient Israel* (New York: Oxford University Press, 2008), 115–16, and Sharon Pace Jeansonne, "Genesis 25:23—The Use of Poetry in the Rebekah Narratives," in *The Psalms and Other Studies on the Old Testament Presented to Joseph I. Hunt*, ed. Jack C. Knight and Lawrence A. Sinclair (Nashotah, Wis.: Nashotah House Seminary, 1990), 149.
5. Jeansonne, "Genesis 25:23—The Use of Poetry," 149.
6. On the masculinity of hair, see Niditch, *My Brother Esau*, 63–80.
7. Susan Niditch, *Underdogs and Tricksters: A Prelude to Biblical Folklore* (San Francisco: Harper and Row, 1987), 99–101.
8. The serpent's punishment in the garden is that God puts "enmity" between his seed and her seed such that "he [the woman's seed] shall bruise your head, and you [the serpent's seed] shall bruise his heel [*'āqēb*]" (Gen 3:15; 25:26).
9. Jacob's "trick" of multiplying his flocks is presented as a divine gift.
10. Even the sound of the verb for Esau's "crying out a great cry" (*wayyiṣ'aq ṣĕ'āqâ*) sounds like his father's name, *yiṣḥāq*.
11. The phrase is nearly replicated in Gen 28:5.
12. The "avuncular (= mother's brother)" relationship within professed patrilineal societies has received considerable scholarly attention. Robert Oden argues that Jacob's relationship with Laban and his cross-cousin marriage with Laban's two daughters "completes a system which is basic to the social nature of kinship itself." With an established avuncular relationship, Jacob can become "Israel," or as Oden puts it, "when Jacob marries his mother's brother's daughter and when he is thereby forced to establish a relationship with his maternal uncle, a complete kinship system is described; and thus Israel properly speaking is born" (Oden, "Jacob as Father, Husband, and Nephew: Kinship Studies and the Patriarchal Narratives," *JBL* 102, no. 2 [1983]: 202). Oden is correct to highlight

the avuncular relationship within the Jacob narrative, but I would argue that "Israel" is not "properly born" until Jacob establishes his house as a continuation of the house of Abraham and Isaac. This is a move that requires him to break with "his mother's brother" and leave "the house of the father of his mother."
13. This is the first of several references to a relative as "bone and flesh," and I examine this kinship designation below.
14. Gen 29:31; 30:17 ["God," not "Yahweh," here]; 30:22–24 ["God" remembers Rachel, and she gives her son a Yahwistic name].
15. A clear parallel is found in the renaming of Solomon "Jedidiah," "Beloved of Yahweh." Solomon's mother, Bathsheba, then secures her son's position as heir to his father, David (2 Sam 12:24–25; 1 Kings 1).
16. Mother of Jacob: Gen 27:11, 13, 24, 29; Mother of Jacob and Esau: Gen 28:2. See Tammi J. Schneider, *Mothers of Promise: Women in the Book of Genesis* (Grand Rapids, Mich.: Baker Academic, 2008), 48–49.
17. In Gen 12:1, Abraham is told to leave his "land and his birthplace and his father's house."
18. The sudden introduction of the "sons of Laban" matches the sudden introduction of a sister of baby Moses (Exod 2:4), a father of Rebekah in her mother's house (Gen 24:50), a wife for Job (Job 2:9), and a sister of Aqhat at the moment of his murder when vengeance is required. In each of these narratives, specific kin are introduced when their related social function is required: Moses's sister rescues her baby brother and secures his place in her mother's house; Bethuel consents to Rebekah's marriage; Job's wife encourages Job to curse God; Pughat avenges the murder of her brother, the "suckling of her mother's clan." The sons of Laban appear here when the wealth of the house of their father is under threat.
19. Jacob refers to Laban as "your father" four times in Gen 31:5–9.
20. This departure notice clearly parallels that of both Abraham and Rebekah (Gen 12:5; 24:59–61).
21. "Fear" is an epithet for a god specific to Isaac.
22. The culmination of the Jacob narrative, where he encounters Esau (Gen 32–33) and establishes his house west of the Jordan, is covered in chapter 9.
23. Summaries of the critical debates surrounding the problems related to Gideon's also being known as Jerubbaal are found in Jack M. Sasson, *Judges 1–12: A New Translation with Introduction and Commentary* (AYB 6D; New Haven, Conn.: Yale University Press, 2014), 344–45; J. Alberto Soggin, *Judges: A Commentary* (OTL; Philadelphia: Westminster, 1981), 103–5; and Daniel I. Block, "Will the Real Gideon Please Stand Up? Narrative Style and Intention in Judges 6–9," *Journal of the Evangelical Theological Society* 40 (September 1997): 353–66. Sasson also considers the possibility that the stories about Gideon heralding from Manasseh, an early settlement area for ancient Israel, and about his son's failed efforts at dynastic succession may belong to early "narratives about the foundation of the Northern Kingdom" (Sasson, *Judges 1–12*, 341).

24. See, e.g., David M. Howard, "The Case for Kingship in Deuteronomy and the Former Prophets," *Westminster Theological Journal* 52 (1990): 101–15, and Barnabas Lindars, "Gideon and Kingship," *Journal of Theological Studies* 16 (1965): 324–26.
25. There are several possible ways to understand Abimelech's name. Most likely the name refers to a divine father such as "My father [Yahweh] is king" or "My father is [the god] Molech." See Robert G. Boling, *Judges: Introduction, Translation, and Commentary* (AB 6A; Garden City, N.Y.: Doubleday, 1975), 163, and Soggin, *Judges*, 167. In Boling's view, the name is used ironically to communicate the narrator's "sustained contempt" for Abimelech, who is called by name thirty-one times in chapter 9 (Boling, *Judges*, 170). Jack M. Sasson suggests that Gideon renamed this son of a concubine Abimelech, signaling his wish that this son, though born of a secondary wife, "might be accorded elite status" (Sasson, *Judges 1–12*, 376–77).
26. In addition to these examples, there are two additional textual hints of Gideon's monarchic connections. The call of Gideon has parallels with the anointing of Saul. He is visited by an angel at the shrine site of the "Oak of Ophrah." The angel greets Gideon with the phrase "The Lord is with you," a phrase that later characterizes God's election of first Saul and then David. Finally, Gideon's initial rejection of the call—"Pray Lord, how can I deliver Israel? Behold, my clan is the weakest in Manasseh, and I am the least in my family" (Judg 6:15)—parallels Saul's response as well: "Am I not a Benjaminite from the least of the tribes of Israel? And is not my family the humblest of all the tribes of Benjamin?" (1 Sam 9:21). A second textual hint is found in Judg 8:18, where Gideon defeats two foreign kings, Zebah and Zalmunna, and asks after his slain brothers. The two kings describe his brothers as looking just like Gideon in that "they resembled *the sons of a king.*"
27. Victor Matthews asserts that children of a concubine had questionable membership in a household and in the inheritance rights. According to Matthews, these children could only share in their father's estate if the father specifically named them as heirs (Matthews, *Judges and Ruth* [NCBC; Cambridge: Cambridge University Press, 2004], 103).
28. I cover the national house of Hagar in chapter 9.
29. It is also possible that as the breadwinner for the family, Rahab is the head of her household, and her mother and father are her dependents.
30. Robert Boling suggests that the use of the phrase "bone and flesh" is covenantal language hearkening back to Gen 2:23a (Boling, *Judges*, 171). At its most basic level, however, the phrase suggests or seeks to establish a claim to common kinship. See the section below on bone and flesh.
31. See Carolyn S. Leeb, "Polygyny: Insights from Rural Haiti," in *Ancient Israel: The Old Testament in Its Social Context,* ed. Philip S. Esler (Minneapolis: Fortress, 2006), 64.

32. Marc Brettler has shown that the book of Judges was redacted such that it expresses a Deuteronomistic bias for Davidic kingship (Brettler, *The Book of Judges* [London: Routledge, 2002], 111–16).
33. Stripped of the support network of the house of the father, non-inheriting sons are often presented as surrounded by "worthless cohorts." Jephthah, for example, is described as going out on "raids" with a band of "worthless fellows" after being kicked out of his father's house (Judg 11:4). The Canaanite Ba'al Cycle shows a similar insider-outsider status for Baal in the house of his father, El, where he is pitted against the seventy sons of Asherah (see chapter 4).
34. On the symbolic interplay of the numbers one and seventy, see Matthews, *Judges and Ruth*, 101, and J. Gerald Janzen, "A Certain Woman in the Rhetoric of Judges 9," *JSOT* 38 (1987): 33–37.
35. The Davidic messiah is heralded as a "shoot from the stump of Jesse" (Isa 11:1). In Jacob's blessing of Joseph, he lauds his favored son as "a fruitful bough" whose "branches run over the wall" (Gen 49:22). The postexilic prophet Zechariah identifies Zerubbabel, a Davidic descendant, as a "branch," suggesting that he will reestablish the Davidic dynasty (Zech 3:8; 6:12). Daniel uses a similar metaphor of a rooted stump as a site where kingship can be reestablished (Dan 4:15, 23, 26). See also 2 Kings 14:9 where a royal cedar disdains a royally aspiring thistle.
36. See Gen 25:6; 37:2, where sons of primary or legitimate wives are contrasted to groups of men who are sons of lower-status wives.
37. Mark S. Smith discusses the way that weapons of warriors become "extra-somatic body parts" and "markers of identity" (Smith, *Poetic Heroes: Literary Commemorations of Warriors and Warrior Culture in the Early Biblical World* [Grand Rapids, Mich.: Eerdmans, 2014], 17, 352n27, citing Fernando Santos-Granero, *Occult Life of Things: Native Amazonian Theories of Materiality and Personhood* [Tucson: University of Arizona Press, 2009], 14). In this case, a millstone is the quintessential woman's tool, an extra-somatic extension of her body and her female identity, and she uses the tool as a weapon to bring down a king.
38. Jon D. Levenson and Baruch Halpern, "The Political Import of David's Marriages," *JBL* 99, no. 4 (1980): 516.
39. The political nature of Amnon's rape of Tamar and of Absalom's avenging the rape through the murder of Ammon has been discussed by several commentators. Victor H. Matthews and Don C. Benjamin correctly note that Amnon's request that Tamar bake bread in his presence and have sexual intercourse with him is an invitation that Tamar "commit Absalom's resources to Amnon's campaign to become monarch in David's place" (Matthews and Benjamin, "Amnon and Tamar: A Matter of Honor [2 Sam 13:1–38]," in *Crossing Boundaries and Linking Horizons: Studies in Honor of Michael C. Astour on His 80th Birthday*, ed. Gordon Young et al. [Bethesda, Md.: Capital Decisions, 1997], 355–60). For a full discussion of the rape of Tamar and the kinship obligations of uterine brothers in the event of rape, see chapter 4.

40. P. Kyle McCarter, Jr., *II Samuel: A New Translation with Introduction, Notes, and Commentary* (AB 9; New York: Doubleday, 1984), 102.
41. In 2 Sam 13:7, 20, we find that both Amnon and Absalom have "houses" that are part of David's royal house.
42. Placing himself at the city gate would recall the rule of the tribal elders and might signal his exploitation of this group's dissatisfaction with royal power.
43. This of course replicates his father David's move when David had himself crowned king in Hebron in a first attempt at usurping Saul's heir Ishbaal (2 Sam 2:1–11).
44. Other verses that explicitly link Absalom with "Israel," "all Israel," or with the "elders of Israel" include 2 Sam 16:15, 22; 17:4, 11, 13, 14, 15, 24, 26; 18: 6, 7, 16, 17.
45. Hans Wilhelm Hertzberg notes that the additional strategic advantage of Hebron is that the residents of this city might have been angry with David for moving the capital to Jerusalem (Hertzberg, *I and II Samuel: A Commentary*, trans. John Bowden [London: SCM Press, 1964], 337). Jon D. Levenson and Baruch Halpern cite the political significance of Absalom choosing to be crowned in Hebron. They also highlight the kinship connections that make sense of Absalom's choice of Amasa to be his military commander, identifying Amasa as the son of Abigail, David's sister (and possibly wife) and of Calebite stock. They argue, "If, in fact, Amasa is of Calebite descent, one can well understand why the rebellious Davidide Absalom, son of the Geshurite princess Maacah, would want this man of old Yhwhistic stock as his commander" (Levenson and Halpern, "The Political Import of David's Marriages," 511).
46. For Ken Stone, Absalom's act serves a "semiotic function" among men, demonstrating David's inability to control sexual access to the women of his household (Stone, *Practicing Safer Texts: Food, Sex and the Bible in Queer Perspective* [London: T&T Clark, 2005], 71–72). See also Victor H. Matthews and Don C. Benjamin, *Social World of Ancient Israel, 1250–587 BCE* (Peabody, Mass.: Hendrickson, 1993), 180. It is also significant that Absalom is advised to defile his father's concubines by Ahitophel, who is the paternal grandfather of Bathsheba, who was similarly defiled by David after he had seen her bathing on a rooftop (David Daube, "Absalom and the Ideal King," *VT* 47 [1998]: 320–25; Hertzberg, *I and II Samuel*, 350). Baruch Halpern notes, "relations with concubines in Samuel represent a claim on the throne" (Halpern, *David's Secret Demons: Messiah, Murderer, Traitor, King* [Grand Rapids, Mich.: Eerdmans, 2001], 29).
47. Riding on the "mule," a sexually non-reproducing animal, prefigures Absalom's ignominious death and burial with "no monument."
48. Robert Alter points to the parallels between Absalom and Samson with regard to their hair. Both leaders had luxuriant heads of hair. Samson was said never to cut his, and Absalom cuts his in a highly narcissistic way, once a year, weighing the sheerings. The two leaders also come to their deaths in a way that is connected to their hair (Alter, *The David Story: A Translation with Commentary of I and II Samuel* [New York: Norton, 1999], 280–81nn26, 30).

49. Alter notes the double use of the word "heart" in this death scene, translating 2 Sam 18:14, "And he [Joab] took three sticks in his palm and he thrust them into Absalom's heart, still alive in the heart of the terebinth" (Alter, *The David Story*, 306).

50. For a discussion of curses that specifically mark a man's failure in the appropriate performance of masculinity, see Cynthia R. Chapman, *The Gendered Language of Warfare in the Israelite-Assyrian Encounter* (HSM 62; Winona Lake, Ind.: Eisenbrauns, 2004), 41–44. P. Kyle McCarter notes that Absalom receives the burial of a "cursed man" and lists parallel examples in Josh 7:26, 8:29, and 10:27 (McCarter, *II Samuel*, 407). The notation of Absalom's lack of a son contradicts an earlier record of his having three sons and a daughter named Tamar (2 Sam 14:27). Most scholars see this as two separate traditions that cannot be easily reconciled, e.g. Alter, *The David Story*, 281n27. The point of view of the redacted document, however, is clear in presenting Absalom as one who died without an heir.

51. For the English translation, see "The Autobiography of Idrimi (1.148)," trans. Tremper Longman III (*COS* 1: 479–80). Akkadian transliteration can be found in Cemil Bulbul, "The Alalakh Kingdom during the Reign of Idrimi," *History Studies* 2, no. 2 (2010): 17–19. I am following Tremper Longman's translation except with regard to the kinship designations, which I have rendered more literally. Scholars have connected the autobiography of Idrimi to several biblical stories of outlaws (Jephthah, David, Jacob) who leave home only to return to establish their sovereignty. Longman sees these biblical parallels not as direct borrowing but rather as the result of a common hero motif that focuses on outlaws who return to their homeland as heroes (Longman, *Fictional Akkadian Autobiography* [Winona Lake, Ind.: Eisenbrauns, 1991], 72–73).

52. Longman, *Fictional Akkadian Autobiography*, 63–66; Mario Liverani, *Myth and Politics in Ancient Near Eastern Historiography* (London: Equinox, 2004), 85–96; Jack M. Sasson, "On Idrimi and Sarruwa, the Scribe," in *Studies on the Civilization and Culture of the Nuzi and the Hurrians in Honor of Ernest R. Lacheman on His Seventy-Fifth Birthday*, ed. M. A. Morrison and D. I. Owen (Winona Lake, Ind.: Eisenbrauns, 1981), 309–24. Michael Astour considers Idrimi's autobiography "a reliable historical text" that dates "shortly after Idrimi's death," which he puts at around 1480 (Astour, *Hittite History and Absolute Chronology of the Bronze Age* [Partille, Sweden: Paul Åström, 1989], 18, 21).

53. "The Autobiography of Idrimi (1.148)" (*COS* 1: 479, lines 5–6).

54. Mario Liverani compares Idrimi's refuge with maternal relatives to Joash's rescue by his aunt and notes the common mythological pattern where a usurping royal hero takes refuge with maternal relatives in order to be "reborn" as a king (Liverani, *Myth and Politics*, 153).

55. According to Mario Liverani, Idrimi's brothers become "antiheroes because of their inability to act." Idrimi is "the hero (who leaves)" and his brothers are the "nonheroes (who stay)" (Liverani, *Myth and Politics*, 90). I would add that the

non-heroes are men who choose maternal links; they stay in their mother's sisters' houses, while Idrimi recognizes he must leave and return to reclaim his father's house.

56. "The Autobiography of Idrimi (1.148)" (*COS* 1: 479–80, lines 25–27).
57. The "brothers" that Idrimi gathers and takes back with him to Alalaḫ are likely his treaty allies, who are referred to as brothers in line 42. His older brothers from his father's house are forgotten once they choose "servitude" in maternally defined space.
58. "The Autobiography of Idrimi (1.148)" (*COS* 1: 479–80, lines 90–91).
59. Some argue that when Satan suggests that if God stretches out his hand and touches "his bone and his flesh," he is in fact referring to Job's wife (Job 2:5). Since it is Job's body that is ultimately struck with boils, the reference to "bone and flesh" more likely refers to Job's physical being and not to his wife.
60. Jephthah, like Abimelech, has to flee his father's house, but there is no indication that the land to which he flees, the land of Tob, is the natal home of his mother (Judg 11:1–3). Phyllis Bird defines the social status of a *zōnâ* as "an outcast, though not an outlaw, a tolerated but dishonored member of society. She normally has the legal status as a free citizen" (Bird, "The Harlot as Heroine," in *Women in the Hebrew Bible: A Reader,* ed. Alice Bach [New York: Routledge, 1999], 100).
61. "Kirta," in Michael D. Coogan and Mark S. Smith, *Stories from Ancient Canaan,* 2nd ed. (Louisville: Westminster John Knox, 2012), 73–74, column 2, lines 1–5; *KTU* 1.14, II, 1–5.

Chapter 9. Like Rachel and Leah Who Together Built Up the House of Israel

1. I discuss Gen 25 in chapter 1 and note that Sarah's name appears only as "Abraham's wife" in reference to Abraham's burial with her in the ancestral cave.
2. A beautiful visual representation of this phenomenon is found on the Zinjirli stele, which shows King Esarhaddon in profile with divine symbols clustered over his right hand showing his favored status. At his feet, tiny versions of the king of Tyre and the crown prince of Egypt are held on a leash. At his sides are the two crown princes that Esarhaddon had named as his heirs in his succession treaty, Ashurbanipal and Shamash-Shum-Ukin. Absent from this stele showing male succession are any mothers. See a discussion and image in Sarah C. Melville, *The Role of Naqia/Zakutu in Sargonid Politics* (SAAS 9; Helsinki: Neo-Assyrian Text Corpus Project, 1999), 47–51.
3. Abraham as a nation founder is promised numerous seed who will possess the gate of their enemies (Gen 22:16–18).
4. The preposition "from upon" (*mēʿālay*) seems to refer to removing a person from a household such that he or she could make no economic claims on that household in the future. Abraham sends Ishmael and the sons of Keturah "eastward"

"from upon" Isaac (Gen 25:6). Amnon, after raping and rejecting Tamar as a potential wife, has his servant send her "from upon him" and bolt the door behind her (2 Sam 13:17).
5. Abraham ultimately has eight sons, but his house in Gen 16–23 is presented as one that produces two sons.
6. Susanne Scholz sees Lot as a victim of rape (Scholz, *Sacred Witness: Rape in the Hebrew Bible* [Minneapolis: Fortress, 2010], 169). Johanna Stiebert notes how unusual it is to find two virgin daughters who take the initiative in sex. She provides an excellent overview of feminist analyses of this story from those that celebrate Lot's daughters' agency to those that see this as emblematic of patriarchy (Seiebert, *Fathers and Daughters in the Hebrew Bible* [Oxford: Oxford University Press, 2013], 131–44).
7. In Hosea's marriage to Gomer, Yahweh commands him to name one of his children *lō' 'ammî*, or "Not My People," to signify that Yahweh has revoked his paternal claim on this people (Hosea 1:9). The name *ben-'ammî* would therefore be the positive form of this name, whereby a god claims a people as his own (see Hosea 2:25).
8. The Amalekites are another hated nation within the biblical tradition, a nation whose memory Yahweh vows to utterly blot out according to Exod 17:14. The genealogy of Esau indicates that they too are sons of a concubine, identifying Amalek as the son of Esau's son Eliphaz with his concubine Timna (Gen 36:12).
9. See the promises made to Abram in Gen 15:5; 22:17.
10. In Phyllis Trible's view, both Sarah and Hagar "pay the price of patriarchy" (Trible, "Ominous Beginnings for a Promise of Blessings," in *Hagar, Sarah, and Their Children: Jewish, Christian, and Muslim Perspectives*, ed. Phyllis Trible and Letty M. Russell [Louisville: Westminster John Knox, 2006], 54). Tikva Frymer-Kensky is too sanguine in her view of the stories of Hagar and Sarah and their respective sons as "a model of separation without denigration" (Frymer-Kensky, "Hagar, My Other Self," in *Reading the Women of the Bible* [New York: Schocken, 2002], 225–37).
11. See chapter 5 text at note 43 and the note.
12. Phyllis Trible notes that Hagar does not simply name the site; she calls directly on the name of the Lord, who spoke to her saying, "You are El Roi." She therefore becomes for Trible a "theologian" (Trible, "Ominous Beginnings," 41). I agree with Trible's evaluation of this scene as being theologically significant to the theme of covenantal promise that weaves through Genesis, but Hagar's direct encounter with Yahweh, and her individualized covenant, ultimately places her son and grandsons under a maternal covenant, and it denies them a claim to their paternal, Abrahamic covenant.
13. This departure notice clearly parallels that of both Abraham and Rebekah (Gen 12:5; 24:59–61).

14. This is the only place in Genesis that Succoth appears. In Pss 60:6 and 108:7, Succoth is used in parallel with Shechem, suggesting a close association between the two cities. In the story of Gideon, Succoth has negative associations when the people of Succoth refuse to provide provisions for Gideon's army (Judg 8:4–7).
15. "'ummâ," BDB: 52; HALOT 1: 62; DCH 1: 312.
16. "gôy," HALOT 1: 62.
17. DCH 1: 312.
18. HALOT 1: 62.
19. The Qumran occurrence is cited in DCH 1: 312, and can be found in 4QD^a 11: 10 (i.e., fragment 11, line 10), DJD 18: 76. The proposed reading of Isa 55:4 as a form of 'ummâ is suggested in HALOT 2: 428.
20. Abraham Malamat, "*Ummatum* in Old Babylonian Texts and Its Ugaritic and Biblical Counterparts," *UF* 11 (1980): 527–36.
21. *CAD* U/W, 116–17.
22. Malamat, "*Ummatum*," 532–33.
23. My discussion of the phrase "*'l 'umty*" is found in chapters 4 and 6.
24. This translation follows the NRSV. JPS reads, "twelve chieftains *of as many tribes.*"
25. In Gen 21:21, we learn that Hagar obtained "a wife" for Ishmael from Egypt. There is no mention of further marriages.
26. "*Ḥāṣēr*," BDB: 347. See also "a permanent settlement, yard without walls," "court, enclosure," *HALOT* 1: 345.
27. "*ṭîrâ*," BDB: 377. The word *ṭîrâ* is used in parallel with "tent(s)" in Ps 69:26 (*HALOT* 2: 374).
28. Baruch Levine, *Numbers 21–36: A New Translation with Introduction and Commentary* (New York: Doubleday, 2000), 290–91.
29. The masculine plural ending on '*ummim* led Mitchell Dahood to repoint the text as *ēmîm*, meaning "gods" or "frightful ones" (Dahood, *Psalms III: 101–150: Introduction, Translation and Notes with an Appendix, The Grammar of the Psalter* [AB 17A; Garden City, N.Y.: Doubleday, 1970], 152).
30. Levine, *Numbers 21–36*, 291.
31. BDB: 1081a. *HALOT* classifies '*ummâ* as part of "Middle Hebrew" and Aramaic, including specifically biblical Aramaic, and defines the term as "tribe, small group of people" ("'*ummâ*," *HALOT* 1: 62).
32. 4QD^a 11: 9–10. See James H. Charlesworth, *Damascus Document II: Some Works of the Torah and Related Documents: The Dead Sea Scrolls: Hebrew, Aramaic, and Greek Texts with English Translations III* (Louisville: Westminster John Knox, 2006), 68–69.
33. "*lĕ'ōm, lĕ'ôm*," BDB: 522; "*lĕ'ōm, lĕ'ôm*," *HALOT* 2: 513; "*lĕ'ōm*," *DCH* 4: 496–97. D. Preuss identifies the term as "poetic" and "late" and suggests that in later Hebrew, the term '*ummâ* may have replaced *lĕ'ōm* (Preuss, "*lĕ'ōm*," *TDOT* 7: 397–98).

There are not enough examples of the term *'ummâ* in late texts to support this thesis.

34. 1 Chron 12:28 [Eng. 12:27], where Jehoiada is "prince of Aaron" (*hannāgîd lĕ'ahărōn*), and 2 Chron 19:11, where Zebediah, son of Ishmael, is "prince of the house of Judah" (*hannāgîd lĕbêt-yĕhûdâ*). In almost every other case where we find the noun "prince" (*nāgîd*), a man is a prince "over" (*'al*) something. The participial noun *mĕṣawwê* is otherwise unattested, so we cannot draw any conclusions about which preposition is most appropriate.

35. E.g., "my brother, the son of my mother" (see chapter 4). *DCH* reads both words as plurals of *lĕ'ōm*: "witness of nations/commander of peoples" but acknowledges the possibility of reading "witness of nations/commander *for* people [= *'ummim*]" ("*lĕ'ōm*," *DCH* 4: 497; "*'ummâ*," *DCH* 1: 312; see also "*lĕ'ōm*," *HALOT* 2: 428). There are also several psalms that contain the phrase *bal-'ummim*, but they are correctly read and translated as *bil'ummim*, "among nations," rather than "no mother-units" (Ps 44:15 [Eng. 44:14]; 57:10 [Eng. 57:9]; 149:7). *DCH* treats these psalms under the term "*lĕ'ōm*" (*DCH* 4: 496–97).

36. The territories of Judah, Benjamin, Ephraim, and Manasseh represent the earliest and most enduring settlements of what becomes the nation of Israel. Together, they are the geographic and ideological center of the nation of Israel. See the maps of early Israelite settlements in Lawrence E. Stager, "Forging an Identity: The Emergence of Ancient Israel," in *The Oxford History of the Biblical World*, ed. Michael D. Coogan (New York: Oxford University Press, 1998), 95–96.

37. Even in Dan's earlier southern, coastal territorial allotment, this tribe was peripheral.

38. Interestingly, the first four judges of note in the book of Judges come from the same four king-making tribes: Othniel (Judah), Ehud (Benjamin), Deborah (Ephraim), and Gideon (Manasseh). The concluding story of the book of Judges is that of the Levite's concubine, and there we find the three king-making tribes together with the priestly tribe: "a certain Levite" from the "hill country of Ephraim" with "a concubine from Bethlehem in Judah," who is ultimately assaulted by the men of "Benjamin." An old man from "the hill country in Ephraim" takes this couple in to protect them, but ultimately the Judean concubine is sexually assaulted to the point of death by Benjaminites (Judg 19).

39. The story of Abimelech's claim to kingship is covered in chapter 8.

40. See chapter 2.

41. When Rachel finally overcomes her barrenness, she names her firstborn son "Joseph," saying, "May the Lord add to me another son" (Gen 30:24). Benjamin is the son who is ultimately added to her house (Gen 35:16–21).

42. David J. Schloen, *The House of the Father as Fact and Symbol: Patrimonialism in Ugarit and the Ancient Near East* (Winona Lake, Ind.: Eisenbrauns, 2001), 154 (citing Mic 5:2 [Eng. 5:1]; 1 Chron 2:19, 24, 50; 4:4). See also the discussion of

Ephratha in Bethlehem in Norman K. Gottwald, *The Tribes of Yahweh: A Sociology of the Religion of Liberated Israel, 1250–1050 B.C.E.* (Maryknoll, N.Y.: Orbis, 1979), 274–75.

43. We see a similarly creative strategy at work in a much later New Testament text when Paul shuffles the maternal sub-houses within the household of Abraham. For Paul, Abraham's two wives represent "two covenants." Moreover, these two wives have distinct geographies: Hagar represents Sinai, bondage, and the "present Jerusalem." Sarah represents freedom and "the Jerusalem above." Paul then identifies those who follow Jesus as children of Sarah, the "freewoman" of Jerusalem, born of "the promise" that was Isaac's. Those Jews who did not follow Jesus were born into a covenant of "bondage" as children of Hagar (Gal 4:21–30).

44. Levine, *Numbers 21–36*, 136.

45. Martin Noth, *Numbers: A Commentary*, trans. James D. Martin (Philadelphia: Westminster, 1968), 24.

46. Levine, *Numbers 21–36*, 144. See also Zecharia Kallai, "The Twelve-Tribe Systems of Israel," *VT* 47, no. 1 (1997): 87.

47. Mary Douglas, *In the Wilderness: The Doctrine of Defilement in the Book of Numbers* (Sheffield, Eng.: JSOT Press, 1993), 177.

48. Levine, *Numbers 21–36*, 142–43; Douglas, *In the Wilderness*, 179.

49. This matches the description of the "molten sea" placed in the courtyard of Solomon's temple. This enormous bronze basin was placed "upon twelve oxen, three facing north, three facing west, three facing south, and three facing east" (1 Kings 7:25). The ordering of the compass points in this text seems to be from least valued to most valued.

50. Michael M. Homan, *To Your Tents, O Israel! Terminology, Function, Form, and Symbolism of Tents in the Hebrew Bible and the Ancient Near East* (Culture and History of the Ancient Near East, vol. 7; Leiden: E. J. Brill, 2002), 32–34. While Homan notes the maternal organization of the tent encampment, he does not account for the placement of Reuben and Simeon in the south or Asher in the north. In what follows, I show how the ordering in Num 2 builds on narrative details found in Gen 35:22; 48:1–7; 49; and Num 25.

51. The northern compass point is less valued because when one faces the preferred east, the south is at one's right hand and is therefore valued over the left-hand-associated north.

52. Jacob Milgrom identifies Gad as "the first alternate" to the biological sons of Leah, completing the second grouping of three (Milgrom, *Numbers: The Traditional Hebrew Text with the New JPS Translation Commentary* [JPS Torah Commentaries; Philadelphia: JPS, 1990], 8). See also Num 26, where Gad replaces Levi in a census in which the Leah tribes are listed by birth order followed by the Rachel tribes. Zecharia Kallai notes that Gad replaces Levi in this tribal organization, but Kallai is not concerned with why Gad is the replace-

ment as opposed to another son of Jacob (Kallai, "The Twelve-Tribe Systems of Israel," 64). The reason Gad is "the first alternate," or the replacement for Levi, is that Gad is the firstborn son of Leah's maidservant, and the southern contingent is the Zilpah contingent.

53. We also find Reuben heading a maidservant grouping of tribes in Deut 27:11–14. Moses tells the Israelites gathered on the eastern side of the Jordan that once they have crossed the Jordan into the Promised Land, six tribes are to stand on Mount Gerizim "to bless the nation" and six tribes are to stand on Mount Ebal "to curse the nation." Reuben, as the Jacob-cursed son, heads the tribal grouping that will "curse the nation," and all four of the maidservant tribes are listed under Reuben in his cursing group. The presence of Zebulun in the maidservant group is harder to explain but could possibly relate to his geographic placement among maidservant tribes. All the tribes in the group that announces a blessing are sons of wives, and several found important royal or priestly houses.

54. Martin Noth summarizes the military arrangement of the tribes, identifying Judah as the "vanguard" and Joseph as the "rearguard" with the northern and southern companies representing the flanks (Noth, *Numbers*, 25).

Index of Subjects

Aaron, 24, 218fig.11, 220, 223, 225, 253n64, 290n3, 299n34

Abigail, 288n69

Abimelech: annihilation of his own *bêt 'āb*, 191; Baal-sponsored efforts of, 186, 187; Deuteronomistic Historian on, 183–84, 186; Gideon's sons murdered by, 167, 185, 186, 197; in house of the father of the mother, 174–75, 185, 186; impact of mother's status on, 197; inheritance claims of, 186–87, 236n18; Jotham, relations with, 186, 187, 197; kinship with Shechemites, 175, 184–85, 186, 187–88, 191–92, 194, 197; name of, 183, 292n25; retreat to Geshurites, 190; royal succession narrative of, 183–84, 186, 190–91, 194, 291n23; Shechemite concubine mother of, 167, 175, 184–86, 190–91, 236n18

Abishai, 97–98, 289n76

Abkhazian culture, 128, 270n17

Abner, 97–98

Abraham/Abram: birth of Isaac, 138, 242n103; childbirth and establishment of his house, 153, 157; dating of narrative, 51–52, 233n51; death and burial of Sarah, 52, 244n120; death of, 41, 52, 211–12; Isaac as heir to, 55, 92, 140, 201, 247n15, 283n15; Jacob as the chosen of, 92, 93; kin relation to Sarah, 138–39; Lot, 162, 203–4, 285n44, 296n4, 297n6; marriage negotiations for Isaac, 53–54; maternal sub-units in house of, 5; New Testament on maternal sub-houses in, 300n43; as remembered by Judean exiles, 35; sends away the sons of his concubine, 99, 211; servant of, 52–55, 57, 73; wealth of, 38–39, 41, 42; Yahweh's covenantal promise to, 92, 139–40, 201, 204–6, 207, 276n65. *See also* Hagar; Keturah, sons of; Sarah/Sarai

Abrahamic covenant, 139–40, 149, 182, 201, 205, 207, 276n65

Absalom, 103fig.7; Amnon murdered by, 100, 102, 175, 260n16; avenges Tamar's rape, 98, 100, 102, 189, 252n59, 260n16, 293n39; as cursed, 191–92, 295n50; David as father of, 98, 191, 194; death of, 191–92, 294n49; Maacah as mother of, 98, 100, 167, 168, 171, 175, 189; refuge in house of the father of the mother, 175, 189–90; royal aspirations of, 190–91, 294nn45,49

Abu-Lughod, Lila, 10, 40, 231n33, 245n128, 254n73

Ackerman, Susan, 26, 130, 137, 275n54

Adad-Guppi, 268n38

303

304   Index of Subjects

ʿAdāyāhû, 285n42
Adonijah, 167, 168fig.8, 171, 172, 228
adoption, 59, 145–46, 148, 270n17, 279n93, 280n101, 282n101
agnatic descent, 10, 127, 230n19, 231n21, 268n45
Ahab, King, 24, 286n56
Ahaziah, 123–24
Ahinoam, 169, 170, 189, 288n69, 289n77
Ahitophel, 294n45
Akkadian, 13, 103–4, 130, 210–12, 267n31, 270n17, 271n29
Albertz, Rainer, 159, 161, 285n42
Alter, Robert, 281n1, 294nn48,49
ʿam (nation or people), 25
ʾāmâ (maidservant), 242n104
Amalekites, 297n8
Amasa (David's military commander), 194, 195, 294n45
Amnon, 103fig.7; Absalom's revenge against, 102, 189; genealogy of, 98, 102, 189, 203; house of, 190; murder of, 171, 175, 289n77; rape of Tamar, 74, 79, 98–102, 189, 243n111, 260n16, 293n39, 296n4; rejection of Tamar, 99–100; Tamar's proposal of marriage, 99–100, 252n59
Amram (Moses's father), 143, 290n3
Anat, 104–5, 107, 108–9, 114–15, 135, 211
Apsu, 131
ʾăqārâ (barren), 93
Aqhat epic, 104–5, 211, 262nn36,37
Arab society, 9–10, 126–27
Aramaic, ʾummâ in, 214, 216
archaeology, 16, 20, 29–31, 86–88, 235n6, 239n56
Arnold, Bill, 229n10
Asher, 23fig.2, 223, 224fig.11
Asherah, 106–8, 130, 131, 267n31, 272n35, 286n56
Ashurbanipal, 103–4, 130–31, 167, 261n29, 270n17, 271n29, 272n31, 296n2
Astour, Michael, 295n52
Athaliah, 102–3, 124

Baal: Anat as sister of, 104–5, 107, 108–9, 114–15, 135, 211; Asherah, 106–8; battle against Mot, 108; battle with sons of Asherah, 167; El, 106, 107, 108, 109, 131; Mot, 95–96, 106–7, 108, 114–15, 211; parentage of, 106; as "your mother's suckling," 108
Baal-berith, 187
Baal Cycle: cohorts of non-inheriting sons in, 293n33; maternal clans in, 108; rivals for kingship in, 106–7; Shapsu, 108, 109; siblings in, 114–15; womb terminology in, 114–15; Yam, 106–7
Baal Peor, 212
Babylonian Chronicles, 288n67
Babylonian creation story, 131
Barbiero, Gianni, 273n42
barren (ʾăqārâ), 93
Bathsheba, 171–72, 189, 228, 242n104, 289n79, 291n15, 294n45
bayit (house): and the birth of children, 151, 282n7; chambers in, 62, 77–81, 84–85, 110, 116–20, 149, 195, 255n16, 266nn28,29; of commoners, 24, 25, 31, 34, 36–38, 81, 87, 237n29; deity makes for a person a house, 162; *gēr* in, 22, 236n21; *ḥeder* in, 79–80, 85, 255n15; hierarchies within, 25–26, 27–28; house societies, 32–33; of King Solomon, 80; origin narratives, 34–35; pillared houses, 16, 20, 29–31, 87–88, 235n6, 239n56; removal from, 203, 296n4, 297n7; as reward for fearing God, 162–63; use of term, 20–22, 24–26, 28, 235n10; of Yahweh, 24, 26, 34, 78, 85, 187, 222, 237n28. See also *bĕkôr;* house of the father; house of the mother; nesting; tent; *tôlēdôt*
Bedouins, 10, 40, 245n128
Beer-lahai-roi, 42–43, 206, 297n12
begats, 1, 2, 4, 53, 203–4, 297n6

běkôr (firstborn or designated heir): defined, 11, 158, 236n17; as designated heir, 22, 236n17; in foundational houses, 21; Joseph as, 44–45; lost status as, 217, 219, 223–25; *peṭer reḥem*, 151, 158; in polygynous households, 158; rite of redemption for, 160; *yôrēš* as, 91, 92; *zeraʿ*, 91, 92
Bēl, 131
Ben-ammi, 204, 297n7
Běnāyāh, 161
Bendor, Shunya, 26, 28, 238n34
Benjamin, 23fig.2, 218fig.11; as king-making tribe, 217–19, 299n38; *raḥămîm* in relation to Joseph, 110, 111; reunion with Joseph, 110–11, 179, 209; territory of, 299n36; as uterine brother to Joseph, 45–46, 47–48, 63, 94, 133, 166–67, 209
Benjamin, Don C., 293n39
Berlin, Adele, 76–77, 287n58
Berquist, Jon, 288n68
bêt ʾāb (house of the father). *See* house of the father
bêt ʾēm (house of the mother). *See* house of the mother
beṭen (belly, womb), 111, 117, 259n3, 264n3, 280n98
Bethlehem, 220–21
Bethuel, 180fig.10; death of, 55, 248n19; genealogy of, 4, 52, 53, 143, 176, 247n9; in Genesis 24 narrative, 53, 55–56, 58; in Jacob narrative, 174; Laban as successor to, 55–56, 179; in Rebekah's *bêt ʾēm*, 55–57; role in Rebekah's marriage negotiations, 57
bêt ʾîšāh (house of her husband), 28–29, 60, 61, 250n39
betrothals, 51–57, 59, 62–63, 64–65
bětûlâ (young woman), 53, 93, 247n10
Bilhah, 23fig.2, 44, 46, 48, 151, 155, 163, 223, 224fig.12
binding of Isaac, 201
Bird, Phyllis, 296n60

Black Obelisk of Shalmaneser III of Assyria, 21
Bloch, Ariel, 119, 255n17
Bloch, Chana, 119, 255n17
Bloch-Smith, Elizabeth, 11, 233n49, 243n113
b-n-h (build), 150, 161, 281nn2,4, 282n10
Boaz: Elimelech replaced by, 144, 152, 166; as father of Obed, 166; Gospel of Matthew on, 166; as house builder, 144, 152, 166; house building for, 166, 222; marriage blessing to, 152, 165, 202, 220–21; Naomi as kin to, 165–66; paternity of, 148
Boling, Robert G., 292nn25,30
"bone and flesh": biblical references to, 189, 195–96, 296n59; as connected to heart, 194–95; in creation narratives, 82, 195, 196; house of the father of the mother, 193–96; in kinship relatedness, 126, 179–81, 185, 193, 194–95, 199, 292n30; in physiological formation, 82, 195
Bonte, Pierre, 82
break forth (*piṣḥi*), 160
breast milk and breastfeeding: as adoption, 145, 270n17, 279n93, 282n101; divine breast milk, 130–31, 271nn24,28; ethnicity received through, 15, 59, 68, 73–74, 126, 139, 141–49, 249n29, 272n35, 277n73, 280nn101,103, 297n6; *ḫêq*, 145, 146, 147, 279n95, 280nn97,98; impact on male children, 129, 270n17; Islamic views of, 127; loyalty pacts, 129, 270n17; milk kinship, 125, 127, 128, 134, 140, 142, 270n17, 273n43, 279n93; naming in narratives, 280n99; Nazirite ritual status established from birth, 134; "nursed at my mother's breasts" indicating uterine brothers, 18, 58, 62–63, 67, 93–94, 105, 118–19, 126, 133–34; nursing at the breasts of goddesses, 130–31, 272n35;

306   Index of Subjects

breast milk and breastfeeding (*continued*) nutrition transmitted by, 137–38; royalty transmitted through, 130–31, 132, 273n40; of Samuel by Hannah, 137; social status and, 126, 140, 276n67; stages of, 116–17, 266n28; traits transmitted through, 126–29, 131–32, 137–38, 142, 272n35, 275n56, 279n92; transformative nature of, 273n37; Trobriand Island peoples on, 129, 271n22; two women who claimed to be mothers of the same infant boy (1 Kings 3:17–18), 113, 147, 184–85, 242n104; weaning, 116–17, 137, 138; wet nurses, 128, 132, 139, 140–42, 145–46, 149, 275n62, 279n90
Brenner, Athalya, 145, 282n8, 287n61
Brettler, Marc, 293n32
"Bridal Songs of Inanna," 249n28
brides, transfer into husband's household, 155, 283n25
bridewealth (*mohar*), 65, 71–72, 248n26, 252n55
b-r-k (to kneel), 52
Brody, Aaron, 87
"brother, son of mother," 13, 76, 91, 93–96, 104, 114, 299n35
brother-brokered marriages, 56, 64–66, 68, 94, 254n73
Bunimovitz, Shlomo, 29, 30, 235n6, 239n56
burial practices, 41–42, 52, 243n113, 244nn116,120

Campbell, Edward, 60, 249n29
Carr, David, 52
chambers (*ḥeder*), 62, 77–81, 84–85, 110, 120, 255nn15,16
childbirth: appositional epithets identifying son of his mother's womb, 121, 268n38; blessings at time of, 163; childlessness, 73–74, 162, 260n22, 266n28, 285nn44,45,46; and the desire to be "built up," 150–52, 154–55, 161–63, 166–67, 173–74, 222, 227, 281nn2,4, 282n10; infertility, 93, 121, 152–54, 156, 160–61, 164, 266n28, 267n37; maternal space associated with, 110; midwives, 117, 162–63; as nation building, 151–52, 161, 201–2, 222, 282nn7,10,11; prestige of, 151, 161–65, 282nn8,10; as raising mothers' status, 159–63; *reḥem*, 111, 112, 264nn1,3; surrogacy, 153–55, 161, 165–66, 283n17, 287n61; traits transmitted through, 122–24, 126–29, 131–32, 137–38, 142, 272n35, 275n56, 279n92; vineyard metaphors, 160; whoredom, 112, 196, 197; and Yahweh, 92, 112–17, 138, 144, 153, 156–57, 159–61, 163
childlessness: *'ăqārâ*, 93; associated with death, 162; in Nuzi marriage contracts, 285n46; and the return of a woman to her uterine household, 73–74, 285nn43,45; *šômēmâ*, 160, 261n22, 285nn39,43,45
children: celebration of birth of, 164; and economic and social prestige, 164–65; establishment of paternity, 158–59; names, 159, 161, 163, 285n42, 297n7; traits transmitted through breast milk, 126–29, 131–32, 137–38, 142, 272n35, 275n56
children of girls (Nuer term), 37, 40
Chileab, 289nn77,79
Chilion, 143
chronological sequence of maternally focused terms, 120–21, 267n37
circumcision, 65, 122, 142, 149, 277n72
clan (*mišpāḥâ*), 12, 25, 105–6, 237n32, 238n34, 291n18
Clements, R. E., 35
cognatic kinship, 123, 177
commoners, houses of, 24–25, 31, 34, 36–38, 81, 87, 237n29
conception, 62, 77, 78–79, 81, 120
concubines, 23fig.2; Abimelech as son of, 175, 184; Abraham's treatment of, 99, 211, 243n113, 244n120;

Index of Subjects   307

distinguished from wives, 184; inheritance claims of sons of, 186–87; Levite's concubine, 250n38; marriage arranged by primary wives, 165; nonresident concubines, 190–91, 236n18; status of children of, 44, 45, 184, 292nn25,27. *See also* Hagar; Keturah, sons of
Conte, Edouard, 9–10, 18, 126–27, 231n21
Coogan, Michael D., 105
covenantal promises, 92, 122, 123, 139–40, 149, 162, 182, 201, 204–7, 268n45, 276n65
Cozbi, 213, 214, 215
creation narrative: begats, 1, 2, 4, 53, 203–4, 297n6; Cain and Abel, 290n3; Eve, 82, 256n28; rib, 82, 282n10; serpent in Eden, 177, 290n8; verbs in, 82, 256n28
curtains (*yĕrîʿōt*), 77–78, 85, 87–88

Dagan, 106
Dahood, Mitchell, 298n29
dam (blood), 126–27
Damkina, 131
Dan, 23fig.2, 163, 223, 224fig.12
dating biblical narratives, 51–52, 59, 61, 221–22, 233n51, 246n3, 249n29, 250n40
Daughter of Zion, 84
daughters of Lot, 162, 203–4, 285n44, 297n6
David, 103fig.7, 169fig.9; Absalom as son of, 98, 191, 194; Bathsheba, 294n45; birth story of, 69–70, 144, 286n56; covenantal promises to, 122, 162; Deuteronomistic bias for Davidic kingdom, 293n32; genealogy of, 59, 68, 73–74, 98, 144, 148, 168, 189, 202, 219–22, 228, 249nn29,31, 280n103, 289n77; and the house of Saul, 70, 167–68, 169fig.9, 170–72, 190, 288n68, 289nn75,76,77; Judean ethnicity of, 166; Maacah as wife of, 98, 100, 103fig.7, 167, 168, 171, 175, 189; Moabite ancestry of, 59, 68, 73–74, 144, 148, 220, 249n29; mourning the death of Amnon, 102; as related to the marriage blessing to Boaz, 220–21; relations with elders of Judah, 194–95; in story of Amnon and Tamar, 99–100, 252n59, 261n20; succession narrative of, 167, 189, 288n68; wives of, 169–72, 189, 228, 242n104, 288n69, 289nn75,77,79, 291n15; womb-opening sons of, 167, 168fig.8, 288n69. *See also* Abimelech; Absalom; Amnon; Tamar (David's daughter)
Davidic messiah, 293n35
Deir ʿAlla inscription, 266n29
Delaney, Carol, 121–22
de Moor, Johannes C., 115
de Vaux, Roland, 21
DH (Deuteronomistic Historian), 168, 183–84, 186, 189–90, 293n32
Dinah, 23fig.2, 66fig.6, 103fig.7; brothers of (*see* Levi; Simeon); brothers refer to her as "our daughter," 260n9; brothers' revenge on behalf of, 65–66, 96–97, 101; childlessness, 260n22; half-brothers, as Jacob's sons, 101; as Jacob's daughter, 64, 96; as Leah's daughter, 64, 67, 251n51; marriage negotiations for Shechem, 64–66; maternal genealogy of, 64, 251nn50,51; Rebekah's marriage negotiations compared with, 66–67. *See also* rape of Dinah
Douglas, Mary, 11
dowry, 71, 74, 248n26
Driver, Samuel Rolles, 276nn64,65, 281n4

Ea, 131
Edom, 114, 277n74; Edom/Esau, 114
El (Baal Cycle), 106, 107, 108, 109, 131, 272n35
Eliakim, 287n67

Elijah, 24
Elimelech, 60, 143, 152, 165, 166
Elkanah, 135, 156, 274nn45,46
El Shaddai, 111–12, 117–18, 264n7
Emar, 192
Enkidu, 131
Enuma Elish (Babylonian creation story), 131
Ephraim, 217, 223, 224fig.12, 280n101, 299nn36,38
Ephrathah, 220–21
Esarhaddon, 103–4, 130, 270n17, 271n29, 296n2
Esau, 42fig.3, 180fig.10; burial of Isaac, 244n116; cognatic descent, 123; genealogy of, 42, 114, 244n116, 297n8; parental pairing with Isaac, 176–77; personality of, 177, 178; physical appearance of, 123, 268n46; relations with Jacob, 69, 95, 114, 176–77, 178, 206–9
Eskenazi, Tamara Cohn, 60
ethnic identity, 122–23, 141–43, 146, 149, 268n45, 277n73
ethnicity: breastfeeding as source of, 15, 59, 68, 73–74, 126, 139, 141–49, 249n29, 272n35, 277n73, 280nn101,103, 297n6; of Moses, 141–42, 277n73
etiologies of names, 163–64
Evans-Pritchard, E. E., 8–9
Eve (Ḥawwâ), 82, 256n28, 282n10
exiles, return of, 22–23, 132, 273n39
Ezekiel, 24, 31, 34, 85, 123, 195, 222, 237n28, 287n67, 288n67

father's house. *See* house of the father
Faust, Avraham, 29, 30, 235n6, 239n56
Feeley-Harnik, Gillian, 288n69
female speaker in Song of Songs: brings lovers into house of the mother, 62–63, 79, 251n45; Daughters of Jerusalem identified with, 62; father of, 261n19; identity of, 68; my mother's sons referred to by, 94; public displays of affection between siblings, 134; uterine brothers of, 61–62, 63, 64, 67, 261n19
firstborn (term). *See bĕkôr*
Fortes, Meyer, 9
Fritz, Volkmar, 235n6
Frymer-Kensky, Tikva, 60, 251n50

Gaal ben Ebed, 187–88
Gad, 23fig.2, 224fig.12
g-b-r (to be manly, to be strong), 154, 283n19
Gĕberet (mistress, lady, queen mother), 154, 283nn20,22
gēr, gērîm (sojourner, alien, resident worker), 22, 236n21
Gerleman, G., 279n93
Gideon (Jerubbaal): Abimelech as son of, 174–75, 183–84, 236n18, 292n25; connections with Manasseh, 218, 219, 291n23, 292n26, 299n38; death of, 185; dynastic rule refused by, 183, 218; in the foundation of the Northern Kingdom, 291n23; Jotham son of, 186, 187, 191, 197; on maternal kinship, 13, 97–98; monarchic connections, 292n6; seventy sons of, 92, 175, 184, 186, 286n56; Shechemite concubine mother of Abimelech, 167, 175, 184–86, 190–91, 236n18
gift giving, 41, 53, 54, 71, 73, 243n110, 248n26
Giladi, Avner, 127, 128
Gilgamesh (hero), 131
Gillespie, Susan D., 31–33, 34–35
God of heaven and earth, 52, 246n3
Good, William, 128
Goshen, 47–48
Gottwald, Norman K., 21
Gôy (nation), 215, 216
Granqvist, Hilma, 71
Greenspahn, Frederick, 26, 236n17

Greenstein, Edward, 287n59
Gruber, Mayer I., 113, 116, 139

Hadad, 277n74
Hagar, 42fig.3; banishment of, 243n113; descendants transporting Joseph to Egypt, 45; foreign status of, 40, 154, 184, 242n105, 287n61; Ishmael as son of, 40, 41–42, 166; Naomi-Ruth story compared with Sarah-Hagar story, 165, 287n61; in New Testament, 300n43; as potential wet nurse for Isaac, 139–40; pregnancy of, 154, 166; Sarai as mistress of, 154, 166, 184; as satellite of the house of the mother, 184, 254n1; as slave girl of Sarai, 155, 205; and the status of Sarah, 153–54, 283n17; as subunit of house of Abraham, 184; as surrogate for Sarah, 154–55, 165, 287n61; theophany at Beer-lahai-roi, 42–43, 205–6, 297n12; as wife, 155, 242n105. *See also* Ishmael
hair, 177, 294n46
Halpern, Baruch, 189, 289n72, 294n46
Hamor, 64–66, 96, 260n9
Hamutal, 287n67
Hannah: appears drunk to Eli, 136–37, 274n53; breast milk of, 275n56; dietary restrictions of, 136–37, 149; prayers of, 121, 136–37, 156; Samuel nursed by, 134, 137; song of, 164, 286nn55,56; special portion offered to, 135, 274nn45,46
Hardin, James W., 30, 87
ḥāṣēr (settlement), 212, 298n26
ḥawwôt (tent villages), 82
heart, use of term, 294n49
Hebron, 167, 189, 190–91, 193, 194, 199, 294n45
ḥeder (chamber), 79–80, 85, 255n15
heirlooms/heirloom valuables, 35–36, 43
heirs. *See* inheritance
Hendel, Ronald S., 4, 11, 35, 233n54

Hendon, Julie, 86, 87
ḥêq, meanings of, 145, 146, 147, 279n95, 280nn97,98
Hertzberg, Hans Wilhelm, 260n16, 294n45
Hoffner, Harry, 82
hôlîd (beget), 4, 40, 229n3
Homan, Michael M., 83
Hosea, 112, 117, 267n37, 297n7
house of her husband (*bêt 'îšāh*), 28–29, 60, 61, 250n39
House of Israel, 12, 34, 206–9
house of the father (*bêt 'āb*), 42fig.3, 58fig.5; Ashurbanipal, 103–4, 130–31, 167, 261n29, 270n17, 271n29, 272n31, 296n2; birth of a son and establishment of, 151–52; bride leaving, 173–74; burial practices, 41–42, 52, 243n113; changing kinship relations in, 101; children in, 152, 157, 162, 260n22; covenantal promises, 122; daughters in, 237n26, 243n111, 252n59; death of the patriarch, 41–42, 52, 211–12, 244n116; disruption of the patriline, 3–4; division into wombs, 255n13; establishment of, 152, 153–54, 282n11, 283n15; flight from, 174, 178, 180–81, 192–93; heirs of, 156–57, 247n8; hierarchies within, 25–27, 46, 165, 184, 209; Kirta Epic, 95, 105–6, 115, 157, 197, 266n18, 286n56; Lamech, 1, 3fig.1, 15, 247n14; language of, in Genesis 24, 53–54; loss of son as threat to, 102, 260n22; marriage negotiations, 52–55, 64–66, 68–70, 253n65; maternal subunits in, 104, 105–6, 170–71, 210, 211–14, 215; in *mišpāḥâ*, 12, 25, 237n32, 238n34; patrilocal marriages, 51–53, 58, 61, 65, 67, 173–74; as pillared house, 29–30; problem wives' return to, 60–61, 237n26, 250n38; *šômēmâ* in, 160, 285n39; sons' houses nested in, 28–29, 30; succession

house of the father (*bêt 'āb*) (*continued*)
narratives in, 104, 166, 183–84, 186, 190–91, 194, 217–18, 268n38, 289n77, 291n23, 294nn45,49; use of term, 28, 51, 237n32; womb openers reflecting strength of, 167–68; Yahweh, 187. *See also* concubines; nesting; *specific paternal houses (e.g., Abraham)*

house of the father of the mother, 174–75, 178, 180, 184–90, 193–94, 199

house of the mother (*bêt 'ēm*), 42fig.3, 58fig.5; adult children in, 81–83; Bethuel in Rebekah's *bêt 'ēm*, 55–57; birth of children and establishment of, 165, 282n7; as chamber, 77, 79, 80, 85; "chamber of her who conceived me," 62, 77, 78–79, 81, 110, 120; clan, 12, 25, 105–6, 237n32, 238n34, 291n18; consummation of marriage in, 244n120; devaluation of significance of, 60; Dinah identified with, 64, 67; fathers in, 56, 277n75; in Genesis *24*, 60–61; house of her husband, 28–29, 60, 61; as kinship group, 67; Laban associated with Rebekah's *bêt 'ēm*, 54–55, 57, 176; male heirs in establishing, 153–54; marriage negotiations in, 57–62, 64, 66, 68, 249n28, 251n50; Moses in, 142, 277n75, 291n18; non-nested houses, 184–85, 292n27; Orpah's return to, 61, 73, 100; Rebekah in, 51–57, 176; as refuge, 60–61, 73–74, 100, 102; as reward for fearing God, 162–63; as satellite houses, 38, 41–42, 49, 75, 184, 201, 228, 254n1; sexual encounters in, 62–63, 77–79, 81–84, 85, 119–20, 134, 251n45; sons protecting the honor of, 66, 97, 101; space in, 63, 64, 67, 77, 81, 134; as spatial unit, 77, 254n6; succession influenced by, 167, 287n67; suckling of my mother's clan, 105, 108, 115, 134, 141, 211, 262n37; tents as, 81–84, 208, 244n120, 255n11, 257n37; use of term, 247n12; as uterine family, 45, 47, 54, 61–67, 72, 73–74; womb-opening children inaugurating, 160. *See also* Song of Songs; uterine brothers; uterine siblings; *specific maternal houses (e.g., Naomi)*

house societies (Lévi-Strauss), 31–32
Humphrey, Carolyn, 89

Idrimi, 192–93, 295nn51,54, 296n57
illegitimate children, 22, 236n18
immaterial wealth, 35–36, 42, 43, 45, 46
infertility, 93, 121, 152, 153–54, 156, 160–61, 164, 267n37
inheritance: blessings for, 117–18, 266n30; break with house of the father of the mother, 174, 175–76, 199; breastfeeding in, 130, 149; cultural value of, 92–93; god-loved son as inheritor, 181; husbands and wives, and their need for, 157, 158; Isaac as Abraham's heir, 55, 140, 201, 247n15, 283n15; male heirs as paternal ideal, 150–52, 153, 282n11; mothers' absence, 201–2, 296n2; mother's ethnicity influencing, 15, 122–23, 139, 141–49, 268n45, 277n73, 280nn101,103; non-inheriting sons, 22, 186, 236n18, 293n33; parents' aspirations for an heir, 151–54; patrilineal, of Maori people, 10; royal succession narratives, 166, 183–84, 186, 190–91, 194, 217–18, 268n38, 291n23, 294nn45,46; status differentiation, 155, 189, 227, 283n23; strategies in quest for, 201, 283n15. See also *běkôr*

'*innâ* (rape), 101, 252n52
Isaac, 180fig.10; as Abraham-begotten son, 40–42, 242n106; as Abraham's heir, 39, 42–43, 55, 140, 201, 244n120, 247n15, 283n15; betrothal to Rebekah, 51–57, 73, 83, 93; binding

of, 201; burial of Abraham, 41–42, 211; concern for Rebekah's barrenness, 156; death of, 244n116; as father of Esau, 176–77; as father of Jacob, 95, 181, 182, 185; genealogy of, 43, 52, 149, 181, 182; geographic associations, 41, 43, 243n111; nursed by woman of status, 140, 276n67; patrilocal marriage of, 53, 58; personality of, 177–78; relations with Ishmael, 41, 140, 243n111; Sarah as mother of, 83, 256n30; Terahite descent of, 140, 143; weaning of, 116, 138, 140; as womb-opening son, 166

Isaiah, book of, 77, 115–16, 130, 132, 273n40

Ishbaal/Esh-baal (son of Saul), 79, 168–69, 169fig.9, 190, 289n72

Ishmael: birth of, 39, 40, 166; expulsion of, 139–40, 296n4; as heir to Abram, 153, 283n15; inheritance of, 42–43, 184; Isaac, relationship with, 41, 140, 243n111; relationship with Abraham, 40, 41–42, 184, 211; sons of, 214, 215; wives of, 212, 298n25; Yahweh's covenantal promise to, 205

Ishmaelites: degradation of, 205–6; descendants transporting Joseph to Egypt, 45; divisions of, 214; under maternal covenant, 206

Ishtar, 130

'iššâ (wife), 82, 154, 155

Issachar, 23fig.2, 163

"I Will Praise the Lord of Wisdom" (Babylonian poem), 267n31

Jabal, 2, 15

Jacob, 23fig.2, 48fig.4, 66fig.6, 103fig.7, 180fig.10; asks El Shaddai to show *raḥămîm*, 112–13; avuncular relationship with Laban, 177–80, 181, 182–83, 193, 290n12; begettings of, 44; burial of Isaac, 244n116; concubines of, 44, 46, 48, 49, 74, 163; dating of narrative, 233n51; Dinah as daughter of, 64–65, 96; etiologies in blessings to sons, 164; genealogy of, 38–39, 44, 123, 181, 182, 207–8, 244n116, 290n12; House of Israel, 12, 206–9; house of Leah as subhouse of, 101; in house of the father of the mother, 174; Isaac's blessing to, 95, 181, 182, 185; as Israel, 207, 290n12; Jacob's sons (use of term), 65, 96–97; Joseph and, 43–45, 111–12, 117–18, 266n30, 280n101; Laban's house as refuge, 174, 178, 180–81; Leah's house nested in, 66fig.6; maternal subunits in, 47–48, 222–23, 255n11; meeting with Rachel, 178–79; origin stories for, 22; personality of, 177, 178; physical appearance of, 123, 180; prayer for Benjamin, 111–12; privileging of Rachel in, 46–47; Rachel, 23, 44, 45; rape of Dinah, 64–68, 101, 252n52, 260n22; reaction to Levi and Simeon's vengeance, 97; reaction to rape of Dinah, 260n22; reaction to slaughter of Shechemites, 66, 252n58; as Rebekah's son, 174, 176–77, 178, 179, 181, 185, 206; relationship with Yahweh, 180–81, 187; relations with Esau, 95, 114, 176–77, 178, 206–9; resettlement in land of Goshen, 47–48; return to the land of his fathers, 181, 182, 291n17; "seed" in covenantal promise to, 122; separation from Laban, 84, 182–83; and the slaughter of Shechemites, 66, 252n58; as son of Isaac, 181, 185; Tamar's half-brothers as David's sons, 101; womb-based allegiance toward house of Rachel, 111–12; wrestling with angels, 208

Jael's tent, 84, 257n37

Jay, Nancy, 268n45

Jehoahaz, 287n67

Jehoiakim, 287n67

Index of Subjects

Jehosheba/Jehoshabeath, 102–3
Jephthah, 159, 197, 293n33, 296n60
Jeremiah, 288n67
Jeroboam, 219
Jerubbaal (Gideon): Abimelech as son of, 174–75, 183–84, 236n18, 292n25; connections with Manasseh, 218, 219, 291n23, 292n26, 299n38; dynastic rule refused by, 183, 218; in the foundation of the Northern Kingdom, 219, 291n23; Jotham son of, 186, 187, 191, 197; on maternal kinship, 13, 97–98; monarchic connections, 292n26; seventy sons of, 92, 184, 186, 286n56
Jerusalem: breastfeeding the returning exiles, 273n41; daughters of, 62, 120; as the mother of Israel, 132; nested households of, 26; return of the exiles to, 132, 273n39; in Song of Songs, 62, 80; temple in, 34; Yahweh's judgment on, 286n56
Joab, 97–98, 195
Joash, 295n54
Job, 157, 195, 259n3, 283n23, 284n28, 286n56, 291n18
Jochebed (Moses's mother), 140–43, 149, 277nn70,77, 290n3, 291n18
Jonadab, 99, 100, 102
Joseph, 23fig.2; as *bĕkôr*, 44–45; Benjamin as uterine brother of, 45, 47–48, 63, 94, 133, 166–67, 209; blessing of, 117–18, 266n30; breastfeeding in birth story, 279n92; dream of, 44–45, 46; Ephraim as the chosen of, 92, 93; half-brothers of, 111–12; house of, 28; name of, 163, 286n51; physical beauty of, 124; *raḥămîm* experienced by, 110, 111; Reuben replaced as heir by sons of, 217, 218; reunion with Benjamin, 110–11, 179, 209; reunion with brothers in Egypt, 45–46, 47–48; sale of, 45; *tôlēdôt* clauses in story of, 43–44; as womb-opening son, 166–67, 217
Josiah, 287n67
Jotham, 186, 187, 191, 197
Joyce, Rosemary A., 35
J source, 39, 246n3
Judah, 23fig.2, 47, 218fig.11, 224fig.12; in Davidic genealogy, 219, 220–21, 222, 228; house of Jacob described by, 47; naming of, 163; Naomi as Judahite, 59, 60, 68, 143–44, 279n93; origin stories for, 22; as royalty, 92, 93, 102–3, 223, 225, 299nn34,38; Tamar (daughter-in-law of Judah), 152, 162, 220, 221, 237n26, 250n38; territory of, 204, 216, 217, 299n36

Keturah, sons of, 42fig.3, 52; in Abrahamic genealogy, 5, 39–40, 45, 226, 242n103, 243n113; death of Keturah, 243n113; descendants of, 45, 205; identity of, 41, 44, 198, 243n109; Joseph transported to Egypt, 45; Midianites, 45, 68, 97, 212–13, 214, 244n115; removed from Isaac's household, 296n4
King, Phillip J., 21
kinship, 3fig.1; ambiguity of sister-brother relationship, 99–101; in Arab texts, 127; aspirations supported by, 106–9; breast milk establishing, 127–28, 270n17, 271n22; defining terms of, 11–12, 25, 27, 76–78, 237n32; feminine kinship terms, 38; identification of Israelite man and Midianite woman (Numbers 25), 212–13, 225; introduction of, 182, 291n18; milk kinship, 125, 127, 128, 134, 140, 142, 270n17, 273n43, 279n93; procreative verbs, 39–40; rejection of, 99–100, 203, 211, 294n4; revenge by brothers, 65–66, 96–98, 101; Ruth's pledge as basis of, 143–44, 277n79; seed, 122–23,

126, 152, 153, 205–6, 268n45, 269n6; shared locality, 51–53, 58, 61, 65, 67, 173–74; through male birth order, 37. *See also* "bone and flesh"; breast milk and breastfeeding; house of the father; house of the mother; nesting

kinship terms, 237n32; ambivalence of, 234n59; Aramaic examples, 214–15; discourse analysis of, 16–19, 234n59; in list of nested units, 211–15; in Maori language, 37; in psalms, 196–97, 214; social organization as, 18; sons of Jacob, 65–66; tribes, 22, 25, 210–13, 222–25, 224fig.12, 298nn29,31; *'ummâ*, 210–13, 214, 215, 298nn29,31. *See also* nesting

Kirta, King, 95, 105–6, 130, 157, 266n18

Kirta Epic, 95, 105–6, 115, 157, 197, 266n18, 286n56

kissing and weeping, 62, 79, 94, 111, 118–19, 134, 179, 209

Kottsieper, Ingo, 56, 100, 261n21

Kugel, James, 76, 95

Kuper, Adam, 126, 231n21

Laban, 180fig.10; associated with Rebekah's *bêt 'ēm*, 54–55, 57, 58; as Bethuel's successor, 179; as father, 69, 182, 291n19; genealogy of, 53, 69; involved in negotiation of daughters' marriages, 68; Jacob's avuncular relationship with, 177–80, 181, 182–83, 193, 290n12; personality of, 177; as Rebekah's brother, 54, 56, 73, 178–79, 248n23, 290n12; as refuge for Jacob, 174, 178, 180–81; resident daughters in house of, 237n26; role in Rebekah's marriage negotiations, 58, 59; sons of, 182, 291n18; tents in narrative of, 84, 257n39

LaCocque, André, 60, 145

Lamech, 1, 3fig.1, 15, 247n14

Lamphere, Louise, 9

land: allotted to maidservants' sons in Jacob's maternal sub-houses, 216–17, 299n36; burial places, 41–42, 52, 243n113; in covenantal promises, 153, 205–6; inheritance of, 42–43, 247n8; Lot's allotment of, 203; in marriage negotiations, 65, 73; material wealth, 41

Landsberger, Benno, 267n36

Leah, 44, 45, 48, 66fig.6, 103fig.7; in Davidic genealogy, 219; Dinah as daughter of, 64, 67, 251n51; in her father's house, 237n26; Laban as father of, 182, 291n19; negotiation of marriage to Jacob, 68; priestly and royal houses descended from, 217, 218fig.11; raised status among women, 163–64; Reuben as womb-opening son, 224; sons of, 156, 163–64; tent of, 84, 208

Leah, house of, 23fig.2, 66fig.6; arrangement of twelve tribes reflecting, 223–24; dishonored by rape of Dinah, 66, 97, 101; Shechem's outrage against, 101; as sub-house of Jacob, 101. *See also* Dinah; Levi; Simeon

Leeb, Carolyn S., 28

Lemche, Niels Peter, 28

Lemos, Tracy, 248n26, 285n50

Lemuel, King of Massa, 120–21, 284n26

lĕ'ōm, lĕ'ummîm (people, nation), 215–16, 299n35

Levenson, Jon, 158, 189

Levi, 23fig.2, 66fig.6, 103fig.7; as Jacob's son, 65; marriage negotiations with Hamor, 65–66; maternally specific kinship terms in, 13; naming of, 163; origin stories for, 22; refuge offered to Dinah, 73, 102; revenge against Shechemites, 65–66, 96–97, 101

Levine, Baruch, 214, 225

Lévi-Strauss, Claude, 31–32

Levites, 141, 143, 277n70

Levite's concubine, 250n38, 299n38

Lewis, Thomas, 272n35
Liverani, Mario, 295n54
Loland, Hanne, 264n3, 265n9
Longman, Tremper, 295n51
Lot, 162, 285n44, 296n4; sexual deception against, 203–4, 297n6
loyalty pacts, 129, 270n17

Maacah, 98, 100, 103fig.7, 167, 168, 171, 175, 189
Machinist, Peter, 271nn24,28
Machpelah, cave of, 41–42, 243n113, 244n120
Mahănāyim, 207
Maher, Vanessa, 113, 116, 126
Mahlon, 60, 143, 152, 166
mahr, meanings and practices connected with, 71
maidservants, 196–97, 206, 216–17, 224fig.12, 242n104
Malamat, Abraham, 210, 211
Manasseh, 82, 217, 280n101, 299nn36,38
Manoah, 156–57
Maori people, 10, 37
Marduk, 131
Margalit, Baruch, 105
marriage: arranged by primary wives, 165; *bayit* formation, 26; betrothals, 51–57, 59, 62–63, 64–65; blessings, 152, 201, 202, 220–21, 282n7; bride price in, 71; brother-brokered marriages, 15, 45, 47–48, 54, 56, 61–62, 64–68, 71–74, 254n73; economics of, 54, 65, 70–73, 74, 261n22, 283n25; *errebu* marriages, 253n62; father-brokered marriages, 68–70; in house of the mother, 57–60, 62, 64, 66; negotiation of, 57–61, 62, 64, 66–67; in Nuzi marriage contracts, 285n46; patrilocal marriages, 51–53, 58, 61, 65, 67, 173–74, 252n59; royal marriages, 68; status of the groom in, 69; Tamar's proposal of marriage to Amnon, 99–100, 252n59; value of, 152; womb-based allegiance, 112
marriage negotiations: affecting status within husband's house, 155; ethnographic studies of, 71–73; expectation for bride to leave natal home, 59, 67; fathers' involvement in, 52–55, 64–70, 252n61, 253n62; gift giving, 41, 54, 71, 73, 243n110; status within husband's house, 155; in Sumerian texts, 249n28
Marsman, Hennie, 262n37
mattānōt (gifts), 41, 53, 54, 71, 73, 243n110, 248n26
Matthew, Gospel of, 166
Matthews, Victor, 60, 292n27, 293n39
McCarter, P. Kyle, 274n48, 286n55, 295n50
McKinnon, Susan, 8–9, 35, 36, 37, 38, 245n128
mē'ālay (from upon), 100, 203, 296n4
Mendenhall, George E., 11
mêneqet (wet nurse), 141, 145
Mesha Stele, 21, 265n16
Meyers, Carol, 28, 77, 86–87, 118–19, 247n12, 275n62, 277n70
Michal, 69, 168, 169fig.9, 170, 285n45
Midianites, 45, 68, 97, 212–13, 214, 244n115
midwives, 117, 162–63
migdānōt (costly ornaments), 52, 57, 248n26
Milcah, 68, 176, 275n59
milk kinship, 125, 127–28, 134, 140, 142, 270n17, 273n43, 279n93
millstone as weapon, 188, 293n37
mišpāḥâ (clan), 12, 25, 237n32, 238n34
Moab: Baal Peor, 212; in Davidic genealogy, 59, 68, 73–74, 144, 148, 249nn29,31, 280n103; Lot, 162, 203–4, 285n44, 297n6; low-status origins of, 203; origin story of, 204; Ruth, ethnic identity of, 59, 68, 73–74, 148, 249n29, 278nn78,79, 280n103; sexual

relations between men of Israel and Moabite women, 212
mohar (bridewealth), 65, 71–72, 248n26, 252n55
Mongolian tents, 89
Montague, Susan, 128–29
Moors, Annelies, 71–72
Mordecai, 146
Morrison, Fynes, 128
Moses: birth of, 141–43, 253n64, 280n99; circumcision of, 142, 277n72; ethnicity of, 141–42, 277n73; Hebrew identity of, 141–42, 277nn70,73; Jochebed as mother of, 140–43, 149, 277nn70,77, 290n3, 291n18; mother as wet nurse of, 140, 141, 142, 149; sister as rescuer of, 291n18; as "wet nurse," 145–46, 147; Zipporah, 68, 244n115
Mot (Baal Cycle), 95–96, 106–7, 108, 114–15, 211
mothers: absence of, 40, 148, 183, 201–2, 209, 242n103, 280nn99,101, 296n2; appositional epithets identifying son of his mother's womb, 121, 268n38; defining sons who fail, 201; divinity of, 130–31, 272n35; ethnicity transmitted through, 15, 59, 68, 73–74, 139, 141–49, 249n29, 277n73, 280nn101,103; etiologies reflecting value of sons, 164; instructive roles of, 118–19, 123; intercession on behalf of sons, 171–72, 201, 282n7; kinship bonds established through breast milk, 128, 271n22; names given to children, 161, 163; and nation building, 151–52, 161, 201–2, 222, 227, 282nn7,10,11; Nazirite requirements observed by, 129, 136–38; *peṭer reḥem* as raising status of, 159–60; prayers on behalf of sons, 121, 268n38; traits transmitted by, 122–24, 126–29, 131–32, 137–38, 142, 177, 272n35, 275n56; tribal identification of, 68, 123, 139, 140, 141, 143, 277n70; as wet nurses, 140, 141, 142, 149; womb-based kinship, 116, 120–21, 268n38. *See also* breast milk and breastfeeding; house of the mother; *specific mothers (e.g., Rachel)*
mother's house. *See* house of the mother
mother's sons (*běnê 'immî*), 62, 63
Mundy, Martha, 71
myth (defined), 186–87

nā'ar, na'ărâ (young woman), 11, 28
Naboth the Jezreelite, 24
Nabu, royal prayer to, 130–31
naḥălâ (paternal inheritance), 56–57
Nahor, 4, 52, 53, 176, 183, 247nn9,12
name-tag objects (heirlooms/heirloom valuables), 35–36
Naomi: Boaz as kin to, 165–66; Elimelech, 60, 143, 152, 165, 166; ethnic identity transferred to Obed, 146–47, 148, 149, 280n103; as giving birth to Obed, 165; hopes for remarriage of Ruth and Orpah, 60–61; Judahite identity of, 59, 68, 143, 146–47, 148, 149; marriage of Boaz and Ruth arranged by, 165–66; maternal blessing given to, 165; as Obed's wet nurse, 144–45, 149, 166, 278n86, 280n103; as post-menopausal, 144–45; Ruth as surrogate of, 165–66, 287n61; Ruth's attachment to, 143–44, 165–66, 277n79; Sarah-Hagar story compared with Naomi-Ruth story, 165–66, 287n61; securing David's Judean ethnicity, 166
Naphtali, 23fig.2, 163, 223, 224fig.11
nasab (agnatic descent), 127
naśî (chief), 213, 214
Nazirites: from birth, 121, 134, 135–36, 274n47, 284n35; dietary restrictions

Nazirites (*continued*)
of, 136–37, 149; mothers of, 129, 136–38, 275n54; requirements of, 135, 274n47; womb openers as, 284n35
nĕbālâ (outrage), 64, 101
neighborhood women, 165, 286n57
nesting, 42fig.3, 58fig.5, 66fig.6, 237n32; architecture and, 16, 20, 29–31, 87–88, 235n6, 239n56; within house of the father, 25, 30–33, 66, 184, 292n27; in Jerusalem, 26; kinship designations, 92–93, 211–15; of maternal houses, 38–39, 41–42, 48–49, 104, 112, 184–85, 189, 244n120; multi-generationality of, 30; non-nested houses in house of the mother, 184, 292n27; satellite houses, 38, 41–42, 49, 75, 184, 201, 228, 254n1; sons' houses nested in house of the father, 28–29, 30
New Testament, 166, 266n28, 273n37, 300n43
Niditch, Susan, 271n23, 285n43
Nielsen, Kirstin, 59, 144, 249n29
non-elite houses, 24, 237n29
non-inheriting sons, 22, 186, 236n18, 293n33
nuclear family. See *bayit*
Nuer people, 8–9, 37, 40, 245n128
Nuzi marriage contracts, 285n46

Obed, 143, 280n99; birth story of, 144; in Davidic genealogy, 202; Judahite ethnicity of, 148, 149; legitimate conception of, 287n59; Naomi's adoption of, 59, 145, 146, 148, 279n93, 280n103, 282n101; paternity of, 166
Oden, Robert, 290n12
Oholah, 24, 85, 123, 222
Oholibah, 24, 85, 123, 222
Olyan, Saul, 274nn46,47
'ōmenet (wet nurse), 128, 139–42, 145–46, 149, 275n62, 279n90

'ōmnim (guardians), 145
origin houses, 34–41. See also specific headings (e.g., Abraham)
Orpah, 60–61, 68, 74, 100

pacts (term), 231n21
Palestinian villages, marriage brokering in, 71–72
parallelism in Hebrew poetry, 62, 76, 77, 78–79, 119–20, 215–16
Pardee, Dennis, 105, 272n35
Parker, Simon B., 262n37
Parkes, Peter, 128, 270n17
paternity: associated with womb openers, 158–59; and mother's ownership of the child, 158–59
patrilineal genealogies: masculinity expressed by, 4; patterns of, 2; Shem-Abram, 4
patrilineal households: status differentiation in, 155; uterine siblings in, 70–71
patrilineality, 5; agnatic descent, 10, 127, 230n19, 231n21, 268n45; begats, 1, 2, 4, 53, 203–4, 297n6; challenges to, 7–11; covenantal promises, 92, 122, 139–40, 149, 162, 182, 201, 204–7, 276n65; Hebrew terms for, 27–28; in kinship studies, 7–11; social status of, 231n33; use of term, 231n21. See also *tôlēdôt*
patrilocal marriages, 51–53, 58, 61, 65, 67, 173–74
Peletz, Michael, 234n59
Perez, 148, 152, 159, 202, 220, 221
pětaḥ (open) as part of a name, 159, 161
peṭer reḥem (the one who opens the womb), 151, 158, 159–60, 175, 284n35, 290n3
Peterson, Brian, 279n95
Pharaoh, 255n14, 287n67
pillared houses, 16, 20, 29–31, 87–88, 235n6, 239n56
piṣḥi (break forth), 160

polygynous households, 15, 27, 49–50, 156, 166, 245n128
Pope, Marvin, 273n43
Pressler, Carolyn, 278n86
prestige of sons, 151, 161–64, 282nn8,10
Preuss, D., 298n33
priestly houses, 24, 218fig.11, 220, 223, 225, 253n64, 290n3, 299n34
problem wives, return of, 60–61, 237n26, 250n38
procreation, 39, 40, 121–22, 268n45
Propp, William H., 277nn69,73
prostitutes, 113, 147, 167, 184–85, 196, 236n18, 254n1
Proverbs, 78, 120–21, 267n36
Psalms, book of, 78, 80–81, 94, 116–17, 173, 195, 196–97, 214, 266n28, 299n35
P source, 4, 39, 139–40, 268n45, 275n63, 276nn63,65, 283n16
Pughat (Aqhat epic), 105, 107, 135, 211, 291n18

qaraba (kinship), 127
q-n-h (creating), 121
Qumran, 117, 123, 279n90
Qur'an, on breastfeeding, 127

Rachel, 23fig.2, 48fig.4, 180fig.10, 218fig.11; arrangement of twelve tribes reflecting, 223–24; Benjamin as son of, 111, 112–13, 221; Bilhah, 23fig.2, 44, 46, 48, 151, 155; children born to Bilhah, 163; death and burial of, 44, 243n113, 244n120; desire to be "built up," 150–51; ethnic formation of Joseph, 279n92; in her father's home, 237n26; Joseph as son of, 45; Joseph as womb-opening son, 166–67; as kinship unit, 47–48, 48fig.4; Laban as father of, 182, 291n19; names given to sons, 163–64; negotiation of marriage to Jacob, 68; origins of Israelite kingship in, 217, 218fig.11; personality of, 177; priestly and royal houses descended from, 217–19; tent of, 84, 208; as wife, 155; womb-based allegiance, 46–48, 48fig.4, 118; womb of, 111, 112–13. *See also* Benjamin; Isaac; Joseph
Radcliffe-Brown, Alfred R., 9
Rahab, 184–85, 292n29
raḥămîm, 48fig.4; *beṭen*, 111, 117, 259n3, 264n3, 280n98; and genuine maternal instinct, 113; as "mercy" or "compassion," 111; *rḥm*, 115, 116, 265nn16,17; two women who claimed to be mothers of the same infant boy (1 Kings 3:17–18), 113, 147, 184–85; womb-based associations, 46–47, 110–16, 264n1, 265nn9,16
Ramras-Rauch, Gila, 252n58
rape of Dinah, 101, 252n52, 261n22; mother's house dishonored by, 66, 97, 101; outrage in, 64, 65, 101; sons of Jacob, 65–66; uterine brothers' revenge for, 65–66, 96–97, 101
rape of Tamar, 74, 79, 98–102, 189, 243n111, 260n16, 293n39, 296n4
Rashkow, Ilana, 254n6
Rebekah, 42fig.3, 180fig.10; as barren, 156; betrothal to Isaac, 51–57, 59, 73, 83, 93; as *bĕtûlâ*, 93; blessings received by, 202, 282n7; dating of the betrothal narrative in Genesis 24, 51–52, 59; disappearance from Jacob's narrative, 183, 202; genealogy of, 51–53, 68, 73, 246n7, 247n9; house of the mother of, 54, 55–56, 57–59, 60–61, 66–67; Jacob as son of, 174, 176–77, 178, 179, 181, 185, 206; Laban associated with house of the mother of, 54–55, 57, 58; marriage negotiations for, 57–59, 60–61, 66–67; *migdānōt* offered to, 52, 57; personality of, 177, 178; pregnancy of, 114; relationship with Esau, 177; relationship with Isaac, 178;

318 Index of Subjects

Rebekah (*continued*)
    relationship with Yahweh, 180–81; runs to her mother's house, 53–54, 55–56, 179; wet nurse of, 275n62
refuge, places of, 73, 100, 102, 174–75, 178, 180, 189–90, 192–93, 199, 250n38
reḥem (womb), 112, 264n1
rēʾšît ʾōn (first fruit of his vigor), 151
Reuben, 23fig.2, 163, 217, 223–24, 224fig.12, 225, 301n53
revenge narratives, 65–66, 96–103, 105, 107, 114–15, 127, 211, 261n21, 291n18
rḥm (womb), 115, 116, 265nn16,17
rivalry between siblings, 95, 106–7, 114, 174–78, 206–9, 290n3
Rofé, Alexander, 52
rōʾš (head), 214
Rosenberg, Joel, 261n20
Roth, W. M., 246n3
royal succession narratives, 166, 183–84, 186, 190–91, 194, 217–18, 268n38, 291n23, 294nn45,49
royalty, 68, 106, 108, 139–40, 149, 266n30
r-q-m (embroidery), 121
Ruane, Nicole, 158–59
Ruth: devotion to Naomi, 143–44, 148, 165–66; disappearance from text, 202, 280n99; foreignness of, 143, 278n78, 287n61; marriage to Boaz, 152, 165–66, 202, 220–21; Moabite ethnicity of, 59, 68, 73–74, 143, 148, 249n29, 280n103; Naomi's hope for remarriage of, 60–61; as surrogate of Naomi, 165, 166, 287n61
Ruth, book of: birth of Obed, 144; Boaz as kinsman, 165–66; dating of, 59, 221–22, 249n29; David's Moabite roots addressed by, 59, 68, 73–74, 144, 148, 220, 249n29; fear of social isolation, 285n45; Genesis 24 compared with, 59, 60–61; in Gospel of Matthew, 166; Judahite family in, 60; marriage blessing in, 202; Moabite ethnicity within, 59, 68, 73–74, 249n29; Naomi as mother of Obed, 59, 165, 280n101, 280n103; Orpah, 60–61, 68, 74, 100; Sarah-Hagar story compared with Naomi-Ruth story, 165–66, 287n61

Sakenfeld, Katharine Doob, 249n29
Salu, 213
Samson, 134, 136, 252n61, 284n35, 294n46
Samuel, 121, 135–38, 149, 274n47, 281n104, 284n35
Sarah/Sarai: death and burial of, 52, 243n113, 244n120; desire to be "built up," 153–55, 161, 283n17; disappearance from narrative, 201–2; Hagar as slave girl of, 155, 205; Hagar as surrogate of, 153–55, 161, 165–66, 197, 283n17, 287n61; Hagar's status as maidservant, 197; infertility of, 93, 153–54; Isaac as womb-opening son, 166; Isaac nursed by, 138–39, 140, 142, 149; as Isaac's mother, 83, 256n30; nested house of, 42fig.3, 244n120; in New Testament, 300n43; related to Abraham, 138–39; as royalty, 139, 140, 149; Sarah-Hagar story compared with Naomi-Ruth story, 165–66, 287n61; tent of, 83, 256n30
Sarna, Nahum, 55–56, 82, 247n15, 276n64
Sasson, Jack M., 292n25
satellite houses, 38, 41–42, 49, 75, 184, 201, 228, 254n1
Saul, 169fig.9; Absalom, 190; Ahinoam as wife of, 169, 170, 189, 288n69, 289n77; Benjaminite genealogy of, 218–19; marriage negotiations, 68; Michal as daughter of, 69, 168, 169fig.9, 170, 285n45; relations with David, 70, 97, 167–68, 170–72, 190, 288n68, 289nn75,76,77
scaling (Gillespie), 33
Schloen, David J., 11, 87, 221, 236–37n21
Schneider, David M., 6–7, 231n21

Schneider, Tammi, 73, 246n7, 251n51
Scholz, Susanne, 297n6
šēbeṭ (tribe), 25
Second Isaiah, 34
seed (*zeraʿ*), 122–23, 126, 152, 153, 205–6, 268n45, 269n6
servant of Abraham, 52–55, 57, 73
seven sons, 164, 175, 286n56
Shahar, 131, 272n35
Shalim, 131, 272n35
Shamash-Shum-Ukin, 272n31, 296n2
Shapsu (Baal Cycle), 108, 109, 115, 211
Shechem (person): concubine mother of Abimelech, 167, 175, 184–86, 190–91, 236n18; as house of the father of the mother, 175, 184, 185, 186, 187–88; marriage negotiations on behalf of, for Dinah, 64–66, 73; murder of, 65–66, 96–97, 101
Shechem (town): home of Abimelech, 167, 175, 184–86, 190–91, 236n18; as house of the father of the mother, 175, 184, 185, 186, 187–88
Simeon, 23fig.2, 66fig.6, 103fig.7, 224fig.12; demotion of, 224–25; Dinah claimed as daughter, 65; as Jacob's son, 65; marriage negotiations with Hamor, 65–66; naming of, 163; refuge offered to Dinah, 73, 102; replaced by Ephraim and Manasseh, 224–25; revenge against Shechemites, 65–66, 67, 96–97, 101; Simeonite bringing a Midianite woman into the Israelite camp, 212–13, 225; in twelve tribes, 223, 224
Simian-Yofre, H., 265n9
Sinclair, Karen, 10, 37, 186–87
šipḥâ (slave girl), 40, 43, 150, 154, 196–97, 206, 216–17, 224fig.12, 242n104, 244nn117,120, 283n20
Sisera, 84
sisters: changes in kinship relations, 99–101, 102; as daughters, 96, 260n9; filial loyalty of, 105, 107, 140, 141, 142, 211, 291n18; as protective, 56, 102–3, 261n24; rejection of, 99–100; "sisters of my mother" as refuge, 192. *See also* Dinah; Leah; Rachel; Rebekah; Tamar (David's daughter)
s-k-k (weaving), 121
slaves, 40, 43, 150, 154, 242n104, 244nn117,120
š-l-ḥ (send out), 99–100
Smith, Mark S., 105, 106, 267n31, 272n35, 278n79, 293n37
Smith, Richard Saumarez, 71
Solomon: Bathsheba as advocate for, 242n104, 291n15; *bayit* of, 25, 80, 85; construction of house for Yahweh, 25–26, 85; references to wife's house, 81; Song of Songs identified with, 13, 61–62, 79–81, 111, 251n17, 255n17; temple built by, 258n40; two women who claimed to be mothers of the same infant boy (1 Kings 3:17–18), 113, 147, 184–85, 242n104; women's chambers in house of, 80, 85
šômēmâ (desolate one), 160, 285nn39,43
son born to a whore (*ben-ʾiššâ zônâ*), 196, 197
Song of Songs: betrothals, 62–63, 67; breast and womb word pair in, 118–20; brother imagined in, 133–34, 273n43; chambers in, 79, 80, 85; dating of, 61, 246n3, 250n40; Daughters of Jerusalem, 62, 68; father absent from, 47, 61, 64, 67; female speaker in, 255n17; house of the mother in, 61–64, 77–79, 81–84, 105, 119–20, 134; marriage in, 62, 67; maternal space associated with childbirth, 110; milk brothers in, 133–34; mother's house as place for lovers' tryst, 83; mother's sons referenced in, 62, 63, 64, 94; parallelism in, 77, 119–20; reciprocal economic and

Song of Songs (*continued*)
  social relationship among uterine siblings, 63, 73; sexual activity in, 81–84, 119–20, 134; sister used in, 93; Solomon referenced in, 13, 61–62, 79–81, 111, 255n17; uterine brothers in, 62–64, 67, 261n19; women associated with instruction, 119; women bringing lovers into house of the mother, 62–63, 79, 251n45. *See also* female speaker in Song of Songs
son of a maidservant (*ben-'ămātô*), 196–97, 216–17
son of his concubines (*běnê happîlagšîm*), 196
son of my womb, 120–21
sons, 174; balance of power among women, 164; battles of succession, 198–99; birth order of, 69–70; as blessings, 136–37, 156–57; brothers as, 260n9; defined by mothers, 201; devalued status of maternally marked sons, 197, 198; in the establishment of the father's house, 151–52; inheritance, 69–70; in multiples of seven, 92, 108, 164, 175, 184, 286n56; prayers for, 136–37, 156–57, 284n26; royal houses of, 106; social value of, 161–63; woman's prestige and sense of security added by, 166
South China, patrilineal households in, 155
Speiser, E. A., 55, 122, 163–64, 248n19, 276n64
Stager, Lawrence E., 11, 21, 25–26, 28, 30–31
Steinberg, Naomi, 56, 122–23, 247n8, 275n58, 283n15
stereometric thinking, 121, 267n36
Stiebert, Johanna, 297n6
Stone, Ken, 14, 294n46
Stone, Linda, 6
Stowers, Stanley K., 17
Stravrakopoulo, Francesca, 243n113

"Stroll" (Egyptian poem), 251n45
succession struggles, 167, 287n67
Succession Treaty of Esarhaddon, 13, 103–4, 130, 270n17, 271n29
Succoth, 209, 298n14
suckling, 104–5, 108, 109, 115, 127–28
suckling of my mother's clan (*'l'umty*), 105, 108, 115, 134, 141, 211, 262n37
surrogacy, 153–55, 161, 165–66, 283n17, 287n61

tabernacles, 78, 85, 255n12
Talmai of Geshur, 98, 100, 167, 168, 171, 175, 189–90
Tamar, 103fig.7
Tamar (daughter-in-law of Judah): Perez, 148, 152, 159, 202, 220, 221; return to her father's house, 237n26, 250n38
Tamar (David's daughter), 103fig.7; Absalom as uterine brother of, 98, 252n59; banishment of, 99–100; childlessness of, 162, 260n22; kinship with Amnon, 99–101, 102; Maacah as mother of, 98; marriage proposal to Amnon, 99–100, 252n59; rape of, 74, 79, 98–102, 189, 243n111, 260n16, 293n39, 296n4; as *šômēmâ*, 160
Tana Toraha (Indonesia), 88
ṭar'um (mother's clan), 105–6
Tekoa, wise woman of, 290n3
Tel Dan Stele (Aramaic), 21
telescoping string of appositional epithets, 268n38
Tel Halif (Iron Age), 30
Tell Al Rimah, 210
tent (*'ōhel*): arrangement of tribes around tent of meeting, 222–23, 224fig.12; defined, 256n23; Eve as derived from, 82; Jacob as dwelling in, 177; in Laban narrative, 84, 257n39; sexual activity in, 81–84; as subdivision of *bayit*, 77–78, 84–85,

255n11; women's tents, 81–84, 208, 256n30, 257n37; Yahweh's house as, 85

Terah: covenantal blessing given to, 123, 268n45; genealogy of, 143, 176, 183; patrilineage of, 4, 143, 246n7, 275n58; Rebekah's genealogy, 68; Sarah descended from, 138–39; tôlēdôt of, 4. See also Abraham/Abram; Bethuel

Thanksgiving Hymns at Qumran, 279n90

Thompson, Thomas, 248n19

ṭirâ (tent encampment), 212, 298n27

tôlēdôt (begettings), 1–4, 53, 201, 203–4, 229n9, 297n6; birth of a son in, 151–52, 201–2; in Genesis, 39–40, 211–12; hôlîd, 4, 39, 40, 229n3; immaterial wealth, 35–36, 42, 43, 45, 46; J source on, 39, 246n3; maternal subunits in, 5; patrilineal genealogies, 2, 4; P source on, 3–4, 268n45; 'ummâ in tôlēdôt of Ishmael, 211–12; translation, challenges of, 17–18, 145, 150, 252n52, 281n2

tribes, 23fig.2, 224fig.12; affiliation of Moses's mother, 141, 143, 277nn70,77; organization of, 222–25, 301n53; sons of Jacob as, 22–23; terms describing, 25, 'ummâ, 210–13, 214, 215, 298nn29,31; 'umt, 105, 108, 134, 211, 262n37

Trible, Phyllis, 47, 61, 111, 113–14, 116, 242nn105,106, 265n9, 297n12

trickery, 13, 66–67, 94, 177–79, 181, 203–4, 297n6

Trobriand Island people, 128–29, 136, 271n22

Ugaritic literature: Aqhatu epic, 104–5, 211, 262nn36,37; Baal Cycle, 106–7, 108, 109, 114–15, 293n33; birth of Shahar and Shalim in, 131, 272n35; Kirta Epic, 95, 105–6, 115, 157, 197,

266n18, 286n56; 'l 'umty in, 105, 134, 211, 262n37

umlālâ (dried up), 286n56

'ummâ, 'ummîm, 'ummōt (tribe, people, mother-unit), 210–13, 214, 215, 216–17, 298nn29,31

ummatum (Akkadian: mother-unit), 210, 211–12

'umt (Ugaritic cognate for Hebrew 'ummâ), 105, 108, 134, 211, 262n37

Urban, Greg, 8, 12, 18

uterine brothers, 103fig.7; as allies in the house of the father, 104; Benjamin as uterine brother to Joseph, 45–46, 47–48, 63, 94, 133, 166–67, 209; brother-brokered marriages, 15, 54, 56, 61–62, 64–68, 71–74, 254n73; economic impact of sister's marriage/dowry shared with, 54, 70–73, 74, 261n22, 283n25; loss of daughter impacting, 261n22; milk siblings, 273n43; "nursed at my mother's breasts" indicating, 18, 58, 62–63, 67, 93–94, 105, 118–19, 126, 133–34, 226, 251n46; physical appearances of, 177; protection of in Succession Treaty of Esarhaddon, 261n27; raḥămîm between, 45–46, 110–11, 115; refuge offered by, 73, 100, 102; revenge by, 65–66, 96–103, 189, 260n16, 261n21, 293n39; revenge for death of, 105; sisters' honor protected by, 63–64, 65–67, 68, 74, 94, 96–97, 251n48; in Song of Songs, 94; womb-based emotion between, 46–47

uterine siblings: affection between, 133–34, 273n43; alliances between, 13, 102–4, 130, 270n17, 271n29; "brother, son of mother," 13, 76, 261n19; kissing and weeping associated with, 62, 79, 94, 111, 118–19, 134, 179, 209; loyalty among, 108–9, 111–12, 114–16, 135, 140; milk kinship, 125, 127–28, 134, 140, 142, 270n17,

Index of Subjects

uterine siblings (*continued*)
273n43, 279n93; parental pairing with, 176–77; refuge offered to, 73, 100, 102; rivalry between, 95, 114, 174–78, 206–9, 290n3; womb-based allegiance between, 46–47, 111–12, 116. *See also* Dinah; Esau; house of the mother; Jacob

valley of the dry bones (Ezekiel 37:7–10), 195
van der Toorn, Karel, 35
van Selms, A., 108–9
vineyard imagery, 73, 94, 160
von Rad, Gerhard, 246n3, 256n30, 276n64

Waterson, Roxana, 33–34, 88
Watson, Rubie, 155
Watson, Wilfred G. E., 111
weaning, 116, 137, 138, 140, 143
weapons, 188, 293n37
Weems, Renita, 252n60
Weingreen, Jacob, 154
Westermann, Claus, 4, 55, 116, 242n103, 246n3, 256n30, 276n64, 281n4, 283n20
wet nurses, 128, 132, 139–41, 145–46, 149, 275n62, 279n90
whore (*zônâ*), whoredom (*zĕnûnim*), 112, 113, 147, 184–85, 196, 197, 296n60
widowhood, 162, 285n45
wife (*'iššâ*), 82, 154, 155
Willett, Elizabeth, 88
Williamson, H. G. M., 237n32
Wilson, Robert, 11, 234n56, 277n77
Wolf, Margery, 9, 10, 248n128
Wolff, Hans Walter, 267n36
womb (*beṭen, reḥem*), 259n3, 264nn1,3; appositional epithets identifying son of his mother's womb, 121, 268n38; belonging to God, 121; *beṭen*, 111, 117, 259n3, 264n3, 280n98; "breasts and womb," 110, 116–20, 149, 195, 266nn28,29; God's control over, 121; nutrition transmitted by, 137–38; opening of, as conception, 159; *raḥămîm* and aspects of/semantic connection to, 113–14; *rḥm*, 115, 116, 265nn16,17; transmission of traits in, 122–24, 128–29, 131–32, 137–38, 177, 279n92; womb-based allegiances, 108–9, 111–12, 114–15, 135, 140; womb-based emotion, 255n13
womb openers, 218fig.11; daughters as, 284n35; of David, 167, 168fig.8, 288n69; dedication as Nazirites, 135–36, 284n35; establishment of paternity associated with, 158–59; hierarchy of, 166–67, 198–99; house of the mother inaugurated by, 160; names of, 159, 161; *peṭer reḥem*, 151, 158, 159–60, 175, 284n35, 290n3; *piṣḥi*, 160; prestige associated with, 164–67, 223, 226–27, 286n55. *See also* Joseph
word pairs: agreement in number, 78, 255n11; "breasts and womb," 110, 116–20, 149, 195, 266nn28,29, 267n31; "brother, son of mother," 13, 76, 91, 94–95, 104, 114; context determining meaning, 76–77; cultural value of, 92–93; feature of deletion in, 76; in female kinship labels, 93; gender-alternating pattern in, 111; "house of the mother/chamber of her who conceived me," 62, 77, 78–79, 81, 120; kinship designations, 91, 92; kinship relatedness, 76–78; nouns in, 78, 255n11; patterns of relatedness, 76; psycholinguistic theory applied to, 76; *raḥămîm/ ḥesed*, 114; seven-to-eight word pair, 95, 259n6; shifts in level of reference, 255n11; single/plural pairs, 77–78; spatial word pairs, 62, 77–79, 81, 110, 116–20, 149, 195, 266nn28,29; three-to-four word pair, 259n6; valued terms in, 78. *See also* "bone and flesh"

Yahweh, 246n3; addressed in prayers for a son, 136–37, 156–57, 284n26; and the birth of Obed, 144, 165, 220–21; and childbirth, 92, 112–17, 138, 144, 153, 156–57, 159–61, 163; covenantal promises made by, 92, 122, 139–40, 162, 201, 204–7, 276n65; in creation narratives/as creator, 195; David's relationship with, 122, 151, 162, 171, 189, 286n56, 289n79; Hannah's prayer to, 121, 135, 137; Hebron as shrine site of, 191; heir identified by, 186; house of, 24, 26, 34, 78, 85, 187, 222, 237n28; Jacob's relationship with, 180–81, 187, 206–7; and Jerusalem, 132, 133; language of judgment against Jerusalem, 286n56; Leah's relationship with, 163; maternal subunits in house of, 24, 85, 123, 222; nation of Israel punished by, 84, 212; paternal claim revoked by, 297n7; in priestly texts, 276n63; psalmist's praise of, 81, 160, 195, 196, 214; *raḥămîm* shown by, 112–13, 114, 117, 289n79; Rebekah's relationship with, 180–81; womb-based emotion expressed by, 265n9; as Yahweh Elohim, 82, 282n10

Yassub, 130
y-l-d (to bear, to give birth), 39, 229n3
y-n-q (suck), 132, 133
yôrēš (heir), 91, 92
"your servant" (use of term), 196–97
y-ṣ-r (forming), 121

Zalmunah (Midianite king), 97
Zarephath, 24
Zebah (Midianite king), 97
Zebidah, 287n67
Zebulun, 163, 301n53
Zechariah, 293n35
Zelophehad's daughters, 253n65, 283n23
zeraʿ (seed), 122–23, 126, 152, 153, 205–6, 268n45, 269n6
Zerah, 159
Zerubbabel, 293n35
Zeruiah, sons of, 97–98, 227, 260n10, 289n76
Zillah, 1, 2
Zilpah, sons of, 23fig.2, 44, 46, 48, 49, 74, 163, 223, 224fig.12
Zimri, identification of, 213
Zinjirli stele, 296n2
Zipporah, 68, 244n115, 277n72
zônâ (whore), whoredom (*zĕnûnîm*), 112, 113, 147, 184–85, 196, 197, 296n60

Index of Ancient Sources

Hebrew Bible

Genesis

2:22	82	13:11	203
2:23	82, 196	13:14–17	205
2:24	82	13:14–18	206
3:20	82	13:15	122
4:1	121	13:16	122
4:18	1	15	152, 153
4:18–22	3	15:1	152
4:19–22	1	15:1–3	157
4:20–21	2	15:2	153
4:22	2	15:2–3	197
4:26	148	15:3	153
9	83	15:3–4	92
9:20–27	83	15:4	153, 158
9:21	83	15:4–5	205
10:21	148	15:5	122
11:10–26	4	15:13	122
11:27	39, 203	15:18	153
11:27–29	176	15:18–21	205
11:27–30	4	16	43, 153, 205
11:29	138	16:1	154, 155
11:30	93	16:2	150, 154
12–50	13	16:3	154, 155
12:1–3	205	16:4	154
12:1–4	203	16:5	147, 154
12:5	138	16:6	154
12:7	205	16:8	154
12:19	139	16:9	154
13:2	139	16:10	205
13:2–13	203	16:11	205
13:9	203	16:12	43, 206

325

Genesis (*continued*)		21:14	140
16:13–14	42	21:15–21	141
17	139, 153	21:18	206
17:1–7	139	21:20–21	206
17:4–8	205	22	201
17:6	139	22:2	121
17:7	122	22:8	177
17:8	122	22:17–18	205
17:8–21	139	22:20–23	176
17:10	122	22:20–24	52
17:15–16	139	23	52
17:15–19	138	23:1–16	42
17:16	153, 161, 201	24	51, 52, 53, 56, 57, 58, 59, 60, 63, 83
17:18	153		
17:19	153	24:2	83
17:21	153	24:2–4	53
18:11	138	24:15	52, 53
19:1–11	24	24:16	53, 93
19:8	203	24:22	54, 73
19:26	203	24:24	52, 53
19:30	203	24:27	53
19:30–37	204	24:28	29, 51, 176, 179
19:32	162	24:28–29	73
19:33–35	204	24:28–32	176
19:34	162	24:28–61	176
20:12	139	24:29	54
21	43, 140, 206	24:30	54
21:1–2	138	24:31	55
21:1–5	140	24:34–36	55
21:1–14	201	24:47	52
21:3	140	24:49	55
21:4	140	24:50–51	55
21:5	140	24:53	73
21:6	161	24:55–60	57
21:7	138	24:60	57, 202
21:8	116, 138	24:67	83, 161
21:8–21	140	25	5, 39, 42, 45, 148, 201, 202, 205, 206, 211, 225, 226
21:9–10	140		
21:10	140, 166, 197		
21:11	140	25:1–4	39, 40
21:12	140	25:5	201
21:13	122, 140, 206	25:6	44, 198, 206

Index of Ancient Sources 327

25:9	41	29	69
25:10	41, 42	29–30	164
25:11	42	29:4–14	180
25:12	40	29:10	179, 182
25:12–18	5, 39	29:12	179, 202
25:16	210, 211, 212, 213, 215, 216	29:12–13	179
		29:13–14	179
25:18	41, 206	29:14–15a	193
25:19	39, 40, 201	29:16	69
25:19–20	52, 73	29:17	45
25:19–24	5	29:21–30	177
25:19–26	39	29:28	155
25:20	73	29:31	159
25:21	156	29:31–30:24	23, 44
25:21–23	178	29:31–34	163
25:21–26	176	29:31–35	151
25:23	114, 180, 207	29:32–35	156
25:25–26	123	29:34	164
25:27–33	69	30:1	156
25:27	177	30:1–24	155
25:28	176	30:2	156
25:29–34	177, 178	30:3	151
25:30	114	30:4	155
25:31–34	69	30:6–8	163
27	148	30:9–13	163
27:5	176	30:17–20	163
27:6	176	30:22	159
27:11	123, 177	30:27	181
27:15	25	30:29–43	70, 177
27:17	176	30:30	28
27:18–29	179	31	181
27:20	181	31:1	56, 69, 182
27:22–23	178	31:3	182
27:29	95	31:14–16	182
27:33–34	178	31:18	182, 187, 202, 206
27:41–45	69, 73, 174	31:19–35	177
27:41–46	177	31:21	202, 206
27:41–28:9	178	31:30	182
28:1–5	180	31:33	84
28:2	174, 178, 202	31:33–35	206
28:6–9	178	31:43	182
28:15	181	31:53	183

Genesis (continued)

31:54–55	183	34:31	66, 97
32:2–3	207	35:2	28
32:4	207	35:16–20	219
32:7	207	35:16–21	23, 44, 221
32:8–9	207	35:22	217, 224
32:10	207	35:26	148
32:11	208	36:1–14	5
32:12	208	36:43	39
32:13	207	37	48
32:23–25	208	37–50	43
32:29	208	37:1–2a	44
32:31	208	37:2	5, 198
33	42	37:2b	44
33:1	208	37:9	44
33:1–2	209	37:10	45
33:1–6	198	37:25	43
33:4	209	37:25–28	45
33:4–16	209	37:36	45
33:15–20	178	38	162, 221
33:17	209	38:7–11	162
33:18–20	209	38:29	159
34	64, 66, 103	39:1	45
34:1	64, 96	39:6	45
34:2	101	41:50	148
34:3	64, 96	42–45	48
34:3–6	65	42:3	45
34:5	64, 96, 101	42:11	46
34:7	64, 65, 96, 101, 182	42:13	46
34:8–9	65	42:38	46
34:9–10	70	43:14	46, 110, 111
34:10	65	43:26–30	79
34:11–17	65	43:29	47, 63, 209
34:13	96, 101, 182	43:29–30	94, 110, 111
34:14	65, 96	43:30	47
34:17	65	43:34	47, 94
34:25	65, 96	44:1–2	47
34:25–26	66, 96	44:20	47
34:26	73, 100	44:27–29	47
34:27	96	45:4	47
34:27–29	66	45:10–11a	48
34:30	28, 66, 101, 164	45:12	48
		45:12–15	94

45:14	48	13:15	158
45:14–15a	179	26:1–13	85
45:15	209	31:18	35
45:22	48	36	85
46:8–27	48	40:21	85
46:15	74, 100		
46:22	148	**Numbers**	
46:30	79	2	222, 224
48:5	217	2:1	225
48:5–6	223	2:3–9	223
49	164, 223, 225	2:17	223
49:3	91, 158	3:38	223
49:3–4	217, 224	4:5	85
49:5–7	224	6	134, 135
49:6	164	6:1–5	135, 136, 137
49:22–25a	118	11:12	145, 147
49:25	118	12:1–3	142
50:8	28	24:5	78
53	57	25	212, 225
		25:1–3	212
Exodus		25:4–9	212
1–6	13	25:14	213
1:19	133	25:15	210, 213, 215, 216
1:21	162		
1:22	141	**Deuteronomy**	
2	143	5:22	35
2:1	141, 143	10:1–5	35
2:2–10	141	13:6	95, 147
2:5	142	20:5–9	26
2:7	141	21:15–17	158
2:9–10	142	21:22–23	191
2:11–12	142	23:4	204
2:11–15	70	28:54	147
2:13–14	143	28:56	147
2:15–22	69	30:6	122
2:16	69	33	164
3:1	70	34:4	142
4:6	147		
4:24–26	142	**Joshua**	
6	143	6:17	185
6:20	143	6:22–25	185
11:5	196, 197		

Joshua (continued)

13–21	212
24:15	25

Judges

3:24	79
4:17	84
6–9	13
6:15	218
6:25–27	183
8:19	18, 97
8:22	218
8:22–23	183
8:24–27	183
8:30	92, 158
8:30–31	167, 184
8:31	175, 183, 184, 197
9	187
9:1–6	218
9:1	175, 185
9:2	182, 185, 193
9:3	185, 194
9:4	186
9:5	186
9:6	186
9:7–15	187
9:18	187, 197
9:26–29	187
9:28	188
9:42–49	188
9:53–55	188
11:1	159
11:1–2	197
11:12	167
13	134, 156
13:2–25	157
13:3	93
13:3–5	136
13:7	136
13:14	136
15:1	80
16:9	79

17–18	26
19:2	29
19:27	24

1 Samuel

1	156
1–2	135
1:1–20	156
1:4–5	135
1:8	156
1:9	137
1:11	135
1:11–20	121
1:13–14	136
1:15	137
1:22	137
1:23	137
1:24	137
2:1–4	164
2:5	164
2:8	164
2:10	168
4:4	168
5:1	196
6:23	168
7:2	21
7:3	21
9:1–2	218
9:20–21	219
10:1–2	219
14:49–50	168
16–23	70
16:1	189, 219
16:11	70
16:12–13	189
16:18	219
17:12	219, 221
17:38–39	170
18:1–4	69
18:2	70
18:4	170
18:17	69

18:17–30	69	12:24	171
18:20	69	13	103, 171
20:30	123	13:1	98, 101, 102, 182
20:42	122	13:2	99
21:8	168	13:2–4	102
31:1–6	169	13:3–6	99
		13:4	99, 102
2 Samuel		13:5	99
1:10	170	13:6	99
1:12	21	13:6–10	79
2:9	190	13:7	99
2:10	169	13:8–9	99
2:12–17	97	13:8–10	79
2:18	97	13:8–19	79
2:18–32	97	13:10	99
3:1	167	13:10–14	80
3:2–4	98	13:11	99
3:2–5	167, 168	13:12	99, 101
3:3	175, 189	13:14–17	99
3:12–16	170	13:14	101
3:27	98	13:18	79
3:30	98	13:19	100
4:4	145	13:20	29, 74, 100, 102, 160, 162
4:5	79		
4:5–8	170	13:22	100
4:7	79	13:23	101, 182
5:1	194	13:23–33	189
5:13–16	189	13:26	100
6:5	21	13:27	101, 182
6:15	21	13:28–29	171
6:20–23	170	13:29	101, 182
7	21	13:30	101, 182
7:4	189	13:31	102
7:11	162	13:32	100, 101, 102, 182
7:11–12	152	13:33	101
7:12	92, 122, 158	13:35	101
9:6–13	170	13:36	101, 102
11	171	13:37	102, 175, 190
12:3	147	13:37–39	189
12:8	21, 147	14:24	190
12:10	171	14:28	190
12:15–19	171	14:28–33	190

2 Samuel (continued)

14:28–15:6	190
15:1	190
15:6	191, 194
15:7–12	190
15:13	191, 194
15:16	191
16:3	21
16:21–22	83
16:22	191
17:25	97, 195
18:6–9	191
18:9	191
18:17–18	191
19:12	194
19:13	195
19:15	195
21:1–6	170
21:7–9	171
21:10–14	171
21:20	148
22:20–51	171
24:14	114

1 Kings

1:2	147
1:11	171
1:15	79, 80
1:21	172
1:30	172
2:13	171
3	184
3:16–18	113
3:20	147
3:26–27	113
6–7	85
7	80
7:1–8	80
8:13	26
8:50	114
10:1	145
11:26	219
12:21	21
12:23	21
17:8–24	24
17:19	147
21:1–4	24
22:25	79

2 Kings

6:12	79
11:1	102
11:1–21	102
11:2	79, 102, 103
19:30	21

Isaiah

9:6	148
26:20	79
40:11	147
44:2	121
44:24	121
46:3	34
48:1	25, 34, 92
48:17–19	122
49	132
49:23	132, 146
49:5	121
49:14–15	117
49:15	116
54	161
54:1–2	160
54:2	77, 84
55:4	210, 215, 216
60	132
60:1	132
60:4–7	132
60:8–14	132
60:9–10	133
60:13–14	132
60:15–16	132
60:16	132
63:16a	92
65:6	147

66	132, 133	Micah	
66:7	133	5:1	221
66:8	133	7:5	147
66:11	133	Psalms	
66:12–13	133	22	116
Jeremiah		22:10	111, 121
1:5	111, 121	22:10–11	117
7:15	92	25:6	114
10:20	78	26:8	78
16:5	114	35:13	147
20:15	148	38:4	195
22:13	78	40:12	114
31	161	45	173
31:4	160	45:11–12	174
32:18	147	45:17–18	173
Ezekiel		50:20	94
8–10	34	51:3	114
8:12	79	51:5	123
16:44–47	123	58:4	111
23	24, 85, 222	69:8–9	94
23:2	123	69:17	114
23:2–4	222	74:11	147
23:5–6	222	77:10	114
23:5–7	85	78:51	91, 158
23:11–17	85	78:67	92
23:12	222	79:8	114
34:8	31	79:12	147
37:7–10	195	83:1	43
40–48	34	83:6	43, 196
Hosea		86	196
1–2	112	86:16	196
1:2	112	87:4	148
2:3–5	112	87:5–6	148
2:6	112	89:19–37	189
9:11–14	117	89:50	147
Amos		103:4	114
1:6	114	105:6	92
1:9	114	105:36	91, 158
1:11	114	106:46	114
		113	161
		113:9	160

Psalms (continued)

116	196
116:16	196
117:1	210
117:1–2	214
119:77	114
128	80
128:1	81
128:2	81
128:3	81, 174
132:3	84
132:7	78
139	195
139:13	121
139:13–15	195
139:15	121
145:9	114
156	114

Proverbs

1–9	119
4:3	93
5:20	147
6:27	147
7:27	78
12:10	114
14:30	195
17:23	147
21:14	147
24:3–4	78
30:21–23	154
31	119
31:1–2	120
31:1–9	120
31:2	18

Job

1:1	157
1:3	157
1:10	157
1:19	157
2:5	195
2:9–10	56
3:11	111
3:11–12	117
10:11	195
15:34	160
15:35	123
19:27	147
31:15	111
33:21	195
42:10–17	157

Song of Songs

1:1–4	68
1:4	80
1:5	85
1:6	62, 63, 64, 73, 94
2:9	81
3:1	81
3:1–4	81
3:4	18, 51, 62, 76, 77, 79, 80, 81, 83, 110, 118
3:11	62
4:8	62, 93
4:9	62, 93
4:10	62, 93
4:11	62, 93
4:12	62, 93
5:1	62, 93
5:2–5	82
6:8–9	62, 68
6:9	110, 118
7:1	68
8:1	18, 105, 119, 125
8:1–2	62, 63, 94, 110, 118, 133
8:2	51, 119, 120
8:5	110
8:8	62, 63
8:8–9	62, 63, 64
8:10	64
8:11–12	73

Ruth

1:1–2	143
1:8–9	60
1:8–14	73, 100
1:9	29
1:11	166
1:16–17	143
1:21	165
2:1	165
2:20	166
3:2	166
4:3–11	144
4:10	152
4:11	202, 220
4:11–12	152, 221
4:13	144
4:13–17	165
4:13–22	144
4:14	165
4:15	148, 165, 166
4:16	145, 146
4:16–17	144, 147, 148
4:17	165
4:17–22	68
4:21	166

Lamentations

2:4	84
2:11–12	147
2:12	147
3:4	195
3:22	114

Ecclesiastes

7:9	147
10:20	79

Esther

2:20	146
2:25	146

Daniel

1:9	114
3:4	214, 216
3:28	215
3:29	214, 216
9:9	114
9:18	114

Ezra

1:1–5	34
4:10	214, 216
10:23	159

Nehemiah

8:1–4	35
9:5	159
9:19	114
9:21	114
9:27	114
9:28	114
11:24	159

1 Chronicles

1:19	148
2:16	195
5:1–2	217
8:33	168
8:34	168
9:39	168
9:40	168
27:30	43

2 Chronicles

2:16	97
22:2–3	124
22:10	102
22:10–23:21	102
22:11	103
30:9	114

Dead Sea Scrolls

4QD[a]	210, 215, 216
4Q507, 2	117, 123

Mesopotamian Sources

The Autobiography of Idrimi	192–93, 199
The Babylonian Gilgamesh Epic	131
Dialogue Between Ashurbanipal and Nabu	130–31
Enuma Elish	131
Esarhaddon's Succession Treaty	103–4, 130–31, 167

Texts from Ugarit

Aqhat
KTU 1.19

I, 7–11	105
I, 32–37	104–5
IV, 34–35	105
IV, 39–40	105

Baal Cycle
KTU 1.2

I, 18–19	106
I, 33	107
I, 36	107
IV, 10	107
IV, 11–30	107

KTU 1.3

II, 28	107
III, 38–39	107
IV	107
IV, 47–48	106, 107
IV, 54	107
V, 1–6	107
V, 27	107
V, 35	106
V, 35–39	107
V, 37	106
V, 38–39	106

KTU 1.4

II, 21–26	107
IV, 50–51	106

KTU 1.5

IV, 44–47	108
V, 28–29	108

KTU 1.6

II, 5–9	115
II, 12	115
II, 13	107
II, 22–23	115
II, 27–35	115
IV, 19	108
VI, 10–11	95–96
VI, 14–15	95–96
VI, 33	108

Kirta
KTU 1.14

I, 8–9	95
II, 1–5	157, 197

KTU 1.15

II, 26–27	130

An Incantation Against Infertility
KTU 1.13, 2   115

The Lovely Gods
KTU 1.23   131